# BEYOND A BORDER

# Sociology for a New Century Series

# BEYOND A BORDER

## The Causes and Consequences of Contemporary Immigration

◆

### PETER KIVISTO
*Augustana College* and *University of Turku, Finland*

### THOMAS FAIST
*Bielefeld University, Germany*

PINE FORGE PRESS
An Imprint of SAGE Publications, Inc.
Los Angeles • London • New Delhi • Singapore • Washington DC

*For information:*

Pine Forge Press
An Imprint of SAGE Publications, Inc.
2455 Teller Road
Thousand Oaks, California 91320
E-mail: order@sagepub.com

SAGE Publications Ltd.
1 Oliver's Yard
55 City Road
London EC1Y 1SP
United Kingdom

SAGE Publications India Pvt. Ltd.
B 1/I 1 Mohan Cooperative
Industrial Area
Mathura Road,
New Delhi 110 044
India

SAGE Publications Asia-Pacific
Pte Ltd
33 Pekin Street #02-01
Far East Square
Singapore 048763

Printed in the United States of America

*Library of Congress Cataloging-in-Publication Data*

Kivisto, Peter, 1948-
Beyond a border: the causes and consequences of contemporary immigration/Peter Kivisto, Thomas Faist.
    p. cm.—(Sociology for a new century series)
Includes bibliographical references and index.
ISBN 978-1-4129-2495-5 (pbk.)
    1. Emigration and immigration—Social aspects. 2. Emigration and immigration—Government policy. 3. Immigrants—Cultural assimilation. 4. Multiculturalism 5. Cultural pluralism. I. Faist, Thomas, 1959- II. Title.

JV6225.K58 2010
304.8—dc22                                        2009023897

This book is printed on acid-free paper.

09   10   11   12   13   10   9   8   7   6   5   4   3   2   1

| | |
|---|---|
| *Acquisitions Editor:* | David Repetto |
| *Editorial Assistant:* | Nancy Scrofano |
| *Production Editor:* | Catherine M. Chilton |
| *Copy Editor:* | Brenda Weight |
| *Typesetter:* | C&M Digitals (P) Ltd. |
| *Proofreader:* | Doris Hus |
| *Indexer:* | Prairie Moon Indexing |
| *Cover Designer:* | Gail Buschman |
| *Marketing Manager:* | Jennifer Reed Banando |

# Contents

# Acknowledgments

Pine Forge Press would like to thank the following reviewers:

David Allen
*Temple University*

Steven P. Dandaneau
*University of Tennessee, Knoxville*

Martha E. Geores
*University of Maryland, College Park*

William J. Haller
*Clemson University*

Ebenezer Obadare
*University of Kansas*

Unnoticed, the narrative has altered,
the displaced of capital have come to the capital.

—Anne Winters

"The Displaced of Capital"


all of us are immigrants
every daughter every son
everyone is everyone
all of us are immigrants

—Steve Earle

"City of Immigrants"

# 1

# Introduction

## Moving Across Borders

The movement of people across national borders represents one of the most vivid dramas of social reality in the contemporary world. If immigrants are the central characters in this drama, there are numerous other dramatic personae whose supporting roles are crucial to determining the ultimate course of events. These include the family and friends left behind in the homeland, government officials and employers in both the sending and receiving countries, other immigrants from the homeland who become part of ethnic communities, sympathetic members of religious and other institutions concerned with assisting newcomers, and people who through either organized or spontaneous means express their hostility toward immigrants. And, as this book seeks to illustrate, the drama also involves social scientists involved in the study of migrants and the migratory process.

People move across borders for a variety of reasons, and in many instances what is involved is a bundle of motives. Some people move because they are, in early sociologist Georg Simmel's terms, adventurers, individuals who are intent on "dropping out of the continuity of life" (Simmel, 1971/1911, p. 187). Those caught up in wanderlust are motivated by a psychological quest for novelty that propels them to seek ever-new experiences in ever-new locales. While such people have existed throughout history, they are such a tiny minority that they cannot account for the large-scale movement of people across national borders. Rather, external forces in their social environments motivate those involved in mass migration.

They move for economic reasons, either because things are sufficiently desperate where they currently reside that exodus appears to be the most viable option for improving the situation or because, in the scheme of things, migration is seen as a way of enhancing the ability to be upwardly mobile. They move for political reasons, during times of revolutionary turmoil or periods of intense political repression. They move because they are prevented from practicing their religious convictions or because their political and social views place them at risk.

Migrations take place within national borders as well and with often profound consequences. The epic movement of victims of the Depression-era Dustbowl of Oklahoma to California is a case in point, one vividly captured in John Steinbeck's classic novel, *The Grapes of Wrath* (1967/1940). Though the geographic distance was not great, the movement of urban dwellers to the suburbs, particularly after World War II, revealed a large social distance between the city and, as Kenneth Jackson (1985) described it, the "crabgrass frontier." Earlier in the 20th century, the "Great Migration" of blacks out of the rural agrarian South to the urban industrial North—seen for a short time by the migrants as the "promised land"—had profound consequences for black identity and the black community, as well as for the larger society. The early American sociologist Robert Park (1914) may have been the first to compare this movement to that of the eastern and southern Europeans then entering the United States in large numbers. Like their European counterparts, blacks were viewed as peasants deeply immersed in the folkways and mores of an agrarian society, and in both cases, they were entering the same urban industrial milieu. The movement of people off the land to the city was one of the major world historical developments of the 20th century—not only in the United States but across the globe. Indeed, it was Park who commented that the world could "be divided between two classes: those who reached the city and those who have not yet arrived" (1950/1935, p. 167).

## The Sociology of Migration

If, as demographer Everett Lee (1966, p. 49) argues, migration refers to a "permanent or semipermanent change of residence," then "a move across the hall from one apartment to another" amounts to the same act as a move "from Bombay, India, to Cedar Rapids, Iowa." While this may at some level be true, we are not concerned in this book with moves across the hall. In fact, using a distinction that has become commonly accepted despite Park's cautionary suggestion about the similarities between some internal and external movements, we will proceed with the assumption that immigration refers (as noted at the outset) to cross-border movements. Thus, we are also not concerned with movements within nations, however distant those moves might be (and a move from Boston to Los Angeles is, in terms of distance, farther than the move from Puebla, Mexico, to Los Angeles). Given that we are interested in movements beyond a border, clearly nation-states need to be seen as playing major roles in either preventing or facilitating immigration, and when it occurs, in shaping it (Joppke, 2001a, p. 7208). As will become clear in due course, the precise role of the state has become a major area of contestation within immigration studies.

The sociological study of immigration is deeply embedded in the history of the discipline. This is particularly so in the United States, where the first major center for the discipline, the Chicago School of Sociology, located at the newly established University of Chicago, took as one of its major areas of empirical and theoretical interest the mass immigration to the country that began around 1880 and continued until the 1924 National Origins Act effectively stopped mass immigration for the next four decades. While other sociologists of that era, such as Franklin Giddings and E. A. Ross, were either hostile or unsympathetic to immigrants and were vigorous proponents of immigration restriction legislation, the key members of the Chicago School over an extended period of time—from the time when W. I. Thomas worked with Florian Znaniecki on their study of Polish immigrants to Robert Park's agenda setting and theoretical framing of the issue for a generation of students, through the leadership of Louis Wirth—were sympathetic to immigrants and supportive of liberal immigration policies. This is not always evident in their work, in no small part because Park in particular sought to distinguish sociological work from social reform, thereby making a clear distinction between research and advocacy. Although the end of the centrality of the Chicago school was evident by the conclusion of World War II, when its decline in reputation meant that it was often forgotten, it had nevertheless managed to establish and entrench in the discipline many of the ways that sociologists study immigration (and for that matter other social phenomena, as well). It did so dispassionately. Moreover, it did so with the goal being to uncover patterns that were capable of generalization. In the process, what was often lost was an explicit concern with the varied ways that concrete individuals experienced immigration at an existential level. Missing are the tears, fears, hopes, plans, aspirations, uncertainties, ambivalences, and the like that are part and parcel of the immigrant experience.

While sociology has proved itself to be a major source for comprehending immigration, it needs to be complemented with other insights. Of course, listening to immigrants themselves or reading diaries and memoirs is one important way to get what might be viewed as a more immediate, unmediated account. Another is to look to literature. In fact, both today and during the last major wave of immigration to the United States and other rapidly industrializing immigrant-receiving nations, an expansive body of fiction has been produced, sometimes by the immigrants themselves, sometimes not.

## Migration as Lived Experience in Recent Fiction

Three recent examples of decidedly nonautobiographical novels illustrate the virtues of fiction for developing a sympathetic understanding of immigration as lived experience. Each of these examples brings the reader into contact with a fictional character from South Asia, one of the major areas in the globe today that is supplying a sizeable percentage of immigrants to western Europe and North America: Kiran Desai's *The Inheritance of Loss* (2006), Hari Kunzru's *Transmission* (2004), and Monica Ali's *Brick Lane: A Novel* (2003).

In Desai's novel, which won the Man Booker Prize, one of the characters departs for the United States with the encouragement of his father, who is an aging cook working for a retired judge in the northeast region of India bordering Nepal, which is plagued by guerrilla activities of Nepalese-origin militants with irredentist or separatist intentions. Biju lands in New York City, an undocumented worker ripe for exploitation—and exploited he is. With limited education, no money, and lacking an effective network of friends and relatives who can assist him in trying to get a foothold in the United States, he moves from dead-end job to dead-end job, never managing to secure a future with promise. Meanwhile, not wanting to disappoint his father, he works hard at giving the impression that things are going well. This fabrication makes his loneliness, anxiety, and despair even more difficult. Living in crowded conditions with others in his situation does not help Biju, for he finds himself incapable of connecting in any genuine way with others. The one person who takes an interest in him is something of a hustler, who, for all of his efforts to project an aura of success, appears in the end to also be living a precarious existence. Haunted by the suspicion that his decision to migrate had been a huge mistake, Biju ponders whether returning home would be a better choice than remaining in such an inhospitable land. In the end, he opts to return, only to discover that the calamitous result of the rebel movement is that his previous existence has been turned upside down, that the world he left has in the interim been irrevocably changed.

Biju's tale is that of one of the world's many poor who set out to try to improve their lot and in the process take care of aging parents and other family members left behind. Coming from somewhere near the bottom of Indian society, he managed to exist only at the margins of American society. He lives in a globalized world, but one quite different from the world of the more affluent. Far from the Internet world where he and his father could have communicated by e-mail every day, he had to rely on prepaid phone cards, calling his father at the public phone in the home village because there was no phone in the judge's home. Given the unreliability of the telephone, more often they relied on letters—many of which never arrived due to the shortcomings of the Indian postal service. Thus, the ways that Biju and his father communicated looked in key respects like the ways immigrants in the past communicated rather than the portrait of the network society that makes possible the emergence of transnational social relations. Biju's life provides vivid testimony that, contrary to neoliberal journalist Thomas Friedman's (2006) claim, the world is not flat, at least not for the vast numbers of people on the wrong side of the digital (and, we would add, financial) divide.

Arjun Mehta, the protagonist in Kunzru's novel, is a graduate of the North Okhla Institute of Technology and a computer geek. In this regard, he is quite different from Biju. Residing in New Delhi, rather than in India's hinterland, Arjun occupies a world of cosmopolitan dreams. He lives in a networked world, as does his sister, who works for a call service whose customers are largely Australian. Thus, as part of her job training, she has acquired an Australian accent and knows a lot about Australian sports, television stars, and the like. But Indian reality cannot match Arjun's dreams: he sees his life stifled in India and his talent squandered. Meanwhile, if Bollywood offers nothing but escapist fantasies, Hollywood appears to depict a real world of success, American-style. Or so it seems to Arjun, who sets out to find his fortune in Silicon Valley.

The experience is, to say the least, jarring. The timing of arrival is crucial here: the protagonist arrives in sunny California as the high-tech bubble is about to burst. Arjun discovers that it takes effort to get acclimated to even the most mundane things. At the same time, landing a job proves to be far more difficult than he anticipated, and considerably more frustrating and disillusioning than he could have imagined. He finds his encounter with America to be increasingly disorienting. Thus, he learns that the apartment he settled into is located in a low-income neighborhood. In other words, his neighbors are poor. Kunzru (2004, p. 41) writes, "The idea of American poverty, especially a poverty that did not exclude cars, refrigerators, cable TV, or obesity, was a new and disturbing paradox, a hint that something ungovernable and threatening lurked beneath the reflective surface of California." From this point forward, the plot moves in an increasingly frenetic and crazed pace, as Arjun's disappointments and failures lead him in frustration and anger to unleash a nasty computer virus that has global consequences.

While Desai's novel is a tragic epic, Kunzru's is a dark, absurdist comedy. In both cases, immigration turns out to be an unmitigated disaster. While this is certainly not the experience of most immigrants, who in fact decide to stay and who do not wreak global havoc, nonetheless many of the experiences—the dilemmas, the ambivalence, the anxieties, the problems—of these two characters will resonate with the lived experiences of actual immigrants. Such is also the case with Ali's controversial novel, which bears the name of the principal London neighborhood for Bangladeshi residents. While today Brick Lane has become somewhat trendy, with its Balti restaurants, renovated flats, and newly marketed identity as "Banglatown," the community Ali describes is one that is largely poor, with its inhabitants living marginal lives in British society. The novel's central figure is Nazneen, who at age 18 migrates to marry Chanu, an older man with a lofty sense of his own prospects that doesn't match reality and a peculiar self-absorption that makes him callous without, curiously enough, making him unlikable.

Nazneen's situation highlights two interconnected issues, gender and Muslim identity. As a woman from a traditional society, she is in all respects ill equipped to deal with an individualistic, modern society. Her marriage, after all, was arranged and thus did not resemble Western romantic ideals. Critics within the Bangladeshi community have challenged what they perceive to be an unflattering portrait of their community, which for some includes the conviction that Ali is unfair to Islam. The intensity of opposition is such that plans to make a film version of the novel by shooting on location had to be changed, with filmmakers forced to find a substitute for Brick Lane.

If these critics knew more about the immigrant experience in historical and comparative terms, they would not only have appreciated Ali's sensitive and convincing depiction of one woman's ability to slowly, fitfully, and at times painfully come to terms with her new environment and in the process come to see it and embrace it as home, but they would have seen this as something shared by many immigrant women from varied cultural and national backgrounds Part of the story is one of loss, seen most vividly throughout the novel in the ongoing though intermittent efforts of Nazneen to keep connected with her one surviving family member, a sister who remained in Bangladesh. Like Biju, the major vehicle for contact is letter writing, something not easy for women with limited educational backgrounds. But both persist, and yet, over time, the gulf between the two—and thus between the old homeland and the new—grows. At the same time, Britain—or at least London—becomes less and less strange, and Nazneen discovers that she is capable to an extent that she couldn't have imagined a few short years earlier of making sense of and adjusting to it. The novel ends sweetly on an ice rink, where she is gently reminded that self-discovery and learning about the possibilities opened up in a liberal pluralist society is an ongoing and never-ending process.

Like so many novels about the immigrant experience past and present, these three recent examples provide poignant testimonies regarding the perils and the promises of the migratory act—and in so doing they keep us focused on the flesh-and-blood nature of that act. But this book is not intended to provide a literary guide. Rather, its focus is the sociology of immigration. The reason for this brief excursus at the beginning of the book is to suggest that the ways that sociology and related social sciences approach this field of inquiry is often at the expense of appreciating the lived experience of concrete individuals—real or fictional. And how can it be otherwise, given that what sociologists are intent on capturing is that which is generalizable. Indeed, one of the first questions that social scientists will ask is the extent to which Biju, Arjun, and Nazneen can be seen as representative of large numbers of immigrants. Are their experiences anomalous or typical? Are they in some sense stock characters or are they particularly unique, idiosyncratic examples?

Beyond this, other questions will inevitably be posed. For example, in what ways is the South Asian immigrant experience similar to and in what ways different from that of immigrants from other points of origin? What difference does it make that one ends up in London rather than New York City—or Barcelona, Berlin, Paris, Sydney, or Toronto? What is the significance of race, class, and gender? How varied are the ways of maintaining homeland ties and how long do those ties persist? What are the ways that immigrants acclimate to their new surroundings and what are the difficulties involved? How significant is prejudice and discrimination? What sorts of roles do states—both sending and receiving—play in encouraging, sustaining, or preventing immigration and in shaping the ways immigrants end up located in and relating to the host society? These and a wide range of related questions are the stock-in-trade of sociologists and their fellow social scientists, and given that immigration is a mass phenomenon, these are essential questions to pose and attempt to answer if we are to adequately understand immigration.

## Overview of the Book

For over a century, sociologists and others have sought to answer such questions, and in so doing they have developed a vast literature that documents empirically the myriad facets of immigration, while at the same time creating theoretical models that serve to inform interpretive and explanatory accounts. This book is intended to survey the state of the field, offering a critical assessment of its achievements and its shortcomings while pointing to what we consider to be both important areas for future research and new theoretical approaches.

In broad brush strokes, it is possible to identify three main topics of inquiry that have preoccupied scholars of immigration, past and present:

- *Movement:* The first topic concerns the factors contributing to migration, which include a consideration of both the causal mechanisms contributing to the flow of migrants across borders and the patterned or structured character of the migratory process over time. Though the focus is on those who opt to migrate, the underlying problematic that needs to be addressed is how to explain, to use the distinction Harrison White (1970) made in a different context, between "stayers and movers." To be more precise, as Thomas Faist (2000a, p. 1) has framed the matter, we need to know, "Why are there so few migrants from so many places and so many from only a few places?" It should be noted that throughout most of the history of immigration studies, sociologists have, to large extent, conceded this particular subject to demographers and economists. It is therefore not surprising that when, in recent years, some sociologists have invested in this matter, they have tended to be individuals with expertise in demography (e.g., Douglas S. Massey) or economic sociology (e.g., Alejandro Portes).

- *Settlement:* The second problematic addresses the matter of immigrant incorporation. Christian Joppke (2001a, p. 7208) points out that immigration "is seen from the perspective of the receiving (rather than the sending) states." In point of fact, he is right. Until very recently, immigration studies have been solely preoccupied with how immigrants do or do not manage to become integrated into the new social order. The impact of migration on sending states would presumably be defined as emigration studies. While no explicit area of inquiry bears that name, as it turns out, the development of transnational studies (which will be discussed in Chapter 5) has called into question the shortcomings of what some see as a container model of immigration studies. Advocates for a transnational perspective argue that we ought not confine our subject matter to the boundaries of nation states, but instead consider the impacts of immigration on transnational social spaces that penetrate into two or more nation-states (Faist, 2000a, 2000b; Glick Schiller, 1999; Glick Schiller & Levitt, 2006; Kivisto, 2001). Within the limitations of a focus on receiving states, this particular topic has generated an array of significant conceptual tools, among the most significant being those that seek to broadly characterize particular modes of incorporation: assimilation, pluralism or hyphenization, and multiculturalism (Alexander,

2006; Kivisto, 2005). Incorporation has been and continues to be the major preoccupation of sociologists of immigration. Although historians tend to eschew theoretical constructs in their work, they too have been deeply involved in answering questions about incorporation—and during the 1960s through the 1980s, the interdisciplinary dialogue between social historians and historical sociologists has proved to be particularly fruitful (Morawska, 1990). Although they have entered the arena of immigration studies some-what more recently, anthropologists, too, have embraced this problem (Brettell & Hollifield, 2000).

- *Control:* The third thematic focus is on the politics of immigration, including considerations of the role of state actions, involving both sending and receiving states. It has been, rather curiously, the least developed of the three, both empirically and theoretically. Controlling borders has been and continues to be a prerogative of nation-states, though as Aristide Zolberg (1989, p. 405) pointed out some time ago, much of classical migration the-ory paid scant attention to this fact. Some regimes have been unwilling to allow their residents to exit and quite adept at preventing them from doing so (Zolberg mentioned Albania during communist rule; one might look today at Myanmar and North Korea as examples). At the same time, though borders in the advanced industrial nations appear in many respects to be quite porous, nonetheless there are some nations that have more lim-ited entrée than others. A research concentration on border controls has increased in recent years (Cornelius, Tsuda, & Martin, 2004; Hollifield, 2004). One of the key figures involved in this trend has suggested that in "bringing the state back in," three themes loom large: the politics of con-trol; the politics of national security and sovereignty; and the politics of incorporation, citizenship, and national identity (Hollifield, 2000; Zolberg, 1981, 1999a, 1999b). Not surprisingly, the scholars most deeply invested in this area are political scientists and legal scholars, though, as is evident, the third theme dovetails with the sociological focus on incorporation.

What follows in the subsequent seven chapters involves an examination of each of these three broad topics. The first section of the book, which we have titled "Movement," will look at immigration flows from the perspec-tive of the history of the modern world. It will also review the most influential theories accounting for immigration. Finally, it will examine contemporary immigration across the globe, focusing on 20 major immigration-receiving nations in the world.

The second section—"Settlement"—is devoted to examining processes of incorporation, which refers to the varied ways immigrants come to be part of a new society. Much of the literature on this topic is laden with preferences, and thus *is* and *ought* are often convoluted. In the three chapters that make up this section, an effort will be made to adjudicate the respective theoretical merits of three concepts that have increasingly come to shape discourse on incorporation: assimilation, transnationalism, and multiculturalism.

Finally, we turn in the last section of the book—"Control"—to the role of states in shaping immigration. For immigration studies during much of the 20th century, this remained an underdeveloped field. We focus on two recent developments in the section's two chapters. The first looks at states as key actors in defining and attempting to structure migratory flows and policies regarding incorporation. The next chapter turns to a discussion of changes in ideas about citizenship, particularly the expansion of dual citizenship around the globe, both as a reality and as something increasingly permitted by states. The book ends with a brief reflection on the need in the new global order/disorder to rethink traditional perspectives about the distinction between citizen and alien.

# SECTION I

## Movement

# 2

# Accounting for Immigration Flows

From the middle of the 20th century to the present, a major wave of immigration has been occurring worldwide, and despite the efforts of some receiving nations to curtail the flow of migrants entering their borders, it has not abated. The major recipients of immigration include virtually all the advanced industrial nations of the world, but it is not limited to them. Not surprisingly, historic settler nations—particularly the United States, Canada, and Australia—have witnessed large influxes of newcomers. So have the nations of western Europe, where even the geographically isolated Iceland has received small numbers of immigrants from such diverse origins as Poland and Vietnam. Despite its hostility to immigration, Japan has received substantial numbers of foreigners into its workforce. However, immigration has not only occurred in the advanced industrial nations. In other regions of the globe, people have left their homes and settled elsewhere, often in neighboring countries. Thus, as the economy collapsed in Zimbabwe and Robert Mugabe's regime employed increasingly repressive measures, many of Zimbabwe's residents moved—often without passports or other documents and thus without legal authorization—to South Africa. Indeed, South Africa has become a destination for Africans from a wide variety of countries, both in southern and western Africa (Kok, Gelderblom, Oucho, & van Zyl, 2006). A similar pattern is evident in Latin America, where, for example, people from the comparatively impoverished nation of Paraguay have immigrated to the more affluent Argentina.

The purpose of this chapter is twofold. First, it will provide a survey of major migratory flows in the past, concentrating on the role of migration since the dawn of modernity. This survey will help to place into historical context the contemporary immigration flows discussed in the next chapter. Second, this chapter will examine the major interpretations of the factors contributing to immigration that have emerged in social scientific discourse from the late 19th century to the present.

## Cultures in Contact

The rise of modernity cannot be fully comprehended if one does not take into account the fact that during the past millennium, people have been on the move. While there were mass movements before, the pace and scope progressively expanded as the modern world took root and developed. Thus, what is occurring today should be seen not as a break with a static past, but as something that emerges out of and is predicated on a long history of migrations.

In this regard, the panoramic research project undertaken by historian Dirk Hoerder, *Cultures in Contact: World Migrations in the Second Millennium* (2002), offers readers a sweeping account of major world migrations from the 11th through the 20th centuries, when the building blocks of the modern world system initially began to take form and shaped subsequent events, including the wide-scale migrations we are witnessing in the world today.

Trade and state building, either jointly or independently, served as the two major forces bringing cultures into contact. In all such cases, migratory movements were part and parcel of the process of contact. Thus, prior to the middle of the 14th century in Europe, the movements of peoples on the continent included the movement of Germans, Frisians, and others eastward to what are present-day Poland, Latvia, and other destinations in eastern Europe. It also involved a Jewish Diaspora that relocated Jews already in Europe from one locale to another while also bringing newcomers to Europe from the Middle East. It involved the movement of Muslims into southern Europe, most notably into Spain. Normans and Varangians took part in movements into Britain, Ireland, Iceland, and beyond. These two groups are a reminder that ethnic or national group formation is a contingent social construct, and thus groups can both appear on the scene at one historical juncture and subsequently disappear. In addition to these voluntary movements of people, slave trade routes linked Africa and Europe, creating the mass involuntary movement of people—or what we today refer to as human trafficking (Hoerder, 2002, pp. 27–58).

But the reasons that motivated human migration were not limited to economic and political considerations. Religion, in particular, played a significant role. Indeed, the previous examples of Jews and Muslims reveal as much. In one instance, the migrations were often prompted by the need to flee religious persecution, while in the case of the Islamic movement into Europe, it was in part the result of a universalistic religion motivated by what Max Weber would refer to as the "warrior ethic" (see Huff & Schluchter, 1999). Similar motivations prompted Christian crusaders to engage in campaigns of conquest in the Holy Land.

At the same time, as Hoerder (2002) stresses, the rest of the world was not static. Thus, not only did trade circuits emerge within Africa, but also similar connections were established that linked parts of the continent to the Middle East and to the Indian subcontinent. India's trade routes did not move simply westward to Africa, but eastward to Southeast Asia and linked to China's coastal trading centers. China's trading circuits expanded into some of the same areas as India's, but in addition they pushed out eastward into the Pacific.

Janet Abu-Lughod (1991) characterized this early period as occurring "before European hegemony." Hoerder's portrait of subsequent developments dovetails with the broad parameters of world systems theory, particularly in its articulation by Immanuel Wallerstein (1974, 1980, 1989), which views the emergence of an integrated world economic system as arising as a consequence of the emergence of the modern capitalist economy, which had its roots in western Europe. Thus, the fluid and disaggregated trade networks that existed prior to the 17th century began to be consolidated. Hoerder (2002, p. 127) aptly captions one of his maps "'Europe Finds the Larger World,' 15th to Early 16th Centuries."

Of particular note, several European powers sent expeditions to the Western Hemisphere—the Americas—where their emissaries' fateful encounter with the indigenous peoples led to the social construction of the racial Other. Similar encounters in other parts of the globe led to similar results. Religion and later science were deployed to provide ideological justifications for colonialism and for its systematic exploitation of the indigenes by offering the substance of racialist ideologies that were an essential component of any "racial formation" (Omi & Winant, 1994). Paul Spickard (2005, p. 2) observes that all colonial systems appear to have generated racial hierarchies, and he contends, *race is about power, and it is written on the body* (italics in original).

The need for cheap labor in the colonies resulted in the creation of a centuries-long Atlantic slave trade. All the major colonial powers in the Americas participated in this trade, including the Portuguese, Spanish, French, Dutch, and British (Hoerder, 2002, pp. 149–157; see also Berlin, 2000; Blackburn, 1998; Horne, 2007; Miller, 1996; Postma, 1990; and Williams, 1994/1944). As Blackburn (1998) has pointed out, commercial interests were prime movers in the establishment and perpetuation of this trade. In the British case, given that 2007 marked the 200th anniversary of the passage of the Abolition of

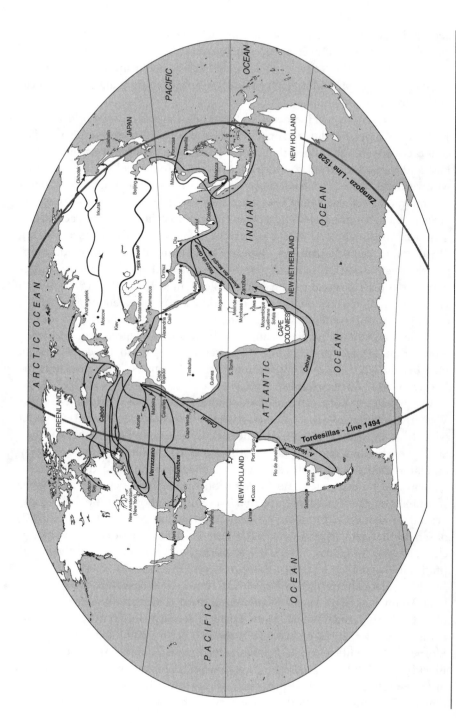

**Figure 2.1**  Migration Flow, 15th and Early 16th Centuries

*Source:* Adapted from Hoerder (2002).

the Slave Trade (the passage of a law actually abolishing slavery had to wait until 1833), the history of the slave trade and the wealth it generated for cities such as London, Liverpool, Bristol, and Cardiff has recently been a topic of journalistic, scholarly, and public interest (the latter being stimulated in no small part by the release of the film *Amazing Grace*, which chronicled the life of the British abolitionist William Wilberforce).

Hoerder (2002, p. 127) concurs with those who put the size of the slave trade from the middle of the 15th century until the last quarter of the 19th at 9.4 million people. While some estimates put the number at 20 million or more, the scholarly consensus tends to set the figure somewhere between 9 and 12 million (Curtin, 1969; Thornton, 1998). The impact of the slave trade was concentrated in West Africa, and as recent scholarship by Gwendolyn Midlo Hall (2007) indicates, the impact was acutely felt by a relatively small number of tribal or ethnic groups in that region of the continent. In the Americas, the vast majority of slaves were destined for Brazil and the Caribbean. Over a third of slaves were taken to Brazil, and similar numbers ended up in the Caribbean, distributed across a number of colonies ruled by various European powers.

Slavery in the Americas was made possible by the involuntary migration of millions whose labor was utilized chiefly (but not solely) in plantation economies. Slavery, thus, was an integral aspect of economic development. In the case of Britain, slavery represented one point in a triangular relationship that made possible the Industrial Revolution (Hobsbawm, 1969), for slave labor produced cotton, the raw material essential if the British textile industry was to succeed. However, at the moment that industrial capitalism came of age, challenges to the slave trade began to change public opinion in favor of ending the trade, a shift that subsequently led to abolishing slavery. In the United States, although the importation of new slaves had been formally ended in 1807, slavery did not actually end until President Lincoln's signing of the Emancipation Proclamation on January 1, 1863. Slavery ultimately ended in the Americas for good when Brazil, the largest importer of slaves, finally ended the practice in 1881. Howard Winant (2001, pp. 71–81) points out that although a key source of resistance came from the slaves themselves as well as "free persons of color," the ultimate success of the abolitionist movement depended on the involvement of whites—in organized form such as the religiously inspired antislavery activities of Quakers and Methodists in the United States and the aspirations for working class solidarity that manifested itself in Britain in the Chartist movement. Brazil's abolitionist movement began later than the rest, promoted chiefly by sectors of the elite and educated middle class.

In these and similar cases elsewhere, the reality was always complex, conflictual, and contradictory. However, in the end, the involuntary movement of people, despite its value to European capitalism up to that point, would cease to be a factor shaping the subsequent mass migrations extending from the late 19th century up to the present. However, as will become evident in subsequent chapters in Section II, modes of incorporation in the 20th and 21st centuries continue to be shaped by the impact of what Winant (2001, p. 81) refers to as a system characterized by a "racial *hegemony*" that relegated nonwhites to social positions characterized by oppression, exploitation, and marginalization.

## Labor in the Service of Capital

It was in the 19th century that what Hoerder (2002, p. 330) refers to as the "proletarian mass migrations in the Atlantic economies" commenced. Winant (2001, p. 81) observes in this regard that abolition "proved to be useful to capital, which could harness anti-slavery logic to equate wage labor with 'freedom' as appropriate: notably in Britain proper and in the U.S. North." Both of these comments highlight a key feature of the migratory movements characteristic of the modern industrial order, which is that movers are voluntary immigrants. Insofar as this is true, they can be seen as actors making decisions about their lives and thus exhibiting what in current sociological parlance is called "agency." It is true that actors make decisions to either stay or to move and, if the latter, about when and where they move. Thus, it is accurate to describe these individuals, in contrast to the movement of slaves, as voluntary migrants. However, it is important to locate these actors within the parameters of a capitalist order in a world system (Sassen, 1999).

The social historian John Bodnar (1985) has aptly characterized the working class immigrants who left Europe for the United States between 1880 and 1930 as "children of capitalism." As such, the decisions they made were structured by the system created by capital—which both enabled and constrained immigrants, setting the parameters for what was and what was not possible. Bodnar stresses the interconnectedness of capitalism and immigration. Immigration occurred because of the dictates and needs of capitalism, and capitalism could not have succeeded if not for immigration.

From 1815 until just before the beginning of World War II, somewhere between 50 and 55 million Europeans left their homelands for destinations in the Americas and elsewhere—constituting about 20% of the continent's population in 1800 (Hoerder, 2002, pp. 331–332). In the earlier stage of this large migratory wave, the emigrants came overwhelmingly from western Europe, while during the second half of the wave, the numbers from eastern Europe rose dramatically and at the same time smaller but still substantial numbers continued to exit western European nations. Historian Brinley Thomas' *Migration and Economic Growth* (1954), a study of Britain in the Atlantic economy, pointed to a situation that Britain shared with other nations on the continent, namely that, as the title of Thomas' book indicates, migration was inextricably connected to economic growth, whether the rationale for moving was the acquisition of land or obtaining work in the emerging capitalist industrial order.

The culturally embedded depiction of the United States as a "nation of immigrants" is well founded, for 70% of European emigrants departed their homelands for the United States (Thistlethwaite, 1960, p. 33; see also Vecoli & Sinke, 1991). It was, indeed, as the preeminent early historian of immigration Marcus Lee Hansen (1940, p. 192; see also Taylor, 1971) described it, "a huge magnet of varying intensity." Other major recipients of migrants included Canada and Argentina, with both receiving around 7 million, while 4.6 million landed in Brazil, and 2.5 million in Australia, New Zealand, and South Africa combined.

Walter Nugent (1992, p. xv) has argued that just as Fernand Braudel's (1972) magisterial study made a convincing claim that the Mediterranean region constituted "the brilliant center of the late sixteenth-century world," so "the Atlantic was the center of the late nineteenth," with the emigration of Europeans to the Americas causing a demographic and social transformation the world had never before seen. Although Nugent's desire to write an Atlantic counterpart to Braudel's work never materialized, his book *Crossings: The Great Transatlantic Migrations, 1870–1914* (1992) provides an invaluable comparative tool. Though brief, it is the only systematic effort to provide a comparative portrait of both the main European emigration nations and the major countries of immigration in both North and South America.

## Leaving Europe

One thing is clear from the outset. Many immigrants arrived in the Americas for political and religious reasons, and a not insubstantial number of prisoners were sent from Britain to its penal colonies in a system known as convict transportation. Nevertheless, the overwhelming majority departing Europe did so primarily for economic factors. This migratory era was predominantly a labor migration, with workers seeking agricultural land and, especially later on, work in the growing industrial sector. Changes in the European agricultural sector in conjunction with the birth of the Industrial Revolution became the two macroeconomic factors that, combined with demographic change, provided the larger causal factors shaping the movement of people out of their homelands for distant lands.

From the middle of the 17th century until the beginning of the 20th, the population of Europe grew dramatically, and this occurred in spite of the exodus of tens of millions. Herbert Moller (1964, pp. 5–7) contends that the population of the continent grew from 140 million in 1750 to 429 million in 1900, which meant that the European population as a proportion of the world's overall population rose from 17% to 25%. Although demographers continue to debate the precise impact of the factors that contributed to this dramatic increase, among the obvious causal forces is the fact that improvements in sanitation and health care resulted in increased life expectancies. During this century and a half, the continent was not struck by the epidemics that—like the Black Death in the 14th century—had drastically reduced the population before. Likewise, although Europe could not be described as peaceful, wars did not take the kind of toll they had earlier— and would again in the 20th century.

The precise role played by fertility rates continues to be debated by demographers. Some have argued, not at first glance unreasonably, that increased fertility rates must have also contributed to the population increase, with reduced death rates alone not being singularly capable of this increase. However, there are many scholars who dispute this assumption. For example, Michael Flinn (1985, p. 90) asserts that "there is generally very little evidence to support the view that the European acceleration in the rate of population growth may be explained in terms of rising fertility: there is indeed more evidence of the reverse happening." Agreeing with this perspective, Jose Moya (1998, p. 14) contends, "In a sense, mass emigration and declining fertility replaced plagues and wars as the checks in this emerging system."

The key point for understanding the significance of migration in this context is that the revolution in agriculture contributed to population growth. It did so because improvements in agricultural technology produced increased yields, which contributed to a healthier populace. However, these changes in commercial agriculture also led to a reduced need for agricultural workers. The enclosure movement asserted the rights of private property over communal ownership, with the result being that smaller farmers were increasingly pushed off the land. From the late 18th century forward, these now landless farmers migrated to cities in search of work. Their ability to find an alternative source of employment depended to large extent on whether or not demand for workers as a result of industrialization was sufficient to absorb this new potential labor force.

The Industrial Revolution took shape at different times and in distinctive ways throughout western Europe. Thus, while Britain was the cradle of the Industrial Revolution, Germany lagged behind at least during the early part of the 19th century, as attested in Marx's discussion of the land of his birth in *The German Ideology*. Moya (1998, p. 32) observes that Spain witnessed the birth of a textile industry around the same time that it emerged in Britain, but the first attempt proved unsuccessful. However, by the middle of the 19th century, a new effort in Catalonia proved more successful, and somewhat later the Basque region became a center for metallurgy and shipbuilding. As a consequence, both of these regions experienced an influx of internal migration as workers sought employment in the industrial sector.

Technological innovations gave the British the lead in industrial development, beginning with such inventions as the spinning jenny and John Kay's creation of the flying shuttle. Watt's steam engine helped set the stage for the transition from textiles to an emphasis on heavy industry based on coal and iron. However, whether leader or laggard in industrialization, the nations of western Europe confronted the prospect of vast reservoirs of surplus labor—what Marx referred to as the reserve army of the unemployed. While on the one hand, such a surplus supply of labor was valuable to capitalists because it served to keep wage levels low, there was considerable concern about the social and possibly political costs associated with the presence of a large sector of unemployed and disgruntled people. It is in this context that the Industrial Revolution became the age of mass migration.

The Atlantic crossing that resulted could not have been possible without major advances in transportation. Key to mass immigration was the replacement of sailing ships with steamships, which reduced the length of the trip considerably, thereby making the voyage considerably less arduous. Nugent (1992, p. 31) writes, "Early in the [19th] century, the voyage from the British Isles to North America took four to six weeks, plenty of time for contagious diseases to ravage passengers and crew," noting that diseases "frequently swept away 10 percent, and occasionally 25 percent, of the passengers during a crossing."

According to Moya (1998, p. 35), "Improvements in transportation were usually designed to move goods rather than people. But as people began to move en masse they, from the perspective of the ship owners, became cargo." The shipping industry increased its capacity to move large numbers of people as a consequence not only of the increased demand to emigrate, but because American raw materials were increasingly in demand in Europe. Indeed, Manchester could not have become the textile center of the world without access to a steady supply of cotton from the Americas. Thus, ship owners were in a position to profit by two types of cargo: human on the trip from Europe to America and raw materials on the return crossing.

Among the largest and most consequential companies that made possible mass migration were the British lines Cunard and White Star and the German Hamburg-Amerika and Norddeutsche Lloyd. Slow to develop their own shipping industry, both Spain and Portugal relied for the earliest phase of mass migration on companies from Britain, Germany, and elsewhere in Europe. Major disembarkation points included Southampton and Liverpool in England and Bremen and Hamburg in Germany, with other locales also playing roles, such as Gothenburg for the Nordic nations and Genoa in Italy. Linked to the increased capacity to move human cargo across the Atlantic were developments in land transportation in both Europe and America, specifically with the expansion of railroad networks. Railroads were instrumental in transporting people from rural hinterlands to port cities and from destination ports to settlement areas in the Americas. In the Americas, the United States developed its railroad network earlier than other countries, some of which did not see the development of a comprehensive railroad network until after the 1880s (Nugent 1992, p. 13).

Yet another factor that made possible this age of migration involved the political decisions of both nations of emigration and receiving states. Regarding the former, Aristide Zolberg (2007) depicts an "exit revolution" that took shape in the wake of the American and French Revolutions. In the American case, one of the colonists' complaints against Britain was that it restricted the free movement of individuals at a time when they sought settlers. The French case revealed the significance of the shift from being subjects to citizens, for what was at stake was the ability of the state to prevent individuals from mobility, both internally and across borders. Prior to the exit revolution, monarchs tended to view their subjects as a resource and as a measure of their power. Thus, they manifested a general unwillingness to permit the mass exodus of people. That being said, with the need to develop their colonies, they found it necessary to establish policies that allowed for some movement, but with the stipulation being that the state, not the individual, was the ultimate arbiter in such determinations. As Zolberg (2007, p. 34) depicts it, "population policy was simultaneously protectionist and acquisitive."

Beginning with the French Constitution of 1791, the right of free movement, including the right to leave one's homeland, began to be viewed as a fundamental right predicated on citizenship, with its emphasis on the notion of self-rule. During the 19th century, this right became increasingly embedded in the political cultures of the western European states, resulting in a progressive but not unilinear move to liberalize existing restrictions on mobility. In some places, such as Prussia, the dismantling of the feudal age with the end of serfdom prodded rulers to relax earlier restrictions on movement, first for internal movement but relatively soon thereafter for exit from the state. The impact of the ideals of the French Revolution reverberated in other parts of the continent (Torpey, 2007, pp. 16–17). Somewhat ironically, France was to later reintroduce restrictive legislation during the 19th century, making it less liberal than most other nations. However, the differences were a matter of degree, as the right to movement became entrenched, though states in various ways sought to exert controls over mobility. The passport, for example, was instrumental in this regard, serving as a tool for individual surveillance and border control (Torpey, 2000). The only exception to this general trend was Russia, which still maintained policies prohibiting emigration. But here, too, there were exceptions insofar as with government permission, ethnic minorities such as Jews, Poles, and Germans were allowed to exit (Schneider, 2007, p. 196).

## Settlement in the Americas

For their part, the nations of the Americas embraced open-door policies, operating with the conviction that in resource-rich but population-poor societies, the influx of newcomers was essential for both economic development and state building. Among historians, dating from Marcus Lee Hansen through such influential works as Maldwyn Jones' classic *American Immigration* (1960) to Roger Daniels' recent *Guarding the Golden Door* (2004), there has been a consensus that despite nativist hostility, the United States did not begin the process of changing its open-door policy until the 1880s, with the passage of the Chinese Exclusion Act of 1882 constituting the first time that the country had signaled out for exclusion groups on the basis of national/ethnic identity.

Recently, Zolberg (2006) has sought to challenge this position by arguing that the national government played a far more activist role in shaping and containing immigration from a very early date. His argument hinges on what he contends is the unappreciated significance of the enactment in 1819 of the Passenger Act. Whereas earlier commentators viewed it as regulatory in nature, Zolberg (2006, pp. 110–113) contends that it amounted to a form of restriction by "remote control." The evidence he presents is somewhat thin and it should be remembered that aside from attempting to prevent the entry of the mentally ill, criminals, and those likely to become paupers, the immigration regime in place throughout the 19th century allowed for a massive influx of newcomers to settle and to naturalize. Thus, it is more reasonable to treat the Passenger Act as a law with rather limited impact that served as a precursor to later developments, when the state undertook a far more activist role in controlling immigration.

In the case of Canada, given the fact that it was a fraction of the size of its neighbor to the south and remained a part of the British Empire, immigration policies were shaped by Britain's realization that the nation's potential was profoundly influenced by its unique relationship to the United States. Indeed, one of the realities that Canada confronted was that large numbers of immigrants did not remain, but headed below the 49th parallel. Nugent (1992, p. 136) has characterized Canadian migration as a "sieve." In the two South American cases he takes up, Argentina and Brazil, relatively weak and sometimes unstable states limited their capacity to control immigration. Thus, their borders remained porous.

This portrait is not meant to suggest that immigration was conflict free; it generated tensions and conflicts in both the sending and receiving nations. In spite of the liberalization of laws related to the right to exit and the open-door policies in the Americas, immigrants often encountered opposition—sometimes violent opposition. In the nation of origin, some cultural elites accused emigrants of being traitors to the homeland. This was particularly common among elites influenced by the nationalist ideologies that took hold in Europe. Religious elites were similarly hostile, in this case because they feared that the immigration setting would undermine religious convictions. Many in Europe's Catholic hierarchy expressed concerns that in the North American context, Protestant proselytizing would undermine migrants' commitment to the one true faith. In the receiving nations, hostility to immigrants varied based on the distinctive characteristics of the particular groups and on whether or not the immigrants were perceived to be competitive threats in the workforce or political rivals. Here, opposition could be seen both among elites, who tended to be primarily concerned about the presumed cultural impacts of newcomers, and ordinary people, who found themselves in competition with immigrants over jobs, housing, and the like.

Within this framework, as Table 2.1 indicates, the United States was the chief beneficiary of the Atlantic migration, followed by Argentina, Canada, Brazil, the British West Indies, and Cuba. Figure 2.2 reveals not only that immigration levels rose and fell over time, achieving a zenith in the early 20th century, but that the pattern for the Americas as a whole closely parallels that of the United States alone. As noted earlier, emigration did not only land migrants in the Americas, as Australia, New Zealand, and South Africa emerged over time as the other primary destinations.

Immigrants came from all the nations of Europe, with the United Kingdom contributing the largest number, followed by Italy, Austria-Hungary, Germany, Spain, Russia, Portugal, and Sweden. Noticeably absent from this list is France. As Figure 2.3 indicates, immigrants predominantly from western Europe defined the earliest phase of the migration. While they continued to arrive throughout

**Table 2.1**   Major Receivers and Donors of Migrants

| Country | Years of Immigration | Number of Immigrants |
|---|---|---|
| Countries Receiving Over 500,000 Immigrants, 1820–1924 | | |
| United States | 1821–1924 | 33,188,000 |
| Argentina | 1857–1924 | 5,486,000 |
| Canada | 1821–1924 | 4,520,000 |
| Brazil | 1821–1924 | 3,855,000 |
| British West Indies | 1836–1924 | 1,470,000 |
| Cuba | 1901–1924 | 766,000 |
| Countries Sending Over 1,000,000 Emigrants, 1846–1924 | | |
| United Kingdom | | 16,974,000 |
| Italy | | 9,474,000 |
| Austria-Hungary | | 4,878,000 |
| Germany | | 4,533,000 |
| Spain | | 4,314,000 |
| Russia | | 2,253,000 |
| Portugal | | 1,633,000 |
| Sweden | | 1,145,000 |

*Source:* Ferenczi (1933, p. 436).

the entire migratory wave, the dramatic increase that occurred in the late 19th and early 20th centuries was primarily due to the large increase in immigrants from eastern and southern Europe. One additional point is in order: not all the immigrants came from Europe. A much smaller but nonetheless significant stream of immigrants arrived from Asia. These "strangers from a different shore," as Ronald Takaki (1989) has characterized them, arrived first from China—beginning with the California Gold Rush—and later from Japan.

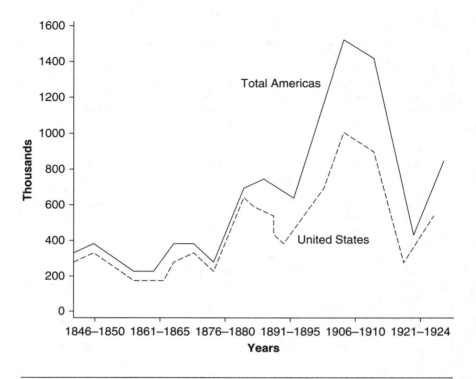

**Figure 2.2**    Immigration to the Americas, 1845–1924 (5-year averages)
*Source:* Ferenczi and Wilcox (1929, pp. 236–237).

Nugent (1992) has pointed out that the difference in the size of the immigrant populations in the American receiving nations is reflected in differences in the amount of scholarly attention that immigration has received in the various nations of the two continents. Thus, a voluminous body of research has been published on the United States, while the size of the body of literature on Canada is reflective of the fact that its population is a tenth of that of the United States. There are considerably smaller bodies of literature devoted to Argentina and Brazil. Nugent's book makes a singular contribution by providing a comprehensive and comparative analysis of the Atlantic migration.

Argentina's population soared from the middle of the 19th century, due in no small part to increases in immigration—rising from 1.7 million in 1860 to 7.9 million in 1914, at which point first- and second-generation immigrants constituted 58% of the total population. No country in the Americas reported a higher percentage of foreign-born and no major cities had a

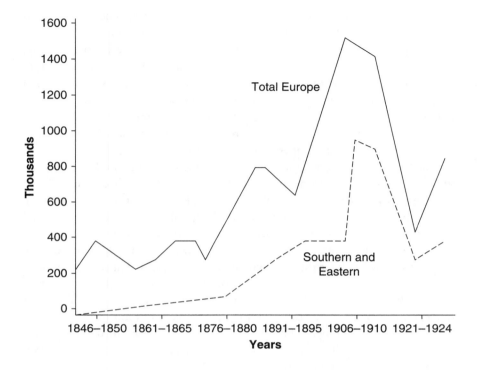

**Figure 2.3**    Emigration From Europe, 1846–1924 (5-year averages)
*Source:* Ferenczi and Wilcox (1929, pp. 230–231).

higher percentage of foreign-born than the 70% level of Buenos Aires. Moreover, 30.3% of the population in 1914 was foreign born. In comparison, the highest percentage ever reached by the United States was less than half that figure (Nugent, 1992, p. 112). By far the largest group in Argentina was the Italians, representing about half of the total immigrant population, followed by Spaniards, with slightly less than a third of the total. The French were the third-largest group, with slightly less than 5% of the total.

Unlike North America, where immigrants seeking land entered an agricultural system characterized by smallholdings (aside from the plantation system in the southern states of the U.S.), the *latifundia* system in Argentina persisted from colonial times and thus most immigrant farmers were renters. On the other hand, urban dwellers often found opportunities for incorporation and upward mobility. Samuel Baily's (1999, p. 119) comparative examination of Italian immigrants in Buenos Aires and New York City found that the former Italians found more opportunities for upward mobility in both skilled occupations and white-collar jobs, while the latter tended to be confined to the unskilled sector of the economy. Buenos Aires' Italians "adjusted more rapidly, effectively, and completely than those in New York" (Baily, 1999, p. 217). The fact that the sheer size of Buenos Aires' immigrant population as a whole and of the Italian population in particular was larger than that in New York City, while perhaps not the whole story, can go far in explaining these differences. Adjustment in the Argentine case was predicated on the fact that immigrants were in a position to have much greater say in forging the content of Argentine identity.

The Brazilian case was in many respects quite different. Unlike Argentina, which became an independent republic early in the 19th century, Brazil experienced throughout that century a difficult transition from Portuguese rule to the establishment of an independent republic. Moreover, Brazil relied more than any other major country in the Americas on slavery. About half of the population was composed of slaves, with the abolition of slavery occurring in 1888, later than elsewhere in the Americas. Thus, even more so than the United States, the nation's history was shaped not only by the role of voluntary immigrants, but by involuntary ones as well. Indeed, the myth of Brazil as a racial democracy, codified in the works of anthropologist and public intellectual Gilberto Freyre, was an explicit effort to depict Brazil's race relations in idyllic terms, distinguishing the nation from the *Herrenvolk* democracy of the United States (Kivisto, 2007a, pp. 229–230).

The earliest European immigrants began to arrive in the 1820s, coming chiefly from Germany and Italy. Both groups clustered in ethnic colonies in the hinterland, thereby living in relative isolation from the larger society. As a result, and this was especially true of the Germans, language and cultural maintenance prevailed at the expense of assimilation. In both instances, the colonies were not especially successful. The real beginning of mass migration occurred late in the 19th century, shortly after the abolition of slavery. The two largest groups were the Italians (33%) and Portuguese (30%), followed by smaller numbers of Poles, Jews, and Germans. In addition, in the second decade of the 20th century, Japanese began arriving, ultimately representing 4.5% of the immigrant population. Brazilian immigration did not have the same powerful impact that it did in Argentina because, demographically, immigrants constituted a far smaller percentage of the population in Brazil. Indeed, the peak moment for immigration took place in 1900, when 6.2% of the population was foreign born (Nugent, 1992, p. 125).

The fact that contemporary Canada has been a leader among the world's liberal democracies in implementing official multicultural policies ought to be seen against the backdrop of its history. Remaining loyal to Britain in the wake of the American Revolution and contending with the fact that the

French, though they lost out in the power struggle for control of the society, could nonetheless claim the status of one of two charter groups, the country's immigration policies have been developed with the realization that what happens in Canada is influenced by what happens in the United States. Until relatively late in the 19th century, Canada did not experience the influx of newcomers to the extent that the United States did prior to 1880. Relatively small numbers of Chinese arrived in midcentury, largely confined to British Columbia. With the expansion of industrialization, labor shortages prompted the government to explore ways to attract newcomers from outside the nation. Indeed, from the late 1890s until the early 1920s, the Canadian government, under the direction of Minister of Interior Clifford Sifton, actively encouraged and structured immigration (Hawkins, 1989, pp. 4–21). Demographic growth as a desideratum was tempered by overtly racist policies that sought to ensure a "white Canada." This meant that preferences were to be given to western Europeans over eastern and southern Europeans. It also meant that anti-Asian immigration laws would stop the flow of the Chinese and other Asian groups.

Nugent (1992, pp. 144–145) focuses on the state's role in shaping policies aimed at settling the Canadian prairie. Noting that the settlement of the Canadian West lagged behind the United States, in part because of the delay in getting an infrastructure, particularly the railroad, in place, he argues that by the end of the 19th century, as land opportunities in the American frontier declined and people began to share Frederick Jackson Turner's (1893) view of the "closing of the frontier," the vast Canadian prairie provinces became the last true frontier in North America. Nugent concurs with Carl Solberg's (1987) comparison of the Canadian case with its Argentinean counterpart. Canada was characterized by an activist state that shaped land distribution and implemented protectionist policies to protect the emerging agricultural sector, while in Argentina the state embraced laissez-faire principles. The net result was that settlers on the Canadian frontier thrived while those on the Argentinean pampas did not and the region stagnated. In parallel fashion, the federal government enacted activist immigration policies that were intended to shape the emerging industrial economy.

In both instances, state policymakers were acutely aware of the need for labor and of the fact that the need could only be met by liberal immigration policies. During the earliest phase of the migration, commencing in the last decades of the 19th century, large influxes of British and U.S. residents added to the size of the Anglophone community, reinforcing it and ensuring the perpetuation of a largely Protestant and English-speaking society. Two and a half million people arrived in Canada prior to World War I, a half million of them from outside the Anglo American orbit. These included sizeable numbers of preferred groups from western Europe, including Germans, the Dutch, and Scandinavian groups. However, over time, the number of immigrants arriving from eastern and southern Europe increased. Among the largest groups from these areas of Europe were Italians, Poles, Ukrainians, and Jews. Collectively, these immigrant communities came to represent a growing "third force"—so named because its members were not part of either of the nation's two charter groups (Kivisto, 2002, pp. 88–90).

The United States shared with all three of the nations discussed in the previous paragraphs the fact that their abundant natural resource base could not be exploited, and later industrialization could not develop without the influx of large numbers of immigrants. It shared with Brazil a legacy of slavery and the enduring impact of former slaves on the nation's subsequent social history. It shared with Canada a deeply rooted cultural history shaped by British influence and the dominance of Protestantism. It also shared with its northern neighbor a desire to privilege white immigrants. What made the United States distinctive was the sheer enormity of the nation, for its population would soon overtake the size of some of the largest European nations. This could not have resulted simply due to high fertility levels, but necessitated mass immigration, which began as early as the 1830s.

As Figure 2.4 indicates, a migratory wave began in the 1830s and ended a century later. It was characterized by peaks and valleys—dramatic increases followed by rapid declines—that moved progressively upward until it reached

**Figure 2.4**    American Immigration: 1820–1970

its zenith in the first decade of the 20th century. Tracing the movement, the first peak was reached in 1854, followed by a decline during the years leading up to and including the Civil War. After the war, immigration rates rose, with dips occurring along the way that reflected changes in the economic climate of the nation. In short, a boom-and-bust economic cycle impacted immigration. During this period, the United States went through two major depressions, 1873–1879 and 1893–1897, and three smaller ones. This migratory wave occurred as an essentially agrarian nation was transformed into what would become the most powerful industrial nation in the world. Immigrants settled in particular on the East Coast, where they confronted and had to adapt to long-established native-born Americans, and in the Midwest, where they arrived at or shortly after the founding of new cities and towns. Later, they also moved westward. The one region that did not experience to any significant degree the impact of immigration was the American South.

The early decades of the wave, up to the Civil War, witnessed a migratory flow that came predominantly from western Europe. The largest groups to arrive during this period included the English, whom historian Charlotte Erickson (1972) aptly labeled "invisible immigrants," invisible because they so readily fit in and blended into a society formed to a significant degree by English folkways, mores, language, and laws. The other two groups of comparable size and significance were the Germans and the Irish. Somewhat smaller in numbers, but nonetheless consequential, particularly for the Upper Midwest, were Scandinavians. Many were motivated by the quest for land, though some nonetheless ended up in industry rather than on the farm.

In many respects, the Civil War was a watershed dividing the nation's agrarian past from its industrial future. Certainly, by the 1880s, industrialization was accelerating at a rapid pace and the demand for labor consequently increased. While immigrants from western Europe never ceased to arrive, their numbers declined over time, and as immigrants from eastern and southern Europe began to arrive in large numbers, the percentage of western European immigrants declined as a proportion of the overall foreign-born population. In 1980, the *Harvard Encyclopedia of American Ethnic Groups* was published, documenting the incredibly diverse array of groups that had contributed to the creation of the composite American identity. Over 100 groups are represented in the volume, ranging from Acadians to Zoroastrians. Many of these groups arrived between 1880 and 1930. Some, although relatively small in number, managed to have an impact in certain geographic locales due to their concentration, such as Icelanders in North Dakota or Acadians in Louisiana. Some, particularly ethno-religious groups like the Amish, managed over time to preserve their distinctive identities, doing so by maintaining considerable distance from the societal mainstream. An abundance of scholarship has been devoted to some groups, while others have received only modest scholarly attention. To cite examples close to home, since one of the authors is half Finnish and half Cornish, there is a substantial body of scholarly work devoted to the Finns, while the Cornish continue from the perspective of scholars (and the general public) to be largely invisible ethnics.

The major point here is simply that the United States is by far the most ethnically diverse nation in the world, and it earned that designation over a century ago. In this context, the largest groups arriving in the second phase of the wave included Italians, Jews (arriving from Russia, Poland, and other points of origin in eastern Europe), and Poles. The Italians were less likely than any other European group to settle in agricultural occupations, finding work instead in a variety of unskilled jobs in factories, in mines, and on "pick and shovel" jobs, with Italian women being well represented in the garment industry (Gabaccia & Iacovetta, 2002; Hutchinson, 1956). "Little Italy"s sprang up in major cities such as New York, Boston, Philadelphia, Baltimore, Chicago, and St. Louis.

In the case of Jews, small numbers had been present in the American colonies, chiefly Sephardic Jews whose origins were from Spain and Portugal. By the late 18th century, Ashkenazic Jews emigrated in relatively small numbers from Germany. They settled along the Atlantic seaboard and in the new commercial cities springing up in the Midwest, often finding success as small business owners, particularly owners of retail stores. The Jewish community changed appreciably after 1880 as a result of the mass immigration of Jews from eastern Europe. These Jews were considerably poorer than those who preceded them, as well as more tradition bound and less educated. They found jobs in semiskilled positions, particularly in the garment industry (Daniels, 1990, 223–232).

When Poles began leaving their homeland in the 19th century, it was often a temporary labor migration to Germany. Over time, these earlier migrations became part of a stage of migration that after 1880 brought increasing numbers of Poles to the United States. By the end of World War I, 2.5 million immigrants had settled in the country, with the community in Chicago being the largest (indeed, more Poles resided in that city than any other city in the world except Warsaw), but with other large Polonias existing in Pittsburgh, Buffalo, Cleveland, Detroit, and Milwaukee. These were overwhelmingly economic migrants who frequently viewed themselves as temporary sojourners who hoped to be able to make money and return home. They were described as *za chlebem* (for bread) immigrants, which historical sociologist Ewa Morawska (1985) has suggested meant that they operated in pragmatic and realistic ways in their efforts to not only survive but improve their economic conditions. Approximately 95% of Poles worked in industry as unskilled laborers; they were heavily concentrated in coal mining, steel production, and slaughtering and meatpacking (Morawska, 1989).

This great migratory wave that constituted the Atlantic crossing came to an end by the third decade of the twentieth century. The worldwide Depression followed by World War II reduced levels, but in the case of the United States, the wave had already wound down due to the passage in 1924 of the National Origins Act. This piece of legislation was the final outcome of the growing anti-immigration movement that had begun to exert political pressure as early as the turn of the century.

It was during this wave that the first efforts were undertaken by the emerging social sciences to understand immigration as a social phenomenon. Sociologists played a lead role, with economists also making substantial contributions. To a lesser extent, political scientists were also involved, though given the fluidity between disciplinary lines at the time, it is sometimes difficult to locate particular contributions squarely within any one discipline's boundaries. That being said, from a very early stage in the emergence of immigration as a topic of inquiry, an implicit division of labor arose. In this division, demographers, economists, and economic sociologists concerned themselves with the causes of immigration, while sociologists concentrated on the impact of the migratory experience on both immigrants and receiving societies. They developed theories to account for immigrant adjustment and incorporation, which included explorations into factors that stymied adjustment and incorporation. In this regard, theoretical developments and research advances in the study of race and ethnicity became closely linked to researchers involved in immigration studies, including work in the areas of prejudice and discrimination. In this chapter devoted to the study of immigrant flows, the former part of the division of labor will be explored, while the latter, what became and remains the primary focus of the sociology of immigration, will be taken up in subsequent chapters.

## Theories of Migration

The first major contribution to a theory of migration is often attributed to Ernst Georg Ravenstein, a German-born geographer who worked at the Royal Geographical Society in London and published two influential articles on "The Laws of Migration" (1885, 1889). According to Ravenstein's own account, he was prompted to theorize about the structured features of migratory movements in response to the contention of William Farr, a contemporary of his, that migrations occurred in basically random or haphazard fashion. Ravenstein was convinced that this was not true and thus sought to articulate a series of laws that could be used to both explain and predict migratory movements, relevant to migrations within and outside of national borders. Using Everett Lee's (1966, p. 48) grouping of Ravenstein's conclusion, we can summarize the main laws as follows:

- *Migration and Distance:* (1) Most migrants travel short distances, (2) while those who do travel long distances prefer major commercial and industrial centers.
- *Migration by Stages:* (1) A current of migration occurs when commercial and industrial centers absorb large numbers of migrants; (2) the closest rural dwellers move to cities, thereby leaving gaps that are filled by the rural population from more remote areas; and (3) the process of dispersion is the reverse of that of absorption.
- *Stream and Counterstream:* Mainstreams of migration produce a counterstream.
- *Urban/Rural Differences in Propensity to Migrate:* Rural dwellers are more likely to migrate than the natives of cities.
- *Predominance of Females Among Short-Distance Movers:* More women make short-distance migrations, particularly within national borders, than males.
- *Technology and Migration:* Improvements in transportation networks and the expansion of industrialization lead to increased levels of migration.
- *Centrality of Economic Factors:* While levels of migration can be influenced by state actions (e.g., laws, tax policies), climate, and geographic factors, they not only are not nearly as consequential as economic considerations, but are often actually intervening obstacles that can sometimes be eliminated, thus permitting economic forces to operate in an essentially unimpeded way.

From the moment it appeared, commentators raised questions about Ravenstein's attempt to provide an account of immigration as a structured phenomenon that operates in law-like fashion. The most fundamental charge leveled against his work was that he had failed to articulate what would generally be construed as theory. Instead, it was argued that what he had actually constructed was a description of various patterns that could be perceived by the empirical evidence available to him. It's not that a description of patterns is unimportant; it's simply to say that it doesn't add up to a theory, or in his terminology, to "laws" (Petersen, 1958, p. 265). While we tend to concur with this assessment, it is nevertheless true that in retrospect, Ravenstein's work influenced two subsequent currents of migration theorizing: the push-pull model and an economic model based on neoclassical economic presuppositions.

## The Push-Pull Model

Turning to the first of these, Lee (1966) is a pivotal figure in giving expression to push-pull theory, although he did not use the term in describing his "theory of migration" (de Haas, 2007, p. 9). He distilled from Ravenstein a model that is predicated on the assumption that the volume, what he called the "stream" (essentially, the direction of migration from point A to point B), and the selection of those who enter the stream is structured by four factors. The factors he identifies are those associated with the point of origin, those with the destination, "intervening obstacles," and the personal characteristics of potential migrants (Lee, 1966, p. 50). Figure 2.5 represents his graphic depiction of what needs to be considered in accounting for any specific migratory flow. In his portrait, three types of factors are operative at both the origin and destination, those that promote migration (+), those that deter or prevent it (-), and those that have no bearing on it (0). As he points out, this figure does not take into account the fourth of his factors, namely, individual attributes. The model's attractiveness for migration research is obvious: it offers a remarkably intuitive and parsimonious account of the process. In short, a major part of the task at hand in accounting for migrations is to provide a cost-benefit calculus.

The assumption is that migrations occur as a consequence of two complementary processes. First, they commence when the weight of the factors pushing people out of one place are more powerful than those keeping them there. Among the most important push factors are rapid population growth, poverty and a lack of economic opportunity, and political repression. In various combinations, these and other factors contribute to the migratory push. Second, it occurs when the weight of factors pulling people into another locale are more powerful than those deterring entry. Among the key factors that pull people to a society are job opportunities, higher wages than in the homeland, the possibility of acquiring land, and political and cultural freedom. The respective intensity of these forces contributes to the volume and defines the particular nature of the stream, moving from A to B rather than

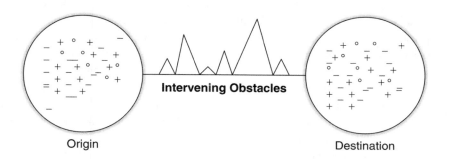

**Figure 2.5**    Origin and Destination Factors and Intervening Obstacles in Migration

*Source:* Lee (1966, p. 50).

to C. This is a model well suited to those disposed to a rational choice perspective, for it assumes that migrations occur as a result of the calculations of individuals who make instrumental decisions intended to enhance their life circumstances.

Lee contends that two additional forces need to be factored into the equation. The first is what he refers to as the "natural inertia" that is a given (Lee, 1966, p. 51). In other words, one of the underlying domain assumptions of his theory is that people are by nature stayers rather than movers. Migrations are thus not persistent features of the modern world, being triggered only in extraordinary rather than ordinary times. The second factor shaping migrations are the "intervening obstacles." Distance is one such obstacle, one that is linked to the state of existing transportation systems. Physical barriers, such as the fence that has been built along sections of the U.S.–Mexican border, represent another obstacle, as do legal barriers.

Figure 2.5 does not depict the matter of the personal attributes of migrants, but Lee is clear that some people are more likely to migrate than others. Migrations are selective. Thus, young people are more likely to migrate than older ones because they are more viable candidates for the receiving society's labor market. Likewise, those with certain types of human capital—educational credentials, employment skills—are far more likely to migrate than those with human capital deficits.

## Neoclassical Economics and Migration

It is common at the moment to dismiss push-pull theory in favor of more recent approaches (Castles & Miller, 2004; de Haas, 2007), most notably network theory as it has been developed in particular by Douglas Massey and colleagues (Massey et al., 1993, 1994; Massey & Taylor, 2004). In part, this is because one variant of the push-pull model is frequently taken to be representative of the model as a whole, an economic theory known as the neoclassical equilibrium perspective. It portrays migration as a consequence of the interplay between the size of the labor supply and wages in two different locales. Simply put, when there is a surplus of labor and wages are consequently depressed in one place, a segment of the surplus population is attracted to a destination characterized by labor shortages and, due to the demand for labor, higher wages.

The earliest articulations of this model were intended for internal migrations within developing nations, specifically the mass movements of workers from rural to urban settings (Harris & Todaro, 1970; Todaro, 1969, 1976), but it has also been applied to international migration (Borjas, 1989, 1990). For both internal and international migration, neoclassical equilibrium theory assumes that the volume of migration is determined by the relative differences in the supply of and demand for labor in different geographic locations. When the differences are great, the volume will be high; when the differences are low, the volume will be low. Of course, would-be migrants need to factor into the equation the cost of migration and potential problems they might encounter before gaining entrée into the destination countries' higher wage labor market. In the case of undocumented migrants, this includes factoring in the potential costs associated with arrest and deportation (Todaro & Maruszko, 1987). Massey and colleagues (1994, p. 701) summarize the essence of neoclassical economics in the following way: "The difference between incomes expected at origin and destination, when summed and discounted over some time horizon and added to the negative costs of movement, yields the expected net gain from movement, which if positive promotes migration."

This theory is predicated on the assumption of a self-regulating market, one in which migrations can be expected to peak before winding down. The reason that migrations are not considered to be perpetual or a constant state is that as more migrants enter a high-demand, higher-wage area, over time their presence reduces demand and thus depresses wages. At the same time, from the point of view of the place of origin, migrants can be seen as surplus labor. Their departure signals a decline in the surplus, which over time will increase the demand for labor, which in turn leads to increases in prevailing wages. Thus, in the end, a new equilibrium is achieved and the migratory wave comes to an end as the incentives to migrate evaporate.

In their review of the literature that has attempted to test the neoclassical equilibrium model in accounting for post-1945 immigration to the United States from elsewhere in the Western Hemisphere, Massey and colleagues (1994, p. 710) conclude that "the accumulated evidence generally supports neoclassical theory's fundamental proposition that immigration is tied to international differences in wage rates." Although it has had a decided impact on both the ways the public thinks about the cause of immigration and has played a role in shaping immigration policy, there are limitations to its utility. Put simply, the central basis of the critique was that due to its singular focus on the individual, neoclassical equilibrium theory is not in itself sufficient to provide a compelling explanation of immigration. One might also note that the theory is only applicable to "voluntary" migratory flows with high degrees of freedom.

## Network Theory and the New Economics of Migration

Economist Oded Stark (1991) became the central figure associated with what has become known as the "new economics of migration." His approach did not seek to reject neoclassical theory *tout court,* but rather to amend it chiefly by complementing its insights with a more empirically grounded theoretical framework. In so doing, one of the domain assumptions of the neoclassical model is challenged. The new economics calls into question the assumption that migration is a phenomenon pursued by individuals. Ignored from the neoclassical perspective is the fact that immigrants are embedded in what Simmel (1955) once called "webs of group-affiliations." Stark's (1991) position concentrated on the role of families. Building on this insight, Massey melded the new economics of migration to sociology by introducing network theory. From his perspective, Simmel's loosely conceived idea of webs takes on analytic rigor as "networks," which he and his associates (Massey et al., 1994, p. 728) define in the following way:

> Migrant networks are sets of interpersonal ties that connect migrants, former migrants, and nonmigrants in origin and destination areas through ties of kinship, friendship, and shared community origin. The existence of these ties is hypothesized to increase the likelihood of emigration by lowering the costs, raising the benefits, and mitigating the risks of international movement. Network connections constitute a valuable form of social capital that people draw upon to gain access to foreign employment and high wages.

Historians of immigration have long been aware of what was once called the "friends and relatives effect" or, alternatively, "chain migration" in creating and sustaining immigration streams (Baines, 1995, pp. 33–38; Hatton & Williamson, 1998, p. 14; Williamson, 1974). Discussing the last great migratory wave in the United States, geographer Robert C. Ostergren (1988, pp. 158–159) described the process as one in which

> the first emigrants from a European community commonly went to some place about which they possessed information. They in turn sent additional information home once they had reached their destination. As new emigrants followed in their footsteps, certain "axes of information" developed between places on either side of the Atlantic. Once the migrant stream began moving along these axes, it became self-reinforcing, ultimately taking on all the attributes of a chain migration.

A substantial body of literature devoted to finely honed analyses of specific ethnic groups who made the Atlantic crossing and settled with their coethnics in various American rural and urban communities reinforces his claim. In addition to Ostergren's (1988) own exploration of Swedes in the Midwest, among some of the most influential and representative studies that stress the significance of migratory chains, one can point to Kathleen Conzen's (1976) work on Germans in Milwaukee, Kerby Miller's (1985) panoramic book on the Irish in America, Jon Gjerde's (1985) examination of Norwegian peasants who settled in the Upper Midwest, Virginia Yans-McLaughlin's (1977) community study of Italians in Buffalo, and Ewa Morawska's (1985) account of Polish and other Slavic immigrants in the mining town of Johnstown, Pennsylvania.

The social ties served to link individual immigrants both to those who remained in the homeland and those who were fellow immigrants. The journey was the result of the economic calculations of a family or other intimates and not made simply by an isolated individual. The significance of prepaid tickets purchased for a potential migrant by friends or family is an indication of the collective nature of the migration decision-making process. The ongoing sharing of information between origin and destination about such matters as whether or not economic and other conditions were conducive to additional immigration was also part of the equation. Likewise, the creation of ethnic enclaves in both urban and rural settings indicates the significance immigrants attached to the maintenance of ethnic connections in the new world.

In contrast to the neoclassical equilibrium model, the new economics framework treats migration as a complex phenomenon that involves both economic and noneconomic factors. While it does not dismiss the role played by wage differentials between geographic locations, it does not conclude that wage differentials are the only cause triggering an initial wave of immigration. In a significant departure from neoclassical economics, the new economics model does not assume that migrations inevitably occur in a wave that ends with the return to wage equilibrium. Instead, advocates of this position contend that whatever sets in motion the initial impetus to migrate, the establishment of migratory networks serves to perpetuate migration because "they lower the costs and risks of movement and increase the expected net returns to migration" (Massey et al., 1993, p. 448). Charles Tilly (1990, p. 84) contends that "networks migrate," by which he means that the network rather than the individual is the proper unit of analysis. In the end, the network can sustain substantial migratory flows even when economic conditions would suggest that migration should either be declining or cease altogether.

Borrowing the idea of "cumulative causation" from Gunnar Myrdal (1957), Massey and associates (1993, pp. 451–454, 1994, pp. 733–738) reinforce the idea that once underway, contemporary migrations tend to become self-perpetuating. Among the explicitly economic factors that contribute to cumulative causation are changes in income distribution, changes in land distribution, and changes in the organization of agricultural production. Key to changes in income distribution patterns at the point of origin is the role played by remittances sent to relatives from migrants. When household incomes rise as a result, those households not receiving remittances suffer from growing relative deprivation, thereby increasing the motive to migrate. Migrants often purchase land back home, which impacts land distribution because it is thought they are less inclined to put such land into agricultural production, instead maintaining it as a place for retirement. When they do work the land productively, they tend to do so in a more capital-intensive way than local owners, thus reducing the number of available agricultural jobs. In either event, the result is added incentive to migrate.

Three other factors also contribute to cumulative causation: a culture of migration, the regional distribution of human capital, and social labeling. The first of these factors refers to the fact that as migration changes the point of origin, those embedded in the migratory network come to see migration as one of a number of viable options. Indeed, in some places, over time an expectation arises that young men will migrate, if only for a time and if only to test the waters. Given the selective character of migration, those with human capital deemed valuable at the receiving location will come first, thereby increasing the level of human capital there while reducing it at the point of origin. Over time, this contributes to economic decline in the sending community, thereby ratcheting up the inducement to migrate. Finally, social labeling refers to the stereotypical matching of immigrants to certain job categories. This is certainly the case with those jobs described as dirty, dangerous, and difficult (such as agricultural work and work on the cutting floors of slaughterhouses), but it also applies to those "brain drain" immigrants who are perceived to possess educational credentials in short supply. Indian computer programmers in Silicon Valley are a case in point.

## Segmented Labor Markets

Contemporary immigration to the world's most economically developed nations differs from the wave of migration to the centers of industry a century ago. The reason is that although newcomers continue to enter capitalist economies, the nature of capitalism has changed in the core nations. While the main demand during the earlier wave was for workers in primary extractive industries such as mining and manufacturing, since the 1970s, those sectors of the economy have witnessed dramatic decreases in the need for labor. During this time, two interconnected ideas took root both within the social sciences and among the public at large: postindustrial society and deindustrialization. The former term, made popular by Daniel Bell (1973) and Alain Touraine (1971), focused on the shift from a manufacturing economy to knowledge production, a view that emphasized the expansion of jobs in science, technology, and administration. Deindustrialization represented the flip side, stressing the dramatic reduction in blue-collar jobs in basic industries, precisely those jobs that had provided sectors of the working class with middle-class standards of living (Bluestone & Harrison, 1982). Those jobs were replaced by expansions in the service sector of the economy, which were typically non-union, low paying, and with few if any benefits. The net result of this transformation, it was argued, was a bifurcated labor market, an "hourglass economy" with substantial numbers of jobs at the top and bottom, but not in the middle.

In terms of immigration, what became known as a segmented labor market meant that immigrant workers were selected for their specific fit within one or another tiers of the economy, that match being predicated on human capital differentials. Michael Piore (1979) and Saskia Sassen (1988) located this movement of workers into the highly skilled and unskilled sectors of the economy in terms of larger flows of labor and capital, or, in short, in terms of the dictates of global capitalism. Both argued that contemporary migration is primarily demand, rather than supply, driven. Although this perspective has been influential in labor studies, it has suffered from various conceptual and methodological shortcomings (Massey et al., 1994, pp. 715–717).

Piore's (1979) initial formulation applicable to immigration per se referred to the dual labor market, consisting of a primary sector providing high salaries, substantial benefits, and reasonable levels of job security, and a secondary sector, characterized by low wage levels, minimal benefits, unpleasant work with little room for advancement, and job insecurity. When Alejandro Portes and Robert Bach (1985) tested the theory using data derived from Cubans in Miami, they found it necessary to revise the theory by factoring into the equation the "enclave economy." This refers to business enterprises owned by ethnics who employ large numbers of coethnics—in this case Cuban owners employing fellow Cubans. What they concluded was that those workers in the ethnic enclave did better than those located in the secondary sector. While the wages paid were low, the enclave economy offered a type of solidarity that increased the prospects for later upward mobility compared to what one could find in the secondary sector.

Portes and Leif Jensen's (1989) replication of the earlier study confirmed the findings. On the other hand, applying the enclave economy model to Chinese immigrants in San Francisco, Jimy Sanders and Victor Nee (1987) concluded that the workers in the ethnic economy did not benefit to the extent reported by Portes and Bach, while Min Zhou and John Logan's (1989) research on New York City's Chinatown found that the returns on participation in the enclave were gendered, with men being able to convert their human capital to higher earnings while women were not. Despite these different conclusions about the impact of the ethnic enclave on those located within it—entrepreneurs and workers alike—there is general consensus that labor markets are indeed segmented, but contrary to the earliest formulations, it is necessary to consider three sectors (Massey et al., 1994, p. 719). This is particularly salient when studying those ethnic groups that contain significant levels of ethnic entrepreneurship, such as Koreans, Cubans, Chinese, Iranians, Pakistanis, and Russians (Portes & Rumbaut, 2006, p. 30).

## Deflecting Immigration: A Case Study

The theoretical frameworks from Ravenstein to the present that have been reviewed in the preceding pages operate at what Robert Merton would call the middle range. This is a level that allows for the construction of testable hypotheses. Not surprisingly, then, a substantive body of literature has accumulated that has tested theories from the neoclassical perspective to the enclave economy. Out of that literature, no consensus has emerged about any theoretical position, though it is quite clear that at the moment the particular significance attached to networks and segmented labor markets plays a significant role in shaping research agendas.

However varied, these theoretical approaches are both rooted in economics and shaped by a sociological concern for social networks. This should not be surprising since most of the world's immigrants during both this current epoch of migration and the one that preceded it are labor migrants. This reality should not obscure the fact that not all the people who move across borders are doing so as voluntary migrants. As a new and growing literature on human trafficking attests, disturbing numbers of people move involuntarily across borders, exploited in various ways by criminal syndicates. Moreover, international migration need not be the outcome of economic factors, but can result from political, religious, cultural, racial, or gender persecution. These theories, simply put, make no effort to account for refugees and asylum seekers or the causal forces contributing to their border crossings.

From an early point in the development of migration theorizing, a distinction was made between voluntary versus forced migrations (Appleyard, 1991; Fairchild, 1925). This is an analytic distinction that is sometimes conflated with the distinction between refugees and labor migrants. The latter refers to terms employed by states in their formulation of policies concerning who will be permitted to enter the country. As such, it is used in a dichotomous manner, with two types of policy being formulated—one for refugees and the other for labor migrants. Astri Suhrke and Aristide Zolberg (1999, p. 143) observe that, "throughout the world of open societies, refugee policy is clearly distinguished from immigration policy."

However, from a sociological perspective, voluntary versus forced migration ought to be treated as a continuum rather than in dichotomous terms. In so doing, this continuum "can be used as an analytical device to determine the degrees of choice or freedom available to potential migrants" (Faist, 2000a, p. 23). William Petersen (1958, p. 261), for example, suggested a middle category in the continuum that he called "impelled migration," by which he meant situations "where the migrants retain some power to decide whether or not to leave." A cursory consideration of concrete cases readily reveals a wide range of degrees of freedom. Thus, the IT person leaving the high-tech sector in Hyderabad for Silicon Valley has a high degree of freedom, while the peasant fleeing drought conditions in the Sahara looks far more like a forced migrant.

One further point is in order: the primary focus of the theories discussed in this chapter reveals a lacuna, which is that the role of the state is given short shrift. The extent to which the policies of sending and receiving countries contribute to immigration flows has been undertheorized, and for that reason, James Hollifield's (2000) call for "bringing the state back in" has led to an increased focus on the role of the state—a topic we turn to in Section III.

A concrete example of the sorts of issues at stake in explaining patterns of migration can serve to illustrate both the strengths and the shortcomings of our current theoretical frameworks. The example we turn to derives from sociologist Ivan Light's book *Deflecting Immigration: Networks, Markets, and Regulation in Los Angeles* (2006). Light attempts to understand why, between 1980 and 2000, nearly a million Mexicans who might have been expected to settle in the Los Angeles metropolitan region did not. The decline in the rate of entry of Mexican immigrants did not mean that levels of immigration to the United States declined, but instead that these immigrants opted to settle in various secondary gateway communities throughout the nation, particularly in the Midwest and South (for research on these new destinations, see Zúñiga & Hernández-León, 2005). Light describes this as deflection, which he views as the end of a four-stage process, the first three being defined as absorption, saturation, and intolerance.

Disagreeing with the position of the new economics of immigration theorists that once networks take root, immigration tends to perpetuate itself, he points out that Los Angeles may be seeing the beginning of the end of the current immigration wave, but he does not suggest that it happens the way neoclassical economics would have it. He describes what has occurred there in the following way. First, he agrees that demand for workers drove immigration at the outset. However, over time, with the saturation of immigrant workers in the labor market, demand declines and the local economic environment becomes less attractive as wage levels are depressed while the cost of living increases. Nonetheless, the network reduces certain costs and risks and thus migration continues after saturation. In part, this is made possible by buffers that permit high levels of migration to continue for a time—transfer payments, welfare benefits, and the ethnic economy itself (including the informal economy). While the neoliberal era has managed to roll back the welfare state somewhat, the benefits nonetheless continue to exceed those available in Mexico.

The transition from demand to network-driven migration resulted in higher levels of poverty. This becomes the key to deflection, for it is by practicing what Light calls "poverty intolerance" that the region becomes an increasingly unattractive settlement area. The enforcement of various municipal codes serves as the policy vehicle for poverty intolerance, including practices such as cracking down on building-code and labor law violations in sweatshops and code enforcement in housing. Once intolerance takes hold, deflection begins.

Light does not claim this is a definitive answer to the question he set out to pursue, merely that it is a plausible one. To the extent that he is right, he points to both the virtue and the inherent weakness of network theory: it can explain why migration can persist after demand declines, but it cannot explain why immigrants moving from A to B shift their destination to C. Roger Waldinger (2007a) and Peter Kivisto (2007b) have agreed with Light's assessment of networks, but questioned whether the local poverty intolerance regime that is so central to his argument for why deflection occurred is convincing. Instead, one alternative would be to view networks as responding to changing economic conditions and making appropriate adjustments, which can include shifting destinations.

One final point is relevant to the earlier discussion of segmented labor markets. Although this is not the main focus of Light's book, from the fact that the deflected were workers located in the labor market's secondary sector, given that demand has not dried up for those in the primary sector, one can account for declines in rates of immigration for one group—Mexicans—while witnessing increases in rates for some Asian groups whose human capital serves to locate them in the primary sector.

## *The Larger Context of Immigration*

If the previous theoretical discussion is located at the level of the middle range, the unanswered question is how should we contextualize immigration in terms of larger, macro-level processes, those operating both at the level of nation-states and at the global level. World-system theory, associated for example with the pioneering work of Immanuel Wallerstein (1998, p. 9), treats the capitalist world order as dating to the 16th century, but becoming "global only in the latter half of the nineteenth century, and it has only been in the second half of the twentieth century that the inner corners and remote regions of the globe have been effectively integrated." Rooted in Marxist tradition, Wallerstein depicts the world-system as a single powerful economic entity supported and sustained by a shifting group of strong nation-states that constitute the wealthy core. The remainder of the world is divided into the periphery and the semiperiphery, both of which are exploited as sources of cheap labor and raw materials by the core.

Although some commentators would prefer to distinguish world-systems theory from globalization theory by contending that the former is too rooted in Marxism or too inclined to economic reductionism, we would point out that they are parallel approaches insofar as both take the globe as the proper unit of analysis (Giddens, 1990, pp. 68–70). Moreover, contrary to critics seeking to bring the state back in, world-systems theory is not necessarily hostile to such an effort. Indeed, as noted previously, the role of the nation-state is central to dividing the world into three types of societies. In terms of immigration, given the fact that most people who are border crossers are labor migrants, a focus on economic factors in shaping migration flows is appropriate—and moreover makes world-systems congruent with the mezzo-level approach of the new economics of migration (Massey & Taylor, 2004; Sassen, 1988).

That being said, as we shall see in subsequent discussions about transnational immigration, some of the insights of globalization theorists distinct from world-systems approaches have proven to be especially valuable for contemporary research agendas. Specifically, what Anthony Giddens (1990) refers to as "time-space distanciation" and David Harvey (1996) calls "time-space compression" points to the fact that the impact of improved transportation networks and enhanced communications systems have led to a dramatic reduction of what Harvey (1996, p. 297) describes as the "monopoly power inherent in place." The emergence of immigrant communities that are transnational in character, with implications for economics, politics, culture, and religion (Glick Schiller & Levitt, 2006; Kivisto, 2001, 2003) is a consequence of the shift from place to space. Before turning to the matter of immigrant incorporation, we turn in Chapter 3 to a survey of the current global migratory flows in order to better appreciate the structural factors underpinning today's "turbulence of migration" (Papastergiadis, 2000).

# 3

# Counting Contemporary
# Immigration Flows

A recent study published by the United Nations reports that in 2005 there were 191 million people worldwide who were living outside of their birth country—a figure that means world migration had doubled over the course of the past half century (United Nations, 2006, p. 5). Who are these people? Do we know how many women are included in that figure? What about racial or religious groups? What are their socioeconomic circumstances? What about their political circumstances? What countries do they come from? Where do they end up? Can we specify the reasons they opted to become immigrants? This chapter is intended to provide a demographic portrait of today's cross-border movers, in an effort to explore the extent to which we can answer these and related questions.

Such an objective might appear to be a straightforward task entailing the collection of the relevant statistics on the topic, synthesizing that data, and presenting it in summary form. However, it turns out that the task is far more complex and the data far more contested or limited than one might have desired. In order to appreciate why this is so, it is necessary to consider where statistics on immigration come from. Most of the data on immigration is collected by national governments, both nations of immigration and nations of emigration (with many countries being, to some extent, both). This is complemented by data gathered by supranational governmental and quasi-governmental entities such as the European Union and the United Nations, as well as data collected by researchers located in universities and think tanks. In all instances, the data are collected with certain purposes in mind and with differing but always limited levels of financial and related resources and with various cultural and political constraints that impinge on the data collection process. For example, to the extent that the quality of surveys and censuses is dependent on available financial resources and human capital levels among the ranks of researchers, it would not be surprising that those from poor countries like Burkina Faso and Namibia would be appreciably different from those from wealthy countries like Belgium and the Netherlands (Bulmer & Warwick, 1993).

Social statistics arose during the 19th century as a tool for governments to assess the current state of affairs, to predict trends, to gain an understanding of the scope of potential social problems, and to inform public policy (Best, 2001, pp. 11–13). Put another way, social statistics were an instrument of control. However, governments differ in terms of how they specify what is and what is not useful information or information that it is appropriate to seek to obtain. Thus, for instance, given the importance attached to the ideal of ethnic homogeneity in Japan, the government does not collect census data on ethnic groups in that nation (Lie, 2001, p. 4). The U.S. Bureau of the Census, similarly, does not collect data on the religious affiliations of either the native-born or immigrants. Many other examples could be offered, but the point is a simple one: different countries collect somewhat different sorts of data depending on differing definitions of purpose. This poses limits to what we know about particular countries and also impacts the ability to do international comparative research.

Complicating statistics on immigration is that the subject matter is, by definition, a moving target. In other words, the 191 million figure cited at the beginning of this chapter refers to the number of global immigrants at a specific point in time, in this instance in 2005. What happened to the level of immigration from the time this was collected until the time it appeared in a United Nations publication a year later or until the moment we write these lines in 2008 or the moment readers read them when this book appears in print? Or, what if what we really wanted to know was the number of immigrants at the very beginning of the new century?

Yet another factor complicating the data on immigration is the fact that many immigrants do not want to be counted. There is general consensus that one particular type of immigrant has grown considerably in recent years: the undocumented or what some would insist on calling illegal immigrants. The idea that these immigrants are undocumented, or as the French refer to them, *sans papiers,* points to the fact that they do not leave a written trace in official statistics. Given their tenuous status, it is not surprising that the undocumented seek to avoid being detected, and among other things this

means that they make it difficult for census takers to count them. Γ
role that the undocumented play in current debates about immigra
there are definite limits to what we know about this particular categoιy. ι-
not that estimates of the size of the undocumented populations in the
advanced industrial nations are so off the mark as to be thoroughly suspect;
it is simply that what we know about this category of immigrant cannot be
based on empirical evidence with the same level of reliability as is the case
with legal immigrants. Indeed, a common method used to gauge the number
of undocumented or irregular migrants is to ask experts, an approach that
has been dubbed the "Delphi method."

## Types of Migrants

As we have stressed from the outset, by definition, immigrants are those who
move across *national* borders, not regional or other boundaries. Thus, excluded
are migrations that occur within national boundaries, such as the movement of
blacks from America's rural south to the urban North during the first half of
the 20th century. As we noted in Chapter 1, Robert Park drew a parallel
between blacks and Poles moving to cities such as Chicago, seeing both as peasants rooted in the soil and in tradition and encountering the jarring impact of a
modern, urban civilization. Nonetheless, by convention these two migrations
have been separated, a practice recently questioned by Ewa Morawska (2008).
With the background provided by the prior historical and theoretical discussion, we are now in a position to reflect further on how to define immigration.
At the outset, one could note that complicating matters is the fact that national
borders are not always fixed. Sometimes people who were residing in their
homeland find that they are residing in another nation despite the fact that they
didn't move—the border did. The shifting Hungarian/Romanian border prior
to World War II is a case in point (Brubaker et al., 2006).

With these provisos, not everyone who crosses an international border is
a migrant. Tourists are not defined as migrants, though they can sometimes
live outside their homeland for extended periods of time. Similarly, students
studying abroad are not migrants, though sometimes their programs of study
keep them abroad for several years. Likewise, diplomats and employees of
embassies are not considered to be immigrants during their postings outside
the country. Border workers—people who commute between their nation of
residence and the nation where they work—are not migrants. If these mobile
border crossers are not considered to be immigrants, why aren't they? What
distinguishes their movements across borders from the movements of those
we do define as immigrants?

Typical definitions of the immigrant always include the following characterization: it is an individual who moves into a country from another country. But this of course is not sufficient because it fails to distinguish immigrants from tourists, students, and the like. For that reason, some definitions go further by stating that the reason for the move is that the person intends to settle there. Still other definitions go even further by contending that the act of settling is intended to be permanent. The matter of settlement, whether defined as permanent or not, serves to differentiate immigration from other border crossings.

However, these amplifications contain ambiguities insofar as they raise questions about the intentions of cross-border movers. What about the international student who overstays a visa and over the long haul remains in the country rather than returning home? When did this person become an immigrant? Or what about the person who leaves the homeland ambivalent about whether she or he will remain abroad or return home? What about so-called "birds of passage"—sojourners who are prepared to move back and forth between two locations or to move from A to B to C? Are they by definition excluded from being defined as immigrants because they do not intend to settle, or at least to settle permanently? Such definitions are problematic due to their subjectivity. In short, if intentionality is a criterion for adjudicating whether or not a person is an immigrant, the individual's perceptions of his or her own situation appear to be determinative.

Christian Joppke has proposed an alternative definition that would seem to offer the basis for a more objective assessment of a person's status as a border crosser. He writes that, "Immigration is the permanent movement of people across states, seen from the perspective of the receiving (rather than sending) states" (Joppke, 2001a, p. 7208). Here it is the state itself (or agents of the state) that establishes a person's status, which Joppke views as a salutary corrective to what he perceives to be a tendency to portray immigration as a "stateless" phenomenon.

The virtue of Joppke's state-focused definition is that it puts squarely into focus the fact that states do, in fact, claim to have a monopoly on defining who is and who is not an immigrant, and beyond this to define different types of immigrants. They do so by enacting laws that have the effect of establishing the parameters of determining the respective status of the foreign-born in their nations. States distinguish immigrants into two broad categories: on the one hand are labor migrants, those who move for economic reasons, while on the other are asylum seekers and refugees, those who are motivated by the conviction that if they remain in their homeland, their lives are at risk (Hollifield, 2004). The fact that there are more of the former than the latter goes far to explain why the theories discussed in the preceding chapter were predicated on this type of immigrant.

States enact immigration laws that are designed in theory to control the flows of labor immigrants, allowing in what are perceived (or hoped) to be adequate numbers to meet the nation's labor demands, while preventing what are perceived to be an excess number from entering. Within the ranks of such immigrants are various subgroups. For example, immigrants can be divided between those granted legal permanent resident status and temporary legal residents. While the former are permitted to remain in the nation as long as they wish, the latter are expected to leave at the end of a specified period of time. Temporary workers include various guest worker schemes, including the bracero program that brought Mexicans to the United States over a two-decade period or the post–World War II guest worker plan in Germany that witnessed the migration of large numbers of workers from Italy, Spain, Portugal, the former Yugoslavia, and Turkey. In practice, the distinction between permanent and temporary immigrants often gets blurred as temporary workers continue residing in the immigration country for long periods, as, for example, the German experience attests. Indeed, it has been said that there is nothing more permanent than a temporary worker (Martin, 1991). In practice, governments repeatedly extend the time period so the result is that often immigrants remain in the country for the duration of their lives. Nevertheless, the distinction is significant, for it is only those immigrants obtaining legal permanent resident status who are eligible to become naturalized citizens.

Second, immigrants are differentiated according to their respective levels of human capital and, related to that, to where they then enter the receiving nation's economy. The migratory wave that occurred in the late 19th and early 20th century was shaped by the early phase of industrialization, where capitalist employers sought workers in primary extractive industries such as mining and lumbering and manufacturing. Thus migrants, whether they were peasants or proletarians in their homelands, entered the ranks of the proletariat in the receiving nations (Kivisto, 1990). In contrast, in today's postindustrial economy, where manufacturing jobs have significantly declined in number, immigrants enter economies in the advanced industrial nations that look increasingly bifurcated between low-paying unskilled labor at the bottom of the economy and well-paying jobs for those with high levels of human capital (specifically, educational credentials and technological skills) at the top. As noted in the preceding chapter, this has been described as an hourglass economy (Portes, 1995; Richmond, 1981). In some cases, the latter group is actively courted by states that create mechanisms designed to select preferentially for them.

The H1B visa program in the United States is one such example. It offers admission slots to highly skilled professionals, with a focus on workers trained in certain occupations, including information technology, computing, finance and accounting, banking, engineering, and the medical and health care

є is a case where the distinction between temporary and per-
ırred, for although the terms of the visa define it as tempo-
ısting 6 years), it is also designed so that it can become a
ᴦo obtaining a green card, which means that the immigrant acquires
ᴦ permanent residency. It should be noted that from the perspective of the
countries of emigration, the highly skilled are often perceived to be "brain
drain" migrants, leaving a poor nation that could use their skills for the
greener economic pastures of the advanced industrial nations. To provide
some sense of what this exodus of skilled professionals can mean for poor
nations, consider the fact that there are at present more Malawian doctors
practicing medicine in Manchester, England, than in the nation of Malawi. Or
consider the fact that only 8% of the doctors trained in Zambia since it became
independent continue to work in that country (United Nations, 2006, p. 8).

The third way of distinguishing labor migrants has become an increasingly
significant part of the public debates on immigration: the distinction between
legal immigrants and undocumented immigrants. The latter group includes
people who for various reasons are in a country without the legal imprimatur
of the state granting them the right to live within its territorial boundaries.
Some of these individuals have crossed borders illegally, either due solely to
their own efforts or with the help of smugglers (what are known, for instance,
as coyotes on the U.S./Mexican border). In many immigrant-receiving
nations, particularly in North America and western Europe, the number of
undocumented workers has risen dramatically since around 1990, a trend
that is linked to the tendency of states to become more restrictive in the number of legal immigrants permitted to enter their respective nations.

Labor migrants are assumed to be voluntary immigrants. Although harsh
economic realities are often at play in shaping an individual's decision to
migrate or remain in place, the general assumption is that such movers are
able to, within various obvious constraints and challenges, exhibit choice. In
contrast, asylum seekers and refugees are perceived to have been forced to
depart from their homeland, often fleeing quickly and without much opportunity to plan. Asylum seekers leave their homes because they believe they
need to do so in order to escape danger, which can include the threat of
involuntary confinement, slavery, physical violence, torture, or death. The
danger can be associated with political upheaval in a nation, with religious
or ethnic sectarian conflict, or with the subjugation of the rights of women.

As individuals, asylum seekers must seek to convince potential receiving
nations that the claims that they are at risk are justified. A high-profile example of what is involved in attempting to convince a state to admit you can be
seen in the case of Ayaan Hirsi Ali, a Somali-born Muslim who requested
asylum in the Netherlands in 1992, claiming that she had fled her homeland
to escape an arranged marriage. She was admitted, and 5 years later became

a citizen. Ali was subsequently elected to the Dutch parliament, and engaged in provocative political challenges to conservative Islam, thereby making her a target of Muslim fundamentalists. In 2002, she informed the media that she had lied on her asylum application. This revelation did not threaten her status until 4 years later when the Dutch Immigration Minister, riding a growing anti-immigration wave, attempted to revoke her citizenship. In the end, as a result of the ensuing political pressure brought to bear by Ali's supporters, the Minister reversed her stand. Ali has since moved to the United States and published *Infidel* (2007), a scathing attack on Islam that, she points out, would put her life in danger should she ever return to Somalia ("Profile: Ayann Hirsi Ali," 2007).

Refugees differ from such asylum seekers insofar as representatives of the international political order have established the fact that they are at risk. The key actor in this process is the Office of the United Nations High Commissioner for Refugees, which since its creation in 1950 has been charged with protecting the rights of people to seek asylum and to find safe refuge in another state. According to the UNHCR Web site (www.unhcr.org/basics.html), "In more than five decades, the agency has helped an estimated 50 million people restart their lives." Refugee status is established collectively rather than on a case-by-case basis and it is done prior to refugees seeking settlement in a safe country. Jeremy Hein's (2006) study of Hmong and Cambodian refugees residing, respectively, in two small midwestern cities, Eau Claire, Wisconsin, and Rochester, Minnesota, is a case in point. The refugee status of both groups, a consequence of the outcome of the war in Southeast Asia during the 1960s and early 1970s, had been established prior to their departure for the United States. One important aspect of the settlement of groups like the Hmong and Khmer that makes their situation quite different from labor migrants is the interventionist role of refugee settlement agencies. Among the key NGOs helping these two groups are Lutheran Immigration and Refugee Services, U.S. Catholic Charities, Church World Relief, and World Relief. In addition, governmental policy has been designed to disperse refugee populations in order to prevent geographic concentration (a policy that has often proven to be unsuccessful).

Given the considerable differences in circumstances between and responses by states and civic organizations to "voluntary" labor migrants and "forced" asylum seekers/refugees, the paths to incorporation into receiving nations and the impediments to incorporation should not be assumed to be the same. In the three following chapters, we will explore modes of incorporation, but when we turn to this topic, it will become apparent that theorizing has had and continues to have voluntary labor migrants in mind.

Here we turn to where contemporary immigrants come from and where they then end up. While it is certainly true that one can find immigrants from virtually every nation in the world, and likewise that a majority of nations have received newcomers, as we shall see in the following sections, a rather limited number of nations represent the main destinations of immigrants, and likewise the majority of migrants come from a select number of countries.

## Immigrant Destinations

Stephen Castles and Mark Miller (2004) have referred to the present as the "age of migration." They are on solid ground when they make this claim, for today there are more people living outside their countries of birth than at any other time in history. While migration rates from certain countries were higher in the 19th century and immigrants came to represent a larger percentage of the overall population compared to today, what is distinctive about the present wave of global migration is that more countries than in the past are impacted by emigration and immigration. Moreover, there are currently more immigrants in the world than the total populations of all of the world's nations save the four largest—China, India, the United States, and Indonesia (United Nations, 2006, p. 6). This book is predicated on the assumption that immigration is having major economic, political, cultural, and social consequences, especially in those nations that are the major destinations of immigrants and those places that have witnessed mass emigration. However, these facts and their presumed implications can be deceiving if they are not put into context. Despite the large number of immigrants, they represent a very small percentage of the world's population. Current estimates place that figure somewhere between 2% and 3%, a range that has not changed appreciably in a half century (United Nations, 2006, p. 6).

Recalling a point we made in the introduction, Thomas Faist (2000a, p. 1) calls attention to what he considers a "baffling puzzle," namely, "Why there are so few migrants from so many places and so many from only a few places?" The relatively low percentage of immigrants compared to the world's population as a whole combined with its distinctive geographic concentrations both in terms of points of debarkation and destination must be seen in light of the fact that "half of the world's population constitute potential international migrants." These are people, he claims, who have the motivation to migrate because they are neither too well off to want to remain in their homeland nor too poor to lack the necessary resources to make emigration possible (Faist, 2000a, p. 4). If half of the world's population is primed to move across international borders, why do so few, comparatively speaking, actually make that move? This disconnection between potential and actual immigrants lends credence to the early theorists of migration who operated with an underlying assumption that staying is the normal thing for people to do and movement is the extraordinary act. However, this is not entirely convincing given that one reason for the relatively low level of international migration is that internal migrations, be they rural to urban or rural to rural, have become more consequential over time, serving as an alternative to international migration.

Within this context, we turn to examining the major destinations of contemporary immigrants as well as identifying the major nations of origin. Beginning with the former, Figure 3.1 reports the 20 countries that have received the largest number of immigrants thus far in the first decade of the 21st century.

## Migration in Sub-Saharan Africa

Rather than beginning with the most obvious findings, which involve the central place of the United States and of other large advanced industrial nations, let's begin by noting that Côte d'Ivoire, a relatively small nation in western

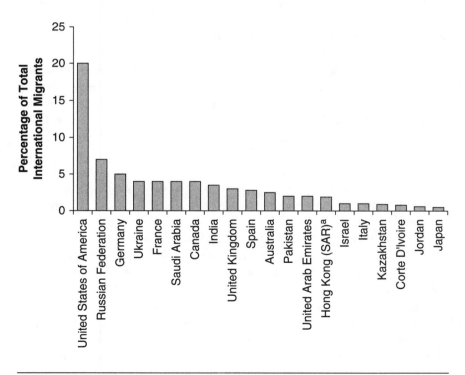

**Figure 3.1**    The 20 Countries or Areas With the Highest Numbers of
International Migrants, 2005

a. Special Administrative Region of China.

Africa with a population in 2007 of 19.3 million, makes it into the top 20. It is the only African country in the top 20. Missing from this list is its much larger and more powerful regional neighbor, Nigeria, which with a population of 148.1 million puts it in the top 10 largest nations in the world. Also missing from the top 20, though nevertheless a significant regional immigration desti- nation, is South Africa (48.6 million people). This begs the question: why is Côte d'Ivoire among the top immigrant-receiving nations in the world? Part of the answer has to do with the fact that it is located in a region composed of a number of smaller nations, the product, according to Aderanti Adepoju (2006, p. 34) of "colonial map-drawers who ignored ethnic demarcations." Thus, this nation is composed of five main and other smaller ethnic groups, many whose historical territories straddle the nation's official borders. Another part of the answer is that the high level of mobility in the subregion is shaped by "cultures of travel" (de Bruijn, van Dijk, & Foeken, 2001) or "cultures of migration" (Hahn & Klute, 2008), based on long-standing traditions of translocal and (since the establishment of contemporary national borders) transnational net- works of trade relations and systems of (mainly seasonal) labor migrations.

The immigrants in Côte d'Ivoire come overwhelmingly from nearby states. Between obtaining independence from France in 1960 and experienc- ing its first military coup in 1999, the nation was considerably more stable than those in the region, and when its export economy based on coffee, cocoa, and palm oil experienced favorable market prices, it needed labor. In short, for decades the nation was receptive to immigrants because of persis- tent labor shortages. The immigrant population rose from 17% in the 1960s to 28% by the latter part of the 1990s (Adepoju, 2006, p. 34). Since the mil- itary coup, the nation has become politically volatile, and thus less attractive for typical labor migrants. On the basis of the concept of "Ivority," which was coined for electoral purposes, xenophobic tendencies, including violence against foreign nationals and massive evictions of migrants from neighbor- ing countries such as Burkina Faso and Mali, have countered the neverthe- less ongoing influx of labor migrants. Given the civil wars in Liberia between 1989 and 2003 and Sierra Leone from 1991 to 2002, Côte d'Ivoire became an important settlement area for refugees from these nations—where many ended up living in refugee camps for a decade or more. In this regard, it rep- resents but one instance of a prevalent phenomenon in sub-Saharan Africa, which is that political instability, often combined with economic collapse, has resulted in masses of people seeking refuge in a nearby state. The flight of undocumented migrants from Zimbabwe into Botswana and South Africa is but a recent example of this tendency.

Before turning to the other countries on the list, it is worth noting that no country in South America is found on it. This is not to suggest that immigration is inconsequential in this region, for it is. Indeed, immigration here points to the reality that more and more countries in the world have been brought into the international migration orbit. However, at present South America is more a continent of emigration than of immigration. Those countries that have received immigrants in sizeable numbers tend to have economies that are more successful than their neighbors and offer relatively greater political and social stability. Thus, Argentina has become a destination for temporary workers from neighboring countries, including Bolivia and Paraguay. However, the point remains that in global comparative terms, the level of immigration overall is not nearly as high as elsewhere.

## The Middle East

Another small nation on the list is Israel, which had a population of 7.2 million in 2007. The term *Diaspora* is used widely in immigration studies today, far too loosely for some people's tastes (Brubaker, 2005; Dufoix, 2008). Its original use was focused very explicitly on Jews, who mark the fall of Jerusalem in 70 CE as the beginning of a millennium and a half during which Jews moved into all parts of the world. The idea of returning to the homeland never disappeared, taking on modern political form in the 19th century with the rise of Zionism as both ideology and a political movement (Dufoix, 2008, pp. 5–10). Responding to the appeal of the movement, Zionists from Europe and North America returned, responding to the idea of *aliyah,* which means a return to the Promised Land. When Israel became a modern state in 1948, enshrined into its immigration and citizenship laws was the entitlement of Jews from anywhere in the world to enter the nation with the right to citizenship. At the same time, Palestinians who left the new Israeli state were not permitted to return and obtain citizenship, though those Palestinians who remained were entitled to citizenship, today constituting 19% of the population (Gold, 2007, p. 284).

During the second half of the 20th century, Diasporic Jews did return, with immigration peaks occurring in the first years of the new state and again in the early 1990s. In the first period, the majority of immigrants came from eastern Europe and various places throughout the Middle East. In the 1990s, in the wake of the collapse of the Soviet Union, it involved large numbers of Jews from Russia. In fact, both the United States and Israel had been open to Russian Jews since the 1960s, but immigration peaked during this uncertain time (Cohen & Haberfeld, 2007). This is relevant because the United States was perceived to be an option for Jews seeking to emigrate alongside Israel, and as the political situation in Israel deteriorated, it became a more attractive choice. Compounding this trend was the fact that Israelis, too, were increasingly inclined to migrate to the United States, in spite of considerable opposition. Although emigration to the United States has been occurring for some time (Shokeid, 1988), it has increased during the past several years as violence and uncertainty in Israel has increased (Lustick, 2004). In 2007, for the first time, emigration from Israel was higher than immigration.

Labor shortages, particularly in the low-paying unskilled sector, were not met, as had been the case in the past, by Jewish immigrants from poor nations in the Middle East and Saharan Africa. As a result, Israel, like the Arab states in the region, has attracted workers from elsewhere. It is estimated that at present, 300,000 such foreign workers reside in Israel, perhaps 60% of which are undocumented. A majority of these foreign workers come in particular from a select number of Asian countries, including China, Thailand, and the Philippines, and the eastern European nations of Romania and Moldova.

In this, Israel is remarkably similar to its Arab neighbors in the region. In fact, three such nations appear among the top 20 countries of international immigration: Saudi Arabia, which has a total population of 24.7 million; the United Arab Emirates (UAE), with 4.4 million residents; and Jordan, with 5.9 million residents. Saudi Arabia and the UAE are part of a group of wealthy Gulf States that, along with Oman, Qatar, Kuwait, and Bahrain, make up the Gulf Cooperation Council (GCC). These were countries made rich by oil, especially after the boom that commenced in 1973. These nations engaged in huge economic development schemes, but with a combined workforce of only 1.36 million, they lacked adequate internal workforces to achieve their development goals. To meet the demand for labor, both skilled and unskilled, all the GCC nations imported temporary contract workers, with Saudi Arabia and the UAE bringing in the largest numbers. As a consequence, their populations grew substantially during the last quarter of the past century. The Saudi population nearly doubled, while in the case of the UAE, the net result was a population in which a staggering 80% was composed of contract laborers. Many of the workers were from Middle Eastern nations, including Egyptians, Yemenis, Palestinians, Jordanians, and Lebanese, and from all four nations on the Indian subcontinent: India, Pakistan, Bangladesh, and Sri Lanka. Add to this mix workers from the Philippines and Nepal (Jureidini, 2003; p. iii; Misra, personal communication, 2009; see also, Fargues, 2006).

As is the case elsewhere, immigrants defined by states as temporary, with their terms of employment based on contracts, are ineligible for citizenship. What makes this situation considerably more precarious is that Saudi Arabia and the UAE are undemocratic. Monitoring organizations such as Human Rights Watch have documented the economic exploitation of these immigrant workers and the unresponsiveness of the respective governments to this situation. Given the lack of transparency regarding human rights violations, researchers confront major challenges in attempting to examine unfree labor and human trafficking. Suffice it to say here that these issues are of particular concern in these two nations and the other members of the GCC.

Jordan presents a different situation. It is not a rich oil-producing nation, and in fact is, in general, natural resource poor. Adjoining Israel, it has literally been at the center of the geopolitical conflict that has defined the region for the past half century. While guest workers from elsewhere in the Middle East and from Asia are present, they are there in comparatively small numbers. The reason that Jordan, a small nation, ranks so high as an immigration destination is that since the founding of Israel up to the present, it has been home to the largest number of Palestinian refugees in the world. These refugees live under the auspices of the United Nations Relief and Works Agency (UNRWA), which has been functioning in Jordan since 1950. Palestinians in Jordan comprise slightly more than 30% of the overall population (Chatelard, 2004, p. 2). More recently, it has increasingly become one of the major settlement nations for Iraqis fleeing the chaos and devastation brought about by the U.S. invasion in 2003 (Human Rights Watch, 2006). Thus, the vast majority of Jordan's immigrants are refugees rather than labor migrants.

## Russia and Former Territories of the Soviet Union

Three other countries on the list were part of the Soviet Union and are now among the 12 members of the Commonwealth of Independent States (CIS): the Russian Federation, Ukraine, and Kazakhstan. Russia has the second largest number of immigrants of all nations, while given their respective overall populations, the impact of recent immigration on Ukraine and Kazakhstan can be expected to be far reaching. Immigration to and emigration from these three countries has been shaped by the profound changes underway in the wake of communism's collapse. The move from command to market economies has created enormous disparities in wealth and income and further fueled endemic corruption. The move from a communist dictatorship to some semblance of democracy has had to counter considerable resistance, and whether or not the future portends western-style democracy is at the moment uncertain. As Durkheim had predicted, rapid social change creates the conditions for anomie, which produces a variety of social problems (see, for example, Pridemore & Kim, 2007, for a discussion of homicide rates in Russia).

Of particular salience for immigration in Russia, the largest of the three countries, with a population of 142.5 million, are two demographic trends: a declining birth rate and an increased death rate coupled with a lowering of the average life span (Pridemore & Kim, 2007, pp. 231–232). Combined with emigration, these trends have led to labor shortages and a concern in policy circles that increased levels of immigration are necessary to meet this challenge. However, at the same time, levels of Russian nationalist xenophobia are very high and violence directed against non-Russian immigrants is common. Thus, the Putin administration has attempted to attract Russian expatriates, many living in independent nations that were once part of the Soviet Union. Based on the evidence to date, this policy of selective immigration will not succeed in its goal of addressing chronic labor shortages.

In Ukraine, with a population of 46.2 million, and the much smaller Kazakhstan (15.4 million), the dynamics differ somewhat but also parallel those of Russia. For example, in less than 20 years, Ukraine's population has declined by approximately 6 million people (Zimmer, 2007, p. 1). In both cases, immigration has been growing in recent years. At the same time, both are also nations of emigration, with many Ukrainians moving westward and southward as well as seeking work in Russia. Women represent a majority of emigrants, with most of these being younger women of childbearing age. There is currently considerable movement among CIS nations, much of it in the form of temporary labor migrations and a growing proportion consisting of the undocumented. Movement across these borders does not require a visa, which makes entry easy, but obtaining work permits is often difficult and thus once in a nation, the person's status is suspect. The movement tends to be to those nations with higher wage levels. Thus, while at the same time that residents of Kazakhstan immigrate to Russia for higher pay, temporary workers flow into that country from neighboring Uzbekistan, which is poorer.

Table 3.1 illustrates the complexity of the situation caused by the dual impact of immigration and emigration. It identifies the five top countries supplying immigrants to Russia. All are part of the former Soviet Union. Despite themselves being in the top 20 immigrant-receiving nations in the

**Table 3.1**    Top Five Sending Countries to Russia as Percentage of Immigrants

| Country | Percentage |
|---------|------------|
| Ukraine | 22.5 |
| Azerbaijan | 15.1 |
| Armenia | 13.3 |
| Uzbekistan | 6.9 |
| Kazakhstan | 6.8 |
| All other | 35.4 |

*Source:* Calculated from the 2002 Russian Census.

world, Ukraine and Kazakhstan are two of the five nations contributing to Russia's immigrant population. Indeed, the former constitutes over 1 in 5 immigrants in Russia and together they represent nearly 30% of the total.

## The Indian Subcontinent

A similar regional pattern of migration exists on the Indian subcontinent, where India and Pakistan are two major destinations for immigrants. Both of these nations have very large populations. India, with a population of 1.2 billion, is the second-largest nation in the world after China, which has 1.3 billion. Given the impact of China's long-standing one child policy, demographers predict that India's population will surpass that of China relatively soon. To indicate how large these nations are, the third-largest country is the United States, whose population of 303.2 million is only a fourth of the size of these giants. What makes the Indian case distinctive is that this vast population lives in a nation with a landmass that is only a third the size of the United States. In short, it is a nation with a high population density. The following comparisons put into perspective India's situation: whereas it has a population density of 386 people per square kilometer, the comparable figure for China is 137, while for the United States it is 31, for Russia it is 8.4, and for Canada it is 7.

India has been a major nation of emigration in recent decades, with large numbers of migrants locating in various destinations in the developed world. At present, Indian immigrants constitute one of the largest groups in the traditional nations of immigration, Australia, Canada, and the United States. In addition, as former colonials, large numbers have settled in Britain, an example of residents of the empire's periphery moving to the center. These immigrants include both poor, unskilled workers and brain-drain immigrants. Some of the latter have also landed in other nations of western Europe, often after having been recruited by high-tech industries.

In this context, where do immigrants to India come from? As is the case with Russia and the CIS nations, migration is a regional phenomenon. Much of the movement across borders needs to be seen in the context of India's modern history. Prior to independence, India included what is contemporary Pakistan and Bangladesh, and thus many people in these two countries—mainly Muslim—have historic attachments to India. Although Sri Lanka, formerly Ceylon, was formally distinct from India during colonial rule, cultural and religious links, especially with Hindu Tamils in both nations, contributed to cross-border movement.

Immigration to India is often irregular, temporary, and illegal. A poor country with a far less developed system of border security than one can find in developed nations, such movement is not surprising. The country that has contributed the largest number of immigrants is Bangladesh, a very poor and densely populated nation (2,850 people per square kilometer). In Indian states located in close proximity to Bangladesh, such as Assam, Bihar, and Nagaland, with borders that are often not clearly marked and extremely porous, migrants appear in large numbers (Ramachandran, 2005, p. 5). However, immigrants do not simply remain near the border, with some moving into the nation's major cities such as Mumbai, Delhi, Kolkata, and Chennai in search of work. Ascertaining with any level of precision the actual number of Bangladeshi immigrants is difficult and fraught with political and religious tensions. The Bangladeshi government minimizes the numbers while right-wing Hindu nationalists in India hostile to the presence of large numbers of Muslim immigrants tend to exaggerate the numbers. In this context, a frequently cited figure that appears in credible sources is 20 million ("Bangladeshis in Assam," 2005).

Sujata Ramachandran (2005, p. 7) describes a structured system of border crossing shaped by a migration industry, which consists of "a well-organized network of *dalals* [consisting of] 'manpower' agencies, recruiters, touts, brokers, 'travel' agents, and their employees or contacts in many Bangladeshi villages." The industry is crucial to the migratory flow of Bangladeshis to India (and elsewhere), functioning in ways that are characteristic of similar operations, both facilitating and exploiting would-be labor migrants while also engaging in trafficking. The latter involves women and children, some being sold as wives to aging widowers and others ending up in India's brothels.

Two other regional sources of new immigrants are Nepal and Sri Lanka. While in both instances, there are parallels to the Bangladeshi case, there is also the additional dimension of political crises in the respective homelands. In the case of Nepal, the Maoist insurgency has dislocated many people, particularly those from rural areas, who found themselves caught between the rebels and Nepalese security forces. The porous border between Nepal and India has meant that, whether formally or informally, many Nepalese enter India as political refugees. A portrait of the Nepalese presence in the Indian borderlands is central to Kirnan Desai's *The Inheritance of Loss* discussed in this book's introduction. The protracted civil war in Sri Lanka between the majority Sinhalese Buddhists and the Hindu Tamil minority has also created dislocations. Given that the south of India is a center of the nation's Tamil ethnic group, it is not surprising that transnational contacts between Tamils in the two countries have contributed to immigration levels, where those in Sri Lanka have viewed India as a place of temporary or permanent refuge.

Turning briefly to Pakistan, Bangladeshi immigrants are the largest immigrant population in a nation of 161.6 million—the sixth-largest nation in the world. Given that from the partition of India in 1947 to the creation of an independent Bangladeshi state in 1972, they were part of a single nation, this is not surprising. Known as East Pakistan, this region chafed at the fact that the West dominated the nation's political scene; ultimately, a separatist movement succeeded in severing political ties with Pakistan and establishing an independent nation—but the two nonetheless remain linked culturally and economically. Bangladeshis seeking entry to Pakistan have to traverse India, which poses a variety of legal and economic hurdles. Despite the difficulties, large numbers make their way into the nation. Given its geopolitical location in the post–9/11 "war on terrorism," another major source of migration to Pakistan—much of it illegal and temporary—is Afghanistan, a nation ravaged by constant internal warfare for three decades. Many of these are refugees who have tribal and kinship ties on both sides of the border, thereby facilitating a back-and-forth movement of peoples.

## Hong Kong

Given that it is a city and not an independent nation, it is quite remarkable that Hong Kong is one of the 20 areas with the highest numbers of immigrants. Yet with a population of 7.2 million, it is demographically larger than Israel, Jordan, and the United Arab Emirates. As a major immigrant destination, this Special Administrative Region of the People's Republic of China is an anomaly in that country, which as a whole has highly restrictive migration policies. However, as a British colony until 1997, when it was turned over to the Chinese, it had become, along with Singapore, an important Asian global city. During British rule, many immigrants were refugees fleeing communist China, and thus although Hong Kong is a city of migrants, its inhabitants are overwhelmingly Chinese. Another refugee community emerged during the Vietnam War as people fled the conflict. In addition to ethnic Vietnamese, some of this cohort included diasporic Chinese who had long lived in Vietnam.

During the past decade of Chinese rule, as China shifted from a command to a market economy, it did not want to kill the golden goose, and thus allowed Hong Kong to maintain a set of relatively autonomous governmental and economic structures. The net result is that Hong Kong continues to prosper. Hong Kong has been a place of emigration during the past half century, and given the uncertainty involved in the transition from British to Chinese rule, Hong Kong experienced a period of increased emigration levels in the years leading up to the departure of the British. Many of these migrants headed for Australia, Canada, the United Kingdom, and the United States.

Despite continued uncertainty about Hong Kong's status, its continuing economic dynamism accounts for the contemporary need for immigrant workers. These include construction workers from various Asian nations, domestics, and women trafficked to work in the city's booming sex industry (Constable, 1997; Ullah & Pamday, 2007). But it also includes immigrants who become part of the highly skilled cadres of economic professionals. Despite the growing diversity of the immigrants' origins, the largest source of migration continues to be mainland China. Even though the percentages have dropped somewhat in recent years, Chinese immigrants constitute about 70% of the total. This raises an interesting question. Prior to 1997, the movement of Chinese into Hong Kong constituted immigration by the definition we offered earlier in this chapter, a definition that differentiated international migration across national borders from internal migrations. Thus, just as migrants from Puerto Rico into the United States do not fit our definition but are nonetheless often counted as immigrants, so it is with the mainland Chinese. Suffice it to say that if we strictly adhere to our definition, Hong Kong quickly falls out of the top 20 immigrant-receiving nations.

## Western Europe

Nine of the 20 nations on the list are the major advanced industrial nations. Five of these are located in western Europe, and are in fact the largest states in the European Union: Germany, France, the United Kingdom, Italy, and Spain. These are listed in order from the largest to the smallest, with Germany registering in with a current population of 82.3 million and, at the other end, Spain reporting 45.1 million. To put into perspective the graph in Figure 3.1 that indicates that the United States absorbs far more immigrants than any other single nation, if we add the populations of these five major western European countries, their combined population would be about 10 million larger than the United States. If at the same time we look at the percentage of total international migrants in these five countries, the figure is approximately 16%. This is less than the 21% U.S. total, but substantial nonetheless. The recent immigration histories of these five nations vary, with France, Germany, and the United Kingdom tracing contemporary immigration to migratory streams that began a half century ago in the wake of World War II. In contrast, mass immigration to Italy and Spain began more recently. In fact, both of these countries were nations of emigration into the 1980s.

These nations are the largest states in the 27-nation European Union (see Table 3.2), which has evolved since the 1950s, when it was founded as an organization committed to economic cooperation and coordination in an effort to compete effectively against international—particularly American—competition. In addition, one of its stated goals was to avoid in the future a repeat of the conditions that led to two world wars during the 20th century. Today, it has the governmental structure of a trans-state, one that does not

**Table 3.2**    European Union Member States by Size

| Country | Populationª | Accession Year |
|---------|------------|----------------|
| Germany | 82.0 million | 1957 |
| France | 64.5 million | 1957 |
| United Kingdom | 61.0 million | 1973 |
| Italy | 59.5 million | 1957 |
| Spain | 46.0 million | 1986 |
| Poland | 38.0 million | 2004 |
| Romania | 21.5 million | 2007 |
| Netherlands | 16.5 million | 1957 |
| Greece | 11.0 million | 1981 |
| Belgium | 10.5 million | 1957 |
| Portugal | 10.5 million | 1986 |
| Czech Republic | 10.5 million | 2004 |
| Hungary | 10.0 million | 2004 |
| Sweden | 9.0 million | 1995 |
| Austria | 8.0 million | 1995 |
| Bulgaria | 7.5 million | 2007 |
| Denmark | 5.5 million | 1973 |
| Slovakia | 5.5 million | 2004 |
| Finland | 5.5 million | 1995 |
| Ireland | 4.5 million | 1973 |
| Lithuania | 3.5 million | 2004 |
| Latvia | 2.0 million | 2004 |
| Slovenia | 2.0 million | 2004 |
| Estonia | 1.5 million | 2004 |
| Cyprus | 1.0 million | 2004 |
| Luxembourg | 0.5 million | 1957 |
| Malta | 0.5 million | 2004 |

a. Rounded to the nearest half million.

deny the sovereignty of the constituent member nations, but has assumed greater governmental authority over time. The organization, once solely located in western Europe, has grown by including nations located in central and eastern Europe. There are currently several other nations seeking entry to the European Union, including Turkey. At the same time, three western European nations have refrained from joining: Iceland, Norway, and Switzerland (although Iceland recently initiated membership talks).

The citizens of member states have the right to move freely within the European Union and to work and take up residence throughout it. They are part of a novel structural arrangement in which citizenship becomes "nested," which means that like Russian dolls, citizenship exists at multiple levels. It exists in all instances at both the national level and the EU level. In some nations where "nations without states" have asserted their identity claims, a subnational citizenship can also exist, as in the case of being a citizen of Catalonia or Scotland (Guibernau, 1999; Kivisto & Faist, 2007). Meanwhile, the European Union has sought to establish a common framework for immigration policy, which has resulted in accentuating the differences between Europeans and non-Europeans.

The current population of the European Union is 492.9 million. If we also consider the three nonmember western European nations, these nations combined account for more than one in three of the world's immigrants. In short, the European continent is the leading immigrant destination in the world, exceeding that of North America, which accounts for one in four of the world's immigrants (United Nations, 2006, p. 6). Given that the levels of economic development of the member states varies considerably, with many of the former Warsaw Pact nations lagging far behind their western European counterparts, there is at present considerable variation in how attractive particular nations are to immigrants.

However, one thing that is shared across the European Union is demographic stagnation, which makes immigration potentially useful to policymakers concerned about population decline. Using data from Eurostat, Rainer Muenz (2007, pp. 1–2) reports that the overall natural increase of population was less than 0.1%. While no country matched Ireland's 8.8% increase, some, such as France, the Netherlands, and Norway, had increases of more than 3%. At the same time, there were countries that experienced natural population declines, including Germany and Italy. Of special note is that some of the largest decreases occurred in eastern Europe, including Lithuania, Latvia, and Hungary, which recorded the largest declines (Muenz, 2007, p. 2). The conclusion to draw from an analysis of natural population change is that immigration has played a more significant role than natural growth in accounting for the expansion of the European population.

Within this context, the impact of immigration varies by place and time. For example, until recently, the nations of the Mediterranean—Italy, Portugal, and Spain—have not been major immigrant-receiving nations. The United Kingdom continues to be a destination choice of current immigrants. Ireland, an economic laggard that has become in recent years the "Celtic Tiger," has shifted from being a historic nation of emigration to one of immigration. Austria, too, has witnessed an increase in migrants entering the nation during the past 15 years. Some countries have experienced declines in the levels of new immigrants arriving, including Germany, the Netherlands, and Belgium. In the end, the five countries on the top 20 international list—Germany, France, the United Kingdom, Italy, and Spain—along with Ireland, Austria, and Portugal, are the countries that have received the largest numbers of new immigrants since the dawn of the new century (Muenz, 2007, p. 3).

What does this mean in terms of the respective sizes of these nations' non-naturalized foreign-born population? First, despite the fact that fewer immigrants are entering Germany than in the recent past, it still is the top country in terms of the size of its foreign-born population. As of 2005, Germany had a foreign-born population of 10.1 million. It was followed by France (6.4 million), the United Kingdom (5.8 million), Spain (4.8 million), Italy (2.5 million), Switzerland (1.7 million), and the Netherlands (1.6 million). These figures are total numbers, and as such do not refer to the percentage of foreign-born in the overall population of specific countries. The microstates of Luxemburg and Liechtenstein are small players in the overall scheme of things, but the foreign-born in these two nations ranges between 33% and 40%. They are followed by Switzerland, with 22.9% of its population being foreign born. While Germany's 12.3% level is shaped by a long process that took form in the aftermath of World War II, and Sweden's 12.4% developed since the 1970s, the 14.1% level reported for Ireland is the result of very recent developments (Muenz, 2007, pp. 3–4).

## Germany

Within the context of the European Union, what are the specific immigration flows characteristic of the five countries with the largest numbers of immigrants? Although there are parallels to be drawn, each nation has its own immigration dynamic. We turn first to Germany. Beginning with the post–World War II reconstruction of Germany, migration played a significant role in meeting the nation's labor demands. Between the division of the nation by the Cold War powers until reunification in 1990, the situation differed in the capitalist Federal Republic of Germany (West Germany) and the Soviet-bloc German Democratic Republic (East Germany). While the former experienced a postwar economic boom that made it the "economic miracle" of western Europe (Heilig, Buttner, & Lutz, 1990) and necessitated the importation of foreign labor in order to make development possible, its communist counterpart lagged behind economically and created a fortresslike border system that made immigration difficult. That being said, during the 1980s there were several hundred thousand contract workers in the German Democratic Republic, mainly from Cuba, Mozambique, Angola, and Vietnam. Thus, for most of the second half of the 20th century, immigration to Germany meant immigration to the Federal Republic.

According to Brubaker's (1992) influential argument, given the nation's long-standing (but at the end of the past century revised) definition of citizenship in ethnic rather than civic terms, only foreigners of German background—collectively defined as *Aussiedler*—were viewed as suitable for permanent residence and the rights of citizenship. We would amend this argument by arguing that the preferred treatment of *Aussiedler* had little to do with the ethnic concept of citizenship. Rather, it had much to do with a "republican" notion in German constitutional law: those persons of German descent who suffered from hardship after World War II because of ethnic persecution could enter Germany (Faist, 2007). During the early years of the Cold War, many such individuals from the Soviet Union and elsewhere in the Warsaw Pact nations moved to Germany. The largest contingents came from Poland, followed by Romania and the Soviet Union (Oezcan, 2004, p. 2). However, communist governments would soon restrict this movement, and thus Germany had to look elsewhere for needed laborers. Thus, the vast majority of immigrants during this period did not come from eastern Europe, but from southern and southeastern Europe, and did not have German ancestry, and therefore were officially categorized as *Gastarbeiter,* or guest workers.

Immigration during the second half of the 20th century occurred in two waves. The first began in the late 1950s and ended in 1975, shortly after the impact of the oil crisis began to be felt and economic restructuring from an industrial to a postindustrial system began to change the dynamics of labor demand. During this quarter of a century, more than 12 million immigrants entered Germany and 8 million left again, leaving a total stock that remained at 3.6 million. The German Federal Labor Office played an activist role in recruitment efforts, negotiating guest worker agreements with a number of countries, beginning in 1955 with neighboring Italy (Kivisto, 2002, p. 161). Other countries that entered into pacts with Germany included Spain, Portugal, Greece, the former Yugoslavia, and Turkey. Over time, the numbers emigrating from European countries decreased while the numbers from Turkey increased. The expectation that workers would return home and the government's general opposition to family reunification were over time relaxed, with the result being that the temporary workers began to look like permanent residents. Indeed, the rotation principle (repatriation built into the guest worker system) was abolished very early. As early as the 1960s, the government ceased to enforce it at the request of employers who wanted to keep their migrant workers. In the wake of the OPEC crisis, with a decline in the demand for labor, public opinion made clear that Germans were opposed to the future settlement of additional workers from Yugoslavia and Turkey (Odmalm, 2005, p. 29). At the same time, the government hesitated to repatriate guest workers already in the country, seeking instead to find ways to improve their social rights. There was an effort on the part of the Kohl government in the 1980s to provide monetary incentives to guest workers to return to their nations of origin. The plan failed miserably. Part of the reason for this was that German unions had made sure that immigrant and native workers obtained the same rights.

In the decade that followed, immigration levels dropped considerably, and in fact during the first half of the 1980s, Germany was actually a nation of emigration rather than immigration. The second wave began in 1985. Between then and the end of the century, 5.5 million immigrants settled in Germany (www.migrationinformation.org). These included *Aussiedler* from Eastern bloc nations who began to arrive when travel restrictions were relaxed prior to the end of communism and continued to arrive after the fall of the Iron Curtain. It also included asylum seekers and refugees—the latter including refugees from Bosnia-Herzegovina who were forced into exile as a result of the ethnic conflict that arose in the aftermath of the collapse of a unified Yugoslav state. The numbers peaked by the mid-1990s, after which the rate of immigration was reduced. In part, this decline was due to the passage of a more restrictive asylum law in 1993 (Siebert, 2003, p. 6), one that reflected the institutionalization of a fortress Europe approach to reducing the number of foreigners from outside the European Union. Nonetheless, between 1990 and 2004, Germany received far more applications for asylum than any other western European nation and the United States. At the same time, the European Union's labor policies called for the free movement of workers among the member states. This meant, for instance, that not only could workers from the less developed nations of the European Union freely enter Germany to seek employment, but so could workers from the more developed ones. Thus, when a decline in the construction industry in Britain led to increased levels of unemployment in that sector of the economy, many British workers took their construction skills to Germany, plying their trade there while awaiting a turnaround in the situation back home.

## France

France has long been viewed as *le creuset français,* the French melting pot—a nation open to all newcomers prepared to embrace the ideals of the republic and in the process to forsake any allegiances to their pasts (Noriel, 1996). France has, in contrast to Germany, long been a nation of immigration. The French state, due to demographic factors, had since the 18th century a long-standing policy of encouraging immigration. During the 19th century it was the most significant immigrant-receiving nation in Europe (Dignan, 1981; Noriel, 1990). The immigrants during this era were overwhelmingly from European points of origin, with Italy providing the greatest numbers, followed by Spain, Portugal, and Poland. Although since the French Revolution the nation has tended to view itself as being particularly open to those seeking political asylum, in fact the vast majority of those entering the nation did so as conventional labor migrants. Prior to World War I, the overall percentage of immigrants remained persistent, but relatively low, amounting to no more than 3% of the total population. Thus, in general the immigrants were accepted, though during periods of economic distress, anti-immigration sentiments would rise, at times leading to violence (Hargreaves, 1995, pp. 7–8).

The labor shortages created by World War I led to a liberalization of immigration laws and as a consequence, during the 1920s the percentage of the population that was foreign born rose to a historic high of 6.6% (Noriel, 1996, p. 64). However, when the Great Depression took hold, once again anti-immigration sentiments surfaced and France became more restrictive in its naturalization policies and hiring practices. Immigration levels would continue to decline throughout both the Depression and World War II. However, by the middle of the 20th century, when the nation began to rebuild, the demand for labor again grew. Low birth rates exacerbated the need to seek sources of labor from outside the nation.

The quarter century beginning in 1950 proved to be the peak point in the history of immigration to France. A steady rise during the first half of the 1950s continued to increase, peaking in the first years of the 1970s and then, in the wake of the OPEC oil crisis, dropping precipitously. While Italy did not prove to be the major source of immigration that it had been in the past, Italians once again became part of the immigrant mix. The Iberian Peninsula once again became one of two major sources of new immigration, with Portugal supplying about three times more workers than Spain. In both instances, these nations were economic laggards in western Europe, and remained so until the respective long-term dictatorships of Salazar and Franco finally ended in the 1970s and democracy took root.

However, the Iberian Peninsula did not in itself meet France's labor needs. The other major source of immigrants was, for the first time in the nation's history, from outside of Europe. Three nations in the North African Maghreb region emerged as major sources of workers; from the largest to the smallest, these were Algeria, Morocco, and Tunisia. Algerian migrants were not simply labor migrants; their move was motivated in part by political events in Algeria leading to independence in 1962. These migrants included *pied-noirs*, French nationals who lived in the former colony, and what were known as *harkis*, indigenous Algerians who had sided with the French during the independence struggle. Shortly after independence, the French and Algerian governments entered into the Evian Agreement, which was designed to establish a formal mechanism for structuring labor recruitment. By 1970, there were nearly a half-million Algerians in France (Hamilton, Simon, & Veniard, 2004, p. 2), at which time the French government increasingly raised concerns about the need to limit immigration levels.

Moroccans and Tunisians began to arrive somewhat later than Algerians. The former found employment in the automotive and coal industries, two sectors that since the 1970s have experienced significant deindustrialization. Thus, by the mid-1970s, unemployment levels for Moroccans increased. Tunisians found work in the construction industry and as unskilled laborers in various settings (Hargreaves, 1995, p. 79). In addition to the Maghreb, 340,000 postcolonials arrived from Departements d'Outre-Mer and Territoiries d'Outre-Mer (DOM-TOM), including the Caribbean nations of Guadeloupe, Martinique, and French Guyana; the island of Reunion in the Indian Ocean; Vietnam; and former colonies in sub-Saharan Africa. Finally, Turks also arrived in significant numbers, though nothing approaching the levels in Germany.

By the early 1970s, as part of a trend occurring throughout EU nations, the French government sought to bring an end to mass immigration. In 1974, it ended its labor migration agreements with other countries, and in a preemptive effort to combat the prospect of rising levels of illegal immigrants, it passed legislation imposing sanctions on employers hiring such migrants. Financial incentives to repatriate were offered. While immigrants from the Iberian Peninsula were attracted to these incentives, immigrants from elsewhere were not. Rather, their numbers increased as they took advantage of family reunification provisions in the law. From the 1990s to the present, French policies have fluctuated, based on whether right-of-center or left-of-center governments were in power. While the former have attempted, in the end unsuccessfully, to put in place what Interior Minister Charles Pasqua called a "zero immigration" policy (Hamilton, Simon, & Veniard, 2004, p. 2), the left's platforms on immigration have been guided by recognition of the fact that the nation needs immigrants, particularly highly skilled ones. The situation during the last quarter of the past century and the first decade of the current one was shaped by a more restrictive climate for labor migrants. During the same time, the number of asylum seekers has increased—and in part this is due to the constriction of the flow of labor migrants. As Lisa Schuster (2004) has pointed out, the increase in asylum seekers in western Europe, including France, has yielded new policies aimed at excluding immigrants.

## The United Kingdom

Since the 19th century, British immigration has been defined to a significant degree but not entirely by its colonial legacy. This is also true of emigration, which prior to the middle of the 20th century experienced considerably higher levels than levels of immigration. One of the most significant destinations of British emigrants was the United States. Other significant destinations included Australia, Canada, New Zealand, and South Africa. The largest immigrant group to Britain during the late 19th and early 20th centuries came from its first colony, Ireland. However, immigrants came from European continental origins as well, including a sizeable number from Italy.

The wave of immigration that commenced after World War II would continue to include Europeans, but what made this a novel migratory wave was the presence of large numbers of people from former colonies—immigrants who as people of color would change the racial composition of the British Isles. Sociologist Paul Gilroy and colleagues at the Centre for Contemporary Cultural Studies (1992) depicted this movement in tongue-in-cheek fashion as "the empire strikes back." This migratory movement's symbolic beginning occurred in 1948, when the *Empire Windrush* arrived in Britain with nearly 500 Jamaicans on board. These passengers, like those who would follow, held British passports because their nations of origin were part of the British Commonwealth nations.

These newcomers arrived from three major points of origin: the British Caribbean, the Indian subcontinent, and various nations in sub-Saharan Africa. English-speaking Caribbeans often opted for the United States, given its geographical proximity and expanding postwar economy, but provisions in the 1952 McCarran-Walter Act served to close the door to such would-be immigrants (Grosfoguel, 1997; Tichenor, 2002, pp. 188–196). Thus, Britain soon became the destination of choice. This was true for Jamaicans, who came to constitute about half, and thus the largest contingent, of immigrants from the Caribbean, but it also was true for migrants from other Commonwealth nations in the region, including Antigua, Barbados, Belize, Dominica, Grenada, St. Kitts, St. Lucia, and Trinidad and Tobago.

During the 1950s, labor recruiters seeking to address acute labor shortages in Britain set their sights on these immigrants. At the same time, despite the fact that they spoke English and were familiar with British culture, these newcomers were forced to confront the reality of unvarnished racism. For many, being British and being white were seen as synonymous, and thus the prospect of blacks integrating into British society was seen as impossible. The demagogic politician Enoch Powell sought to incite fears of a racial war in which the nation would witness "rivers of blood" as it was overrun by a "colored population." Despite racist animosity, Caribbeans continued to enter the country. During the 1950s, they constituted by far the largest of the nonwhite groups entering the nation, their numbers rising to a half million by 1990 (Goulbourne, 1998, pp. 42–43) and to over three quarters of a million by the end of the past century, though in recent years the numbers have tapered off (Sriskandarajah & Road, 2005).

The Indian subcontinent also became the major source of what became known in the United Kingdom as Asians. The largest numbers arrived from India, with substantial flows also entering the nation from Pakistan and somewhat later Bangladesh and in smaller numbers from Sri Lanka. This migratory stream was religiously diverse, including Hindus, Muslims, and Sikhs. While many of the earliest arrivals were young men destined for the unskilled sector of the labor market, over time the migrants became more diverse in terms of human capital levels, including more highly educated professionals and businesspersons. In addition, family reunification led to the establishment of internally complex ethnic communities in major cities, with London not surprisingly constituting the major settlement area.

The third source of postcolonial immigrants was sub-Saharan Africa. This migratory stream included Indians forced out of various locales in Africa due to policies that called for the "Africanization" of local economies. As middleman minorities in nations such as Kenya and Uganda, they were targeted by nationalists and forced out of the countries, becoming in effect "twice migrants." While some returned to their homeland, many ended up in the United Kingdom (Goulbourne, 1998, p. 44). Added to this exodus, Africans from former British colonies also joined the migratory stream, adding numerically to the size of what became known as the Afro-Caribbean population.

The combined impact of these three migratory sources was that the United Kingdom became considerably more diverse in terms of race and religion. Yet, however significant this transformation was, in terms of sheer numbers, the largest single national source of immigrants throughout the second half of the 20th century up to the present derived from nearby Ireland. As the nation's first colony, Ireland had long been a source of labor migrants. As an economically struggling nation for most of this period, conditions in Ireland were conducive for emigration and given both the proximity and the intertwined histories of the United Kingdom and Ireland, it is not surprising that many emigrants simply crossed the Irish Sea (others did seek more distant destinations, including the United States). By the middle of the 1980s, the number of Irish residents in the United Kingdom was over a half million. More recently, as Ireland has become an economic success story, immigration levels have declined and, in fact, some Irish living abroad have returned home.

In contrast to the Irish, some of the new EU member states have taken advantage of the ability to move freely across borders in order to access labor markets in the wealthier nations in the confederation. When several new central and eastern European countries joined the European Union, several of the wealthier member nations placed restrictions on the flow of workers from these countries. The United Kingdom resisted pressures to act similarly, in part because in contrast to some of those nations, it enjoyed a growing economy and a low unemployment level. It did, however, limit the ability of migrants from the new member states to have ready or complete access to the nation's package of social benefits, in an effort to address what was referred to as "benefits tourism" (Sriskandarajah & Road, 2005, p. 7).

In addition to legal migrants, the numbers of undocumented have risen in recent years, which includes evidence of human trafficking, smuggling, and forced labor. Of particular concern to authorities are undocumented people entering from either China or various points in eastern Europe. While reliable estimates of the undocumented are hard to come by, a study conducted by the Institute for Public Policy Research reports that estimates range from 310,000 to 570,000, with the median estimate being 430,000. While it is also difficult to determine with any precision the origins of the undocumented, based on evidence obtained from people the authorities have detained, the largest percentage originated in Africa, followed by Asia, Europe, the Americas, and the Middle East (Farrant, Grieve, & Sriskandarajah, 2006, pp. 9–10). In this regard, the United Kingdom is no different from the rest of the wealthy countries of western Europe. Estimates of undocumented migrants in Germany, for example, are higher than estimates of those in the United Kingdom. Unsurprisingly, for this reason, the undocumented have become a policy priority not only for the nations involved, but within the European Union itself.

In terms of asylum seekers, the 1990s witnessed an increase in the number of applications, peaking at about 40,000 applicants per year, and with it, growing public sentiment that this constituted a problem. As Lisa Schuster (2004) has documented, the Blair administration responded to this growing chorus by instituting policies intended to reduce the number of applicants, streamline the process, and enhance the ability to deport unsuccessful applicants. The detention of asylum seekers has become more common since the beginning of the new century. This shift in policy was intended to make it more difficult for asylum seekers to have their applications approved.

## Italy and Spain

While mass immigration to Germany, France, and the United Kingdom has been occurring for a half century, this is not true of the other two major immigrant-receiving nations in western Europe, Italy and Spain. Both of them have until relatively recently been predominantly nations of emigration rather than of immigration. This has changed during the past two decades. In the case of Italy, its geographic location defines it as the closest point of entry for immigrants from both North Africa and eastern Europe. This accounts for the distinctive nature of the migratory streams that have emerged in recent decades. Four such streams have been identified. The first one is the oldest, with roots dating to as early as the 1960s. It linked migrants from Tunisia to Sicily and involved Italian merchants living in Tunisia who returned to Italy because of nationalization policies implemented in that country. Many of these migrants found employment opportunities awaiting them in the fishing and agricultural sectors. While this stream reflected the connection across the Mediterranean between Italy and Africa, the second one involved a similar connection between both sides of the Adriatic. After a devastating earthquake in Friuli in 1976, the demand for construction workers was met in part by laborers from Yugoslavia (Caponia, 2008; Colombo & Sciortino, 2004).

The third stream was defined by Italy's colonial past, as immigrants arrived from Eritrea, Ethiopia, and Somalia. Many of these immigrants settled in Milan and Rome, where they found work in the unskilled sector and in the ethnic enclave economy. In terms of the latter, they became a visible presence as street peddlers. The fourth migratory stream differs from the previous three insofar as the immigrants in it did not originate in places close to Italy. Rather, it involved people in countries that had experienced a history of Catholic missions in which Italian priests, nuns, and monks had played a prominent role. Thus, this stream included migrants from places such as Cape Verde and the Philippines (Caponia, 2008; Colombo & Sciortino, 2004).

The comparative newness of Italian immigration has resulted in a lag in establishing policies concerning preferred modes of incorporation and has created uncertainty both in policy circles and among the public. What is clear is that immigrants have come to constitute a significant presence in a nation whose population had been declining due to low birth rates. In 2005, there were 5.8 migrants per 1,000 in Italy, which is considerably higher than Germany's 1.2, France's 1.7, and the United Kingdom's 3.3. In absolute numbers, Italy's 338,000 immigrants in that year was the second-highest level in Europe (Muenz, 2007, pp. 2–3).

Ahead of Italy numerically was Spain, with an absolute total of 652,000 and a remarkable net migration per 1,000 of 15.0. This latter figure is quite remarkable, with Ireland's 11.4 being the only other western European country with a number in double digits. The end of the Franco dictatorship and the rapid economic modernization of Spain resulted in a dramatic reduction of Spaniards emigrating, whether it be within western Europe or elsewhere; many émigrés returned home to Spain. By the 1990s, Spain had became an immigrant-receiving state. At first, immigrants often treated Spain as a jumping-off point for a subsequent move to somewhere else in Europe. This changed by the mid-1980s, a time when those other ultimate destinations became more restrictive and ended guest worker programs that had been created shortly after World War II.

Given both Spain's proximity to the Maghreb and historic ties to the countries of the region, this area became one of its major sources of immigrants, with Morocco constituting the largest immigrant group from that region. Indeed, as the flow of Moroccans into Spain has continued, they are now the largest foreign nationality. South America and the Spanish Caribbean have also become major points of origin, with Ecuador emerging as the largest contributor, but also including sizeable contingents from Peru, Colombia, Cuba, Argentina, and the Dominican Republic. These are largely labor migrants heavily concentrated in the service sector and agriculture.

Europeans represent about 40% of the immigrant population, with the largest groups coming from Romania, Britain, Bulgaria, Italy, Portugal, and Germany (Pérez, 2003, p. 2). While the Portuguese, like Africans and immigrants from the Western Hemisphere, are labor immigrants, this is only partially true for the British, who are the second-largest European group, and German immigrants. In the case of these two groups—along with smaller numbers from elsewhere in northern Europe—many who have settled in Spain are retirees who have purchased homes or condominiums along the Mediterranean coast. It's for this reason that in some towns and cities on the Costa del Sol, one can find pubs, fish-and-chip shops and other manifestations of everyday British life.

As with Italy, Spain is wrestling with policies aimed at immigration control. Given the increase in undocumented migrants, many of whom enter Spain after treacherous journeys across the Mediterranean, controlling the border has become a matter of public concern. Thus, the focus of both legislators and the public has been on legislation regulating immigration flows. Due to the relative newness of mass immigration, Spain is only beginning to consider matters related to immigrant incorporation. Founded in 1994, the National Integration Forum has been charged with responsibility for formulating policy regarding immigrant inclusion. Its most current effort is the "Strategic Plan on Citizenship and Integration, 2007–2010."

## *Canada and Australia: Two Historic Settler Nations*

Canada and Australia constitute two very large land masses containing relatively few people. In 2007, Canada's population was 33 million, while Australia's was 21 million. As parts of the former British Empire, their historical trajectories have been shaped culturally, politically, and socially by that fact. Unlike the United States, which severed its political ties to the United Kingdom in a revolutionary upheaval, both Canada and Australia maintained their connections, and are thus today part of the Commonwealth of Nations. One significant difference between the two nations that the British government was cognizant of from an early point was the fact that Canada's proximity to the United States (indeed, its population is heavily concentrated along the border with its southern neighbor) meant that its future would in ways both predictable and unpredictable be shaped by that geographic reality. In contrast, Australia, an island continent, was more isolated and its future would be influenced by the character of its relationships with its closest Asian neighbors.

In Chapter 2, the history of Canadian immigration from the arrival of the nation's two charter groups to the formation of the "third force" in the late 19th and early 20th centuries was discussed. Picking up that history from where we left off, we begin with the following: From the onset of the Depression until the end of World War II, immigration levels were quite low. This changed quickly after the war as a large influx of displaced persons fled war-ravaged Eastern Europe and more traditional labor migrants also began to arrive. Among the largest groups entering Canada during this time were Italians, Greeks, Poles, and Portuguese. One consequence of these new arrivals was that the size and impact of the "third force" expanded (Elliott, 1983). At the same time, the United Kingdom continued to provide the largest percentage of new arrivals.

Canadian political and economic elites have long been cognizant of the need to enlarge the population, at times promoting various efforts to liberalize immigration policies by invoking the rhetoric of "populate or perish" (Hawkins, 1989, p. 38). The current wave of immigration has taken place in a far more liberal policy and cultural environment than was the case at the middle of the 20th century. This wave, which has entered Canada during the past three decades, amounts in effect to both an expansion and a recasting of the third force. The nation has experienced a dramatic increase of immigrants from Asia and the Caribbean. The largest Asian groups are the Chinese, Indian, Pakistani, Filipino, and Vietnamese, while the largest Caribbean groups are from Jamaica, Trinidad and Tobago, and Haiti. By the beginning of the 21st century, 5.4 million people had been born outside of the country, which represented over 18% of the population. This constituted the highest percentage of foreign-born for seven decades.

Figure 3.2 provides a graphic picture of the shifting demographics of Canadian immigration. Simply put, Europe has contributed a smaller percentage of immigrants over time, while Asians have contributed the largest percentages. During the last decade of the 20th century, immigrants from the People's Republic of China constituted, at 10.8%, the largest group. If the number of Chinese from Hong Kong and Taiwan is added to this figure, the total percentage of Chinese immigrants that entered Canada during this time period was 20.2%. The second-largest contingent came from India, at 8.5%. Other groups in the top 10 included arrivals from the Philippines, Sri Lanka, Pakistan, the United States, Iran, and Poland. A major consequence of this change in the national origins of new immigrants is that the racial composition of the nation has changed, with what the Canadian government calls the "visible minority population" rising threefold during the past quarter century

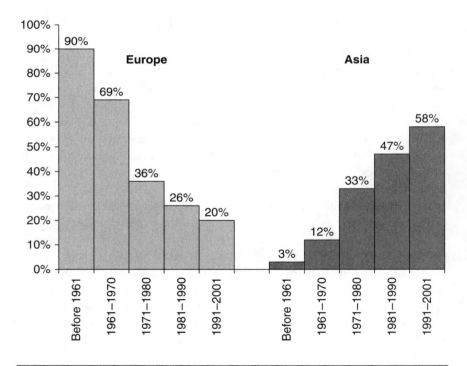

**Figure 3.2**    Proportion of Canadian Immigrants Born in Europe and Asia by Period of Immigration

(http://www12statcan.ca). It is within this context that the Canadian experiment with multiculturalism, which will be discussed in Chapter 6, needs to be understood.

Canada's foreign-born population at the beginning of the 20th century was 18%, which makes it the nation with the second-highest percentage of foreign-born among the advanced industrial nations, following the country we turn to now, Australia, which reports that 22% of its population is foreign born (http://www12.statcan.ca). Beginning as a British prison colony, Australia's population grew more slowly than Canada's during the 19th century, primarily because it was so distant from Europe. Nonetheless, the growth of the immigrant population paralleled that experienced by both Canada and the United States: first arrivals came primarily from western Europe and later this shifted to a growing segment of eastern Europeans. Fears of being inundated with migrants from nearby Asian countries led Australia to pass stringent racist immigration laws that were intended to ensure that Australia remained white. The whites-only policies remained in place until the 1970s, after which time more liberal laws were enacted, a reaction to the growing realization that the nation could not meet its labor needs if it relied solely on European and North American immigration sources. The White Australia Policy was dismantled in 1972, and subsequent steps were taken to remove race as a criterion for admission.

Approximately 6 million settlers entered the country from the end of World War II until the close of the past century (Department of Immigration and Multicultural Affairs, 2001, p. i). They entered a country that allows legal immigrants comparatively easy access to citizenship, as newcomers are eligible to apply for citizenship status after only 3 years' residence. During the 1970s, when these changes commenced, the nation also confronted the reality of refugee crises in Indo-China, and among those entering the nation in the latter part of that decade were refugees from Vietnam and Thailand. Refugees from Lebanon's civil war and the crises in both East Timor and Cyprus also arrived during this period. Refugees from El Salvador and Sri Lanka were added to the list during the following decade. During the last two decades of the past century, increasing numbers of Chinese arrived, along with Indonesians, Vietnamese, and Filipinos. The largest population actually came from New Zealand, which replaced the United Kingdom as the largest supplier of new immigrants. Anti-immigration sentiment rose and, as a consequence, Australia became less receptive to refugee settlement. At the same time, aware of the need for immigrants, an effort was made to establish entry policies along labor market needs, with particular emphasis granted to enlarging the "skills stream" (Department of Immigration and Multicultural Affairs, 2001, p. 15). By 2007, the number of skilled immigrants that had entered Australia during the first years of the 21st century was six times larger than the comparable figure for those entering the country for humanitarian reasons. The number entering under family reunification provisions was almost four times larger than the humanitarian figure (Department of Immigration and Citizenship, 2007, p. 2).

## The United States

We complete this survey of the top 20 contemporary immigrant-receiving countries with the United States, the nation that has throughout its entire history been defined by the impact of mass immigration and which today is the largest immigrant-receiving nation in the world. Two pieces of legislation serve to frame two great immigration waves. The first was passed in 1924, and as noted in the previous chapter, it brought to an end the great migratory wave that began during the 1880s as the nation made the transition from an agrarian to industrial economy. The second immigration law, the Hart-Cellar Act, was passed in 1965. The two legislators for whom the act is named were liberals intent on ending the racist character of the quotas that were implemented in the 1924 legislation. At the same time, it was based on a conviction that the United States needed to open its doors in order to address labor shortages in some sectors of the economy, which included in part areas that required skilled workers. According to Daniel Tichenor (2002), the bill's sponsors did not think that the law would result in the unleashing of a new huge migratory wave. Indeed, the young Senator Edward Kennedy, who worked for passage, contended on the Senate floor that the bill would not lead to the migration of large numbers of very poor immigrants from Africa.

While this proved to be true insofar as Africa has not become a major source of immigrants, in fact the law set in motion a new wave that began to grow each decade from the 1970s. The last decade of the 20th century witnessed more immigrants entering the United States than entered during the century's first decade, which had heretofore been the peak immigration decade in American history. During the first half of the first decade of the 21st century, the numbers continued to increase, reaching a level of 35.2 million. This led to a situation where more newcomers entered the United States during this 5-year period than at any 5-year period in the nation's history (Camarota, 2005, p. 1). Figure 3.3 places the sheer volume of immigration into context. Given that the overall size of the United States population is much larger today than it was a century ago, immigrants as a percentage of the overall population constitute at the moment 12.1%, lower than during the peak percentage historically, which was 14.7% in 1910. At the same time,

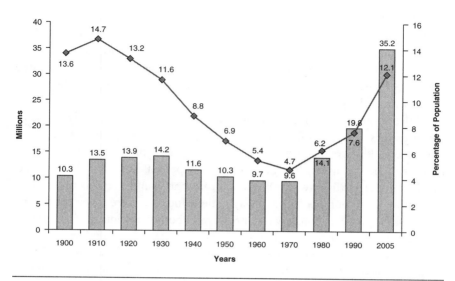

**Figure 3.3**    Immigrants in the United States, Number and Percentage of
Population, 1900–2005

the current figure is higher than any percentage since 1930—after which the
impact of the 1924 immigration restriction legislation began to be felt.

As with the other settler nations examined in this chapter, the majority of
the new wave of immigrants to the United States did not come from Europe.
Whereas Europeans accounted for over 50% of immigrants during the previous wave of migration, now they amount to around 15% (Clark, Hatton,
& Williamson, 2002, p. 1). Replacing Europeans were immigrants from
Latin America and Asia. The proximity of Mexico led to a situation where
that one particular nation played a particularly significant role. At present,
they account for somewhat more than two out of five of the nation's foreign-
born. Their presence in the nation skews many immigration statistics, such
as mean incomes, educational levels, and so forth. Mexican immigrants are
poorer, less well educated, and more likely to be located in the unskilled sector of the economy than immigrants as a whole.

Among the other largest immigrant groups that have arrived in the United
States since 1970 are Chinese (from the People's Republic, Taiwan, and
Hong Kong), Filipinos, South Koreans, Vietnamese, Indians, Salvadorans,
Cubans, and Dominicans, along with other groups from Central and South
America and the Caribbean. The actual mix of immigrants is very diverse,

including substantial numbers from Canada and the United Kingdom, as well as others from Europe. Senator Kennedy was right about Africans, for although immigrants from that continent, such as refugees from Somalia, have entered the country, no group from that country finds its way into the top 20 immigrant groups in the United States (Lyman, 2006, p. A16).

Over time, the percentages of some groups waned while others waxed. For example, South Korean immigration grew quickly during the early phase of the migratory wave, but declined in recent years as the South Korean economy emerged as a regional powerhouse. At the same time, immigration from India remained relatively low during the early period, but expanded dramatically from the 1990s onward. While Koreans had found a role as middleman minorities in a number of gateway cities, Indians were overrepresented among skilled professionals, with a presence in both medicine and in the high-tech sector. These examples are reflections of the fact that immigrants to the United States are overwhelmingly labor migrants. Indeed, in comparison to its European counterparts and Australia, refugees and asylum seekers constitute a smaller percentage of the overall migratory mix in the United States.

In Chapter 4, we will discuss the concept of segmented assimilation. At this point, it suffices to note that in an economy characterized by labor demand at both the top end of the occupational scale and at the bottom—among both highly skilled professionals and unskilled workers who will perform the dirty, difficult, and dangerous work that native workers avoid—immigrants will be attracted to both sectors. Given the significance of both ends of the occupational hierarchy, there are significantly different economic outcomes. Linked to this fact are differences in terms of levels of incorporation into the country's social and cultural fabric.

Two other developments have reconfigured immigration in recent years. First, in contrast to the earlier phase of the wave when immigrants were heavily concentrated in six states—California, New York, Texas, Florida, New Jersey, and Illinois—more recent arrivals are increasingly likely to avoid traditional gateway cities and settle instead in smaller cities and towns, particularly in the South and Midwest (Massey, 2008). The net result is that immigrants are becoming more evenly distributed across the country than was the case during the 1970s and 1980s. Second, the number of undocumented immigrants has increased (Van Hook, Bean, & Passel, 2005, p. 2). Figure 3.4 provides a portrait of the legal status of immigrants during the first decade of the present century. A large majority of the 10.3 million undocumented immigrants have entered the United States since 1990. While there are undocumented immigrants from Asia, Europe, and Africa, this is chiefly a phenomenon confined to the Western Hemisphere. Indeed, 57% of the total is from Mexico. With an additional 24% from other countries in Latin America,

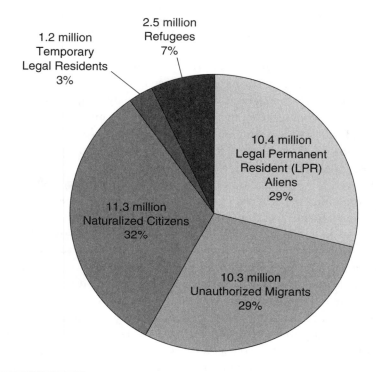

**Figure 3.4**    Legal Status of Immigrants in the United States

this means that 81% of the undocumented are from nations south of the U.S. border. Since 1995, more undocumented immigrants have entered the nation than legals (Passel, 2005, pp. 4–6). A legislative effort was initiated during George Bush's first term in office to reform immigration laws, the substance of which was to create a guest worker scheme that would meet the labor demands of certain sectors of the economy and to find a pathway to legalization for undocumented immigrants. Growing anti-immigration sentiment stymied the attempt, and thus immigration continues apace, as do calls to "secure" the borders.

## Conclusion

Immigration is a worldwide phenomenon, but to large extent contemporary flows are characterized by migrants from a relatively select number of countries moving to an even smaller number of nations—even though more and more nations have been drawn into the migratory orbit. Despite growing anti-immigration sentiment, there is no indication that the current flow is about to end. Indeed, it's fair to say that for the foreseeable future, immigration levels will remain high. Not surprisingly, despite the significance of immigration in the other top 20 immigrant-receiving nations and their regional counterparts (where immigrants are overwhelmingly temporary workers or refugees and asylum seekers), the bulk of the world's immigrants—estimated at around 60%—have entered western Europe, North America, and Oceania—or in short, those nations of the world characterized both as advanced industrial economies and liberal democracies.

Moreover, these particular nations have been the primary focus of sociological attention, and when we turn in a later section to modes of incorporation, the theoretical articulations of different modes derive from particular reference—sometimes explicitly—to these nations. In the following three chapters, three primary theoretical constructs will be analyzed: assimilation, transnationalism, and multiculturalism. While there is a lively debate about each of these modes, in which analysis and prescription often get intertwined, most involved in the debates are concerned with the advanced industrial liberal democracies. Thus, it remains an open question whether these concepts have applicability to countries such as Côte d'Ivoire or Saudi Arabia. To answer this question, at the outset it is necessary to consider the political system and national culture at hand in order to see if they are congruent with or antithetical to those of the nations that have been and continue to be the referents for conceptualizing various modes of incorporation—for a domain assumption of these concepts is that the receiving nations are modern liberal democracies.

# SECTION II

## Settlement

# 4

# Assimilation

## Historical Perspective and Contemporary Reframing

The preceding section was concerned with *movement* across borders, exploring the development over time of increasingly complex accounts of the dynamics of migration and reviewing contemporary migratory flows with these accounts in mind. As noted earlier, this work has primarily been the focus of demographers and economic sociologists. This section is concerned with *settlement*. As will quickly become evident, the patterns or modes of settlement involve not only the immigrant generation, but also their generational offspring as well—the second and third generations and beyond. This section's three chapters represent an examination of what might be called the bread and butter of sociology from the earliest studies of immigration a century ago to the present, because it is clear that what sociology has been chiefly preoccupied with is a conceptual framework for explaining if and how new forms of inclusive solidarity manage to be achieved once immigrants establish roots in a new homeland. This is a remarkably contested field, far more so than the debates that preoccupy those concerned with accounting for immigration flows. At bedrock, the issue at stake concerns the dialectic between inclusion and exclusion.

Charles Taylor has pointed out that democratic societies are inclusive insofar as they promote popular sovereignty, but this paradoxically also contributes to exclusion. This is the case, he contends, because "of the need, in self-governing societies, of a high degree of social cohesion. Democratic states need something like a common identity" (Taylor, 1998, p. 143). If current members define an outside group seeking entry as a threat to that common identity, they seek to effect closure rather than attempting to expand the bonds of solidarity. Groups can be excluded in a variety of ways, with such practices extending to three main groups: indigenous peoples, ethnonational minorities, and immigrants. In the case of immigrants, they can be denied entrance to a nation. If they are already present in the nation, they can be expelled. Or they can be allowed to remain, usually with the assumption that their presence is temporary, and that they are not in a position to acquire full societal membership. Moreover, they are not in a position to be involved in political decisions impacting their lives (Benhabib, 2008; Bosniak, 2006). The category of "guest workers"—a remarkable euphemism given that such migrants are permitted to enter a country solely because their labor is desired, but their presence in other respects is not valued—constitutes perhaps the best example of such border crossers.

Returning to the discussion in the preceding chapter about definitions, by some definitions guest workers would not be considered true immigrants since their intention is presumably not to settle permanently. While, as we've noted, such conclusions may be suspect insofar as they tend to convolute the intentions of movers with the state-defined terms of entry into a new nation, it is clear that being defined as temporary by the host society means that guest workers are not eligible to become fully integrated members of the society they have entered. A similar fate awaits undocumented migrants, who are forced to live their lives in the shadows, working and in many ways establishing stakes in the new society while also always being acutely aware of the fact that their legal circumstances make them both vulnerable and ineligible for full societal membership.

But what about those immigrants and their offspring who settle and sooner or later become included in some fashion into the new society? To begin to answer this question requires considering two underlying ones. First, what does inclusion mean, and second, how does inclusion occur? For much of the past century, inclusion was framed in terms of assimilation, a concept that took center stage in the work of Chicago School sociologists and continued as the hegemonic account of inclusion for a half century (Kivisto, 2005; Rumbaut, 1997). More recently, two concepts have emerged as challengers to assimilation: transnationalism and multiculturalism. This chapter takes up the history and recent reconsideration of assimilation, while Chapter 5 is devoted to exploring the development of transnationalist theory during the past two decades. Chapter 6 takes up the topic of multiculturalism, concluding with an attempt to tease out an account of inclusion that views assimilation and multiculturalism as potentially connected rather than antithetical modes of incorporation.

## To Be an Immigrant

What are the fundamental, recurring characteristics of the immigrant experience? This is a basic question sociologists of immigration have asked from the beginning of immigration research conducted by the members of the Chicago School up to the present. While the answers vary to some extent, there is a shared perspective that a movement beyond borders entails psychological, social, and cultural dislocations as one leaves the familiar and is forced to encounter that which is new, strange, sometimes enticing, and sometimes repugnant. This is clearly evident in what is generally regarded as the first major empirical research project on immigrant adjustment, W. I. Thomas and Florian Znaniecki's *The Polish Peasant in Europe and America* (1918–1920). In their account, immigration is depicted as a three-stage process in which the organization that gave coherence to the lives of premigration individuals leads to disorganization brought about by the very act of migration. This, in turn, in the proper circumstances where the impediments are not too great, leads over time—and from the immigrant generation to the second and beyond—to reorganization as settlers and their offspring find ways to accommodate to and achieve incorporation into the new society. This is not a cost-free process, for disorganization entails psychological imbalances, cultural loss, and in many instances a variety of social problems.

Norbert Wiley (1986) points out that the authors of the book—a native-born American and an elite Polish émigré who was socially distant from peasant coethnics—were not always sympathetic to their subjects and moreover did not adequately connect their conceptual framework to their data (which consisted most significantly of a treasure trove of immigrant letters). Nonetheless, their emphasis on the difficulties typical immigrants were likely to encounter became the received wisdom for sociologists and historians for decades to come.

Nowhere was this more evident than in Harvard historian Oscar Handlin's Pulitzer Prize–winning book, *The Uprooted* (1951). Influenced by the Chicago School in general and the work of Thomas and Znaniecki in particular, he preferred to use the language of alienation and anomie, drawing upon the mass-society literature of the time (Gleason, 1983; Kivisto, 1990, p. 467). The book sought to offer an account of the ideal-typical peasant immigrant who arrived on America's shores during the late 19th and early 20th centuries. Handlin contended that the sea change produced a dramatic disjuncture in the consciousness of these immigrants as the world-view of the peasant village was challenged by the impersonal nexus of an urban/industrial society. A tradition-oriented, religious, deferential world-view rooted in the soil and in the intimate relationships of family and community underwent a rapid process of deracination. The immigrant generation was portrayed as living in but not of the new society; inclusion eluded it, as did the reorganization described by Thomas and Znaniecki. The process of assimilation that Handlin thought would unfold only did so as the second generation came of age.

This is a "dark view" of the immigration experience (Deaux, 2006, p. 11). As will be seen in the following paragraphs, such a view has been challenged in recent decades by social historians, sociologists, and social psychologists. However, it is worth noting that this position has not disappeared, though it is no longer linked to the Chicago School formulation or to the particularities of the U.S. context. Pointing to one exemplary case, the title of the late Algerian sociologist Abdelmalek Sayad says it all: *The Suffering of the Immigrant* (2004). Influenced by the theoretical orientation of Pierre Bourdieu, the book focuses on the painful transformation Algerian peasants have experienced since they began to enter France in large numbers after World War II. Sayad stresses the ambivalence of the immigrants' situation, captured well in the following passage:

> Torn between two "times," between two countries and between two condi-tions, an entire community lives as though it were "in transit." Being con-demned to refer simultaneously to two societies, emigrants dream, without noticing the contradiction, of combining the incompatible advantages of two conflicting choices. At times, they idealize France and would like it to have, in addition to the advantages it gives them (a stable job, a wage, etc.), that other quality of being a "second" land of their birth—which would be enough to transfigure the relationship and to magically transform all the reasons for the dissatisfaction they experience in France. At other times, they idealize Algeria in their dreams after spending time there during their annual holidays. (Sayad, 2004, p. 58)

Neil Smelser (1998) describes ambivalence as an affective state character-ized by simultaneously holding two opposed emotions toward an object: attraction and repulsion; love and hate. While it would be a mistake to claim that all immigrants react ambivalently to their homeland and their new place of residence, there is abundant evidence not only in the work of social his-torians and sociologists but also in fictional accounts of immigrant life, past and present, that ambivalence is a very common emotional reaction to migration. Borrowing from Albert Hirschman (1970), Smelser contends that there are three responses to ambivalence: by exit (which stresses the negative side of ambivalence), loyalty (which represses the negative side), and voice (which seeks to steer a middle course between the positive and negative). These options are more complicated for immigrants given that they can feel ambivalent toward their place of origin, their destination, or both.

Elizabeth Aranda's (2007a, 2007b) research on contemporary Puerto Rican professionals who often move several times between the island and the mainland provides a telling example of the struggles involved in responding to ambivalence. That her subjects are not by our definition true immigrants since they are U.S. citizens is not relevant here; their ability to move freely back and forth offers a particularly telling instance of how difficult it can be for people attempting to sort out their emotional attachments and their prospects for reconfiguring a sense of belonging.

The consensus among scholars today is that immigrants deal with ambivalence with more resources than scholars such as Thomas and Znaniecki, Handlin, and Sayad took into account. This consensus, while recognizing the fact that immigrants frequently confront nativist hostility, economic exploitation, and political and cultural marginalization, contends that they nonetheless have generally managed to be agents of their own lives. In other words, they play an active role in the process of adjustment and becoming a part of their new homeland. John Bodnar's *The Transplanted* (1985) presents a synthesis of the work of social historians and historical sociologists dating from the 1960s forward. As the title of his book suggests, it is meant to be in part a critique of Handlin's ideal-typical portrait of an uprooted generation. While it is true that many immigrants opted for exit, returning to their origins (Wyman, 1993), and others sought to express their loyalty by rejecting their roots in an effort to fit in, the typical immigrant in Bodnar's account exhibited voice, seeking to negotiate the terms of incorporation predicated on a selective embrace of the host society's institutions and values, while picking and choosing which aspects of their cultural heritage to transplant and which to abandon. They did so, he argued, with a *mentalité* that he characterizes as pragmatic.

Two central features of his work serve to distance it from the earlier generation of immigration scholarship. First, while his predecessors tended to either ignore the macro context of migration or located it in terms of modernization theory, as noted in Chapter 2, Bodnar stresses the specific linkages between the rise of industrial capitalism and immigration. Second, he treats the negotiation process as a group endeavor and not an individual initiative. In so doing, he focuses on the ethnic community as both resource and agent. Although he didn't use the language of networks, the affiliations made possible by a complex of ethnic institutions and social relationships that made up ethnic communities was seen as playing a profound role in the precise way that different groups ended up over time becoming incorporated into American society. The community served to buffer the difficulties immigrants inevitably encountered and, in so doing, assisted in the process of becoming members of the wider society—a phenomenon that Barbara Ballis Lal (1990, p. 96) has referred to as the "ethnicity paradox." What she meant by this term is that ethnic communities, rather than retarding incorporation, actually were important for making incorporation possible.

Social psychologist Kay Deaux's (2006) recent work reinforces Bodnar's stress on the negotiated character of immigrant behavior. Focusing on contemporary immigrants in the world's liberal democracies, she finds that the vast majority of immigrants do not seek to remain separate from the wider society. Indeed, the only exception she reports is that of Turks in Germany who prefer separation to incorporation. We would point out that there is abundant evidence that challenges the view of Turks in Germany as an exception to the general inclination to seek inclusion. Whether the immigrants call it integration or assimilation, the major conclusion to be drawn from her work is that voluntary labor migrants are prepared to some extent to be transformed in order to become part of the settlement society. That the preferred term, especially outside the United States, tends to be integration rather than assimilation is due to the fact that while the former is defined as permitting immigrants to maintain their cultural identity, assimilation is by many seen as entailing a loss of such identity (Deaux, 2006, pp. 60–61). Whether this is an accurate depiction of assimilation—in either its canonical formulation or current usage—will be addressed in the following paragraphs.

Of significance here is the fact that outcomes are dependent on several factors, including the obstacles to inclusion posed by the receiving society. Deaux pays particular attention to public opinion and the stereotypes and prejudices harbored by citizens toward newcomers. In addition, it is important to factor into the equation what immigrants bring to the table—motivations, skills, expectations, values, and needs—and what they encounter, which includes social networks, a particular opportunity structure, and a climate shaping interpersonal relationships. At the social psychological level, these factors serve to shape the varied ways immigrants negotiate their identity while at the level of social interaction they influence relationships with group members and with members of the wider society, which includes the sorts of collective action generated by the immigrant community.

A major lesson to be derived from both Bodnar and Deaux is that for most immigrants, being an immigrant means being prepared to be transformed. However, this seldom means that immigrants think that the transformation in question calls for a complete repudiation—a forgetting—of the preimmigration past. Rather, the process of becoming incorporated into the new setting requires a sifting and choosing of which aspects of one's cultural background to preserve and which social ties to maintain. This is an inherently complex undertaking, made even more complex when immigrants must reckon with their ambivalent feelings about both their homeland and the land of settlement. Given the layers of complexity, it is not surprising that assimilation, transnationalism, and multiculturalism offer theoretical accounts of the incorporation of immigrants and their offspring that are highly contested.

## The Return to Assimilation?

We turn to assimilation. The goal of the remainder of this chapter is first to offer a portrait of the so-called canonical view of assimilation. The purpose of this account is to achieve greater clarity about a concept that is often misunderstood. Second, we will examine the two most significant contemporary efforts to reframe assimilation theory, the idea of segmented assimilation developed by Alejandro Portes and associates (e.g., Portes & Rumbaut, 2001) and Richard Alba and Victor Nee's (2003) work on the redefining of the "American mainstream."

In the final decade of the 20th century—a decade that witnessed more newcomers arriving in the United States than at any point in its history— Richard Alba referred to the impact on the nation brought about by assimilation as a "quiet tide" and a "dirty little secret" (1995a, p. 3). What he was reflecting on was a growing realization that despite an aversion among many scholars to employ assimilation theory in accounting for immigrant incorporation, in fact, there was abundant evidence to suggest that assimilation was occurring. Within a decade, the secret was out in the open. Assimilation was once again a topic of interest within sociology and related disciplines. For example, this was evident in the title of an article appearing in *The Chronicle of Higher Education*: "Scholars Cook Up a New Melting Pot" (Glenn, 2004) as well as in the title of a collection of essays edited by Tamar Jacoby of the Manhattan Institute, *Reinventing the Melting Pot* (2004). Among the contributors to Jacoby's book are such prominent immigration scholars as, in addition to Alba, Herbert Gans, Nathan Glazer, Douglas Massey, Alejandro Portes, Stephen Steinberg, Stephan Thernstrom, Roger Waldinger, and Min Zhou. Nevertheless, considerable debate persists about what assimilation actually means and many scholars remain suspicious about assimilation, either for its presumed ideological biases or empirical inadequacies.

Clearly, any effort to make sense of the analytical utility of assimilation must be pursued first by recognizing the three incontrovertible facts about assimilation that we have just identified: (1) there is little consensus about what we mean by the term; (2) it remains highly contentious; and (3) it continues to shape contemporary research agendas (e.g., Chiswick, Lee, & Miller, 2005; Waters & Jiménez, 2005). In the following pages, we will attempt to sketch out the historical trajectory of this concept. This will involve tracing the career of the concept beginning in the late 19th century and culminating in an effort to account for the return of assimilation among scholars of migration and ethnicity since the 1980s, despite confusion about what exactly it means and in spite of the controversies that surround it.

## The Canonical Formulation of Assimilation Theory

Robert Park, in conjunction with key colleagues of his at the University of Chicago such as W. I. Thomas and Ernest Burgess, is generally and appropriately considered to be the sociologist most responsible for the canonical formulation of assimilation theory (Hirschman, 1983; Kazal, 1995; Kivisto, 2004; Lal, 1990; Lyman, 1972; Matthews, 1977; Persons, 1987; Rumbaut, 1999). However, there is less consensus about both what Park had in mind when he described assimilation and to what extent he merely presented a summary of prevailing views or developed an original position. His perspective has been portrayed by some as a theoretical articulation of the melting pot, as a synonym for Americanization, the final outcome of a "race relations cycle," and an expression of a "straight-line" process of incorporation (Gans, 1992a; Lyman, 1972; Portes, 1995). In these various interpretations, it has been assumed that his particular perspective on assimilation is incongruent with, if not antithetical to, cultural pluralism or its more recent parallel concept, multiculturalism (Gordon, 1964; Kivisto, 2002).

### Park's Precursors

Earlier uses of assimilation as a sociological concept predate Park's contribution by three decades. The appearance of assimilation, both in popular usage and among social scientists, coincided with the beginning of a great migratory wave around 1880. Regarding the former, Rubén Rumbaut (2001, p. 845) cites an editorial in *The New York Times* from this era that expressed concern about the capacity of the nation to assimilate many of the new immigrants then arriving in the United States. Within the social sciences, the term was commonly used, though seldom explicitly defined. James McKee (1993, p. 122) contends that "assimilation became a central concept in sociology without prolonged debate and without much concern for any preciseness of definition." This is not entirely true insofar as in at least two instances, sustained systematic attempts were made to both add clarity and to employ assimilation as a concept accounting for the processes associated with immigrant incorporation.

The earliest such effort was political economist Richmond Mayo-Smith's "Assimilation of Nationalities in the United States," which appeared in 1894 as a two-part installment in the *Political Science Quarterly*. According to Mayo-Smith, there were three primary forces promoting assimilation: intermarriage, physical environment, and social environment. He ignored the first factor due to a lack of adequate data, and thus did not examine the biological mixing of peoples, but rather focused on whether or not members of the varied ethnic groups in the United States were adapting to and embracing the customs, laws, and institutions of the nation, and thus were fusing culturally into an American nationality (Mayo-Smith, 1894, p. 431). Like Frederick Jackson Turner, he argued that with the passing of the frontier, the role of the physical environment receded, leaving the social environment as the primary factor promoting assimilation.

More specifically, Mayo-Smith (1894, pp. 652–669) identified two primary factors that contribute to assimilation: education and the exercise of citizenship rights. In this discussion, it is clear that assimilation is construed to be a one-way process wherein the newcomers transform themselves, but there is no reciprocal process affecting the members of the host society. His version of what Milton Gordon (1964) would seven decades later refer to as "Anglo-conformity" appeared to be the outcome of a relatively easy, seamless, and unidirectional process. Indeed, although he supported some form of immigration control, he was critical of those among his contemporaries who feared some of the new immigrants—whom they accused, among other things, of being prone to political radicalism and being responsible for rising crime rates—because he was confident that the social environment would serve as an antidote to these problems. Because of this, he assumed that assimilation was "natural and almost inevitable" (Mayo-Smith, 1894, p. 670). This conviction was predicated on the capacity of the nation to socialize newcomers into its folkways and mores and on the presumed willingness of immigrants to be so resocialized.

The second significant contribution to the early development of assimilation theory was Sarah Simons' five-part article on "Social Assimilation" that was published in the *American Journal of Sociology* during 1901 and 1902. It was a detailed, richly documented, and theoretically sophisticated essay that explored assimilation in world historical terms. Part of the rationale for the essay was to provide conceptual clarity to a term that was viewed as important for both sociological and historical research (Simons, 1901–1902, pp. 790–791). Simons defined assimilation as "that process of adjustment or accommodation which occurs between the members of two different races, if their contact is prolonged and if the necessary psychic conditions are present," with the result being "group-homogeneity to a greater or less degree" (Simons 1901–1902, pp. 791–792).

Assimilation was construed to have both a social and a psychological dimension. Moreover, it was seen as having two aspects, the first of which entails an unconscious or unplanned social process that occurs in situations where sustained contact between groups exists. The second is a volitional aspect, and in this regard Simons (1901–1902, p. 793) is especially interested in "purposive assimilation" that is "directed by the state." Social contact is regarded as becoming more frequent and intense in modern societies as a result of improvements in transportation brought about by the railroad and steamship and in communications by such factors as the availability of mass-produced newspapers and the telegraph. Sounding like a precursor to contemporary globalization theorists, Simons wrote, in language that offers a remarkably prescient account of globalization akin to such contemporary accounts as those found in the work of Anthony Giddens and David Harvey, that developments in transport and communication technologies have resulted in "a system which does much toward annihilating the barriers of space and time" (Simons, 1901–1902, p. 800).

Simons (1901–1902, p. 803) treated assimilation as a reciprocal process, but she posed it in an unusual way insofar as she described those involved in the assimilation of others as constituting the active factor while those being assimilated were the passive factor. The attractive assimilation of modern societies relies primarily on education and the political and civic involvements of newcomers. They become incorporated largely due to imitation, and thus assimilation is reactive, or in her terms, passive. In the conclusion of her theoretical discussion, she contended that the creation of group homogeneity does not necessarily mean that all group differences are eliminated. While a universal civic culture is essential, which means a shared language and an embracing of democratic values, she asserted that "in personal matters of religion and habits of life, however, individuality shall be allowed free play" (Simons, 1901–1902, p. 821). While it is clear that Simons' view of assimilation is not the melting-pot variety, what is left unclear is the extent to which difference is a group or an individual phenomenon.

## Park's Theory of Assimilation

It is in the context of these two predecessors that Park's distinctive contribution to assimilation theory needs to be understood. Although he used the term repeatedly in many of his publications, Park explicitly and in a sustained way addressed assimilation as a topic in only three publications that span the course of his career at the University of Chicago. Two of these are very brief, including a section introduction to the textbook he coauthored with Ernest W. Burgess and an encyclopedia article (Park, 1930; Park & Burgess, 1969/1921). His earliest treatment, appearing in the Chicago flagship journal, the *American Journal of Sociology*, is clearly his most sustained and arguably his most original and theoretically sophisticated analysis of the topic (Park, 1914).

Before proceeding to summarize Park's argument in this seminal essay, an observation is in order. Contrary to a commonly held view that was advanced in particular by Stanford Lyman (1972, pp. 27–70), Park's theory of assimilation is not inextricably linked to the "race-relations cycle," which entails a four-stage teleological process that has groups moving slowly and gradually from contact to conflict, to accommodation, and culminating in assimilation. Park used the idea of a cycle in only two publications, and in only one did this process seem to be what he had in mind. In none of the previously noted articles explicitly concerned with assimilation does he mention the term. For this reason, it is reasonable to concur with Barbara Ballis Lal (1990, pp. 5, 41–42) that the race-relations cycle idea served only a minor role in Park's work and does not inform his conceptual discussions of assimilation.

In "Racial Assimilation in Secondary Groups With Particular Reference to the Negro" (1914), Park identified three objectives. First, he sought to clarify the significance of assimilation as a category of sociological analysis, implicitly distinguishing it from assimilation as a normative concept. Second, he articulated a theory that treated assimilation as a process. Third, he presented his understanding of the implications of racial impediments to assimilation. Park noted that two different meanings of assimilation coexist. The first is "to make like" and the second is "to take up and incorporate." Both represent societal processes. The former operates more or less spontaneously as individuals "acquire one another's language, characteristic attitudes, and modes of behavior." The latter is more volitional, involving the incorporation of both individuals and ethnic groups into "larger groups." In combination, these two processes are responsible for the construction of national identities in the modern world (Park, 1914, p. 606).

As with Durkheim, Park considered changes in the division of labor in society as creating a new structural matrix for social relations. He saw homogeneity as the predominant feature of the premodern world, while in modern societies, increasing heterogeneity among individuals becomes typical. In such societies, social solidarity no longer demanded the "consciousness of kind" characteristic of the past. Rather, the interdependencies made possible by the new economic order serve as a powerful basis for a new form of solidarity characterized by the potential for considerable diversity. Because modern societies are able to accommodate to far greater levels of diversity, individuals are increasingly free to develop autonomously.

One of the ways they do so is by emancipating themselves from the constraints of parochial groups that constrain expressions of individualism. In place of such groups, individuals are inclined to become voluntary members of what Park (1914, p. 607) described as larger and more inclusive "cosmopolitan groups." What he had in mind appears to be connected to two insights of Simmel (1971/1911, pp. 252, 274): first, that increases in individualism coincide with the expansion of the "social circle encompassing the individual," and second, that individualism and a "cosmopolitan disposition" are intimately intertwined. Park (1914, pp. 607–608) made the following observation:

> What one actually finds in cosmopolitan groups, then, is a superficial uniformity, a homogeneity in manners and fashion, associated with relatively profound differences in individual opinions, sentiments, and beliefs. . . . So far as it makes each individual look like every other—no matter how different under the skin—homogeneity mobilizes the individual man. It removes the taboo, permits the individual to move in strange groups, and thus facilitates new and adventurous contacts.

Thus, assimilation is conceived to be a process wherein individual social horizons expand and, simultaneously, increasingly complex webs of social interaction and affiliation arise. In other words, although it might appear paradoxical, assimilation signals the proliferation of diversity. Rather than enforced conformity, it makes possible a greater degree of autonomy.

At the same time, Park described a relationship between assimilation and social solidarity by arguing that in societies characterized by mutual interdependence, sentiments and habits develop that encourage pragmatic working relationships. Assimilation understood in terms of such relations creates the precondition for a situation wherein "groups of individuals, originally indifferent or perhaps hostile, achieve the corporate character," by which he meant that social groups, including ethnic groups, can persist in exhibiting their collective distinctiveness due to the fact that they buy into an overarching national sensibility of live and let live—or in other words a cultural climate predicated on pluralism and toleration (Park, 1914, p. 610). Thus, contained in Park's formulation is an explanation for how cultural pluralism or multiculturalism can coexist with assimilation—though not the essentialist version of pluralism associated with Horace Kallen (1924) or the parallel essentialism evident in some strong multiculturalist theorizing.

As the title of the essay indicated, Park treated assimilation as a process relevant to all ethnic groups, and not only voluntary immigrants and their offspring. Indeed, here he specifically used the concept for an analysis of the situation of blacks in the United States, the only nonvoluntary migrant group in the nation. In this discussion, he identified what he considered to be the chief obstacle to incorporation, which was predicated on invidious comparisons made on the basis of external features such as skin color. The consequence of race prejudice is that the member of the marginalized group cannot be seen as an individual, but merely as a representation of the collectivity. This constitutes the social psychological underpinning of racial prejudice, for insofar as people are not capable of viewing the other as an individual, they are unable to establish patterns of interaction based on reciprocity and respect—a theme he returned to in 1926 in his essay "Behind Our Masks." Park (1914, p. 611) did not explore the causes or varied manifestations of prejudice, focusing instead on the interactional implications of the color line that separates the races.

In applying assimilation theory to blacks, Park claimed that assimilation, at some level, takes place even in a situation of intense prejudice. He was clear that the aspect of assimilation that "goes on silently and unconsciously" and results in the acquisition of the dominant culture's language, religion, and values was quite thoroughgoing (Park, 1914, p. 611). On the other hand, blacks had not assimilated structurally because they had been denied entrée to and membership in the secondary groups of the dominant society. The result was the emergence of a sense of group identity associated with the idea of racial pride, a phenomenon akin to the nationalist movements among Europe's "nations without states." In this regard, Park concluded his essay with an intriguing speculation about the prospect of a multiethnic state wherein nationality groups maintain their distinctive identities while at the same time being committed to the interests and ideals of the state, a situation that is possible only if the state is prepared to deal with the demands of the nationality group for redistribution of resources and recognition (Park, 1914, p. 623).

## What Is the Canonical Formulation of Assimilation?

Mayo-Smith, Simons, and Park rejected the view that assimilation was a theoretical expression of the melting pot, or what Park and Burgess (1969/1921, p. 735) disparagingly referred to as the "magic crucible" version of assimilation that they associated with theories of "like-mindedness." All three emphasized the role of culture over biology, though only in Park can one detect a genuine break with biological determinism.

Park's position, in contrast to his predecessors, advances the theory of assimilation in significant ways. First, he understood migration to be a group phenomenon, and not merely an individual one. Second, he disagreed with the Anglo-conformity view of assimilation that was explicitly articulated in Mayo-Smith and was certainly a large part of what Simons had in mind. Third, Park granted agency to ethnics. Finally, he articulated his position in a manner that very consciously sought to divorce sociological analysis from moral preferences and ideology.

His is, to borrow Herbert Gans' (1992a) term, a "bumpy-line" version of assimilation, not as some commentators have assumed (including Gans), a "straight-line" approach. Assimilation is the product of interaction and thus has a reciprocal character, although Park understood that differences in group location and power and status differences would affect outcomes. Racial hostility (he leaves out of consideration religious hostility) was consistently described as the major impediment to assimilation.

Assimilation boiled down to finding a way to live together cooperatively, playing by common rules that define the parameters of intergroup conflict. It entailed the creation of a shared national identity, which of necessity required certain commonalities, such as a shared language and core cultural values. However, it also permitted the persistence of ethnic identities and affiliations. Assimilation thus is not considered to be antithetical to a multicultural society; it does not require cultural homogeneity.

The unappreciated aspect of Park's contribution to this dialogue is his explanation for why modern societies can tolerate diversity and his account of why assimilation propels so many individuals to exit—totally or partially—their ethnic groups. Park was insistent that due to the division of labor in modern societies, assimilation did not entail homogeneity, and that considerable individual and group differences can persist without impairing national unity. The reverse side of the coin involves the lure of assimilation. Park thought assimilation was attractive because modern societies are individualistic. What this means is that people will seek to enhance their own opportunities and expand their life options, and that one way of doing so is to refuse to permit the parochial constraints of the ethnic group to limit self-realization. It means that individuals will seek to expand their social circles and will treat the ethnic group not as a community of fate, but as one of a variety of possible affiliations and sources of personal identity. The cosmopolitan group, in contrast to the parochial group, is one in which individuals possess options, including the options of loyalty, voice, and exit.

One of the unfortunate features of Park's discussion is that he failed to adequately define what he meant by cosmopolitan groups. In part, this was a failure to take up the research agenda presented by Arthur Schlesinger, Sr., in the pages of *The American Journal of Sociology*. The task of scholars, he contended, was not only to explore "the influence of America on the ever-changing composite population," but also to examine "the influence of immigration on American life and institutions" (Schlesinger, 1924, p. 71). Park ignored the latter. More specifically, he failed to understand the implications for American identity of cosmopolitan groups being receptive to being transformed as a result of their encounters with groups from outside the mainstream. In this regard, the insights of social critic Randolph Bourne (1916), in his advocacy on behalf of a "trans-national America," could have served Park well in amplifying his thesis. Unlike Kallen, who tended to view ethnic identities as fixed and distinct, Bourne had a more dynamic view in mind, one that presumed that not only would ethnic groups be transformed as a result of their encounter with the larger society, but that American society would also be transformed positively as a consequence of the encounter between the core culture and outsiders moving in. Park appears to have had something similar in mind, but unfortunately his argument in this regard remained woefully underdeveloped.

## The Impact of the Paradigm

The version of assimilation articulated by Park can be seen as a theory of the middle range developed under the influence of those grand narratives of modernity associated particularly with the work of Durkheim and Simmel. For the first two-thirds of the 20th century, it constituted the hegemonic theory used by both sociologists and historians to study ethnicity in America.

Most sociologists spent little time refining or revising the theory, concentrating primarily on operationalizing it. This was clearly the case among Chicago School sociologists, as can be seen, for instance, in the social distance scale developed by Emory Bogardus (1933) and in the wedding of assimilation to the ecological focus on the spatial patterns of cities in the work of Louis Wirth (1928). The apogee of such work was W. Lloyd Warner and Leo Srole's *The Social Systems of American Ethnic Groups* (1945), which was a part of their Yankee City Series.

They offered a complex conceptual scheme to account for the likely assimilative trajectories of a wide range of groups that they broadly distinguished into three categories: ethnic, racial, and ethnoracial (this is not well defined, but represents something of an interstitial category). The focus of their study was on the differential barriers to incorporation confronting various groups. Key to defining the strength of the barrier was the level and degree of subordination each group confronts, but factored into the equation was the impact of the relative strength of the group's communal bonds. Located in the social distance tradition, the traits that made incorporation difficult for ethnic groups were cultural in nature, and, therefore, subject to change. In contrast, the racial traits that worked against assimilation were rooted in biology, and thus would remain persistent handicaps for racial groups. The ethnoracial groups (the two examples in the study were "Spanish Americans" in the Southwest and "mixed bloods" from Latin America) had sufficiently ambiguous identities that their futures might either look like the futures of ethnic groups or the futures of racial groups (Warner & Srole, 1945, pp. 284–292).

In their "scale of subordination and assimilation," Warner and Srole combined racial and cultural types to form a grid in which they located each specific group. They offered both a prognosis of the length of time it would take to assimilate (ranging from "very short" to "very slow") and their pre-dicted future social location. In the case of ethnic groups, the movement over time would be from the ethnic group into specific social class locations. At the other end of the spectrum, for blacks it would be a movement from the racial group to a "color caste" location. Asians were destined to enter a "semi-caste" condition, while Latinos would either end up in a class or color caste location. Thus, they concluded, "The future of American ethnic groups seems to be limited; it is likely that they will be quickly absorbed. When this happens one of the great epochs of American history will have ended and another, that of race, will begin" (Warner & Srole, 1945, p. 295). This is a rather odd formulation given the prominent role race has played throughout American history, but it does serve to differentiate the future historical tra-jectories of white ethnics and people of color.

Both methodologically and in terms of the theoretical assumptions shaping their work, Warner and Srole's study can be viewed as emblematic of a tradi-tion of sociological research that extended into the 1960s. A parallel connec-tion to the canon can also be seen among historians of the era. This is especially evident in the seminal essay of Marcus Lee Hansen, "The Problem of the Third Generation Immigrant" (1938), whose thesis challenges the idea of straight-line assimilation, offering instead an account for why a renewal of interest in ethnic origins might materialize. Thus, his thesis has often been regarded as offering an explanation for ethnic revivals (for a retrospective account of the Hansen thesis, see the essays in Kivisto & Blanck, 1990). Hansen argued that unlike the second generation, which repudiated its ethnic-ity due to insecurity and a desire to be accepted into the mainstream, individ-uals of the third generation were inclined to manifest a renewal of interest in their ethnic identity precisely because they had adjusted to and been accepted by the mainstream society. However, this did not amount to a repudiation of assimilation theory. Rather, it signaled the fact that the third generation inhabited a unique historical moment, one that was not likely to be replayed in subsequent generations. Although he posed his thesis in generational terms, the impact of specific historical events ought also to be factored into any analysis of the likelihood of ethnic return. In any event, Hansen assumed the overarching trend was toward acculturation and incorporation.

A similar assumption can be found in the work of the other major historian of immigration at midcentury, a scholar we have discussed earlier: Oscar Handlin. As Russell Kazal (1995, p. 446) has pointed out, both of Handlin's significant books on immigration, *Boston's Immigrants, 1790–1865: A Study in Acculturation* (1941) and *The Uprooted* (1951), "contained a healthy dose of Chicago-style sociology." If the first emphasized, as the subtitle indicates, the adjustment process, the latter was structured around the concept of alienation, and thus focused on the existential tensions, conflicts, and suffering experienced by the immigrant generation— those people whom, as noted earlier, he depicted as being consigned to forever live in two worlds without feeling truly at home in either.

Handlin did not focus, as did Hansen, on the American-born generations. Among those that have picked up on Hansen's theme of generational transformation, none have offered a more cogent sociological account than Vladimir Nahirny and Joshua Fishman (1965) in their reappraisal of the Hansen thesis. As they point out, since assimilation takes place over time, it is essential to take into account both history and generational transition. Nahirny and Fishman consider Hansen's social psychological explanation to be oversimplistic, and in its place they offer a far more complex portrait, one that arrived at what they describe as a paradoxical conclusion: "despite acculturation . . . the sons continued to remain acutely conscious of their ethnic identity." More than merely challenging the Hansen account of children forgetting and grandchildren remembering, in their phenomenological emphasis on lived experience, they have offered a sociologically informed explanation for why individual experience and social structural factors combine to yield the paradox of acculturation occurring simultaneously with the maintenance of a keen sense of ethnic identity.

In a parallel effort published in the same year, Tomatsu Shibutani and Kian Kwan (1965) offered an approach that weds the Chicago School version of assimilation similar to that developed by Park to symbolic interactionism. They advanced the theory of assimilation in part by moving from a singular focus on the United States to explore its applicability to a wide range of locations around the globe. In a recent reappreciation of their work, Richard Alba and Victor Nee (2003, p. 34) contend that their social constructionist approach adds several features that are missing in the canonical account. One is a complex, causal analysis that allows for contingency. . . . Another is the preservation of the distinctions among levels of aggregation so that the interaction among individuals, groups, and the larger social environment is incorporated into the analytic accounting. . . . Finally, their analysis quite explicitly recognizes the centrality of stratification [and power] in the ethnic experience.

## Gordon's Typology of Assimilation

These works are representative of the central orientation of the majority of sociologists and historians into the 1960s and a reflection of the hegemony exerted by assimilation theory decades after its canonical formulation. A half century after Park's initial formulation, Milton Gordon's seminal study, *Assimilation in American Life* (1964), both codified and systematized the theory of assimilation. However valuable this work may be, Roger Waldinger's (2003, p. 250) observation is on point, namely that Gordon "provided a typology of assimilation and its components, not a theory." Gordon (1964, p. 71) identified seven types of assimilation: (1) cultural or behavioral—also known as acculturation; (2) structural; (3) marital—or amalgamation; (4) identificational, which means creating a shared sense of peoplehood at the societal level; (5) attitude receptional; (6) behavioral receptional; and (7) civic, where interethnic conflicts over values and power are overcome by the shared identity of citizenship. Two of these, in our estimation, do not refer to assimilation per se, but rather to preconditions for assimilation, which have to do with the absence of various impediments to incorporation: attitude receptional assimilation refers to the lack of prejudice while behavioral receptional assimilation concerns the related absence of discrimination.

One of the intriguing aspects of Gordon's thesis is that he located cultural pluralism within this schema. This is because he did not think that there was a straight and uniform path to assimilation, but rather assumed as others before had that it would occur along a variety of different avenues and at differing speeds. Moreover, if persistent levels of prejudice and discrimination characterize interethnic relations, all or some types of assimilation would be stymied. Thus, assimilation did not necessarily mean that ethnic identities and affiliations would disappear or become irrelevant.

Gordon referred to these aspects of assimilation not simply as types, but also as stages, and thus he did have a sense that assimilation might in some circumstances signal the demise of ethnic allegiances. He hedged his bets on how the process of assimilation would occur, though he was clear about two things. First, he thought that marital assimilation would be the last to occur (on this score, see David Hollinger, 2003, for a reconsideration of the history of amalgamation). Second, he contended that the type of assimilation most crucial to the process was structural assimilation. Once it occurs, he argued, all the others will inevitably follow: "Structural assimilation, then, rather than acculturation, is seen to be the keystone in the arch of assimilation" (Gordon, 1964, p. 81). In this regard, what Gordon had done was to codify and add analytical rigor to Park's formulation. If acculturation can be seen as that aspect of assimilation that Park described as occurring spontaneously, structural assimilation entails volition on the part of ethnics and members of the larger society.

The point at which Gordon adds a significant dimension to the matrix missing in Park is when he separates out civic assimilation from structural assimilation. Park's discussion of assimilation had a curiously apolitical quality to it—one that ignored entirely the significance of the role of citizen. He did deal with the identificational side of this when discussing the significance of national identity as a unifying and thus assimilating force. However, the extent to which the idea of the citizen as actor might override or complicate the idea of the ethnic as actor is not advanced in his formulation. In Gordon's case, he laid it out but does not develop it, implicitly agreeing with Talcott Parsons' contention that the salience of ethnicity progressively gives way to citizenship as the principal basis of solidarity in liberal democracies (Parsons, 1971, p. 92). It should be stressed that for both, it was not an either/or proposition pitting ethnicity against citizenship. Rather, what they had in mind was the capacity of citizenship to reduce levels of interethnic hostility and conflict. The enhanced salience of citizenship did not mean that the memories of ancestors and the embracing of one's cultural roots would necessarily disappear.

## Assimilation Abandoned?

Within a decade after the publication of Gordon's book, assimilation theory's hegemonic status came under attack. Given that difficulties associated with dissociating the theory of assimilation from assimilation as ideology and policy, this is not surprising. According to Gary Gerstle (2001, p. 327), the civic nationalism that took hold during the administration of Theodore Roosevelt (who, incidentally, attended a performance of and had high praise for Israel Zangwill's *The Melting Pot*) and defined American national identity until the 1960s came under attack in what amounted to a "revolt against assimilation." This was due chiefly to the combined impact of the civil rights and the anti–Vietnam War movements. In the case of the former, ideas associated with black pride (recall Park on this score) and with the critiques of white America offered by militant black nationalists signaled an end to the idea that "assimilation into the national culture took precedence over the maintenance of cultural or religious particularity" (Gerstle, 2001, p. 330). Opposition to the Vietnam War furthered this trend, especially insofar as the "best and the brightest" who had led the nation into the quagmire were associated in the minds of many antiwar activists with the WASP elite (as, coincidentally, were many antiwar activists, such as William Sloane Coffin and Robert Lowell).

Related to these developments, in part as a reaction to them in a context where the center did not hold, by the early 1970s there was considerable discussion about an ethnic revival among the southern and eastern European ethnics whose ancestors had arrived in the nation between 1880 and 1930. Reviving the essentialist argument that Horace Kallen (1924) had advanced on behalf of cultural pluralism shortly after World War I, polemicists such as Michael Novak (1972) depicted groups such as Greeks, Italians, Jews, and Poles as "unmeltable ethnics." Part of the heightened sense of ethnicity among these ethnics entailed a benign search for roots. However, it also signaled a reaction to the perceived gains achieved by blacks in the immediate aftermath of the civil rights movement and a resistance to integration (Rieder, 1985).

## Assimilation Challenged

The zeitgeist of this era, not surprisingly, filtered into scholarship on ethnicity. Within both sociology and history, there was a rather widespread abandonment of assimilationist theory in favor of variant versions of pluralism. The idea of ethnic persistence gained currency with the publication—at virtually the same time that Gordon's book appeared—of Nathan Glazer and Daniel Patrick Moynihan's *Beyond the Melting Pot* (1963), which examined five ethnic groups in New York City (Italians, Irish, Jews, blacks, and Puerto Ricans) and concluded, in a richly documented and nuanced thesis, that these groups functioned to large extent as interest groups. One could draw the conclusion that to the extent that this instrumentalist *raison d'être* persisted, so would the saliency of ethnic identities and affiliations. Despite the book's provocative title, the authors did not offer an explicit pluralist alternative to assimilation at the theoretical level. Reflecting on the book 35 years after its publication, Glazer (2000, p. 270) remarked that it was "clear how much it is a book of its time."

The sociologist most responsible for the promotion of a research agenda that sought to indicate the persistence of ethnicity, rather than its erosion, was Andrew Greeley (1971, 1974; Greeley & McCready, 1975), who relied on National Opinion Research Center surveys to examine a wide array of attitudinal and behavioral topics, all of which were intended to ascertain the extent to which ethnicity still mattered. Greeley limited his subjects to European-origin ethnics, excluding from consideration racial minorities that have not been able to assimilate structurally due to externally imposed barriers. His findings did not lend much validation to the idea that assimilation theory was irrelevant. Indeed, his results about the persistence of ethnicity were mixed at best, and moreover, crucial issues that would call the thesis into question, such as intermarriage rates, were largely ignored. Greeley's findings pointed to little more than the obvious fact that assimilation had not yet reached its end stage, but no serious sociologist actually made such a claim. Greeley, too, did not attempt to offer a theoretical alternative to assimilation.

Pluralists who did attempt to provide theoretical explanations were divided between two alternative accounts of ethnic persistence. Some theorists, including Harold Isaacs (1975) and Pierre van den Berghe (1981), embraced what has been described as a primordialist perspective (though the current terminology that could be used to describe this camp is essentialist). Ethnicity from this perspective is considered to be deeply rooted in the psyche or from a sociobiological perspective in the genes, and, as such, is an immutable and universal given. Ethnic attachments are the result of a little understood but nonetheless extraordinarily powerful psychological attachment to the group. This position is problematic insofar as it devalues the role played by both historical events and social structural factors and because it fails to appreciate the mutability of human attachments and loyalties.

For this reason, most sociologists who embraced pluralist theory did so from what became known as a circumstantionalist (Glazer & Moynihan, 1975, pp. 19–20) or optionalist (Gleason, 1983, p. 919) perspective, which provided a more compelling sociological basis for understanding ethnicity. This version of pluralist theory looked to those social, cultural, and political factors that created conditions that either sustained or undermined ethnic attachments for particular groups at particular times.

### Assimilation Ignored

It also dovetails with the work of social historians of ethnicity during this time period, who, by being sensitive to the distinctive features of specific groups, the particularities of time and place, and the significance of complexity and contingency, added to the appreciation of the variability of possible outcomes (Higham, 1982). Olivier Zunz (1985, p. 53) correctly contends that this generation of social historians to large extent neglected assimilation. In their effort to write history from the bottom up, they gave voice to the ethnics, stressing the choices they made, the strategies they employed, the resources they mustered, the ambiguities they felt, the coalitions they formed, and the constraints they encountered. This is clearly the case in John Bodnar's "transplanted" thesis discussed earlier, which like much of the best social history of this period represents a fruitful interplay between ethnic history and labor history (Higham, 1990; Kivisto, 1990). His portrait of the immigrant generation—the "children of capitalism"—is one in which they reacted pragmatically to the larger society's institutions and values, creating a world as best they could that was "an amalgam of past and present, acceptance and resistance" (Bodnar, 1985, p. 210). He did not raise the prospect that, as Warner and Srole predicted, European ethnics would shift from a primary identity rooted in ethnicity to one located in class, but rather concentrated on the dialectical tension and mutual reinforcement of these two aspects of individual identity. Kazal (1995, p. 456) writes, "When Bodnar used the terms 'Americanization' and 'assimilation,' he appeared to distinguish them from the larger process of immigrant adjustment and to deny that they happened for the majority of immigrants and their children."

Perhaps because there is a tendency among historians to focus on the particular and to resist the temptation to generalize about larger social processes, social historians such as Bodnar did not offer a frontal rebuttal of assimilation theory. Nor did they explicitly embrace cultural pluralism or propose an alternative. Rather, as Zunz (1985) has argued, they tended to simply ignore assimilation, thereby implicitly casting into question its utility as a concept for understanding the incorporation of immigrants and their offspring into the larger society.

## Rethinking the Theoretical Legacy

By the 1990s, a growing number of sociologists and historians, reacting to the critiques and the neglect of assimilation theory, began to express their conviction that a reconsideration of its utility and validity was in order. This included some scholars who had remained supporters of assimilation theory throughout this period, such as Herbert Gans, Nathan Glazer, John Higham, and Stephen Steinberg, in addition to a younger generation that included Richard Alba, Rogers Brubaker, Douglas Massey, Ewa Morawska, Victor Nee, Alejandro Portes, Rubén Rumbaut, Roger Waldinger, and Min Zhou (Jacoby, 2004). In reacting to what Rogers Brubaker (2001, p. 531) referred to as the "massive differentialist turn" that occurred during the latter part of the 20th century, these figures are among those most responsible for the "return of assimilation." The idea of a return stimulated an effort to rethink and reappropriate a line of thought dating back to Park (Rumbaut, 2005).

In part, this disparate group of thinkers was challenging the theoretical adequacy of cultural pluralism in accounting for the fate of ethnicity over time for European-origin groups. At some level, the argument advanced was quite simple: assimilation had proved to be a far more useful analytical tool for understanding the historical trajectories of these groups. Glazer (1993, p. 123) answered his own question about whether assimilation was dead by contending that however unpopular the term might be at the moment, if "properly understood, assimilation is still the most powerful force affecting the ethnic and racial elements of the United States." The fact that blacks have not been successfully incorporated into the mainstream of American society accounts for much of the criticism of assimilation, but according to Glazer, this does not undermine assimilation theory but illustrates the fact that, as he notes Park had already stressed, prejudice and discrimination stymie assimilation. In other words, assimilation is a powerful force, but not inevitable.

Glazer's argument dovetailed with Ewa Morawksa's (1994) defense of assimilation, in which she called for its resuscitation. She also called for correcting what she saw as certain problematic features of the "classical" theory of assimilation. These included that it was too simplistic and ahistorical, that its efforts to understand the dominant group and what it is that groups are assimilating into were insufficient, and that it exhibited a lack of concern about the role of gender in the assimilation process. In a similar vein, Marcelo M. Suárez-Orozco (2002) pointed to questionable assumptions that have underpinned much work in assimilation (though, we would point out, not necessarily to the canonical formulation): (1) the clean-break assumption, which suggests that immigrants quickly and thoroughly sever their ties to their homeland; (2) the homogeneity assumption, which fails to appreciate that the host society is multilayered and diverse; and (3) the progress assumption, which views the length of time in the host society as key to the improvement of the socioeconomic circumstances of the group.

Still other scholars cast a sympathetic but simultaneously critical perspective on assimilation theory from Park to Gordon, addressing, as Rumbaut (1999) described it, the "ironies and paradoxes" of assimilation. Rumbaut argued that rather than seeing it in terms of a terminal end state, it ought instead to be imaginatively conceived as an analytical construct of an "endlessly astonishing synthesis" (Rumbaut, 1999, p. 191). Efforts to make the concept more complex and less unidirectional included Gans' (1997, 1999a) effort to expand upon Gordon's (1964) attempt to reconcile assimilation and pluralism. Milton Yinger (1994, pp. 38–55) offered a similar effort by treating assimilation and "dissimilation" as operating in a state of dialectical tension.

Gans (1979), responding to the claims made in the 1970s about an ethnic revival among European-origin ethnics, developed the idea of "symbolic ethnicity." It was intended to account for both the indicators of the persistence of various manifestations of ethnicity and the simultaneous gradual decline of ethnic affiliations and behaviors. He thought it was especially apt in describing the significance of ethnicity for the third generation and beyond. In Gans' view, by the latter part of the 20th century, the ethnicity of these offspring of immigrants could be characterized as manifesting a low-level intensity—occupying an individual's attention only periodically. The decline in ethnic organizations and cultures no longer permitted more substantive expressions of ethnic identity or affiliation. Rather than relying on community or culture, these latter generations used symbols, primarily out of a sense of nostalgia for the traditions of the immigrant generation. According to Gans (1979),

> Most people look for easy and intermittent ways of expressing their identity, for ways that do not conflict with other ways of life. As a result, they refrain from ethnic behaviors that require an arduous or time-consuming commitment, either to a culture that must be practiced constantly, or to organizations that demand active membership. Second, because people's concern is with identity, rather than with cultural practices or group relationships, they are free to look for ways of expressing that identity which suit them best, thus opening up the possibility of voluntary, diverse, or individualistic ethnicity.

Mary Waters described such an ethnicity in terms of "ethnic options," whereby individuals pick and choose from their ancestral cultural traditions. Like Gans, her portrait is one of an ethnicity predicated on *feeling* (at least periodically) ethnic rather than having to permanently *be* ethnic. This emptying out of a once-robust ethnicity would appear innocuous except that it serves to create a sense of "us" versus "them," wherein the "us" includes all white European-origin groups while "them" includes blacks and new immigrants. Waters (1990, pp. 147, 155) contends that "symbolic ethnicity persists because of its ideological 'fit' with racist beliefs," offering these ethnics "a potent combination" entailing both "a community without cost and a specialness that comes to you just by virtue of being born." This conclusion is reinforced in Matthew Frye Jacobson's *Roots Too*, a study of the ethnic revival of the 1960s and 1970s in which he sees the drawing of boundaries in terms of invidious comparisons: "we" are hard-working, law-abiding, religiously devout, family-oriented people, while "they" lack these virtues (Jacobson, 2006, p. 150). In this regard, assimilation is seen in terms of boundary drawing, a topic we turn to later in the chapter when we examine the work of Alba and Nee.

The most sustained attempt to offer a systematic rethinking of assimilation theory rooted in the tradition was that offered by historian Elliott Barkan (1995). On the surface, it appears to represent an effort to revive the race relations cycle that, as noted earlier, has been inappropriately associated with Park, insofar as it involves a model consisting of six stages: contact, acculturation, adaptation, accommodation, integration, and assimilation into the core society/core culture. However, Barkan insisted that this model ought not to be construed as a cycle or a straight-line teleological process, writing that *"there has been no one pattern, no cycle, no one outcome that uniformly encompasses all ethnic experiences"* (Barkan, 1995, p. 46; italics in original).

The analytical purpose of the model is to identify both those patterns that occur with a certain regularity as well as the exceptions to the patterns. By noting the exceptions and by being attuned to the impact of prejudice and discrimination as well as individual choices on the part of marginalized people to either seek incorporation or to resist it, the model is designed to link assimilation to pluralism. He saw assimilation as a two-way process, entailing both the level of openness on the part of the host society and the extent to which there is a desire to incorporate on the part of marginalized individuals. More than that, as an effort to remedy a particular shortcoming in the canonical model, he viewed assimilation as "a bidirectional phenomenon in that the general society and culture are affected by the heritages of those who assimilate" while recognizing that the interplay between newcomer and host is not an equal exchange (Barkan, 1995, p. 49). Barkan was less attentive to the fact that the host society is multifarious and thus outsiders who assimilate do so into differing sectors of the society, thus making assimilation a far more complex and varied phenomenon, and one that does not necessarily signal a successful entry into the societal mainstream.

Critics have identified problematic features of Barkan's model. Its inattentiveness to class and gender has been noted (Vecoli, 1995). Likewise, its singular focus on the individual over the group has been criticized (Alba, 1995b). Finally, the model appears to be intended primarily to account for the historical trajectories of voluntary immigrants. This raises concerns about whether or not it can be proven suitable in accounting for the historical experiences of nonvoluntary immigrants such as blacks, indigenous peoples, or ethnonationalist minorities.

Nevertheless, the model served to amplify the argument that assimilation and pluralism were interrelated phenomena, and not either/or propositions. In a sense, it can be read as a culmination of a rethinking of conceptual frameworks dating from the early part of the 20th century. It can also be seen as offering a theoretical account of the historical fates of European-origin ethnics in the United States, and in so doing provides a theoretical framework for locating such studies as Richard Alba's *Ethnic Identity* (1990). This study was perhaps the most influential research project that mounted compelling empirical evidence for the erosion of ethnic institutions and neighborhoods, the declining role of ethnic cultures, the progressive decline in ethnic identities and loyalties, the concurrent increase in intermarriage rates, and substantial evidence of social assimilation.

During the past several years, two projects aimed at building on a long history of work on assimilation while pushing it in new directions. We turn to them in what follows.

## New Directions I: Segmented or Downward Assimilation

Segmented or downward assimilation is a concept developed by Alejandro Portes and various colleagues, including Patricia Fernandez-Kelly, Rubén Rumbaut, and Min Zhou. However, one can turn to a speculative essay by Herbert Gans (1992b) for a precursor discussion about the potential differential occupational and socioeconomic outcomes of contemporary immigrants. This article was part of a growing body of work devoted to exploring the possibility of second-generation socioeconomic decline. Gans describes six potential scenarios, three positive and three negative. The positive, involving outcomes resulting in intergenerational upward mobility, can be (1) education driven; (2) succession driven (moving up into more attractive jobs as the native-born exit them in their own quest for upward mobility); and (3) due to niche improvement (remaining in the jobs occupied by parents and using them for economic advance). The possible negative scenarios are the reverse of the positive: (1) educational failure (such as high dropout rates); (2) the stalling of ethnic succession; and (3) niche shrinkage. The reason for concern about the prospects of decline had to do with a sense that the changes in the American economy that led to positive outcomes for the earlier wave of European immigrants no longer exist, and instead the emergence of a postindustrial economy called into question whether contemporary immigrants were likely to follow the upward mobility pattern of the past.

In the first articulation of the segmented assimilation thesis, Portes and Zhou (1993, p. 76) point out that for the first time since Irving Child's work of a half century earlier, sociologists were turning their attention to the second generation. They contend that in contrast to the Italians that were the focus of his work, the situation for many contemporary immigrants differs in two ways. First, many of today's immigrants are defined as nonwhite and thus race must be factored into the equation. Second, the economy has changed as a result of deindustrialization, which has drastically reduced the number of available jobs in the manufacturing sector. The idea of segmented assimilation was born of the idea that the incorporative trajectories of contemporary immigrant children might take three possible paths. As Portes and Zhou (1993, p. 82) put it, "One of them replicates the time-honored portrayal of growing acculturation and parallel integration into the white middle-class; a second leads straight in the opposite direction to permanent poverty and assimilation into the underclass; still a third associates rapid economic advancement with deliberate preservation of the immigrant community's values and tight solidarity." By being "absorbed" into "different segments of American society," immigrants are being socialized into different subcultures (Zhou, 1997, p. 999).

In considering the factors that can be expected to yield different outcomes, Portes and Rumbaut point first to the relationship between the first and second generations. Immigrants arrive with differing stocks of human capital, and these differences serve to locate them both in terms of occupations and residency. Related to parental human capital is family structure, which in large part means whether or not the family is headed by one (usually female) or two parents. Put simply, those second-generation children living in families whose parents possess high levels of human capital are expected to do better than children of those with lower levels. Likewise, dual-parent families offer a stronger system of parental guidance than do single-parent families, and they provide a richer network of social ties. In terms of their location in different sorts of families, gender is also salient insofar as socialization differs for boys and girls (Portes & Rumbaut, 2001, p. 64). As Figure 4.1 reveals, the third background variable they specify is modes of incorporation, which refers to the varied types of reception of immigrants by the state, the society at large, and the immigrants' preexisting ethnic community. In terms of state and society, some immigrant groups are favored and others are not. Thus, during the Cold War, the earliest waves of Cuban refugees were greeted warmly, while since 9/11 immigrants from the Middle East have not been.

The acculturation of the second generation is viewed as the outcome of the complex interplay of the three background factors. Portes and Rumbaut stress the relationship between the two generations that results from this interplay, distinguishing three types of acculturation: dissonant, consonant, and selective. Dissonant refers to a situation where the children become rapidly acclimated to the language and ways of life of the new society and at the same time experience a dramatic loss of their cultural heritage. At the

**First Generation** | **Second Generation**

| Background Factors | Intergenerational Patterns | External Obstacles | | | Expected Outcomes |
| | | Racial Discrimination | Bifurcated Labor Markets | Inner-City Subcultures | |
|---|---|---|---|---|---|
| Parental human capital | Dissonant acculturation | Confronted directly and without support | Met with individual resources alone | No countervailing messages to adversarial attitudes and lifestyles | Downward assimilation |
| Modes of incorporation | Consonant acculturation | Confronted directly with family support | Met with parental guidance and family resources | Countervailing message based on family aspirations | Mostly upward assimilation, blocked at times by discrimination |
| Family structure | Selective acculturation | Filtered through ethnic networks and confronted with family and community support | Met with parental guidance backed by family and community resources | Countervailing message based on family aspirations and community networks | Upward assimilation combined with biculturalism |

**Figure 4.1** The Process of Segmented Assimilation

*Source:* Portes and Rumbaut (2001, p. 63).

same time, their parents find getting acclimated difficult and thus remain rooted in the premigration worldview. In this setting, parents become dependent on their children, thus establishing a "role reversal, especially where parents lack other means to maneuver in the host society without the help of their children" (Portes & Rumbaut, 2001, p. 54). In such a context, the second generation confronts three primary external obstacles—racial discrimination, a bifurcated labor market, and inner-city subcultures—on its own, without sufficient support from parents because there is either a generational rupture or a lack of parental authority and without support from the ethnic community. Thus, dissonant acculturation can lead to downward assimilation, particularly if the children embrace the adversarial lifestyle associated with what Elijah Anderson (2000) calls the "code of the street." Downward assimilation contributes to gang involvement, drug activities, unplanned pregnancies, and dropping out of school.

In contrast, one version of consonant acculturation results when parents and children acclimate to their new setting in more or less parallel fashion, both managing to become culturally and socially competent in the new society and at the same time exiting the ethnic community together. In this scenario, parents and children are on the same page insofar as both generations are seeking integration into the American mainstream. This particular trajectory is most likely among families whose parents possess high levels of human capital, and are thus from the outset poised to enter the middle class and to experience upward mobility (Portes & Rumbaut, 2001, pp. 52, 54). In the other form of consonant acculturation, parents and children are again coming to terms with the new society congruently. However, in this version, both are slow to make a language transition and to embrace the host society's values and lifestyle. At the same time, both remain embedded in the ethnic community. These immigrants and their offspring remain isolated from the larger society, dependent on the ethnic enclave. One outcome of such acculturation is that mobility and integration into the larger society are blocked. If the sense of isolation becomes sufficiently pronounced and unattractive, it can prove to be an incentive to return to the homeland.

Finally, selective acculturation entails a successful balancing act on the part of both immigrants and their children between embracing the cultural values and language of the society and remaining embedded in the ethnic community. Thus, assimilation occurs gradually and without the anomic dislocations that can occur in consonant or dissonant acculturation. The ethnic community in this case serves as a decompression chamber that helps ease the transition into the larger society. In this scenario, there is very little intergenerational conflict, the second-generation children count many coethnics among their friends, and they tend to be genuinely bilingual (Portes &

Rumbaut, 2001, p. 54). R. Stephen Warner (2007, p. 108) summarizes the virtues of selective acculturation in the following passage:

> [It] is the most promising trajectory for those families with at least a modicum of resources and the chance of escaping the worst forms of treatment by the host society. . . . Insofar as acculturation of the second generation is all but inevitable but also fraught with danger, selective acculturation—which slows the process of Americanization, promotes ethnic pride in ethnic identity, and helps parents maintain their authority while both they and their children accommodate to the new society—would seem to be the wiser course for those who can manage it.

The three obstacles identified earlier serve to establish what Portes and Rumbaut view as the novel features making contemporary immigrant incorporation different than it was in the past. Thus, they contend that "while assimilation may still represent the master concept in the study of today's immigrants, the image of a relatively uniform and straightforward path is questionable given the many contingencies and novel forces affecting the process" (Portes & Rumbaut, 2005, p. 986). In their Children of Immigrants Longitudinal Study, a study of second-generation students in Miami/Ft. Lauderdale and San Diego, they found that a majority of these youth are poised to experience a successful entry into the mainstream. They are acquiring educations that can serve them well in that quest, and their early occupational experiences suggest they are moving in a positive direction. On the other hand, "a significant minority is being left behind" (Portes, Fernández-Kelly, & Haller, 2005, p. 1000).

Whether or not these findings ought to be read optimistically or pessimistically is open to question. Charles Hirschman (2001) focused on educational attainment and concluded that there was partial support for optimism and partial support for pessimism. In a major research project on new immigrants in New York City—one of the nation's two primary gateway cities—Philip Kasinitz, John Mollenkopf, Mary Waters, and Jennifer Holdaway (2008, p. 16) conclude that their evidence leads them to be "guardedly optimistic about the second generation." They contend that the portrait of entry into an oppositional culture that can over time reproduce downward assimilation is too negative. It overstates the significance of an adversarial subculture among both native minorities, particularly blacks, and second-generation immigrants and, conversely, fails to appreciate the fact that native-born whites, too, can be found embracing an oppositional identity (Kasinitz, Mollenkopf, & Waters, 2002, p. 1030; see also, Kasinitz, Mollenkopf, & Waters, 2004).

Two other studies have addressed the theory to determine if the American-specific focus of its formulators meant that it had little applicability in other national contexts. Monica Boyd (2002) concluded that in the Canadian context, segmented assimilation did not appear to be evident. On the other hand, Roxane Silberman, Richard Alba, and Irene Fournier (2007; see also Alba & Silberman, 2002) found evidence of downward assimilation among Muslim immigrants in France who came from former French colonies. They question the applicability of one of the central obstacles in Portes and Rumbaut's formulation: race. Rather than racial markers based on such features as skin color, the salient obstacles in the French context appeared to revolve around ethnic markers, with people's names serving as a key divider between in-group and out-group members.

This leads to explorations conducted independently and jointly by Joel Perlmann and Roger Waldinger that call into question the assumption that segmented assimilation is a novel phenomenon characteristic of today's immigrants versus the presumably more uniform assimilation that occurred several decades earlier and involved European-origin immigrants. Of particular note, they question the assumption that the racial makeup of contemporary immigrants—defined as nonwhite—puts them at a distinct disadvantage compared to their white European predecessors. As whiteness studies research argues, eastern and southern European immigrants from the 19th century and early 20th were often defined upon arrival as nonwhite. As such, they were treated as racial outsiders by the hegemonic culture. Thus, the process over time of becoming assimilated meant in part "becoming white" (Roediger, 2005; see Guglielmo, 2003, for a critique). The wide variety of racial categories employed a century ago—Nordic, Mediterranean, Slavic, Semitic, and the like—as the markers used to distinguish those who were white from those who were not declined in significance. Increasingly, they were replaced by a perspective that treated all European-origin groups as white, with Jews probably entering that side of the racial divide last due to the more durable character of anti-Semitism.

Gans (1999b) raises the possibility that something similar might be occurring at present in pondering whether or not a new racial hierarchy might be in the process of formation. Specifically, he speculates about the prospect of a new racial divide that no longer is framed in terms of white/nonwhite, but instead in terms of black/nonblack. If, for example, Asian immigrants—sometimes depicted as the "model minority"—find themselves as "honorary whites," this would suggest that for them, at least, the significance of race is a declining barrier to incorporation. They would not actually have to be defined as white: the key to their acceptance is that they are on the nonblack side of the divide. Though their situation is not the same, a similar process might be underway for Latinos, which if true would mean that for the new immigrants as a whole, race will prove to be less and less of an obstacle, while for their part, native-born blacks will end up being more socially isolated. Gans is not claiming that such a new racial formation already exists, merely that such a scenario is a realistic possibility.

Perlmann and Waldinger (1997, 1998) contend that if taken as a whole, today's immigrants show little evidence of being uniquely disadvantaged. In fact, "the children of the post-1965 immigration began with disadvantages no greater than those encountered by immigrant children before." However, if there is one stark difference between the old immigrants versus the new, it is that today there are far more middle-class immigrants who come poised for upward mobility. Thus, generalizations about the new immigrants must be made carefully and with this reality in mind. Given the fact that Mexican immigrants in the United States represent by far the largest component of the new immigration and that they are considerably poorer and possess far less human capital than the new immigrants overall, it is reasonable to question whether they might be uniquely disadvantaged, and thus particularly likely to experience downward assimilation.

It is with this in mind that Perlmann (2005) engaged in a comparative study of the Italian second generation of the past and today's second-generation Mexicans. When Handlin created his ideal-typical portrait of the "uprooted" immigrant, Italians constituted a paradigmatic example. So, too, do Mexicans. Thus, this is a particularly apt comparison in testing whether or not the chances for intergenerational upward mobility today have declined compared to those in the preceding migratory wave. Perlmann's study reveals two things. First, the progress made by Italians was slower and more difficult than is often seen in retrospect. Second, although Mexican progress has been slower than that of their Italian counterparts, nonetheless the trend is in the same direction. Without discounting the fact that the society Mexicans have entered in recent years is in many ways different from the one Italians entered earlier, Perlmann's study calls into question the view that upward mobility is less likely today than in the past—and implicitly challenges the claim that segmented assimilation is only applicable to the present.

One of the key assumptions of segmented assimilation is that contemporary immigrants confront a major economic obstacle due to the economic restructuring that has been underway since the early 1970s. The portrait of an hourglass economy is central to this conviction, for the precipitous decline in manufacturing jobs is considered to be a major barrier to mobility. This particular assumption has been widely accepted by immigration scholars, though it has not until recently been subjected to empirical investigation. The untested assumption underlying this view is that manufacturing jobs proved to be the route to upward mobility for earlier immigrants. Waldinger (2007b) has raised the fundamental question: "did manufacturing matter?" He observes that a key difference between traditional assimilation theory and segmental assimilation is that while the former does not, the latter has an explanation for how the children and grandchildren of immigrants in the past improved their economic lot: it was as a result of obtaining jobs in the manufacturing sector, which, it is claimed, provided them with wage levels that served to narrow the economic gap between them and native-born whites. He points out that this focus on the role of factory work in heavy industry "has a muscularly proletarian feel," an account of male rather than female (other than during World War II) workers (Waldinger, 2007b, p. 9).

Waldinger contrasts two of the largest immigrants groups from that era, Italians and Poles. He found a pronounced difference between the two in terms of their respective locations in the manufacturing sector. While second- and 2.5-generation Poles were twice as likely as native white, native parentage (NWNP) workers to be located in manufacturing, Italians were less likely (Waldinger, 2007b, pp. 18–21). This would imply, from the segmented assimilation perspective, that Poles should have had higher incomes than Italians. In fact, the reverse was the case. Moreover, Poles did not narrow the income gap between themselves and NWNP workers, while Italians did. Thus, while finding work in the manufacturing sector did not produce the expected results, it appears that Italians found an alternative route to economic advancement. Precisely what this finding means for contemporary immigrants inhabiting a society that has been transformed by deindustrialization is not clear. However, one reasonable conclusion to be drawn is that the relationship between manufacturing jobs and upward mobility has been overstated.

Despite these problems with segmented assimilation theory, it has the virtue of attempting to connect immigrant socioeconomic destinations to different social class locations. If classical assimilation theory paid scant attention to class, even with Gordon's (1964) call for consideration of what he called "ethclass," this is a salutary development—one that represents less of a break with the older theoretical tradition than an emendation of it.

One problematic feature of the idea of segmented assimilation is that, in offering a dichotomous description of entry into either the upwardly mobile middle class or the underclass, the model oversimplifies a more complex picture (Waldinger & Feliciano, 2004). Although it may be that the economy looks more like an hourglass than it did before, the metaphor can mislead insofar as immigrants are to be found in the working class as well as the underclass and the educated middle class. As Alba and Nee (2003, p. 8) point out, the concept also carries the risk of treating the culture of the underclass as static and immune to outside cultural influences. Related to this point, it also carries with it a tendency to overlook the fact that not all members of the underclass are embedded in an adversarial culture. Nevertheless, the significance of segmented assimilation is that it calls attention to the fact that the location of immigrants in the class structure plays a significant role in shaping distinctive incorporative paths.

That being said, Gans (2007) has recently reminded immigration scholars that assimilation and economic mobility are interrelated but distinct processes. He suggests that during the earlier phase of immigration research, it was presumed that upward mobility would occur over time and across generations, and therefore there was a tendency to convolute assimilation and mobility. Stepping back from this tendency, he suggests that one of the tasks today is to consider the extent to which assimilation leads to mobility, and vice versa—or in other words, without using such Weberian language, he calls for a consideration of the nature of the elective affinity between the two. In making this case, Gans (2007, p. 161) stresses that cultural assimilation (acculturation) and structural assimilation "refer to people's adaptation to changing conditions, and all those who undergo any kind of adaptation are thus likely to acculturate and assimilate as a result."

## New Directions II: Boundaries and the Mainstream

In comparison to segmented assimilation's focus on the connection between assimilation and mobility, Richard Alba and Victor Nee (2003, pp. 35–66; for earlier versions, see Alba, 1998, and Alba & Nee, 1997) have produced a revisionist theory of assimilation that gets at Gans' point in the preceding paragraphs, an approach that they refer to simply as "new assimilation theory." Influenced by the new institutionalism in sociology and building on the "forms-of-capital" model formulated by Nee and Sanders (2001), their theory is intended to both link agency to structure and the microlevel to the macrolevel. Furthermore, the theory is intended to be sensitive to historical and structural contexts.

Alba and Nee (2003, p. 38) distinguish between proximate and distal causes, the former referring to factors operating at the individual and group network level and the latter to the macrostructural level, focusing for instance on the role of major societal institutions, particularly the state and the economy. From the agency side of the equation, their framework calls for considering differentials in financial, human, and social capital among immigrants and the varied ways these resources are deployed, both by individuals and collectivities (this is an approach that Alba and Nee clearly share with segmented assimilation theorists). From the structure side, they seek to locate these deployments in terms of the existing institutional mechanisms that either facilitate or inhibit assimilation. Of particular significance in the post–civil rights United States is the impact that the rights revolution has had on both the potential for and modes of incorporation of immigrants and other minorities. In this regard, the state plays a critical role in structuring and enforcing mechanisms for incorporation, and its impact has been profound in challenging discrimination, particularly in the workplace (Alba & Nee, 2003, pp. 53–55; see also Collins, 2001).

The central concept employed in the new assimilation theory is that of boundaries, which in the area of ethnic studies is usually associated with the work of Fredrik Barth (1969). Barth famously argued that the boundaries dividing ethnic groups are more significant than cultural similarities or differences. The idea that boundaries are socially constructed rather than being givens has since become a taken-for-granted assumption in ethnic and racial studies. In this regard, this subfield is not so unique for, as Michèle Lamont and Virág Molnár (2002) have illustrated, boundaries and the related concept of borders have increasingly been employed by social scientists in a wide range of fields, including social and collective identity; class, ethnic/racial, and gender/sexual identity inequalities; the professions; science; communities; and national identity. Andreas Wimmer (2008, p. 970) has recently attempted to move beyond constructivism, treating boundaries as the outcome of "the classificatory struggles and negotiations between actors situated in a social field." In this article, Wimmer (2008, p. 985) notes that Alba's recent work (he cites a solo-authored article rather than the coauthored work with Nee) can be seen as emerging out of an intellectual heritage that begins with Weber and leads to Barth.

Boundaries are central to Alba and Nee's *Remaking the American Mainstream*. In this work, they "distinguish among three boundary-related processes: boundary crossing, boundary blurring, and boundary shifting" (Alba & Nee, 2003, p. 60). This is not an original formulation, but rather builds on the work of Rainer Bauböck (1994) and in particular that of Aristide Zolberg and Long Litt Woon (1999). Bauböck distinguished between the first two types of boundary process. The first of these processes—boundary crossing—occurs at the individual level and does not entail the altering of the boundary itself. It does not make a bright boundary blurry nor does it either expand the boundary or shift its location. Rather, the boundary remains intact as an individual opts to exit one group and enter into another. Assimilation posed in terms of boundary crossing means that the individual departs the marginalized outside group and enters the mainstream. The second process is blurring, which is a group phenomenon brought about by situations in which the boundary demarcating "us" and "them" becomes less clear, and thus calls into question where people are located. Zolberg and Woon (1999) add to Bauböck's two boundary processes the third: boundary shifting. Here, as the term implies, the boundary moves rather than individuals moving.

It is worth quoting Zolberg and Woon at length to understand these three processes and their implications for evolving relationships between immigrants and the host society:

1. Individual *boundary crossing*, without any change in the structure of the receiving society and leaving the distinction between insiders and outsiders unaffected. This is the commonplace process whereby immigrants change themselves by acquiring some of the attributes of the host identity. Examples include replacing their mother tongue with the host language, naturalization, and religious conversion.

2. *Boundary blurring*, based on a broader definition of integration—one that affects the structure (i.e., the legal, social, and cultural boundaries) of the receiving society. Its core feature is the tolerance of multiple memberships and an overlapping of collective identities hitherto thought to be separate and mutually exclusive; it is the taming or domestication of what was once seen as "alien" differences. Examples include formal or informal public bilingualism, the possibility of dual nationality, and the institutionalization of immigrant faiths (including public recognition, where relevant).

3. *Boundary shifting*, which denotes a reconstruction of a group's identity, whereby the line differentiating members from nonmembers is relocated, either in the direction of inclusion or exclusion. This is a more comprehensive process, which brings about a more fundamental redefinition of the situation. By and large, the rhetoric of pro-immigration activists and of immigrants themselves can be read as arguments on behalf of the expansion of boundaries to encompass newcomers, while that of the anti-immigrant groups can be read as an attempt to redefine them restrictively in order to exclude them. (Zolberg & Woon, 1999, pp. 8–9)

Alba and Nee accept this model, as well as Zolberg and Woon's (1999, p. 9) claim that "boundary shifting can occur only after substantial boundary crossing and boundary blurring have taken place." Their empirical focus for the post-1965 immigrants is on boundary blurring, which they consider to be distinctly characteristic of the contemporary second generation, which has entered a society more receptive to difference than in the past. In contrast, boundary shifting is little discussed.

Boundary crossing is perceived as having been far more characteristic of immigrants and their children during the last great migratory wave to the United States, and as less common today. Alba and Nee (2003, p. 63) cite as an example the attempts made in the past to make physical changes by resorting to cosmetic surgery in order to eliminate what was seen as a distinctly ethnic look. They point to the popularity among Jews of "nose jobs." Another common form of boundary crossing occurred when individuals shed their ethnic-sounding names for WASP substitutes. While this was commonplace among movie stars and entertainers, it was not limited to this group. One could find it, for example, among sociologists, witnessed in Milton Meyer Goldberg's decision in 1941 to legally change his name to Milton Myron Gordon (Gordon, 1978, p. vii) and when Meyer R. Schkolnick was transformed into Robert K. Merton.

Boundary crossing was the likely option for Jews seeking to assimilate in a context characterized by a bright boundary. Alba (2006, p. 349) points to Philip Roth's *The Plot Against America,* a novel located in the Nazi era, as "a reminder of the bright boundaries that once governed Jewish-Gentile relations in the U.S." However, he contends that the bright boundary has in recent decades given way to boundary blurring, which leads to a situation in which ethnic distinctions come to play a less significant role in shaping intergroup relations. The form of assimilation resulting from blurring differs from that characteristic of crossing. In the latter, the conversionlike move across boundaries produces a radical disjuncture between people's past identities and their new identities, the consequence of being *"forced to choose* between the mainstream and their group of origin" (Alba, 2006, p. 351).

By contrast, blurring occurs when the mainstream's boundary is "relatively porous and absorbs elements of the minority culture. In other words, boundary blurring is brought about because cultural change is not limited to the minority group; it occurs to the majority group as well, and therefore the process of acculturation is to some extent a two-sided affair" (Alba, 2006, p. 351). The sort of assimilation made possibly by boundary blurring can lead to the maintenance of a meaningful and substantive minority group identity, something that Alba thinks can be more substantive than the thinner version of ethnic identity maintenance depicted in Gans' (1979) symbolic ethnicity and Waters' (1990) "ethnic options" thesis. Alba (2006, p. 356) suggests that it "lends itself to hyphenated, if not hybrid, identities, which allow individuals to feel that they remain part of the group of origin." Although he does not offer much by way of empirical contrast, he appears to think that blurred-boundary assimilation leads to a form of assimilation that not only differs from the bright boundary conversion version, but also from a "vaguely imagined multiculturalism" (Alba, 2006, p. 357).

In a comparative study of Mexicans immigrants in the United States, Turks in Germany, and North Africans in France, Alba (2005) attempts to illustrate the comparative utility of the boundary concept for research on assimilation.

He discusses citizenship, race, language, and religion as the three most salient markers used in the construction of boundaries and observes that they are deployed in different ways in different societal contexts. The question he poses is whether these three groups confront bright or blurred boundaries in their efforts to become incorporated into their host society's respective mainstreams. His conclusion is that to large extent Mexicans confront a blurred-boundary situation, with race confounding that somewhat. On the other hand, the two Muslim groups in France and Germany to large extent inhabit societies in which the boundaries remain bright.

The main criticism to date of the new assimilation theory does not challenge its approach to boundaries. Indeed, if Wimmer's (2008) earlier mentioned article is any indication, the present constitutes a return on the part of immigration scholars to boundaries—whether it be articulated in terms of a return to the Weber/Barth tradition or an embrace of a perspective most closely associated with Bourdieu. Rather than taking exception to the idea of boundaries, Waldinger (2003) has questioned the idea of a mainstream. Linked to this, he argues that Alba and Nee are mistaken when they contend that assimilation entails a "decline of an ethnic distinction" (Alba & Nee, 2003, p. 11). Rather, Waldinger (2003, p. 255) contends, it refers to a "transmutation." Arguing that there cannot be a mainstream without a sidestream, he concludes that this means that ethnicity persists, both at the center and on the periphery.

In a subsequent article, Waldinger (2007c, p. 366) argues that the key point about assimilation is that it involves transforming foreigners into Americans, imbuing them with a particularistic identity that sets them apart from non-Americans and as such is connected to the state's process of closure whereby it seeks to create and maintain a "container society." Alba's (2008) response is that in "two-way" assimilation, the majority also changes as a result of boundary blurring.

## Conclusion

This comment leads from these recent efforts to revise assimilation theory in order to address its presumed earlier defects while also recasting it to address that which is distinctive about contemporary immigrant incorporation. By using the term "container society," Waldinger is raising a key issue developed by theorists of transnationalism, to which we turn in the following chapter. Neither spokespersons for segmented assimilation or new assimilation theory have attempted to link these concepts to transnationalism (it should be noted that although Portes is a theorist of transnationalism, his work has not attempted to connect assimilation and transnationalism). In focusing on how immigrants and their offspring do or do not manage to become incorporated and on what terms, the role of the state, the larger public, and transnational actors have been largely undeveloped, despite the stated intentions of its key advocates. As will be seen in Chapter 5, such is not the case for transnational theorists. Some central figures associated with transnationalism have been critics of assimilation theory in its various guises. However, others agree with Waldinger (2007c, p. 343; see also Waldinger & Fitzgerald, 2004) that assimilation and transnationalism ought to be construed as processes that are "inextricably intertwined." We will explore Waldinger's claim.

Given that the focus of this recent work has been on the new second generation, new assimilation theory has not attended to concrete instances of boundary shifting. Agreeing with Zolberg and Woon (1999) that this is only likely to occur after considerable crossing and blurring, the idea that boundaries can be reconfigured in such a way that the society either expands the prospects of inclusion or, conversely, that it becomes more exclusive is postulated but remains underdeveloped. Alba and Nee (2003, pp. 141–145; see also Alba, 1999) pay relatively scant attention to multiculturalism, and generally they view it as a political project rather than a useful concept relevant to incorporation. In Chapter 6, we take up the topic of multiculturalism, and when we do so, we will see whether it has relevance for the idea of boundary shifting.

In short, in the next two chapters we will attempt to review the histories of two recent and highly contested concepts. In this regard, the objective is the same as in this chapter: to achieve greater clarity in order to better appreciate a concept's relevance for understanding the process of immigrant settlement. Beyond that, we will make an effort to indicate in what ways transnationalism and multiculturalism should be seen as potentially operating as processes in tandem with assimilation rather than as alternatives to it.

# 5

# Transnationalism and the Persistence of Homeland Ties

*Transnationalism* entered the lexicon of immigration studies in the early 1990s, more than a century after earlier generations of immigration researchers had introduced and made extensive use of the concept of assimilation. It did so in rather different circumstances, for whereas assimilation gained currency with relatively little reflection or debate at the moment that immigration research was in its early formative period, transnationalism entered a well-developed sociological subfield. It was assertively promoted by several principal advocates and rather quickly embraced by many scholars. However, it was also confronted by critics and skeptics. The result is that the concept has undergone substantial revision since its earliest formulations, the consequence of an often spirited dialogue (for an updated summary, see Levitt & Jaworsky, 2007).

In tracing the origins of the use of the term, scholars often point to social critic Randolph Bourne's essay advancing the idea of a "trans-national America," which was intended to challenge the Americanization campaigns of the early part of the 20th century that were intent on "washing out the memories of Europe" (Bourne, 1916, p. 86). Equating assimilation with the ideology of the melting pot (which historian Philip Gleason, 1964, aptly characterized as a symbol of fusion and confusion), Bourne saw the new immigrants that entered the United States during his lifetime as an antidote to what he feared was the petrification of the national culture. Immigrants were necessary to "save us from our own stagnation" (Bourne, 1916, p. 87), something that can only happen if a more cosmopolitan perspective is embraced by the host society. Although Bourne does mention in passing the fact that the rate of dual citizenship will likely rise and immigrants will move back and forth between the United States and their native lands, his real focus is not on the forging of transnational ties between the homeland and host society, but rather on something that looks very much like what today would be called multiculturalism. Thus, it is not surprising that contemporary proponents of transnationalism tend to nod toward his seminal work, but in fact make no effort to build on it in developing the concept of transnational migration.

Between his essay and the early 1990s, however, transnationalism was used in a variety of other contexts—again making its career as a concept different from that of assimilation. The *Oxford Dictionary of English* dates the emergence of the term *transnational* to circa 1920, documenting it with a quotation from an economics text from the era that characterized Europe after World War I by its "international or more correctly transnational economy" (Oxford University Press, 2003, p. 1762). It did not gain intellectual traction at that point. Rather, the term reemerged in the late 1960s, used to denote the increasing economic and political interdependence among industrialized countries (Keohane & Nye, 1977; for an updated extension, see Risse-Kappen, 1995). Transnational relations in political science pointed beyond the state centrism and billiard-ball models employed by mainstream international relations scholars. In short, it held that nonstate relations crossing the borders of states would lead to the accentuation of interdependence among states (Nye & Keohane, 1971).

More recently, the term has been employed in an ever-expanding variety of contexts. In what has been called transnationalism-from-above, one line of inquiry has focused attention on the transnational capitalist class (Sklair, 2001; Staples, 2008), and, related to it, transnational financial flows (Held, McCrew, Goldblatt, & Perraton, 1999). Beyond this usage, works have appeared discussing transnational wars (Kaldor, 1999), transnational nongovernmental organizations (Boli & Thomas, 1997), transnational think tanks (Struyck, 2002), transnational social movements (Kriesberg, 1997; Smith, 2001), transnational counterhegemonic networks (Evans, 2000), transnational terrorist and criminal networks (Shelley, 1995), and transnational religious communities (Rudolph, 1997). The list could go on. The development of work devoted to transnational migration must be seen in terms of this larger context. It must also be seen in light of the fact that citizenship regimes in the world's liberal democracies are changing, while at the same time we are witnessing the new modes of transnational cultural diffusion characterized by increasing hybridization or creolization (Appadurai, 1996; Castells, 1996, 1997; Hannerz, 1996; Kaufman & Patterson, 2005; Sassen, 1996; Soysal, 1994).

Those scholars who initially embraced the idea of transnational immigration did so because of a conviction that it was necessary to capture the distinctive and characteristic features of the new immigrant communities that have developed in the advanced industrial nations at the core of the capitalist world system (Faist, 2000a; Glick Schiller, 1997; Portes, 1999a, 1999b; Roberts, 1995; Urry, 2000; Vertovec, 1999). The term has emerged and evolved at a time characterized by high levels of labor migration from economically less developed nations to the most developed and from similarly high levels of political refugees fleeing conflicts and instability in former communist and third world nations (Castles & Miller, 2004). The influx of these new labor migrants and refugees has reshaped the ethnic mixes not only of nations with long histories of immigration, the settler states of the United States, Canada, and Australia, but also of states that have not been notable as immigrant-receiving nations in the earlier phases of industrialization, those of western Europe and to a lesser extent, Japan. The high levels of migration, the new locales of settlement, changes in the nature of capitalist economies in a new industrial epoch, changes in the meaning and significance attached to the idea of citizenship, and the potency of a globalized popular culture have contributed to the conviction that what is novel about the present requires equally novel conceptual tools if we are to make sense of the impact of the new immigration on both the receiving and sending countries.

Steven Vertovec (1999, pp. 449–456), who in his former capacity as director of the ESRC's Research Programme on Transnational Communities has been from the beginning an active promoter of the concept, points out several recurring themes that shape the ways the term is employed. He identifies six distinct, albeit potentially overlapping or intertwined, uses of the term: (1) as a social morphology focused on a new border spanning social formation; (2) as diasporic consciousness; (3) as a mode of cultural reproduction variously identified as syncretism, creolization, bricolage, cultural translation, and hybridity; (4) as an avenue of capital for transnational corporations, and in a smaller but significant way in the form of remittances sent by immigrants to family and friends in their homelands; (5) as a site of political engagement, both in terms of homeland politics and the politics of homeland governments vis-à-vis their émigré communities, and in terms of the expanded role of international nongovernmental organizations (INGOs); and (6) as a reconfiguration of the notion of place from an emphasis on the local to the translocal.

Our concern in this chapter is with the implications of transnationalism for modes of immigrant incorporation. Is it a distinct mode of incorporation? If so, is it an alternative to assimilation? If not, what exactly is the relationship between the two? Is it something other than a mode of incorporation? If so, is it an impediment to assimilation or does it actually facilitate assimilation? Or, alternatively, does it have little impact one way or the other? In order to adequately answer these questions, we will proceed by examining (1) the initial conceptualization of transnational immigration, (2) the critiques, and (3) the revisionist impulse that has characterized recent conceptualizations. This will lead to an analysis of what has become known as the *transnational optic,* and when this is accomplished, we will be in a position to address what transnationalism means for immigrant incorporation.

# The Initial Conceptualization of Transnational Immigration

The initial phase of theorizing transnational immigration ran from the early 1990s until the dawn of the new century. While a number of scholars contributed to this development, three stand out as being of singular significance: (1) cultural anthropologist Nina Glick Schiller and her colleagues Linda Basch and Christina Szanton Blanc (1992, 1995; see also Basch, Glick Schiller, & Szanton Blanc, 1994, and Glick Schiller, 1997); (2) Alejandro Portes and colleagues (Portes, 1995, 1996a, 1996b, 1998, 1999; Portes, Guarnizo, & Landolt, 1999; Portes & Zhou, 1999); and (3) Thomas Faist (1998, 2000a, 2000b, 2000c).

## Transnationalism as a New Mode of Incorporation: Glick Schiller and Colleagues

Though one may quibble about the date that transnationalism made its first appearance, a fairly convincing case can be made for the period between 1990 and 1994 as its debut years, for it was during these years that the first articles appeared attempting to lay out the conceptual parameters defining transnational immigrants and their communities. It was in 1990 that cultural anthropologists Nina Glick Schiller, Linda Basch, and Christina Szanton Blanc organized a conference on transnationalism that was cosponsored by the New York Academy of Sciences, the Wenner-Gren Foundation, and the Institute for the Study of Man. Two years later, they edited a collection based on conference papers titled *Towards a Transnational Perspective on Migration* (Glick Schiller et al., 1992), in which their introduction and lead article presented transnationalism as a novel analytic approach to understanding contemporary migration. Two years later, they again organized a conference, a Wenner-Gren–sponsored symposium held in Mijas, Spain, on "Transnationalism, Nation-Building, and Culture" and in the same year published another book, *Nations*

*Unbound* (Basch, Glick Schiller, & Szanton Blanc, 1994). These two publications constitute the first theoretical articulations of the transnational perspective on contemporary migration.

Glick Schiller and her colleagues, in the lead article to their 1992 collection, "Transnationalism: A New Analytic Framework for Understanding Migration," made clear that they sought to articulate a new conceptual model for interpreting contemporary migration. They reiterated and in some minor ways amplified their position in the two introductory articles of *Nations Unbound*, "Transnational Projects: A New Perspective" and "Theoretical Premises." These three articles in tandem represent a unified statement of the authors' position.

Glick Schiller et al. made two initial points, one historical and the other theoretical. Historically, they contended that there is something qualitatively different about immigrants today compared to their late 19th- and early 20th-century counterparts. Implicitly agreeing with Oscar Handlin's (1951) depiction of the latter group as "uprooted," Glick Schiller et al. were prepared to view this earlier era's immigrants as having broken off all homeland social relations and cultural ties, thereby locating themselves solely within the sociocultural, economic, and political orbit of the receiving society. By contrast, they contended, today's immigrants are "composed of those whose networks, activities, and patterns of life encompass both their host and home societies. Their lives cut across national boundaries and bring two societies into a single social field" (Glick Schiller et al., 1992, p. 1; see also Glick Schiller, 1997, p. 158).

From this historical comparison, Glick Schiller et al. offered a rationale for a new analytic framework, making a case for the introduction of two new terms: *transnationalism* and *transmigrants*. The former refers to "the process by which immigrants build social fields that link together their country of origin and their country of settlement," while the latter refers to the "immigrants who build such social fields" by maintaining a wide range of affective and instrumental social relationships spanning borders (Basch et al., 1994, p. 27; Glick Schiller et al, 1992, p. 1). Implicitly, the introduction of these new concepts suggested that existing theoretical frameworks are not up to the task of analyzing the new immigrants. Glick Schiller (1997, p. 158) made this more explicit when she contended that by embracing these concepts, scholars are "discarding previous categorizations of return, circulatory, or permanent immigration."

To make their case, the authors offered three vignettes (Glick Schiller et al., 1992, pp. 2–4). The first involved a Haitian hometown association located in New York City. While the activities of the association clearly have something to do with immigrant adjustment, it has also initiated various projects in Haiti. This, Glick Schiller et al. contended, distinguishes contemporary mutual aid societies from those in the past, which, they argued, were solely designed to address the adjustment needs of the immigrants themselves (a more sustained treatment of the Haitian case is found in Basch et al., 1994, pp. 145–224). The second example involved white-collar Grenadian immigrants being addressed by Grenada's Minister of Agriculture and Development. The point of this illustration is that the immigrants are at once both Grenadian nationals with an ability to influence friends and relatives who have remained in the homeland and American ethnics capable of undertaking efforts to shape economic and political decisions in the host society (see Basch et al., 1994, pp. 49–144). The third example looked to Filipinos and the *Balikbayan* box, a formalized and regulated form of remittance. The main point of this illustration is that remittances are not new, but that homeland governments are increasingly likely to embrace their expatriate communities when such an embrace can be economically beneficial.

From these illustrations, the authors made two main conceptual points. The first, and the most original and crucial for their case, is that social science must become "unbound." The argument is that the problem with theories operating as closed systems in which the unit of analysis is ultimately the nation-state is that they fail to provide room for the wider field of action occupied by contemporary immigrants. Such theoretical perspectives are faulted for their failure to provide an adequate basis for comprehending the dialectical interplay between homeland concerns and receiving nation realities and the impact this interplay has on immigrants. Thus, Glick Schiller et al. argued for the necessity of recasting theory from the national to a global or world systems perspective. In this regard, they noted that Wallerstein's world systems theory is a useful corrective to closed systems, but in their view it suffers from a tendency toward economic reductionism. Nonetheless, they stressed that transnationalism is the product of world capitalism that has produced economic dislocations making immigrants economically vulnerable (Basch et al., 1994, pp. 30–34; Glick Schiller et al., 1992, pp. 5–12). The result is a "new and different phenomenon, . . . a new type of migrant experience"(Glick Schiller et al., 1992, pp. 8–9).

While sympathetic to the discussions of transnationalism as cultural flows, seen in the work of figures such as Arjun Appadurai (1996) and Ulf Hannerz (1996), the main thrust of the authors' argument involved an articulation of a notion of transnational migration that focuses primarily on social relations. Finally, the authors pointed to the multiple and fluid identities of contemporary transmigrants, contending that their manipulation of identities reveals a resistance on the part of transmigrants to "the global political and economic situations that engulf them" (Glick Schiller et al., 1992, p. 11; see also Glick Schiller, 1997, p. 164).

This led to the second conceptual point: the need to rethink received ideas regarding class, nationalism, ethnicity, and race. Relying on the Gramscian idea of hegemony, the authors treated each of these aspects of identity as contested and pliable. The real significance of the discussion is that assimilation and cultural pluralism are inadequate to account for the distinctive character of contemporary immigration. From this perspective, whereas assimilation implies the loss of past identity, cultural pluralism advances an essentialist perspective that treats ethnic identities as immutable (Glick Schiller et al., 1992, pp. 13–19). The crux of Glick Schiller et al.'s thesis is that new times and new sociohistorical circumstances demand a new theoretical paradigm.

## Transnationalism as Middle-Range Theory: Portes and Associates

Perhaps the person most responsible for popularizing and expanding the use of the transnational perspective is Princeton sociologist Alejandro Portes (1996a, 1996b, 1998, 1999a, 1999b; Portes et al., 1999). The focus of Portes' research has been the new, post-1965 immigration to the United States. He has sought to expand our understanding of the role of ethnic enclave economies for these newcomers (Portes & Zhou, 1999), has sought to offer a more complex notion of assimilative outcomes by introducing the idea of segmented assimilation (Portes, 1995), and has urged a shift in research agendas from the immigrant generation to the second generation (Portes, 1998). Though he has not done original research on the last great wave of immigration to the United States, as the book he coauthored with Ruben Rumbaut on *Immigrant America* (2006) reveals, he brings to his understanding of contemporary immigration a sophisticated comparative historical perspective. Portes has emerged as the preeminent scholar of the new immigration, and has served as something of a magnet for numerous social scientists engaged in empirical studies of new immigrant communities.

Herein we explore only one aspect of Portes' work: his advocacy on behalf of claims for the utility of employing the idea of transnationalism in analyzing some new immigrant communities. His most definitive early formulations were contained in two articles—a coauthored introduction and a solely authored conclusion—that framed a special issue of *Ethnic and Racial Studies* devoted to the study of transnationalism. In these two essays, Portes offered an overview of what he means by the term and why he thought it is a useful addition to the conceptual tool bag of scholars of immigration and ethnicity (Portes, 1999a; Portes et al., 1999). We focus primary attention on these essays, but also refer to his use of the term in a few articles that preceded them (Portes, 1996a, 1996b, 1998).

Before examining the two key articles, it is instructive to explore earlier manifestations of interest in transnational discourse that preceded these more fully developed conceptual statements. As with Glick Schiller and her colleagues, Portes has made use of vignettes to illustrate the phenomenon. His examples included a Mexican enclave in Brooklyn working to create a safe water system for their Mexican village of origin; Dominican entrepreneurs who spent time in the United States but returned home to operate small businesses there, with economic support from the expatriate community; Otavalo traders from Ecuador who sell their ethnic wares in street markets in North America and western Europe; and the new Chinatowns in suburban Monterey Park, California, and Flushing, New York (Portes, 1996a, 1996b, 1998, 1999b). Three of these nicely illustrate certain central points that Portes made in developing his case on behalf of transnationalism.

The Mexican example reflects a case in which immigrants remained actively engaged in homeland concerns, and in this respect is not unlike the Haitian example used by Glick Schiller et al. In this case, the Mexican community in Brooklyn not only raised over $50,000 to improve the waterworks of their hometown of Ticuani, but a committee was actively engaged in the design of the plan in an ongoing way (for a complete account of this immigrant group, see Smith, 2006). Central to the viability of transnational communities, Portes contended, are improved communication and transportation networks. This made possible not only continuing oversight of the project from Brooklyn, but also the inspection of the materials and the actual installation of pipes by a committee that flew from New York to Mexico. Reflecting the desire to maintain homeland ties, a seal was designed that read, "For the Progress of Ticuani: The Absent Ones, Always Present." Thus, rather than claim that earlier immigrants lacked a desire to be involved in homeland issues, Portes' argument was that what makes the situation different today is that improved communications channels and transportation systems make it possible to more readily act on that desire.

The Dominican example concerns the economic rather than the sociocultural. Hundreds of small business owners of factories, commercial enterprises, and financial organizations in the Dominican Republic maintain close social relationships with the expatriate community in the United States, which serves as a vital source of investment capital and as a market for goods and services. Thus, though their operations are physically located in the Dominican Republic, the geographic field of reference of these entrepreneurs is transnational. Portes suggested that "transnational communities are in a sense labor's analog to the multinational corporation" (1996a, p. 74).

This example, however, does not involve a global proletariat, but rather international small business operatives.

The third example looks at the birth of new Chinatowns outside of the older central city locales of the long-established Chinatowns. Robert E. Park (1935/1950, p. 151) had predicted the demise of Chinatowns as a result of immigrant restriction; with the post-1965 resumption of immigration, older Chinatowns have been revitalized and new ones have emerged. The rather limited research to date on these new communities has tended to focus on the new patterns of accommodation to the United States that serve to differentiate immigration today from the past (Chen, 1992; Fong, 2000). Portes' interest in these communities arose as a result of the role played by Taiwanese- and Hong Kong–financed banks in these communities and the business "astronauts" who travel frequently between the United States and Asia. The former is reminiscent of the rotating credit associations that have characterized Chinese immigrant communities since the 19th century (Takaki, 1989, p. 241). The latter, however, is a new phenomenon. Part of the reason for their existence was the export of capital out of Hong Kong prior to the PRC takeover of the colony.

With these examples in mind, we now turn to the earlier-mentioned *Ethnic and Racial Studies* framing essays, wherein Portes offered his most sustained articulation of transnationalism, explaining why it is unique, and what its implications are for ethnic communities over time. At the outset, the distinctiveness of this phenomenon is described in historical comparative terms.

> While back and forth movements by immigrants have always existed, they have not acquired until recently the critical mass and complexity necessary to speak of an emergent social field. This field is composed of a growing number of persons who live dual lives: speaking two languages, having homes in two countries, and making a living through continuous regular contact across national borders. (Portes et al., 1999, p. 217)

Noting the varied and sometimes contradictory ways the term has been put to use, Portes and his colleagues sought to offer a middle-range theory of transnationalism capable of shaping research agendas. They invoked Merton (1987) to suggest the circumstances in which it is appropriate to create a new concept: (1) if a significant percentage of immigrants are involved in the process, (2) if the activities they engage in exhibit persistence over time, and (3) if existing concepts fail to capture the content of these activities (Portes et al., 1999, pp. 218–219).

Assuming that each of these criteria has been met, they proceeded to refine and delimit the broad definition inherited from Glick Schiller et al. and evident in much of the literature during this early phase. This began with a decision to abandon the term *transmigrant,* suggesting that the word *immigrant* suffices and does not need to be supplemented or replaced. Next, they limited the use of the term *transnationalism* to include only those activities that involve continuity of social relationships across national borders over time. In other words, in contrast to Glick Schiller et al., only some, but not all, contemporary immigrants are transnationals. As an example of who would not count, they point to immigrants who on occasion send gifts to family and friends back home. Whether or not this would exclude Filipinos sending *Balikbayan* boxes is not obvious, since these are sent only periodically, but have acquired a formalized and regulated character.

A final form of definitional delimitation identified individuals and their support networks as the appropriate units of analysis, thereby excluding communities and more overarching structural units such as governments (Portes et al., 1999, pp. 219–220). The authors' separation of topics is designed to reinforce the idea that transnationalism as applied to immigration is transnationalism "from below," in contrast to the transnationalism "from above" that is manifested by global corporations and governments (Guarnizo, 1997; Smith & Guarnizo, 1998). In the interest of forging a theory of the middle ground, the exclusion of communities and so forth was done, not for theoretical reasons, but as a methodological strategy, based on a conviction that it was advisable in the formative stage of transnational research to concentrate on individuals and families.

Portes and his colleagues (1999, p. 221) distinguished three different types of transnationalism: (1) economic, (2) political, and (3) sociocultural. Economic transnationalism involves entrepreneurs whose network of suppliers, capital, and markets crosses nation-state borders. Of interest here is that Portes (1996a, p. 74; 1996b, p. 151; see also Portes et al., 1999, p. 227) had made the point elsewhere that the idea that capital is global while labor is local is called into question by the advent of transnational communities, which he described as "labor's analog to the multinational corporation." However, in this definition of economic transnationalism it is not labor migrants—a global proletariat—but mobile capitalist entrepreneurs that become the sole representation of this type of transnationalism. In addition, missing from this formulation are members of the professional middle class—brain-drain immigrants—that have proven to be an important component of some contemporary migratory flows. Political transnationalism was defined as involving "the political activities of party officials, governmental functionaries, or community leaders whose main goals are the achievement of political power and influence in the sending or receiving countries" (Portes et al., 1999, p. 221). The sociocultural refers to activities "oriented towards the reinforcement of a national identity abroad or the collective enjoyment of cultural events and goods" (Portes et al., 1999, p. 221).

The net result of this operational definition is that no longer was it necessary to view present migration as necessarily qualitatively different from the preceding era's migrants. While conceived as more common today than in the past, the historically dichotomous assumption underpinning Glick Schiller et al. is modified. Nevertheless, in describing the necessary conditions for transnationalism, Portes and his colleagues pointed to the advances in transportation and communications technologies as making possible today a time-space compression unheard of in earlier times. Thus, they contended that the scope of transnationalism is far more extensive today than a century ago (Portes et al., 1999, pp. 223–227).

At the same time, as a cursory examination of the way the three types of transnational immigration are described suggests, it is clear that not all contemporary immigrants ought to be seen as transnationals. Portes et al. differentiated immigrants in terms of their access to the technological prerequisites for transnationalism. Those with higher levels of social capital would be more likely to forge transnational linkages than those with less capital. At the same time, proximity continues to count: groups with homelands closer to the receiving nation will be the most likely candidates for establishing transnational ties (Portes et al., 1999, p. 224). Given these stipulations, it would appear that those that can actually be defined as transnational immigrants might from this vantage constitute a minority of today's total immigrant population.

Despite the actual number of transnational immigrants, the authors pointed to the potential impact they might have on forging novel boundary-breaking social fields by serving as the facilitators making possible the development and possible institutionalization over time of various translocal economic, political, and cultural ties (Portes et al., 1999, pp. 228–229). To the extent that this process occurs, Portes et al. contended that received versions of assimilation theory needed to be revisited in order to consider the possibility of new modes of adaptation to the receiving country. They pointed to four possible outcomes, only one of which actually suggests transnationalism is both new and relatively permanent. The three that do not include the return home of transnational entrepreneurs with their families; the abandonment of transnationalism in favor of full assimilation into the receiving country; and the rejection of transnationalism by the children of transnational immigrants in favor of assimilation. The one that does consider transnationalism as novel and enduring entails the generational transmission of a transnational perspective and the knowledge needed to promote it. It is this latter prospect that they concluded may well become the most common accommodative path chosen by immigrants in the future (Portes et al., 1999, p. 229).

In his conclusion, Portes (1999a, pp. 464–466) treated transnationalism as one possible outcome out of several, and summarized the factors that shape the choices individuals make. These include the forces contributing to migration, the extent to which homeland issues remain salient for immigrants, and the role of nativist hostility to newcomers. These factors, of course, are not new to today's immigrants; rather they can be and indeed have been employed to explain the differing modes of adaptation and acculturation among earlier immigrant groups. What is new is the role some homeland governments are playing in attempting to encourage ongoing connections with their expatriate communities. Emigrants a century ago confronted governments and cultural elites that tended to be overtly hostile; today's counterparts, in contrast, frequently find their emigrants to be useful economically, and sometimes politically and culturally as well. Thus, rather than condemning their decision to exit or enticing them to return, they instead work to create relationships with the immigrants that are beneficial to the homeland. To the extent that immigrants perceive these relationships to be mutually beneficial, the potential for a transnational social field arises.

At the same time, Portes viewed assimilation as a powerful force, particularly for the second generation and beyond. Insofar as this is the case, he presented transnationalism less as an alternative to assimilation than as an "antidote to the tendency towards downward assimilation"—or, in other words, as a way of combating the consequences of what he has elsewhere referred to as "segmented assimilation" (Portes, 1995; Portes, 1999a, pp. 446–473; see the discussion on this topic in the preceding chapter). Here Portes appeared prepared to treat transnationalism as one variant of assimilation, in contrast to elsewhere where it is posed as an alternative to assimilation. In the end, it was not always clear whether Portes viewed transnationalism as an alternative outcome to assimilation or as a new type or form of assimilation. Nor was it obvious, given the expected impact of acculturation on the second generation and beyond, why he thought that transnationalism as one of several possible outcomes might actually become normative.

One aspect of his theory involved the use of the idea of social fields. While relying on this concept, he did not actually develop it. However, the third early formulation of transnationalism did so, and thus we now turn to that work.

## Immigration and Transnational Social Spaces

By far the most sustained attempt at clarifying and developing the idea of the social field during this period was undertaken by Thomas Faist (2000a), though he recast the term by presenting the idea of "transnational social spaces" rather than social fields (see a related discussion in Beck, 2000, p. 26).

In a series of articles and papers, he developed the contours for a systematic theory of transnationalism predicated on the idea of the construction of border-crossing social spaces (Faist, 1998, 2000b, 2000c). However, it was in *The Volume and Dynamics of International Migration and Transnational Social Spaces* (2000a) that his position achieved its most complete articulation, and thus it will be the focus of this analysis.

For Faist, the idea of transnational spaces entailed considering the migratory system as a boundary-breaking process in which two (usually) or more nation states are penetrated by and become a part of a singular new social space. This space involves in part "the circulation of ideas, symbols, and material culture" (Faist, 2000a, p. 13). It also involves the border-crossing movements of people who then come to engage in transnational social relations. To the degree that this occurs, a theory of transnational social relations is needed, and it should be seen as yet another possible outcome of immigrant adaptation to the receiving country, one that "supplements the canonical concepts of assimilation and ethnic pluralism" (Faist, 2000a, p. 29). This meant that Faist considered both assimilation and ethnic pluralism as potential outcomes for contemporary migrants. Moreover, he disputed the claim that transnationalism is a new phenomenon that only applies to post–World War II south-north migrations. Instead, he insisted that transnationalism clearly could be found in the migratory wave of a century ago to white settler states. However, he also concurred with Portes that the relative ease of long-distance travel and improved communication technologies means that transnationalism today has achieved the critical mass that makes it more extensive and consequential than its earlier manifestations (Faist, 2000a, pp. 211–212).

A third type of complementarity involves the relationship between transnationalism and both world systems theory and globalization. Faist contended that these three concepts should be seen as distinct but overlapping. His understanding of world systems theory locates it in the center-periphery model. Though advocates of world systems theory might disagree, his argument was that this paradigm is rooted in a perspective that looks solely at the symbiotic relationship between a particular nation from the periphery and a particular core nation. What makes transnationalism different, he suggests, is that in contrast to world systems theory, it opens to consideration the possibility that migrants from a nation in the periphery may end up in several destinations that create a complex transnational space involving more than two nation-states. In this regard, it offers a broader vision than world systems theory (Faist, 2000a, p. 210).

In contrast, transnationalism is seen as offering a more limited perspective than globalization theory. While the two processes can overlap, Faist distinguished them by contending that globalization involves, referring to Marx's phrase from the *Grundrisse* (1973, p. 423), the "annihilation of space and time." More contemporary characterizations of this shift include David Harvey's (1989) "time-space compression" and Anthony Giddens' (1984) "time-space distanciation." For postmodern theorists such as Harvey and theorists of high modernity such as Giddens (1990, 1999), globalization referred to a process that makes possible the proliferation of social relations across great distances. These relationships "are becoming more intense and robust rather than stretched and attenuated" (Waters, 1995, p. 58). In this regard, the terms *transnationalism* and *globalization* might appear to be virtual synonyms (Bauman, 1998; Robertson, 1992). However, Faist (2000a, pp. 210–211) rejected this conclusion by claiming that globalization tends to refer to processes that are "decentered" or "deterritorialized," while "transnational processes are anchored in and span two or more nation-states" and thus are not "denationalized."

The linchpin of Faist's thesis was the concept of transnational social spaces. It is his articulation of a systematic theory of such spaces that is the product of what Glick Schiller and her colleagues (1992, p. 5) identified as the desideratum of a "social science unbound." Faist (2000a, p. 243) described this as going beyond the "container concept of space" (see also Beck, 2000) that he thought characterized both assimilation theory and ethnic pluralism. Moreover, it can be seen as a parallel to what Glick Schiller et al. and Portes describe as "social fields." While the intellectual lineage of social fields derives from Bourdieu, Faist's use of the term *space* has been influenced by the work of the Swedish school of time-geographers, particularly the work of Torsten Hagerstrand (1976). From this theoretical perspective, space is not equivalent to place. Faist (2000a, pp. 45–46) described the difference in the following way:

> Space here does not only refer to physical features, but also to larger opportunity structures, the social life and the subjective images, values, and meanings that the specific and limited place represents to migrants. Space is thus different from place in that it encompasses or spans various territorial locations. It includes two or more places. Space has a social meaning that extends beyond simple territoriality; only with concrete social or symbolic ties does it gain meaning for potential migrants.

Two things stand out that differentiated Faist's position from that of Portes. First, he explicitly included transnational immigrant communities in his framework—and not simply individuals and families—and second, he insisted that such communities must be theoretically linked to what Portes describes as transnationalism from above, rather than treating transnationalism from above and below as discrete parallel phenomena. Portes treated transnationalism from above and transnationalism from below as interrelated phenomena, but his middle-range theory encouraged—at the very least at the methodological level—an approach that did not lend itself to a fuller theoretical articulation of the nature of the interrelationship. Faist, by contrast, sought to articulate a theoretical position that addressed such connections.

In Faist's earliest definition, transnational social spaces were defined as "combinations of social and symbolic ties, positions in networks and organizations, and networks of organizations that can be found in at least two geographically and internationally distinct places" (Faist, 1998, p. 216). This differed little from subsequent formulations (Faist, 2000a, p. 197). However, in identifying the component groups involved in these spaces, he amended his earlier characterization of a triadic relationship consisting of groups and institutions of the receiving nation, the homeland state, and the immigrant group itself to a pentagonic relationship. In this revised formulation, he separated the state from civil society in both the homeland and host society, thus adding four units of analysis to the immigrant group (Faist, 1998, p. 217; Faist, 2000a, p. 200).

The social construction of enduring transnational social spaces requires the sustainability of various types of ties. Faist identified three types of transnational social spaces, each with a characteristic tie. Kinship groups, he contended, are predicated on ties of reciprocity, as can be seen in the form of remittances. Transnational circuits, in contrast, require instrumental exchange ties such as those structuring trading networks. Finally, transnational communities are predicated on the solidarity derived from a shared conception of collective identity, such communities constituting a parallel to ethnic communities located in one place rather than transnational space (Faist, 2000a, pp. 202–210).

Undertheorized in this formulation was the affective element contained in each of these ties. Thus, while a norm of reciprocity may define the structured pattern of remittances sent to family members, this is not simply an instrumental transaction, but one based on an emotional attachment to those left behind. It is a tie predicated on emotions related to longing, the sorrow of absence, and the desire to remain bonded to one's family. As E. K. Francis (1947) pointed out long ago, while ethnic groups are secondary groups, they share with kinship groups collective attachments and interpersonal relationships that are emotionally charged. Moreover, kinship networks can appropriately be seen not as distinct from the transnational ethnic community, but as a constituent part of it. But can the same affective character be said to characterize transnational trading circuits? Are these ties different: merely instrumental arrangements based on the profit motive? Not when one considers the role that trust plays in economic exchange. Trust is an essential ingredient in combating economic risk, and insofar as ethnic affiliations facilitate a requisite level of trust, they serve to underpin and make possible instrumental transactions. Once again, this would imply that transnational circuits are embedded in transnational communities, and can only be separated from them analytically.

Thus, transnational immigrant social spaces require the creation of a new form of ethnic community. What makes it different from the more familiar form that typified immigrant enclaves in industrializing nations a century ago is that it is located in a space that encompasses two or more nation-states, a situation made possible by time-space compression. These are, in a well-selected phrase, "communities without propinquity" (Faist, 2000a, p. 197). But, of course, in a fashion, so were ethnic communities forged within the borders of particular nations. For example, European-origin immigrants to the United States forged a collective ethnic identity that linked fellow ethnics regardless of where in the United States they lived. This type of collective identity was the product of an exit from the home-land and the migration to a particular place. In contrast, migrants in transnational spaces are seen as being engaged in a more fluid and syn-cretistic process of adaptation. Metaphorically, assimilation is associated with the image of "the uprooted" (Handlin, 1973), and cultural pluralism with "the transplanted" (Bodnar, 1985). Faist (1998, p. 239) proposed as an appropriate transnational metaphorical alternative—borrowing from the novelist Salman Rushdie—the idea of "translated people," writing, "Migrants are continually engaged in translating languages, cultures, norms, and social and symbolic ties." In other words, transnational migrants forge their sense of identity and their community not out of a loss or mere replication, but out of something that is at once new and familiar—a *bricolage* constructed of cultural elements from both the homeland and the receiving nation.

Crucially for this thesis, it is not simply individuals living with one foot in two places that constitute the sole occupants of transnational communities. Rather, Faist (2000a, pp. 207–208) wrote,

> Transnational communities characterize situations in which international movers and stayers are connected by dense and strong social and symbolic ties over time and across space to patterns of networks and circuits in two coun-tries. . . . Such communities without propinquity do not necessarily require individual persons living in two worlds simultaneously or between cultures in a total "global village" of de-territorialized space. What is required, however, is that communities without propinquity link through exchange, reciprocity,

and solidarity to achieve a high degree of social cohesion, and a common repertoire of symbolic and collective representations.

Moreover, for a viable transnational community to be established and to sustain itself over time, a continual pattern of involvement with both governmental and civic institutions in the homeland and receiving country are essential (Faist, 2000a, p. 208). This is due to the fact that transnational immigrants qua transnational immigrants are engaged in activities designed to define and enhance their position in the receiving nation, while simultaneously seeking to remain embedded in a participatory way in the everyday affairs of the homeland community. What is distinctive about this type of community is that over time the transnational social space thus carved out makes the dichotomous character of host society concerns versus homeland concerns if not irrelevant, at least less pronounced and at some level part of a transcendent structure of border-crossing social relations.

Over time also means generational succession. The unanswerable question at present is whether or not transnational social spaces, to the extent that they have been created, will prove to be little more than a phenomenon describing the immigrant generation. Faist (2000a, p. 238), more forcefully than the previous theorists, put on the table the matter of the durability of transnational ties with the passage of time, suggesting that "we should not lose sight of the ever-present lures of cultural adaptation."

## Critiques and Revisions

Two responses to these earliest conceptual articulations of transnational migration were quickly in evidence. On the one hand, a growing number of immigration scholars began to deploy the concept in empirical research. On the other hand, several recurring criticisms of the approach emerged. We turn in this section to the criticisms leveled against the concept, coupled with the responses to these criticisms by key proponents that have resulted in significant revisions. An early cautionary question was posed by Ninna Nyberg-Sørensen (2000), when she speculated about whether it was a "useful approach or trendy rubbish." However, in reality, most critics were usually not inclined to see the approach as rubbish, but rather as being in need of refinement and revision. For their part, the proponents proved to be remarkably willing to engage the critics by frequently revisiting and reformulating their earlier work. This resulted in moving the concept into a second stage—one of maturation (see, for example, the stock taking in Portes, 2003). We turn to it, but only after we review the major criticisms and responses.

## *Immigration Past and Present*

One of the claims, made most explicitly in the early Glick Schiller formulation, is that transnationalism is a novel phenomenon, characteristic of this era's immigrants but not evident among those in the migratory wave that occurred during the late 19th and early 20th centuries. This was challenged by historical sociologists, who argued that it was a mistake to concur with Handlin's portrait of immigrants from the past who were presumed to quickly and permanently sever their ties to the old world (Barkan, 2004, 2006; Foner, 2005, 2001; Kivisto, 2001; Morawska, 2001, 2003). Indeed, there was abundant evidence of the persistence of cross-border ties over time, including not only ties to kin, but also an engagement in homeland politics and in some instances in maintaining economic connections (see, for example, the following synthetic accounts: Bodnar, 1985; Daniels, 1990; Fuchs, 1990; Portes & Rumbaut, 2006; Takaki, 1993). Wyman (1993) has documented that return migration and back-and-forth movement were characteristic features during this time, the latter including seasonal migrations. DeConde (1992) and Jones (1976) have illustrated the extensive engagements in homeland politics. Immigrants sent money and goods to relatives and friends in the homeland. Joppke and Morawska (2003, p. 22) have described many of these immigrants as "closet transnationalists." By this, they meant that their transnational aspirations were circumscribed by "the exclusionary demands from home and host states regarding their national commitments."

Connected to this comparison between past and present is the claim that today's transnational migrants are engaged in a form of resistance to capitalism (Glick Schiller et al., 1992). As Delmos Jones (1992, p. 223), an early commentator on this assertion, pointed out, contemporary immigrants are far more likely to simply seek incorporation into the capitalist system rather than resisting it. Waldinger (2003) suggests that the reason for this is simply because labor migrants are first and foremost about improving their lives by finding employment opportunities abroad that are an improvement on what is available at home.

In this regard, it is worth pointing out that Bodnar's (1985) portrait of the "transplanted" revealed that most of the earlier wave of immigrants, too, were pragmatists, seeking to find a way of becoming integrated into the new economic setting in ways that were seen as advantageous to themselves. However, there is one feature of the past wave that makes it different from the present: there was more overt resistance to capitalism then than now. This was because those immigrants were able to collectively embrace vibrant ideological alternatives to capitalism, be it socialism, communism, anarchism, or industrial unionism. Within all of the European-origin groups in the United

States, one could find a radical presence, and in the case of a few groups—Jews and Finns in particular—a significant percentage of the community affiliated with one or another expression of anticapitalism (Kivisto, 1984; Miller, 1974; Rosenbaum, 1973). However, despite their dreams of a radiant future free of capitalist exploitation, in the end, as Seymour Martin Lipset and Gary Marks (2000) put it, "it didn't happen here" (or, for that matter, in other immigrant-receiving nations).

In response to this line of criticism, transnational theorists have conceded that transnationalism is not new. In fact, one of the outgrowths of this dialogue is that historians of immigration have increasingly come to employ a transnational perspective in their work, viewing it as a useful corrective to earlier generations of scholars who were so focused on modes of incorporation into the host society that they tended to pay scant attention to the study of the persistence of homeland connections. At the same time, this does not mean that the past is simply being repeated today. Foner (2005, pp. 69–70) offers a cogent analysis of what's new today, writing,

> Clearly, transnationalism was alive and well a hundred years ago. But if there are parallels with the past, there is also much that is new at the beginning of the twenty-first century. Advances in transportation and communication technologies have made it possible for immigrants to maintain more frequent, immediate, and closer contact with their home societies, and in a real sense, have changed the very nature of transnational connections. Today's global economy encourages international business operations; the large number of professional and prosperous immigrants in contemporary America are well positioned to operate in a transnational field. Dual nationality provisions, in conjunction with other changes in the national and international political context, have added new dimensions to and altered the scope and thrust of transnational political involvements.

Foner also notes that today's immigrants need not be "closeted" because the host societies are more ethnically tolerant and sympathetic to diversity. In addition, sending states have changed their view of their émigré populations. Whereas in the past they were viewed as traitors to the homeland, they are increasingly seen as "potential lobbies to influence U.S. policy" (Foner, 2005, p. 75). We turn to the role that states play in transnationalism in the third section of this book, where we focus on control.

## Avoiding Technological Determinism

As is evident in the previous discussion, one recurring thread running through much of the work on transnationalism is the role played by new communications technologies and modes of transportation that make cross-border contacts easier today than in the past. Air travel rather than travel by ship makes it easier to contemplate recurring cross-border movements, while telephones, faxes, and e-mail suggest the ability to engage in ongoing, sustained communication with people in the homeland. This stands in stark contrast to the letter writing of the earlier era—a slow process that was particularly daunting for illiterate immigrants who had to rely on professional letter writers to communicate with friends and family in the homeland.

While these developments no doubt make possible a dramatic expansion in transnational connections, they are not inevitable. No transnational scholars, to our knowledge, explicitly advocate on behalf of an argument that is predicated on technological determinism. However, there is an implicit tendency to assume that the existence of these new technologies inevitably produces transnational social relations (Kivisto, 2003; Waldinger & Fitzgerald, 2004, p. 1188). Claude Fischer's (1992) social history of the telephone is a useful corrective to this way of thinking, for it reminds us that communication technologies do not determine if they will be used, how they will be used, and how frequently they will be used. The uses of technology are ultimately socially determined and will be shaped by, among other things, the social class location of the individuals in question. Thus, it is not surprising that an Indian businessman running a global import-export company out of Bangalore with operations in Singapore, Belize, and Côte d'Ivoire would rack up huge numbers of frequent flyer miles, while maintaining daily contact with his offices abroad by phone, e-mail, and fax. On the other hand, it's useful to remember Biju from *The Inheritance of Loss*. This fictional character reflects the reality of millions of poor immigrants today, who find that it is not easy to make telephone calls to a homeland where not everyone has ready access to a phone.

Recently, researchers have begun to explore the extent to which immigrants have access to and actually use the new communications technologies. Thus, Steven Vertovec (2004) has written about cheap international phone calls as the "social glue of migrant transnationalism." Noting that international phone calls overall have grown from 12.7 billion call minutes in 1982 to 154 billion by 2001, he points to the fact that the use by migrants can be inferred from looking at nation-specific patterns. Thus, for example, the increase in calls between Germany and Turkey, between India and the United Kingdom, and between Mexico and the United States are reflections of specific migratory flows. In addition, some phone card companies report that they sell either exclusively or extensively to ethnic markets. Pointing to the "grossly uneven distribution of telecommunications infrastructure," Vertovec's (2004, p. 222) research note leads to the conclusion that the mere existence of new technologies is insufficient to account for their role in transnational relations. Explicitly social factors must also be part of the equation.

## How Many Transnational Immigrants?

The guiding assumption of the first phase of transnational theorizing was that all, most, or at least a significant percentage of contemporary immigrants were transnational. Critics pointed out that such claims needed empirical verification. In fact, two proponents of transnationalism were quick to raise this issue. Portes pointed out that research to date had tended to draw evidence from the dependent variable, thereby exaggerating the extent to which transnationalism was present, noting that there was abundant evidence of immigrants who were only marginally involved in transnational activities or not at all. He concluded that it was important to view transnationalism as but one type of immigrant adaptation, one that "co-exists with other more traditional forms" (Portes, 2001, p. 183). In a similar vein, Peggy Levitt (2001a) warned against the tendency to see transnationalism everywhere.

Portes and associates were among the first scholars to offer empirical evidence about the scope of transnationalism. In two major articles, they sought to explore transnational *practices*, rather than transnational communities or social fields. Specifically, they examined economic practices in one article (Portes, Haller, & Guarnizo, 2002) and political practices in the other (Guarnizo, Portes, & Haller, 2003), studying three specific immigrant groups in the United States: Colombian, Salvadorans, and Dominicans.

Their conclusion in both articles was that a relatively small minority of immigrants can be defined as transnational. Looking at the economic realm, transnational entrepreneurs are defined as "self-employed immigrants whose business activities require frequent travel abroad and who depend for the success of their firms on their contacts and associates in another country, primarily their country of origin" (Portes et al., 2002, p. 287). They discovered that the percentage of immigrants from each group that were transnational entrepreneurs was very small, with Salvadorans registering 5.3%, Dominicans 4.8%, and Colombians 4.3%.

Similar results were obtained in their examination of the political activities of these three groups. The study examined such practices as memberships in home country political parties, giving money to those parties, taking part in home country electoral activities, membership in civic hometown associations and charity organizations, and giving money to such nonelectoral organizations. The percentages of immigrants involved in regular engagements with these practices ranged from 7.2% to 14.3%, leading the authors to conclude "that the transnational political field is not as extensive or evenly distributed among contemporary immigrants as proposed by previous accounts. In fact, the number of immigrants who are regularly involved in cross-border activism is relatively small" (Guarnizo et al., 2003, p. 1238).

The number of people engaged in routine and sustained cross-border activities may be small, but this does not necessarily lead to the conclusion that transnationalism is a minor sidestream. Portes (2003, p. 877) is clear about this when he writes, "Despite its limited numerical character, the combination of a cadre of regular transnational activists with the occasional activities of other migrants adds up to a social process of significant economic and social impact for communities and even nations." We will turn to the evidence to date that supports Portes' claim in the following section on social spaces. However, before doing so, we turn to the final topic of critique: the relationship between transnationalism and assimilation.

## Transnationalism and Assimilation

What is the relationship between transnationalism and assimilation? The early Glick Schiller and colleagues (1992, 1995; see also Appadurai, 1993; Basch et al., 1994) formulation viewed the two as contrasting, antithetical modes of incorporation, the former being at the least an alternative to the latter and perhaps—as a form of resistance—a direct challenge to it. On the other hand, there are those who think that transnationalism is of limited import and offers little by way of an alternative to assimilation (Bommes, 2005; Esser, 2004). Both of these positions have progressively given way to a view that sees the two not as mutually exclusive, but rather as interconnected (Kivisto, 2003, p. 19). The call has been to overcome what Levitt (2003, p. 178) refers to as the "false dichotomy between assimilation and transnationalism." Portes et al. (2002, p. 294) make such a case in arguing that transnationalism, rather than being seen as something that slows assimilation, might actually accelerate the process. For example, he and a team of researchers concluded that for Colombian, Dominican, and Mexican immigrants, transnational engagements appeared to work in tandem with political incorporation into the United States (Portes, Escobar, & Arana, 2008).

The key, but generally unstated, point is that transnationalism is not to be conceived as a mode of incorporation akin to assimilation, but rather, as Portes (2001, p. 188) puts it, "immigrant transnationalism is significant in that it can alter, in various ways, the process of integration to the host society of both first-generation immigrants and their offspring." Some have questioned the efficacy of transnationalism for the second generation, suggesting that it is likely to wane in salience with the passage of time and especially with the transition of generations (Kasinitz et al., 2004). However, as Levitt (2001a, p. 212) has pointed out, this remains an open empirical question, and a collection of essays edited by Levitt and Waters (2002) provides preliminary indications that transnationalism is capable of persisting into the second generation, although there is little consensus about its significance. At one end of the spectrum are those who are most skeptical about transnationalism's long-term impact. Rumbaut (2002, p. 90), relying on data from the Census Bureau's Current Population Survey, concludes that for the vast majority of the new second generation (including the 1.5 and 2.5 generations), "theirs is an American future, not a bilingual or binational one." This overall assessment is echoed by Joel Perlmann (2002) and Michael Jones-Correa (2002). At the other end are articles that express the view that transnationalism may well have greater staying power over time and across generations than skeptics think is likely (Espiritu & Tran, 2002; Fouron & Glick Schiller, 2002).

Ewa Morawska (2003, p. 133) contends that "transnational involvements of immigrants and their children and their assimilation into the host society typically are concurrent." However, since both are multipath processes, a number of outcomes are possible:

> These two processes form differently textured combinations as each of them takes different forms: mainstream or adhesive, "upward" and "downward" or oppositional assimilation, optional or oppositional transnationalism with an encompassing or focused range of engagements, and so on. And . . . these particular forms and "contents" of T/A combinations are context-dependent, that is, contingent on different constellations of features of the economies, politics, and cultures of sender and receiver societies and local communities and of the immigrants (or the second generation) themselves. (Morawska, 2003, p. 162)

Teasing out these various possible combinations has only begun in research agendas, thus far largely explored in ethnographic research. Two notable studies have done just that. Both Levitt's (2001b) study of Dominicans from the village of Miraflores who emigrated to the Jamaica Plain neighborhood of Boston and Robert C. Smith's (2006) study of villagers from Ticuani, located in the Mexican state of Puebla, who migrated to New York City offer thick descriptions of the complex processes involved in both remaining connected to the homeland and adjusting and seeking to find a place in the host society. While both studies are intentionally focused on the transnational side of the equation, they also address the relationship between transnationalism and assimilation. Levitt (2001b, p. 5) writes that "transnational practices are not just another way station along the path to assimilation. Rather, assimilation and transnational practices are not incompatible." Smith (2006, p. 52) elaborates by contending that

> transnational life is anchored simultaneously in the assimilation of Ticuanese migrants and their children in New York and in the transformation of Ticuani

and the Mixteca by migration. In New York, assimilation does not preclude involvement in transnational life. Rather, it provides a context that makes transnational attachments valuable for immigrants and their children.

These two studies represent the general consensus that has emerged among key proponents of transnationalism, that "simultaneity" is the characteristic relationship between assimilation and transnationalism (Levitt & Glick Schiller, 2004). Glick Schiller and Levitt (2006, p. 14) have noted, "There is no doubt that transnational migration scholars did not document migrant incorporation with the same fervor as transnational connections. Most researchers, however, assumed simultaneity and documented it in their work." The point that needs to be stressed here is that assimilation and transnationalism ought not to be construed as competing alternatives, and the reason is clear: whereas assimilation refers to a mode of immigrant incorporation into a receiving society, transnationalism does not. Rather, it is a mode of connection between the homeland and the settlement society, a mode of connectedness that is achieved to the extent that a dialectical relationship between the movers and stayers in the two worlds is achieved in one or more arenas of social life: familial, religious, economic, political, cultural, and so forth.

## Transnational Social Spaces and Development

By focusing primarily on the adjustment process in the postmigration setting, earlier generations of immigration scholars paid insufficient attention to the ongoing connections between homeland and postimmigration settings. What has become known as the "transnational optic" has sought to redress this lacuna—an optic that requires seeing "beyond the nation-state" as a unit of analysis (Glick Schiller, 2007). Faist's (1998, 2000a) work, discussed earlier in this chapter, provided one of the most fully articulated discussions of transnational social spaces, but others have also contributed to the discussion (e.g., Bretell, 2006; Glick Schiller, 2005; Morawska, 2003; Pries, 2005; Wimmer & Glick Schiller, 2002).

A line of inquiry that has emerged in recent years concerns the connection between immigration and economic development, and it has sought to carve out a research agenda that is framed in terms of whether or not contemporary immigrants are creating communities within the transnational social spaces linking homelands and settlement nations (Portes, 2009). At its most elemental, what is at issue is whether or not remittances are a developmental tool in poor nations. Clearly, for some state actors and officials in such trans-state organizations as the World Bank and the International Monetary

Fund, remittances have become, in the words of Deresh Kapur (2005), "the new development mantra." The assumption is that remittances can only work as a developmental tool to the extent that transnational communities are forged and sustained over time. To appreciate the ideational shift implied in linking development to transnational immigrant communities, one need only consider the fact that twice before in the second half of the 20th century was a connection made between migration and development.

During the 1960s, public policy emphasized "labor gaps" in the wealthy nations and the need for "development" in poor ones. During this era, the role of remittances was understood to be important, but only over the short term, for in the end there was an expectation that return migration would occur, and with it the subsequent transfer not only of human capital but also the cultural diffusion of a worldview that emphasized that package of ideas associated with modernization theory (Kindleberger, 1967). Such a perspective was congruent with the demographic model that depicted the emigration of surplus labor from underdeveloped areas as leading over time to a new equilibrium between labor and capital (Lewis, 1954). This was seen as occurring because as labor moved from poor to wealthy nations, labor scarcities in the former led to inflows of capital investment, which in turn led to economic development that drew émigrés back home (Hamilton & Whaley, 1984).

When reality undercut this optimistic scenario, a new line of thought took hold during the 1970s. Influenced by currents of Marxism rather than modernization theory, the idea of development was replaced by that of "dependency," which was depicted as a structural condition of the periphery dominated by a center, with "underdevelopment" seen as the inevitable result (Wallerstein, 1974). From this theoretical viewpoint, it was no longer argued that migration led to development. On the contrary, underdevelopment produced migration (for an example, see Portes & Walton, 1981). In terms of the public policy implications, financial remittances were not considered to be appreciably beneficial. Instead, dependency theory highlighted the fact that underdevelopment led to the loss of highly skilled workers who migrated from the periphery to the center. This out-migration—the "brain drain"—was thought to contribute to even more underdevelopment and increased migration flows through the asymmetric distribution of benefits and resources (Delgado-Wise & Covarrubias, 2005; Martin, 1991).

Near the end of the past century, a rejection of the development of underdevelopment thesis appeared on the scene. It was associated with the idea of codevelopment (Naïr, 1997), which was an apt characterization of a new approach to development. It focuses on the mediation of village associations in development cooperation, a model whose origins are rooted in associations from Mali that have been located in France since the colonial era. From this model, international migration is treated as having the capacity to fuel development in the poor nations of the south and east—sometimes referred to as the "Global South." The role of states, both receiving and sending, as well as INGOs, is crucial to this development. However, equally important is the role of transnational immigrants and the trans-state communities they create.

One of the most significant shifts in the approaches of sending states to their émigré populations is that they no longer seek to encourage permanent return migration. This change is on display in the People's Republic of China's official stance toward their emigrants. Whereas in the recent past, the state's propaganda slogan was "return to serve" (*huiguo fuwu*), it has been replaced by a new one that calls upon the Chinese diaspora to "serve the country" (*wei guo fuwu*). Similar rhetorical shifts can be detected in numerous countries, and they have been complemented by public policy changes. One example that will be explored more fully later in this book involves the growing support of dual citizenship (Faist & Kivisto, 2007b). Additional policy changes include extending voting rights to absentees; tax incentives directed to citizens abroad; and the creation of ties to migrant organizations on the part of local, regional, and national governments. Instead of calling for an eventual permanent return to the homeland, states are far more inclined to encourage temporary returns. In this regard, they have been supported by INGOs, such as the International Organization of Migration's (IOM) Migration and Development in Africa (MIDA) program, which sends migrants as experts back to their countries of origin for short periods of time. In similar ways, sending nations have sought to promote the sending of remittances to the homeland.

## Remittances and Development

There is little wonder that governments and INGOs have begun to consider the development potential of remittances. According to Samuel Maimbo and Dilip Ratha (2005, p. 2), the official figure for remittances to developing nations "exceeded US$125 billion in 2004, making them the second largest source of development finance after foreign direct investment." This is an undercount of the actual figure because a substantial level of remittances moves through informal channels such as the Islamic transfer system known as *hawala*. Figures 5.1 and 5.2 reveal, respectively, the top 20 nations that are sources of remittances and the top 20 nations that are recipients of remittances. The two top source nations for remittances are the United States and Saudi Arabia, while the top two recipients of remittances are India and Mexico (Ratha, 2005, pp. 24–25).

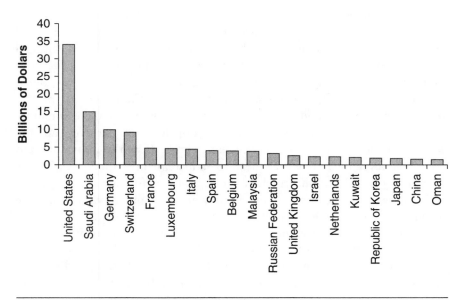

**Figure 5.1**     Main Sources of Remittances, 2003

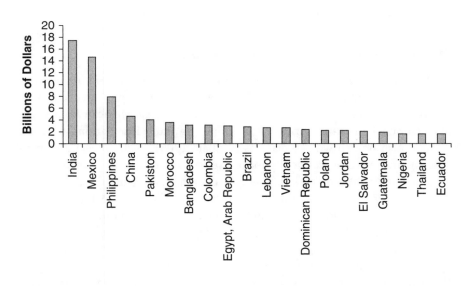

**Figure 5.2**     Main Recipients of Remittances, 2003

The uses of remittances can be divided into two broad categories, one relating to consumption and the other to investment. This is true at the level of individuals and households, at the community level, and at the national level. In terms of individuals and households, this can involve acquiring consumer goods, including those that might be categorized as luxuries, but it also involves reducing or eliminating debt. It can make possible improved access to health care and to educational opportunities. At the community level, it can involve making improvements in the local infrastructure and the creation of new markets for services and goods. If at the individual and household level, the outcome can lead to an increase in inequality within the community based on who receives substantial benefits due to remittances and who does not; remittances functioning at the community level have the potential for reducing levels of inequality.

To the extent that development occurs at these two levels, their combined impact manifests itself at the national level by increasing the flow of foreign currency into the economy, creating employment possibilities, and enhancing levels of human and social capital. This represents the optimistic scenario that portrays remittances as an across-the-board benefit. However, there are grounds for caution. For example, Çaglar Özden and Maurice Schiff (2007, p. 5) point out that the "poverty-reduction impact of remittances is much larger if measured only for recipient households rather than for the population as a whole." In more general terms, the reality is that much remains unknown at present about the actual developmental impact of remittances.

## Hometown Associations and Remittances

With this in mind, we turn to an examination of the role of communities within transnational social spaces associated with hometown or village associations. Examples are numerous and varied, including Mexican hometown associations, Jamaican returnee associations, charitable foundations in Egypt, and Turkish hometown associations (Cağlar, 2006). Such associations provide significant resources at the local level by, for example, providing construction materials for their hometown church, raising money to improve water and sewage systems or health and educational services, helping to organize relief efforts following natural disasters, or in various other ways channeling remittances in specific directions and for specific purposes.

While traditional emigration countries, such as Italy, have long had policies and programs for their émigré populations, it is only relatively recently that emigration states have redefined their relationship to hometown associations in ways that seek to create a symbiotic relationship between the associations and the state (see, for example, Goldring, 2002, on Mexico). In the not-too-distant past, INGOs were primarily preoccupied with the possibility that transplanted hometown communities could be useful in the maintenance of culture (Moya, 2005). What's new today is that the same INGOs look at these associations with the view that they have the capacity to play a crucial role in economic development. Some hometown associations and states have established formal policies of cooperation aimed to improve the infrastructure in hometown regions. A well-known example is Mexico's "3 for 1 Program," a model for the much-touted public-private partnership (PPP) initiatives in developmental policy. In this program, every dollar of remittances from hometown associations that is targeted for government-approved development projects receives matching funds from the federal, state, and local governments.

The response of states to their emigrants has evolved over time. For instance, from the 1960s through the 1980s, Morocco viewed its diaspora with suspicion, enacting policies of repression and surveillance toward those who had migrated to France. By the 1990s, this had given way to a new attitude, one that involved "courting the diaspora" (de Haas, 2006). Such a shift could also be observed in the cases of Mexico, Haiti, and the Dominican Republic as they responded to their emigrant communities in the United States. Mexico, for example, has made efforts in recent years to increase support of Mexicans living outside the country by delivering various services through their consular institutions and by encouraging dual citizenship. Thus, migration states such as Zacatecas, Jalisco, Michoacan, Guanajuato, and Puebla have created centers in major U.S. cities with large numbers of migrants from each respective state. The state of Guanajuato, for example, has created 45 Casas Guanajuato across the United States (Portes, Escobar, & Radford, 2005, p. 32).

Yet potential conflicts between homeland associations and the communities of origin persist. Transnational organizations and groups are able to link exit and voice, and often do so. To the extent that transnationalism has empowered those who are mobile, it can create tensions between mobile and relatively immobile people remaining in the country of origin. Indeed, Roger Waldinger, Eric Popkin, and Hector Aquiles Magana (2008, p. 855) contend that such conflict is inevitable. At stake here is the fact that while transnational immigrants may have a voice in decision making in the homeland, they are not necessarily impacted by those decisions the way those in the homeland are. In addition, the relationship between the immigrants and those who remained behind is often an unequal one in which the former are accorded—and expect—leadership roles and command respect (Waldinger et al., p. 867).

Another source of conflict concerns the transformation of gender relations in the migratory setting, which can over time impact gender relations in the homeland as well. For example, the migration of women from Bangladesh to Malaysia has led to changes in traditional social practices. As a result of increased economic independence in the migratory setting, women who remained in Bangladesh have revealed a greater likelihood of participation in the paid labor force (Dannecker, 2004). On the other hand, in some cases transnational practices exacerbated existing gendered power relations, especially when control over financial remittances continues to rest with men (Mahler & Pessar, 2001; Walton-Roberts, 2004).

## Business Networks

Networks of businesspersons from emigration states who live abroad constitute an important source of financial transfer and investment, both as immigrant entrepreneurs in their new societies of settlement and for their countries of origin. The governments of sending nations have increasingly initiated programs to attract emigrants' investments. By far the largest set of transnational networks—a set of interlinked local, national, and regional networks—in the world is that of the Overseas Chinese. They promote trade by providing market information and matching and referral services by utilizing their coethnic ties. Numerous studies provide evidence that transnational business networks promote international trade by alleviating the problems associated with contract enforcement and by providing information about trading opportunities (Rauch, 2001, pp. 1180, 1200).

Historically, business networks functioned by relying on social mechanisms ensuring trust predicated on the norm of reciprocity, which was based on two mechanisms, the moral community and the prospect of collective punishment. First, trade in most parts of the world until the 19th century rested on a moral community, which could be found, for example, in northern Europe's Hanseatic League, the Hausas in Africa, and the aforementioned Overseas Chinese in Southeast Asia. Among ethnic groups, maintaining a sense of distinctiveness from the host society (sometimes reinforced by host society hostility) served to strengthen in-group ties. Second, transaction costs are lowered by collective punishment of transgressors by all merchants, which deters opportunistic behavior. Contrary to the claim that such networks are vestigial, cultural-bound phenomena that will wither away under the impact of modernization, such practices are in fact quite common in transnational settings. At present, there is evidence that new telecommunications technology serves to sustain such relationships, complementing rather than substituting for face-to-face interaction.

The governments of origin sometimes see their emigrants and their emigrants' children as potential middlemen who can play two valuable roles: in brokering foreign investments or investing themselves, and by helping to diffuse an entrepreneurial spirit into the homeland (cf. Hirschman, 1958). Indians who settled in California's Silicon Valley, for example, contributed to the rise of the high-tech hubs in Bangalore and Hyderabad. Over time, Indian immigrants who worked as highly skilled specialists began to invest in the burgeoning IT industry in India. They could take advantage of a trained workforce that was already employed by foreign companies in data processing and computer programming jobs (Leclerc & Meyer, 2007). The Indian investors added a new dimension by setting up their own companies in India. Other multinational companies followed suit (Cornelius, Espenshade, & Salehyan, 2001). A parallel experience can be found in Taiwan (Tseng, 2000).

In those cases where the immigrant group contains a large number of well-educated emigrants, the potential for foreign investment is high. About 20 million Indians live abroad, second in size only to the Chinese. It is estimated that the income of Indian immigrants amounts to more than a third of India's GDP. It is no surprise that these "nonresident Indians" (NRI) provide about 10% of the foreign direct investment (FDI) in India and a sizeable part of venture capital. The People's Republic of China provides a case par excellence: about 50% of FDI comes from some 30 million Chinese immigrants. Not surprisingly, successive Chinese governments have created incentives for capital investment in selective enterprise areas (Saxenian, 2002). But financial remittances are not the only type of flow. In addition, flows of human capital and social remittances (the transfer of ideas and practices) are also being encouraged. China is but one instance of a trend among emigrant nations, where governments have implemented policies designed to attract highly skilled emigrants as returnees and, more frequently, to entice those who stay overseas to maintain productive links with the homeland. For example, the Indian government offers tax incentives for emigrants and tries to use their expertise, advice, and ideas to equip Indian companies and to create opportunities for overseas Indian companies.

## The Transnational Optic

As this review of homeland associations and business networks indicates, when transnational immigration takes institutional form, actions from below generally become intertwined with actions from above, particularly the actions of the sending states who have decided that it is in their interest to facilitate and support transnational engagements. But also requiring consideration are the respective roles sometimes played by INGOs and by receiving states. Thus, it is quite clear that by employing a transnational optic, which calls for moving beyond the state, it does not mean that states are ignored. To the contrary, the social spaces created from below by transnational immigrants are also shaped by other actors from above, including state actors.

Whether in the longer term the current efforts to link transnational immigration to development will be deemed successful is impossible at present to determine. Indeed, current research efforts, which have only recently begun, have focused on documenting the existence of the institutionalization of transnationalism, not on its sustainability over time. A review of this work indicates how difficult it is to determine just how robust such transnational immigrant institutions actually are. The study cited previously by Waldinger et al. (2008) can be seen as a cautionary tale. Exploring Salvadoran homeland associations in the Los Angeles region, they point to a number of inherent dilemmas confronting such organization, which includes low levels of participation, free riding, internal competition, the prospect of opportunism, inequality between immigrants and stay-at-homes, and the complexities inherent in the long-distance coordination of activities. This is not to suggest that such organizations are fated to be first-generation phenomena, but rather that there is a tendency for them to be inherently fragile and thus difficult to maintain over time. Business networks may or may not tend to experience a similar set of dilemmas and thus may prove to be less subject to the vicissitudes of hometown associations.

In a report based on the results of the Pew Hispanic Center's *2006 National Survey of Latinos,* Waldinger (2007d, pp. ii–iii) notes that only 9% of Latinos send remittances home, travel to the homeland, and telephone relatives in the homeland. While many more do one or two of these activities, 28% are involved in none of them. Those most fully engaged in transnational activities are more weakly attached to the United States, a finding supported by Smith's (2006, p. 53) ethnography, which revealed that those most active in the New York Committee, the Ticuani hometown association, were not inclined to participate in local politics, concentrating their energies on being "the absent ones always present." Waldinger (2007d, p. 22) concludes that the general trend is toward a "steadily deepening commitment to the U.S.," while as the length of time in the United States increases, transnational activities decrease.

It is possible to speculate about what the future of transnationalism is likely to be, not only for Latinos in the United States, but other immigrants in both the United States and elsewhere. However, it is difficult to predict what the future might hold, for there are many variables that must be taken into account. These include considering whether immigration flows continue or are curtailed, whether sending and receiving states encourage or discourage transnational practices and institution building, the state of the economy, the political context, and so forth (Pries, 2004). This is true not only in considering the long-term relationship between transnational immigration and development, but in other arenas of social life as well. This includes political and religious transnationalism (see Kurien, 2007, for an example in which the two are linked: émigré Hindu nationalists in the United States supporting the right-wing Bharitiya Janata Party).

What is clear is that as the concept of transnationalism has been further developed and refined and as a rich and growing body of empirical research has been produced, immigration studies have begun to be complemented by emigration studies. In other words, whereas assimilation attempts to explore if and how immigrants fit into and carve out a place for themselves in the receiving society, so transnationalism has provided a lens on when and how immigrants have managed to remain connected to and involved in their homelands.

# 6

# Multiculturalism

## A New Mode of Incorporation

When Raymond Williams published *Keywords* (1976), his widely read guide to cultural studies, the term *multiculturalism* did not find its way into the book. Nonetheless, the contemporary use of the term actually dates to this era, when in the early 1970s (actually, some date the beginning as early as 1965) the Canadian government began to use it to characterize policies it was enacting that were intended to promote tolerance and respect for difference while simultaneously advancing the idea of a shared national project. This observation about the policy origins of the term in one particular nation is laid out at the beginning of Ien Ang's entry on multiculturalism in *New Keywords: A Revised Vocabulary of Culture and Society* (2005). Between the publication dates of these two books, a huge body of scholarship has been produced on multiculturalism, which has often been overshadowed by polemical condemnations of the idea.

A cursory examination of the first 200 of the estimated 4,420,000 entries on multiculturalism in a Google search reveals that the most vociferous critics of the concept have an overwrought sense of its presumed pernicious character. Thus, one can find entries depicting multiculturalism as "madness," "a destructive doctrine," "a tool of collectivism," the "bane of the West," a "political danger," and "an experiment as dangerous as communism." It has been accused of perpetrating a "fraud" in its "dishonest pretense" that all cultures are equal. It has been described as a "threat to liberal democracy" and as encouraging a "legal apartheid" that "chains people to their roots"—and insofar as it does so, it amounts to the "racism of anti-racists." Central to these criticisms is the assumption that multiculturalism constitutes a threat to nothing less than the civilizational roots of contemporary liberal democracies. While many of these arguments might easily be written off as emanating from the fringe right wing, in fact, views not much different have been embraced by members of more mainstream conservatism as well.

One prominent example, written specifically about the United States in the post-9/11 context, is Harvard political scientist Samuel Huntington, who has been a key spokesperson for the "clash of civilizations" thesis. In *Who Are We?* (2004), he addresses what is perceived to be the serious threat to security and national identity that the nation confronts. While one might have thought that in the "age of terror" the threat is represented in the form of Islamic extremists with allegiances to Al Qaeda, curiously the focus of his concern is with Mexican immigrants. Arguing that the United States has been from its birth up to the present a nation fundamentally shaped by its Anglo-Protestant roots, he sees the presence of large numbers of Mexican immigrants as posing a distinct threat to that culture. In a nation that has proven to be a graveyard for languages other than English, the fact that Spanish can be heard on the streets of America is portrayed as a disturbing development. Although for an earlier era of Catholic immigrants, Americanization was the order of the day, Huntington (2004, p. 254) seems convinced that Mexico's "culture of Catholicism" will for the foreseeable future work against today's Catholic immigrants following the same path to inclusion as their predecessors. In the case of language, he ignores the evidence of rather rapid transition to English by the second generation, while in terms of the second generation, he appears to think that Mexicans are the deterministic product of their (static) culture, in contrast, for example, to earlier Catholic groups such as the Italians.

Huntington's relevance for the topic at hand is that he considers multiculturalism to be a "challenge to the core culture." It is worth quoting him at length to get a sense of why he thinks this is so:

> Multiculturalism is in its essence anti-European civilization. It is, as one scholar said, a "movement opposed to the monocultural hegemony of Eurocentric values, which has generally resulted in the marginalization of other ethnic cultural values. . . . [It is opposed to] narrow Eurocentric concepts of American democratic principles, culture, and identity." It is basically an anti-Western ideology. Multiculturalists advance several propositions. First, America is composed of many different ethnic and racial groups. Second, each of these groups has its own distinctive culture. Third, the white Anglo elite dominant in American society has suppressed these cultures and compelled or induced those belonging to

other ethnic or racial groups to accept the elite's Anglo-Protestant culture. Fourth, justice, equality, and the rights of minorities demand that these suppressed cultures be liberated and that governments and private institutions encourage and support their revitalization. America is not and should not be a society with a single national culture. (Huntington, 2004, p. 171)

As we proceed to examine philosophical arguments on behalf of multiculturalism and the ways multiculturalism has been put into actual practice in a select number of nations, we will be in a position to see that, contrary to Huntington's argument, these four points do not inevitably and necessarily lead to the utter fragmentation of a national culture into a congeries of particularistic ethnic cultures and likewise that the idea of maintaining differences can exist simultaneously with a shared national identity. Suffice it to say at this point that each of the world's liberal democracies is home to intellectual counterparts to Huntington, equally critical of the multicultural experiment.

The purpose of this chapter is to treat multiculturalism as a mode of incorporation, and as such, as an approach to inclusion that either constitutes an alternative to assimilation, a complement to it, or a new version of assimilation. It should be noted at the outset that this is not the way many commentators have construed multiculturalism. Tempered critics of multiculturalism—those not prepared to see it as a threat to civilization—seldom consider the possibility that it might constitute a mode of democratic inclusion. While we focused on conservative challenges previously, in fact, such critics are varied and can be found across the political spectrum, though it is true that those on the political right are more inclined to be hostile to multiculturalism both as an ideal and as policy. The arguments against multiculturalism fall into four broad categories of complaint. The first argument is that multiculturalism is divisive and, as such, it threatens national unity. This was the crux of Huntington's argument.

It was also the thesis advanced in far more circumspect terms by the late historian Arthur Schlesinger, Jr., advocate for the "vital center," in his highly influential *The Disuniting of America* (1992). Counterparts to this thesis have been advanced for other nations, such as Reginald Bibby's critique of Canadian multiculturalism in *Mosaic Madness* (1990). Second, the inverse of this argument is that multiculturalism results in the ghettoization of marginalized populations. The assumption in this claim is that promoting tolerance for other cultures and advancing programs intended to shore them up over time leads to the members of those cultures being locked in the ethnic community, without the prospect of exit (Bissoondath, 2002; Malik, 2002).

Another critique of multiculturalism originates in the political left. Although often intertwined, this critique actually contains two complaints.

First is the charge that the differentialist focus of multiculturalism results in the erosion of the possibility of forming progressive alliances and coalitions. A particularly influential argument along these lines is Todd Gitlin's (1995) contention that multiculturalism has contributed to the "twilight of common dreams." This argument parallels that of Schlesinger insofar as the assumption is that multiculturalism divides rather than unites—in this case dividing not the nation, but the progressive political left. Put differently, Gitlin thinks that the quest for justice and solidarity posed in universalistic terms yields to aspirations rooted in particularistic cultural values. The second aspect of the left's concerns with multiculturalism—clearly absent in conservative thought—is that one of the unintended consequences of the promotion of a politics of recognition (Taylor, Gutmann, Rockefeller, Walzer, & Wolf, 1992) is that in the process a politics of redistribution is ignored or placed on the back burner (Fraser, 1995; see also Barry, 2001, & Wieviorka, 1998).

Given the controversies surrounding multiculturalism, it is not surprising that when it has taken concrete form in educational curriculums, cultural organizations, the arts, and governmental policies, it has routinely elicited opposition. Such opposition has been most vigorous, not surprisingly, in the wake of traumatic events. Thus, as Tariq Modood (2005) has chronicled, in the wake of the July 7, 2005, Underground and bus bombings in London, some commentators were quick to blame multiculturalism for being an incubator of terrorism. However, it does not require a trauma for intense controversy to materialize in the mass media. Such was the case when Rowan Williams, the Archbishop of Canterbury, in a lecture at the Royal Courts of Justice, explored the idea of the legal recognition of religious identities and touched on the role of sharia law within the Muslim community. Although he did not propose to introduce sharia as a parallel legal structure in Britain, the speech produced a firestorm of protest (Modood, 2008). Media pundits and political activists alike have increasingly begun to talk frankly about what they see as the demise of multiculturalism. In the February 28, 2005, European edition of *Time* magazine, a special report exploring "Europe's identity crisis," asked on the cover, "Is multiculturalism dead?" More recently, Ernst Hillebrand (2008, p. 43), a director of the Friedrich Ebert Foundation, the party foundation of the German Social Democratic Party, wrote, "Multiculturalism—the left's answer to the significant rise in European immigration in recent decades—has failed. It has led to fragmented societies and ghettos of marginalized minorities in which the mutual frustrations of indigenous populations and immigrants have increased."

Those sympathetic to multiculturalism have increasingly come to share the view with the critics that multiculturalism is eroding. For example, in reviewing the short history of official multiculturalism in Australia, Brian

Galligan and Winsome Roberts (2003) describe it in terms of its "rise and demise." In the country where support for multiculturalism remains highest, Canada, a reporter titled an article in the *Toronto Star,* "Canada Could Lose Multiculturalism Critics Warn" (Oliveira, 2008). Given these nationally and regionally specific examples, some recent commentators who have set their sights more broadly on all of the major liberal democracies in the world have concluded that the multicultural moment is over as state policy, social practice, and perhaps as theoretical construct as well (Joppke, 2004; Wolfe, 2003). If true, these assessments signal a radical departure from the earlier purchase of this term in both the academic and public arenas.

Multiculturalism had generated during the past two decades a veritable cottage industry of scholarly and popular publications, primarily but not solely focusing on the advanced industrial nations of the globe. It has been widely used in various ways during the past two decades, including in the depiction of interethnic relations, in the defense of group rights, as a valorization of difference, and as a rationale for new state policies of incorporation. Not long ago, Nathan Glazer (1997) proclaimed that "we are all multiculturalists now," and others have argued that however fitfully and fraught with conflict and unease, the world's liberal democracies have imbibed what might be seen as a multicultural sensibility, even if they have not instituted official policies or offered explicit endorsements of multiculturalism (Joppke & Morawska, 2003; Kivisto, 2002; Pearson, 2001). If more recent critics are correct, these earlier assessments merely managed to capture a fleeting moment that we have now moved beyond.

One conclusion that might be drawn from these potential reversals of fortune is that the term has been the victim of a certain intellectual fashion consciousness. One can, for instance, point to current efforts to find what can be depicted as alternatives to multiculturalism, such as cosmopolitanism (Vertovec & Cohen, 2002) or conviviality (Gilroy, 2005, pp. 121–151). Another reasonable conclusion that might be drawn is that multiculturalism is so tainted by ideological baggage that it can no longer reasonably be assumed to offer the sort of conceptual clarity needed to be a constructive guide to theory construction and empirical research programs, let alone to sound policy. Yet another possible conclusion is that after 9/11, we have entered an "age of terror" that affects a sharp break with the recent past and therefore renders obsolete calls for a politics of difference or for the recognition of group rights.

While clearly plausible accounts, one might question the bottom line conclusion, which contends that multiculturalism has outlived its intellectual utility. Compounding the difficulty in making sense of the term is the fact that in its typical articulation, multiculturalism is generally presented in a fashion that manages to blend or blur its utility as an analytical concept with its expression as a normative precept. David Pearson (2001, p. 129) also notes the significance of context in coming to terms with the particular meaning attached to this "highly contested and chameleon-like neologism whose colours change to suit the complexion of local conditions." Despite these difficulties, we don't think the concept has outlived its significance. Indeed, we suspect that its significance might increase in the future and will attempt to indicate why this might be the case in this chapter. To do so requires acquiring (1) a clearer understanding of the intellectual origins of multiculturalism, (2) the main contours of its most important contemporary philosophical expressions, and (3) the form and content of multicultural policies as they have been implemented in a number of liberal democracies. When these analyses have been completed, we will be in a position to examine multiculturalism as a sociological concept reflecting a new potential mode of immigrant incorporation.

## Cultural Pluralism as Precursor to Multiculturalism

In immigration studies and more generally in the study of race and ethnicity—particularly in the American context—cultural pluralism historically represented the main alternative to assimilation, particularly to the melting pot version of assimilation. The origins of the term occurred not in sociological theorizing, but in moral argument. The principal advocate of cultural pluralism was Horace Kallen, a Harvard-trained philosopher of German-Jewish background. He advanced his argument on behalf of cultural pluralism around the same time that Bourne's case for a "trans-national America" appeared. The argument was first advanced in an article titled "Democracy Versus the Melting Pot," which appeared in *The Nation* in 1915 (later to be republished in a book). During this time, the tide of anti-immigration sentiment was on the rise, and in particular, as a consequence of World War I, German Americans—the second largest European-origin group after the English—found their culture and their social location in the United States under siege. It was a historical juncture when calls for "100 percent Americanization" were widespread. In the article, Kallen contended that the radical demands for the complete deracination of ancestral cultures were antithetical to democratic ideals. Moreover, in what can be read as an early expression of identity politics, he contended that such calls were contrary to an important sense of self-identity, which he saw as based on an appreciation of and identification with one's ancestral heritage. Defining his position as one favoring "cultural pluralism," he sought to provide an alternative to the imagery of the melting pot. In its place, he suggested that America should more correctly be seen as an orchestra. He wrote, "As in an orchestra every type of instrument has its specific *timbre* and *tonality*, . . . so in society, each ethnic group may be the natural instrument, its temper and culture may be its theme and melody and the harmony and dissonances and discords of them all may make the symphony of civilization" (Kallen, 1924, p. 125).

Kallen's orchestra, however, was solely composed of European musicians. He was tone deaf to race. His attempt to find a mode of inclusion that expanded the sphere of social solidarity while simultaneously permitting, indeed encouraging, the preservation of ethnic cultural particularism did not extend to blacks, Native Americans, or non-European-origin immigrants (Schuck, 2003, p. 44; see also Hollinger, 1995). Indeed, Stephen Steinberg (2007, p. 118) has recently pointed out that the subtitle of the previously noted article in *The Nation* was "With Special Reference to the Jewish Group," leading him to ponder, "Was cultural pluralism a specifically Jewish project?" He asked further, "Did it entail an ideology and a politics that were particularly congenial to Jews, given their experiences as a perennial minority that wrestled with the dilemma of maintaining ethnic loyalties while demanding the full rights of citizenship?" (Steinberg, 2007, pp. 118–119). Insofar as this is an accurate characterization of "the project," it called for inclusion into the public sphere and the preservation of ethnic distinctiveness in the private realm.

If cultural pluralism had particular salience for Jews, it was definitely not solely a Jewish project. Rather, over time, it was embraced by many ethnic leaders and opinion makers from the ranks of immigrant groups from eastern and southern Europe. This was evident during the 1940s in the multiethnic circle affiliated with the magazine *Common Ground* that was edited by the Slovenian immigrant Louis Adamic. It was even more evident during what became known as the "ethnic revival" in the late 1960s and 1970s. A key spokesperson for that movement was Michael Novak (noted in Chapter 4); his polemical screed, *The Rise of the Unmeltable Ethnics* (1972), argued that the forced efforts to destroy the ethnic attachments of European immigrants in America had proved to be a decided failure. The reason, he contended, was due to the deeply rooted psychic need to maintain ethnic attachments in order to stave off alienation and meaninglessness. Novak's attachment to the ethnic revival was part of his move from the political left to the right during that time, and he saw in white ethnics a counterforce to the hegemonic liberalism of the era.

Cultural pluralism was, thus, a political project from its inception at least through the fading of the ethnic revival. Was it also an academic project, one that worked at developing it conceptually as a mode of incorporation distinct from, and indeed as an alternative to, assimilation? Steinberg (2007, p. 120) suggests that it was, pointing to the work of Isaac Berkson, particularly his book *Theories of Americanization* (1920), which distinguished between three types of adjustment: Americanization, the melting pot, and a "federation of nationalities" (the last being an idea favored by both Berkson and Kallen).

This idea didn't gain traction until the post–World War II era. Then, scholars such as Nathan Glazer and Daniel P. Moynihan (1963), in their "beyond the melting pot" thesis, and Gordon, in his (1964) earlier-discussed book on assimilation, offered new sociological interpretations of cultural pluralism. Unlike those scholars who saw cultural pluralism as an alternative to assimilation, predicated on essentialist assumptions, these sociologists considered the two to be mutually compatible rather than mutually exclusive; more specifically, they treated cultural pluralism as a phenomenon capable of persisting for some considerable amount of time within the parameters of the trend toward assimilation. Exclusion from the mainstream due to prejudice and discrimination can serve to reinforce ethnic loyalties and attachments. Similarly, homeland politics can strengthen such connections. On the other hand, other powerful forces can be at play undermining such attachments, including a desire to be free from what is perceived to be a limiting and parochial world or a rejection of certain significant ethnic values, such as those pertaining to religion or to gender relations. For those who have not been prevented from entering the mainstream and who are not engulfed in homeland politics, cultural pluralism could largely manifest itself as a backward-looking nostalgia, the stuff of Gans' (1979) symbolic ethnicity.

An intellectual historian looking back on the period dating from the early 1980s would conclude that at the moment the term *cultural pluralism* declined in usage among scholars of immigration (and ethnic relations more generally), the employment of the term *multiculturalism* increased. Indeed, for some observers, it appeared that the latter was merely a synonym for the former. There was one marked difference, which was that people of color were included under the multicultural rubric in contradistinction to the tendency to use cultural pluralism in contexts limited to white ethnics. But is it a synonym? Steinberg, for one, appears to think so.

Writing when pluralist thought was ascendant in American sociology, Steinberg, in *The Ethnic Myth* (1981), argued that the problem with the concept was that it tended to reify culture at the expense of social structure. Put more simply, one cannot understand the character of ethnic life without grounding analysis in terms of the dictates of capitalism and the class structure that it establishes. Class location is the source of social inequality. In his view, "democracy and pluralism are not compatible . . . because pluralist structures tend to reinforce existing class inequalities" (Steinberg, 1981, p. 260).

Writing more than a quarter of a century later, when given the evidence for the erosion of ethnic structures among white ethnics, he contends that proponents of cultural pluralism were advancing an "epistemology of wishful thinking" (Steinberg, 2007, p. 111) insofar as they denied the reality of assimilation's impact. He thinks the same is true of multiculturalism's advocates today (Steinberg, 2007, pp. 124–133). With this charge in mind, we turn to multiculturalism, beginning with a summary account of the main claims of key theorists of multiculturalism.

## The Philosophic Case for Multiculturalism

An immediate challenge to any effort to offer a brief overview of the main propositions of multiculturalism is that the key theorists associated with it are often at pains to differentiate their particular takes on multiculturalism from that of other multicultural theorists. Given that some of these debates strike us as having the character of what Freud called the "narcissism of small differences," it is our goal in this section to lay out as simply and cogently as possible the elements of multicultural theory that are embraced by a wide variety of theorists. In doing so, we should note at the outset that there is a difference between what are sometimes called hard and soft multiculturalists. The emphasis herein is on the latter, the reason of which will become evident when two sections from now we address the topic of modes of incorporation. That being said, we begin with a scholar often located in the camp of the hard multiculturalists: the late Iris Marion Young (1990, 2000). What follows in this section derives chiefly though not entirely from the work of three scholars: the Canadian philosophers Charles Taylor (1998; see also Taylor et al., 1992) and Will Kymlicka (1995, 2001, 2007), and the British social theorist and member of the House of Lords Bhikhu Parekh (2000a, 2000b, 2008). We do not intend to summarize and then compare and contrast the work of these figures. Rather, we will distill from them what we take to be the major component parts of the philosophical argument in support of multiculturalism.

Multiculturalism, as a philosophical position that underpins a political project, begins with a specific answer to the question, "Can people with diverse cultural identities be viewed as equal if in the public sphere they are only considered in terms of universal values, and that which makes them distinctive is ignored?" The answer is, "No." The question is relevant insofar as most of the world's liberal democracies are composed of a multiplicity of cultures. Few places today can be accurately defined as monocultural, with a relatively isolated and small nation like Iceland serving as the exception to the general rule.

Young's (1990) rejection of the claims of universalism begins by questioning whether it can amount to anything other than a disguised form of particularism, namely, the particularism of any society's hegemonic group. What she calls for is a politics of the oppressed that is predicated on the idea of "differentiated citizenship." This type of citizenship plays out in a heterogeneous public sphere where the valorization of different attributes and values in different sectors of that sphere ensure a pluralist politics. In this context, oppressed groups can lay claim to distinctive rights of representation.

Two aspects of her argument have been subject to repeated critiques. The first is that she operates with a remarkably expansive view of which groups are to be included under the rubric of oppressed groups, and thus of who qualifies for the rights of differentiated citizenship. Her American-specific list includes "women, blacks, Native Americans, Chicanos, Puerto Ricans and other Spanish-speaking Americans, Asian Americans, gay men, lesbians, working-class people, poor people, old people, and mentally and physically disabled people" (Young, 1989, p. 261). Joppke (2001b, p. 433) observes that on the basis of this list, something like three quarters of the U.S. population would appear to be candidates for differentiated citizenship.

Second, the rejection of universalism and the embrace of heterogeneity strike critics as a call for group isolation and social fragmentation, which threatens to yield a politics of aggressive self-interest. Anne Phillips (1993, p. 117) contends that Young fails to appreciate the fact that "democracy also includes a vision of people coming to perceive the limits of their own specific interests and concerns, learning to recognize the potential conflicts between their own position and that adopted by others, and acknowledging the wider community to which we all ultimately belong." Jeffrey Alexander (2006, p. 398) sees Young's position as amounting to a call for "recognition without solidarity." He elaborates further in the following passage:

> Contra such group-centered theorists as Iris Marion Young, justice has not become simply a matter of accepting the politics of difference. The goal is not to allow group cultures to become so distanced from one another that their particularity can be recognized and separation assured. Difference can be positively recognized only if the particular is viewed, to again paraphrase Hegel, as a concrete manifestation of the universal. This becomes possible only if civil discourse is expanded to include subaltern communities, an expansion that de-essentializes and "purifies" polluted identities, recognizing differences as legitimate by constructing them as variations on the theme of a common humanity. (Alexander, 2006, p. 259)

Phillips and Alexander have critiqued Young, not as opponents of multiculturalism, but rather as defenders of the soft multiculturalism to which we now turn. Alexander's own perspective on multiculturalism will be discussed in greater detail later in this chapter. At this point, suffice it to say that according to Alexander, his chief criticism of Young's position has to do with its "empirical validity," including her understanding of the ways that culture, institutions, and social movements actually work (Alexander, 2006, p. 400). The linkage between the universal and the particular that he notes in his paraphrasing of Hegel can be seen as a shared ethical perspective of soft multiculturalists, but he insists that not only is it morally preferable but also an empirically accurate assessment of real existing multiculturalisms (see also Lemert, 2004).

Multiculturalism as practice manifests itself in two ways—from minority groups making demands and from the state seeking to manage diversity—that are inherently interdependent. Philosophical arguments on behalf of multiculturalism begin with the former, concentrating on articulating the rationale for such claims. As such, Giuseppe Sciortino (2003) is correct when he describes multiculturalism as "a field for claims-making." More specifically, multiculturalist claims are "political claims expressed by actors on behalf of a social category." According to Taylor et al. (1992), those claims are of a particular type that constitutes a "politics of recognition," or what more commonly has become known as "identity politics" (Kenny, 2004). There is a complex philosophical background to Taylor's ideas, but given our sole focus on multiculturalism as a potential mode of incorporation for contemporary immigrants, we will dispense with reviewing it, simply noting that Taylor's perspective on the self is grounded in a view that stresses its socially and culturally embedded character. From his perspective, one's social and cultural grounding is an essential feature in how one constructs a meaningful existence. At the same time, he does not think that cultures and social locations are deterministic; nor do they necessarily limit one's ability to interact in constructive and beneficial ways with individuals who in terms of backgrounds are different. Rather than repudiate the universal as a sham, as Young was inclined to do, Taylor (implicitly concurring with Alexander) considers the potential for the universal and particular to play out simultaneously.

Recognition refers to the ways that others respond to the individual. On the one hand, recognition entails a call for equal dignity. This appeal is to that which "is meant to be universally the same, an identical basket of rights and immunities" (Taylor et al., 1992, p. 38). Here the politics of recognition calls for seeing beyond that which makes us different—race, gender, religion, and so forth—in order to grasp the significance of a shared humanity. Soft multiculturalists see this as one aspect of a multicultural politics of recognition. In itself, it does not move us past traditional liberal perspectives, which see the goal as to arrive at a state of color blindness, gender blindness, and so forth (Modood, 2007, p. 51). What does distinguish multiculturalism from traditional liberalism is that the call for equal dignity is complemented by a call for equal respect, which is predicated on an appreciation of difference. Taylor et al. (1992, p. 38) write that "with the politics of difference, what we are asked to recognize is the unique identity of this *individual or group*, their distinctiveness from everyone else" (italics added). To act otherwise, he continues, is to repudiate the "ideal of authenticity." Note that two different recognitions are possible here, one that concerns the individual and the other that concerns the group.

The idea of equal respect for groups leads to the need to consider the significance of culture in multiculturalism. Kymlicka (1995) is the multicultural theorist who has most explicitly addressed this topic. Indeed, for him, the starting point involves defining *culture,* which he considers to be "synonymous with 'a nation' or 'a people'—that is, as an intergenerational community, more or less institutionally complete, occupying a given territory or homeland, sharing a distinct language and history" (Kymlicka, 1995, p. 18). This definition serves to limit the type of groups that qualify for multicultural rights to ethnic groups, which can be divided into three types: ethnonational minorities, indigenous peoples, and immigrants. In this regard, he stands in contrast to Young's expansive view, for all the other groups she is prepared to include are excluded from consideration as multicultural claims-makers. As he puts it, "I am not including the sorts of lifestyle enclaves, social movements, and voluntary associations which others include within the ambit of multiculturalism" (Kymlicka, 1995, p. 19).

What claims are appropriate for multicultural groups? Put another way, what are the legitimate rights that such groups, in the interest of justice, demand? In answering this question, Kymlicka makes an important distinction with relevance to immigrant incorporation. He distinguishes between "multination states" and "polyethnic states" (Kymlicka, 1995, p. 11). Multination states are composed of minority groups that have long histories and territorial claims within those states. This includes indigenous peoples such as Native Americans in the United States, First Nations people in Canada, and the Sami in Finland. It also includes ethnonational groups—or nations without states. Examples include Scots and the Welsh in Britain and Catalans and Basques in Spain.

Polyethnic states are composed of groups that reside there because of immigration. While the analytic distinction can be readily understood, when applied to actual existing states, it is difficult to determine which best characterizes any particular state. For example, is Britain a multination or a polyethnic state? If one focuses on the previously noted ethnonational groups, the former seems appropriate, but when one factors in immigrants who have settled in Britain during the past half century from the Indian subcontinent, the Caribbean, and Africa, it is clear that both designations are applicable. That being said, operating at the group and not state level, the distinction between national minorities (the group counterpart to the multination states) and ethnic groups (the group counterpart to polyethnic states) is an important one for Kymlicka because within the distinction is a differentiation of appropriate group rights.

Kymlicka (1995, p. 76) further refines what he means by culture by introducing the idea of "societal culture," which he describes as "a culture which provides its members with meaningful ways of life across the full range of human activities, including social, educational, religious, recreational, and economic life, encompassing both public and private spheres. These cultures tend to be territorially concentrated, and based on a shared language." While national minorities would appear to qualify as instances of societal culture, it is not clear whether the term is appropriate to immigrant groups. Some would claim that it does not seem to apply. Thus, Modood (2007, p. 34) suspects that Kymlicka's work—with perhaps Canada's long-standing struggle with the Québécois independence movement in mind—exhibits a "multinational bias," while Joppke (2001b, p. 435) wonders how immigrants can qualify for minority rights if the purpose of those rights is "access to their own societal culture" and yet such a culture does not exist in the migratory context.

Kymlicka disagrees with the idea that immigrants do not have the potential to access their own societal culture. He does, however, think that their relationship to that culture is different than it is for national minorities insofar as by "deciding to uproot themselves, immigrants voluntarily relinquish some of the rights that go along with their original national membership." But, he goes on, "This does not mean that voluntary immigrants have no claims regarding the expression of their identity." The net result is that his understanding of multicultural rights is that they are differentiated between these two categories of groups, with national minorities legitimately laying claim to a more robust package of rights, while immigrants can only justifiably claim a more limited set of rights.

The signal difference between national minorities and immigrants is that only the former are appropriate candidates for group representation in the political system and thus for some semblance of self-government (Kymlicka, 1995, pp. 144–145). Immigrants have no claim to territorial rights and thus policies providing for regional autonomy, self-rule, and the like (as with Britain's policy of devolution) are inapplicable. What then are the rights that immigrants can reasonably lay claim to? Noting that very few voluntary immigrants seek to avoid integration into the host society's societal culture (the Amish being a classic example of a group that has consciously and assertively opted to avoid inclusion), immigrant multiculturalism concerns what Kymlicka (2001, p. 162) refers to as the "fair terms of integration." Some of the policies that have been enacted that are intended to promote integration in ways that reveal a respect for cultural diversity include antiracist and affirmative action programs designed to combat prejudice and discrimination that leads to marginalization. Multicultural policies are closely linked to educational campaigns, which can include curricular changes in schools to include units on an appreciation of cultural diversity, funding of ethnic festivals, cultural sensitivity seminars in the workplace, and so forth. Yet another aspect of fair terms involves being prepared in various ways to accommodate different cultural practices in public life, in schools, and in the workplace. This can entail offering religious minorities days off from work on important religious holidays or revising dress codes. Finally, though Kymlicka does not stress this point, immigrants can demand and obtain certain group-specific policies aimed at ensuring that they have genuine political voice. This can include special sections in political parties or the design of electoral districts in a manner designed to enhance minority representation in legislative bodies. Throughout this discussion, Kymlicka is insistent on one point: such multicultural policies are not intended to promote marginalization but, on the contrary, to facilitate integration in ways that respect diversity.

Some critics of Kymlicka portray his understanding of culture as too static, monolithic, and what Seyla Benhabib (2002, p. 67) calls "preservationist"— or in short as infected with essentializing tendencies. Benhabib (2002, p. 60) calls into question the very existence of Kymlicka's societal culture, arguing that he "has conflated institutionalized forms of collective public identities with the concept of culture." In a similar vein, Phillips (2007) has recently made a case for "multiculturalism without culture." She doesn't actually mean that culture is irrelevant, but rather that she wants to dispense with reified versions of culture in order to approach "people as agents, not as captives of their culture or robots programmed by cultural rules" (Phillips, 2007, p. 176).

What such an approach fosters is an appreciation of the capacity for intercultural dialogue. If there is one thing that philosophers of multiculturalism share, it is a desire to ground their theorizing in very concrete practices. To that end, in the work of all the figures noted in this section and others as well, one finds case after case that raises questions about how to address the claims making of minority groups. Underlying this focus is a conviction that culture ought not to be construed as an obstacle to intercultural communication. For this to be possible, Parekh (2000a, p. 219) asserts that "a multicultural society needs a broadly shared culture to sustain it. Since it involves several cultures, the shared culture can only grow out of their interaction and should both respect and nurture their diversity and unite them around a common way of life."

Multiculturalism so conceived is thus about the mutual negotiation of the terms of integration, which often involves the extent to which the society will find ways to accommodate particular culturally rooted practices and in other instances requiring the minority culture members to change their practices. We turn to a few examples of some of the issues that have attracted public scrutiny in one or more countries, issues that in various ways get at some of the reasons that multiculturalism is contested and thus politically charged.

The first deals with the issue of whether Muslim schoolgirls (or teachers) should be permitted to wear the *hijab,* or headscarf, in school. This has been in recent years a highly contested issue, especially in France, but in a few other nations of western Europe as well. The reason that this has been so contested in France is due to the nation's commitment to *laïcté,* their version of protecting a secular society by establishing a powerful wall between church and state. Opponents of the *hijab* contend that wearing what is construed to be a religious symbol violates this principle. In addition, some feminist opponents see the practice as serving to perpetuate cultural values that are oppressive to women.

Proponents, on the other hand, argue that wearing a headscarf, just like a Christian wearing a crucifix or a Jew wearing a yarmulke, amounts to no more than an individual seeking to make an expression of religious faith—which ought to be a protected right. They dispute the assertion that religion must be relegated solely to the private sphere, or that a symbolic statement of one's religious identity constitutes a threat to the idea of a secular state. While most proponents do not explicitly note it, they assume that the secular character of modern liberal democracies is not at risk. If it was, they perhaps might reconsider. John Gray (2004, p. 14), for example, is critical of attempts to forbid the headscarf in European schools, contending that "monolithic secularism" is unnecessary and counterproductive and that "religious pluralism" is a far more reasonable approach to religious diversity. However, he thinks that such a prohibition might be appropriate in Turkey, a nation with a more fragile democracy and where there is a struggle over the secular state, with a politically ascendant religious party that is considered by some—including Gray—to be a threat to the secular state. The situation in Europe has been a fluid one, reflecting the fact that public opinion is divided over the issue, and that division has played out in a seesaw shifting between permitting and forbidding the wearing of the *hijab.*

It is worth noting that this has been a contested issue in some European countries but not others. For example, it has not sparked the sort of controversy in Britain that it has in France. Moreover, it has not generated conflict in either Canada or the United States. In the latter, the only real challenge to religious clothing occurred when a woman wearing a full burka that covered her face did not want to remove it to have her photo taken for a driver's license. This, as Phillips has pointed out, is not a matter of keeping religion out of the public arena, but rather is concerned with security. As she put it, "I believe it reasonable to expect citizens not to cover their faces in photographs taken for identity purposes" (Phillips, 2007, p. 165).

Our second example is related to this case insofar as it raises a different type of conflict than that involving the separation of religion and the state, pitting the right to wear a religious symbol against a law intended to promote public safety. In 1972, Britain passed a law requiring that motorcyclists wear helmets as a safety requirement akin to requiring the use of seatbelts in cars. Soon thereafter, Sikhs were arrested for refusing to comply with the law and they protested it on the ground that wearing helmets would require adult males to remove the turbans that the religion requires them to wear at all times. They asked for an exemption to the law.

Those opposed to such an exemption did so by arguing that the state has a right and a duty to ensure the safety of citizens, helmets have proven to be an important element of motorcycle safety, and such laws ought to be applicable to everyone. The counterargument was that if an adult male Sikh capable of making an informed decision concludes that remaining faithful to the dictates of religious practice are more compelling than the safety afforded him by a helmet, he ought to be permitted to wear his turban without risk of arrest for violating the helmet law. In addition, turbans did offer some protection—not as much as a helmet, but protection nevertheless. Four years later, lawmakers concluded that an accommodation was warranted and thus they amended the law to exempt Sikhs from wearing helmets. Parekh (2001a, pp. 243–244) points out that this arrangement was subsequently extended to an exemption to wearing hardhats at construction sites. In both instances, the law stipulated that if a turban-wearing Sikh was injured, he or she could only claim damages for injuries that would have been inflicted had the individual been wearing a helmet or hardhat. "Such an arrangement," he concluded, "respects difference without violating the principle of equality, and accommodates individual choice without imposing unfair financial and other burdens on the rest of their fellow-citizens." On the other hand, Phillips (2007, pp. 112, 165) observes that the decision to create an exemption was made with the advice of scientific experts informing MPs that a turban afforded a degree of protection. She concludes that if experience indicated that Sikh cyclists and construction workers were incurring far more head injuries than the rest of the population, it would be right for the Parliament to revisit the exemption.

A different form of accommodation involves dietary requirements based on religious regulation. Muslim parents in Britain petitioned to have *halal* meat served in the cafeterias of state schools. The plan was challenged by animal rights advocates who contend that the slaughtering practices used to produce *halal* meat (and *kosher* meat) inflict unacceptable levels of pain and suffering. In both instances, animals are not stunned before being slaughtered and thus are conscious when their throats are slit. In this instance, the conflict pits a religiously defined practice against the ethical standards of the host society.

Given that not everyone in the host society agrees with the views of the animal rights movement, there is nothing approaching consensus about whether a ban on such slaughtering practices ought to be enacted. Thus, in Britain it remains permissible to both engage in such practices at the abattoir and to serve meat from these sources in state-funded schools. While this has not been an issue that has elicited much public debate in the United States, because of the fact that the largest *kosher* meat-processing plant in the country in Postville, Iowa, engages in practices that meet state requirements, the outcome would likely be the same there. However, as Parekh (2001a, p. 274) points out, if public opinion changed such that a majority of people in a society were opposed to actions that increased the likelihood that animals would suffer unduly, a prohibition on such slaughtering practices would be appropriate. He notes that such was the case in Norway. After extensive intercultural dialogues that included the Jewish and Muslim communities in the nation, a ban was enacted with the consent of both religious groups.

In contrast to animal slaughter, Western nations have uniformly been opposed to permitting female circumcision. There are three forms of female circumcision, with the "traditional" form being the least radical (it has been described as a parallel to male circumcision). The other two amount to more radical procedures: one involves the removal of the clitoris and all or part of the labia minor, while infibulation entails removing the clitoris, labia minor, and part of the labia major, and requires stitching the two sides of the vulva. The two more radical forms of circumcision are practiced in about 25 countries; some nations with large Muslim populations practice one or both of these forms, while others do not. Parekh (2001a, p. 276) summarizes the major arguments advanced in favor of the practice. One claims female circumcision is a religious or cultural requirement and is linked to a way of life. Another states that in regulating sexuality, it protects the girl's virginity and thus enhances her marriage prospects, while simultaneously tampering down her sexual urges.

Agreeing with Taylor that we need not treat all cultures and all cultural practices as equal and as worthy of respect, Parekh (2001a, pp. 277–278) engages in an "intercultural evaluation" and concludes that the practice cannot be condoned. He argues that the harm—both physical and psychological—far outweighs the case on behalf of religion, culture, or a way of life. Although Parekh does not elaborate on the health risks, these include the potential for excessive bleeding and infection, traumatizing pain, and an increased potential for contracting HIV/AIDS and other sexually transmitted diseases. Likewise, he disputes the claim that this is a legitimate form of sexual regulation. Moreover, given that the practice generally applies to young girls, the fact that they are not in a position to make an informed independent decision also weights heavily in his assessment. His opposition is far from controversial. In fact, female circumcision is illegal in many countries. It is a federal crime in the United States to perform either of the two radical procedures on a minor. It has been a crime in Britain since 1985, and recently efforts have been made to address underground circumcisions and the practice of taking young girls to Africa to have the procedure performed. Similar prohibitions can be found in other liberal democracies. Moreover, a joint report prepared by several United Nations agencies, including the Office of the High Commissioner for Human Rights, UNESCO, and WHO, calls for the "elimination of female genital mutilation" (United Nations, 2008). The shift in language from talk about female circumcision to that of genital mutilation is revealing about the extent to which the practice is condemned.

These and numerous other examples reveal the negotiated character of multicultural practice. When multiculturalism becomes state policy or practice that is not part of formal state policy, it does so in ways that reflect the particularities of national social conditions and cultures. As a consequence, there is no single, uniform type of multiculturalism. The next section offers thumbnail sketches of the emergence of multiculturalism in a select number of countries. This will be followed by an attempt to offer a sociological typology of multiculturalism in an effort to understand what it means to treat it as a mode of incorporation.

## Multiculturalism as Policy and Practice

Although multiculturalism's origins as social policy and state practice are varied, it is generally agreed that the first nation to sketch out the contours of what has come to be defined as multiculturalism is Canada. Multiculturalism in Canada was conceived as an alternative to the assimilationist model of the United States. Multiculturalism's ideological roots are located in the popular understanding of the nation as a mosaic—with the idea of an identity based on discrete tiles constituting the constituent elements of a national portrait—rather than a melting pot (Kivisto, 2002, pp. 85–101; Porter, 1965). The underlying historical context involved policy efforts on the part of the Canadian government to respond to an increasingly restive and militant Québécois nationalist movement.

Canadian national identity had been defined in terms of the distinctive identities of the nation's two "charter groups," the English and the French. According to Gilles Bourque and Jules Duchastel (1999, p. 185) the bifurcated model "made very poor use of the concept of nation; rather, it focused on the idea of a *community of citizens*," which contained an understanding of a shared system of universal entitlements brought about by the welfare state. However, the bifurcation was based on an asymmetrical relationship wherein the Anglophone community occupied a superordinate position vis-à-vis the Francophone community.

This was the context wherein the mobilization of the Francophone community began first with a movement of civil rights known as the Quiet Revolution that in effect was a counterpart to the civil rights movement in the United States and moved in short order to a more militant phase that called for the independence of Québec. The left-of-center Canadian government reacted to this incipient ethnonationalist movement by promoting a policy of biculturalism. This included downplaying the hegemony of British influence in various symbolic forms, such as changing the Canadian flag from a modified Union Jack to an innocuous maple leaf. It also involved more substantive policy initiatives aimed at elevating the status of French Canadian culture, seen most explicitly in the inauguration of policies promoting official bilingualism.

Biculturalism was, however, short lived due to the combined impact of mobilized First Nations people and the new immigrants arriving in Canada during this time who revitalized what had become known as the Third Force—immigrant groups other than the English and French. The latter had until the 1960s chiefly been composed of European immigrants, including large numbers of displaced persons from Eastern Europe who arrived in Canada in the immediate aftermath of World War II. However, a new wave began to arrive from the nations of the south, and they transformed the ethnic dynamics of the nation, particularly its major cities. Thus, Canada was confronted not only by an ethnonationalist movement with a separatist agenda embraced by many Francophones, but by an aboriginal rights movement and the presence of new immigrants demanding integration policies that respected their cultural backgrounds. In short order, biculturalism gave way to multiculturalism, particularly under the Trudeau administration (Breton, 1986).

Canada became the first nation in the developed world to officially enshrine multiculturalism into its constitution, doing so in 1982. In 1988, this multicultural provision took legislative form in the Multiculturalism Act. As part of a national identity-building project, multiculturalism meant that the official stance of the Canadian government was to repudiate the earlier valorization of a homogeneous Anglophone culture in favor of a plurality of cultures. To this end, unlike the United States, Canada appeared prepared to promote ethnic group rights as well as individual rights. However, from the point of view of elected officials and government bureaucrats, the purpose of multiculturalism was not to balkanize the nation, but rather to find a new modus vivendi for achieving national unity. At its most elemental, it was intended to ensure that Québécois nationalism did not result in the breakup of Canada, but beyond ethnonationalism, it saw in multiculturalism a way of dealing with what the left-of-center sector of the dominant culture saw as the legitimate grievances advanced by First Nation's advocates and the need to find new tools to integrate the current wave of immigrants (Harles, 1997).

According to a summary report written for the Canadian Parliament, there were four key policy objectives: (1) to help cultural groups preserve and nurture their identities, (2) to overcome barriers to full societal inclusion, (3) to facilitate intercultural exchanges, and (4) to prepare immigrants to succeed in Canada by learning "at least one of the official languages" (Dewing & Leman, 2006, p. 4). Thus, multiculturalism in practice has meant that ethnic groups are permitted to maintain aspects of their ancestral heritages, and that at times the state will play an interventionist role in protecting ethnic group claims. Such has been the case in terms of federal legislation designed to elevate the status of French as one of the nation's two official languages. Multiculturalism led to the ill-fated effort to have Québec defined as a "distinct society" with veto powers unavailable to other provinces in a series of proposed constitutional amendments known as the Meech Lake Accord. On the other hand, it has provided the rationale for the funding of a wide range of ethnic cultural pursuits, particularly such symbolic practices as ethnic festivals and the promotion of ethnic art, music, and so forth. In the case of aboriginal peoples, it led to the creation of Nunavut, a new political jurisdiction for the Inuit carved out of the Northwest Territories.

Canada was not alone in becoming a multicultural nation. Australia, though lacking an ethnonationalist separatist movement, was similar to Canada insofar as it confronted an increasingly restive Aboriginal rights movement and the impact of mass immigration, particularly the migration of non-whites, particularly Asians. Patterning their legislation after the Canadian model, Australia became the second, and, to date, only other developed nation to develop an official multicultural policy. In doing so, it replaced the short-lived policy of integration. While there were similarities between integration and multiculturalism, there were two significant differences. First, based on the assumption that multiculturalism necessitated a reduction in racism, the government assumed a more proactive role in the protection of rights of individual minority members than it had in the past. Second, multiculturalism meant not merely tolerating the presence of difference, but viewing the core of

Australian national identity as embedded in the notion of diversity. This implied that national identity was not to be construed as fixed in the past, but rather as fluid and future oriented.

Canadians are more supportive of multiculturalism than are the citizens of other liberal democracies. That being said, they often embrace the ideal of a diverse and multicultural society more than they are prepared to endorse specific state-sponsored multicultural policies. Residents of Québec are the least sympathetic to multiculturalism. Rather than following the other provinces by establishing a multicultural plank that parallels the federal government, they call their policy "interculturalism," and as Michael Dewing and Marc Leman (2006, p. 12) observe, "Diversity is tolerated and encouraged, but only within a framework that establishes the unquestioned supremacy of French in the language and culture of Québec." There are critics of multiculturalism in Canada, including very vocal ones, but in general a majority of the population is supportive of a Canadian identity that is inherently multicultural in character.

Stephen Castles (1997, p. 15) has pointed out that multiculturalism in Australia did not promote minority group rights, but rather was articulated at the level of individual rights and obligations and was premised on a commitment to the nation and its legal system, along with "the acceptance of basic principles such as tolerance and equality, English as the national language and equality of sexes." As the New Agenda of 1997 made clear, multiculturalism was to be understood in relationship to "civic duty," which is the term used to locate cultural diversity within a framework of shared values and orientations as citizens. If we accept Russell Ward's (1978) thesis, underlying this articulation of democratic citizenship and solidarity is the frontier-based myth of "mateship." Multiculturalism in the Australian version encourages cultural pluralism or diversity, accepts structural pluralism, and necessitates civic assimilation.

Although the United States did not become an officially, state-sanctioned multicultural society, due to a number of causal variables, it increasingly came to exhibit a multicultural sensibility. Like Australia, the United States did not confront an ethnonationalist challenge, while it was forced to deal with an increasingly mobilized indigenous population and a major new migratory wave. What made the U.S. case distinctive was the emergence of a civil rights movement from within the black community—a movement created by the only involuntary migrants in the nation. This movement originally pressed for equality and integration, but a more militant black power phase would question the desirability of the latter.

Criticism of Anglo-conformity as the appropriate model of incorporation into American society grew from the 1960s, when it was challenged both by white ethnics from southern and eastern Europe (the "unmeltable ethnics" of Michael Novak's title) and by the rise of black nationalism. The red power and Chicano movements would also play roles in critiquing it. Even without multicultural legislation, the federal government, paralleling the attitudes of the general public, was increasingly willing to tolerate and even support manifestations of symbolic ethnicity (the proactive role of the federal government became especially evident with the passage of the Ethnic Heritage Studies Act in 1972).

However, multiculturalism was not merely advanced symbolically. Rather, it took more substantive form in policies that came to constitute "the minority rights revolution," which John Skrentny (2002, p. 4) depicts as rising very quickly during the 1960s as a result of a congeries of "federal legislation, presidential executive orders, bureaucratic rulings, and court decisions that established nondiscrimination rights." The minority rights revolution was generally not equated with multiculturalism, though the parallels to policies elsewhere that were so designated are quite clear. A distinctive feature of these efforts, Skrentny (2002, p. 4) went on to note, was that they "targeted groups of Americans understood as disadvantaged but not defined by socioeconomic class." While many accounts of multiculturalism view it as promoting identity politics in contradistinction to interest politics, this example provides compelling evidence that it is a mistake to treat "identity" and "interest" as antithetical (see, for example, Sciortino, 2003).

Two particular policies stand out as being of singular importance: affirmative action and bilingual education. At least from the perspective of state intent—however difficult it is to specify state intentionality—these policies resemble those enacted in Australia insofar as the focus is on individual members of disadvantaged groups, and not the groups themselves. Thus, the legislative purpose of affirmative action was to assist minority individuals to obtain university admission, employment slots, and business ownership opportunities through a variety of administrative devices. In other words, its purpose is to assist individual upward social mobility. Likewise, the Bilingual Education Act of 1968 was conceived as assisting individual immigrants—chiefly Latinos and Asians—in making the transition from their native languages to English language proficiency. Lawmakers did not see the act as designed to protect or preserve native languages over time. Perhaps the only significant exception to this focus on minority individual rights was the gerrymandering of electoral districts to enhance the likelihood of increasing minority membership in Congress.

Turning to a nonsettler nation, as noted earlier, during the second half of the past century Britain became a site of both ethnonationalist movements and, coincident with the collapse of empire, the mass immigration of residents from various Commonwealth nations. Regarding the former, three movements arose with differing goals and approaches to pursuing those objectives: (1) the irredentism and violence of the republicans in northern Ireland, (2) the peaceful pursuit of greater political autonomy and perhaps independence by Scottish nationalists, and (2) the equally peaceful cultural-ist preservation efforts of Welsh ethnonationalists. Regarding the latter, the initial reaction of exclusionary British politicians and citizens was that the arrival of blacks (the then-blanket term for virtually all immigrants) would lead to, in Enoch Powell's hyperbolic phrase, "rivers of blood." The response of the British government to ethnonationalism varied depending on the particular movement and in part whether the Tories or Labour were in power. Dealings with the IRA ranged from the use of massive force to seeking a negotiated settlement, while the Scottish and Welsh nationalists were variously ignored, challenged, and accommodated (the last with "New Labour" via a policy of "devolution"). Meanwhile, the response to the new immigrants was twofold. First, highly restrictive immigration policies were enacted to stem the flow of new arrivals. Second, there was a concerted effort—grounded in the Race Relations Act and administratively promoted by the Commission for Racial Inequality and Race Relations Councils—to reduce racism and intergroup tensions (Favell, 1998; Solomos, 2003).

None of this was viewed as advancing a multicultural agenda, but as with the United States, Britain increasingly exhibited a multicultural sensibility. In part, this was because many of the initiatives advancing multiculturalism took place in educational institutions, which had been important sites for the percolation of a multiculturalist agenda (Modood, 2005, p. 171). Despite the persistence of racism, the social exclusion of immigrants, and ethnic-based inequalities in socioeconomic well-being, Bhiku Parekh, the lead author of a Runnymede Trust study on multicultural Britain, concluded that it is possible to conceive of a "relaxed and self-confident multicultural Britain with which all its citizens can identify" (Parekh, 2000b, p. x). Indeed, the rationale for the report, *The Future of Multi-Ethnic Britain*, was to identify the chief obstacles to achieving this state and to lay out a wide range of policy initiatives concerning such topics as policing and the criminal justice system, education, the media and entertainment, health and welfare, employment, political representation, and religious pluralism. What is clear from this report is that the advocates of multiculturalism thought it possible and desirable to both promote and sustain diversity while forging a shared sense of what it meant to be British.

As these examples indicate, whether as official state policies or as implicit approaches to ethnic diversity, multiculturalism in practice has meant that at the same time that differences were to be not only tolerated but valorized, there was also an expectation that such an approach would serve the interests of the state insofar as it simultaneously constitutes what Alexander (2001) calls a "mode of incorporation." Alexander treats modes of incorporation in general as processes that bring heretofore excluded, marginalized, and oppressed groups into civic life in terms that make them the relative equals of established members and at the same time facilitates the emergence of new patterns of societal solidarity. Multiculturalism represents but one possible mode of incorporation. As the experiences not only in the previously noted advanced industrial nations, but in many other similar nations as well as poorer nations indicates, the logic of such an approach is predicated on the assumption that multiculturalism threatens neither the core values of liberal democratic societies nor the incorporation of ethnically marginalized groups—both "multinational" and "polyethnic" ethnics, to use Kymlicka's (1995, p. 17) terminology.

## Charting Modes of Incorporation

Kymlicka (2007, p. 108) is quite right that "really-existing multiculturalism in the West is liberal multiculturalism." If there is a lesson to be learned from existing practice-related formulations of racial democracy and multiculturalism, it is that they are designed to serve a dual purpose. On the one hand, they are a response to the demands on the part of marginalized ethnic groups for collective rather than merely individualistic solutions to inequality and exclusion. In other words, they are responses to the claims-making efforts of mobilized groups for recognition and/or redistribution. On the other hand, at least from the perspective of decision makers, policy formulators, and most of the political advocates of some version of group rights, the other objective is to bring heretofore-marginalized groups into the societal mainstream. Moreover, as Alexander and Smelser (1999, pp. 14–15) observe about the United States, but we would argue is more generally applicable, "Although the radical multicultural position advocated by many spokespersons for minority groups seems to contradict [the sense of] connectivity, the actual political and social movements advocating multiculturalism consistently employ a civil-society discourse." In other words, multiculturalism constitutes a "mode of incorporation" that is characterized by a particular type of civil participation. In this formulation, multiculturalism constitutes a complex of strategies pursued by social movement actors, the state, or both in an effort to move toward an ideal of society framed by the ideal of justice and a more expansive understanding of social solidarity.

What follows in this section is an effort to sketch out what is distinctive about this particular mode of incorporation. To do so, it is necessary to move beyond both polemics and the philosophical controversies surrounding multiculturalism in its varied forms, ranging from, to use the distinction employed by Kwame Anthony Appiah (2005, pp. 73–79), "hard pluralism" (e.g., Young and Gray) to "soft pluralism" (e.g., Kymlicka, Parekh, Raz, and Taylor), if a distinctly sociological theoretical framework for multiculturalism is possible. Two such efforts at mapping the terrain offer particularly useful guideposts: Alexander's (2001) essay on modes of incorporation, which received further empirical elaboration in *The Civil Sphere* (Alexander, 2006), and Douglas Hartmann and Joseph Gerteis' (2005) article on "mapping multiculturalism" (which builds on Alexander's work). We turn to these two efforts.

Alexander's thesis, which is intended to offer a theoretical rejoinder to both multiculturalism's conservative critics and to radical multiculturalists (here his exemplar is Young's *Justice and the Politics of Difference* [1990]), is structured around the centrality he accords the civil sphere, which is portrayed by his concept of "fragmented civil societies" (which, as Patricia Hill Collins [personal communication, 2006] has pointed out, is similar to the idea of "imagined communities). "An impartial civil sphere," he contends, "does not necessarily rest upon the kind of undifferentiated, homogeneous, melted social values that conservatives recommend and radicals deplore." His definition of the civil sphere locates it squarely within the parameters of a modern liberal democratic society, as is evident in his emphasis on the individual over the group, and on the reciprocal notions of respect and trust. Thus, he writes that this sphere

is organized around a particular kind of solidarity, one whose members are symbolically represented as independent and self-motivating persons individually responsible for their actions, yet also as actors who feel themselves, at the same time, bound by collective obligations to all the other individuals who compose this sphere. The existence of such a civil sphere suggests tremendous respect for individual capacities and rationality and also a highly idealistic and trusting understanding of the goodwill of others. For how can we grant a wide scope for freedom of action and expression to unknown others—as the democratic notion of civil society implies—if we did not, in principle, trust in their rationality and goodwill? (Alexander, 2001, pp. 239–240)

In this scenario, incorporation entails the permitting of out-group members to move into the civil sphere. This occurs in one of two ways, either because core group members become convinced that the out-group members share a "common humanity" and are thus "worthy of respect" or because they have been required by wielders of power to act as if this was the case (reminiscent of Merton's idea of prejudiced nondiscriminators). Alexander writes,

Incorporation points to the possibility of closing the gap between stigmatized categories of persons—persons whose particular identities have been relegated to the invisibility of private life—and the utopian promises that in principle regulate civil life, principles that imply equality, solidarity, and respect among members of society. (Alexander, 2001, p. 242)

He identifies three incorporation regimes, which he treats as ideal types: assimilation, ethnic hyphenation, and multiculturalism. The first two have had lengthy histories in the United States and elsewhere, while multiculturalism is a historically novel mode of incorporation. By assimilation, Alexander (2001, p. 243) means that individuals are admitted into the civil sphere only when and insofar as they are willing and able to shed their ethnic cultural heritages—in his language, replacing their "polluted primordial identities" with the "civilizing" identity of the core group. In this scenario, there is no intercultural dialogue between the center and the periphery. Instead, the out-group remains forever the alien "other," while its members opt to engage in a strategy of exit in order to obtain an admission ticket to the center. Assimilation thus defined requires that the ticket can only be purchased once the deracination of those traits associated with the marginalized ethnic group has been accomplished.

Although at one level, Alexander's account of assimilation appears to parallel that of many other versions, in fact his view is quite unique. This can be seen in terms of how he locates assimilation historically. Rather than treating it as the dominant mode of incorporation well into the 20th century, at least until the passage of immigration restriction legislation in 1924, he sees it as losing out to the next mode of incorporation by the end of the Civil War, due in part to its inherent instability (Alexander, 2006, pp. 443–450). He distinguishes assimilation from the idea of the melting pot. In so doing, he assumes that it is empirically accurate to conclude that the thorough deracination of old-world traits on the part of marginalized groups proved to be something that to large extent did not happen.

In contrast, the ethnic hyphenation model allows for greater fluidity insofar as it permits to varied degrees the maintenance of certain "primordial" features as the individual outsider is also taking on the cultural characteristics of the core. This mode becomes increasingly viable as the civil sphere gains strength and the core society is less inclined to see itself threatened by the presence of the other. There is some level of tolerance for the cultural traits of outsiders and a lessened demand to abandon all such group attributes. It's this mode and not assimilation that Alexander thinks should be associated with the popular image of the melting pot. Here ethnic identities can be maintained as long as they are confined to the private realm and people embrace the values of the core while in the public realm, thus making "outsider qualities invisible" (Alexander, 2006, p. 432). In his view, American history during the first part of the 20th century can be described as one in which European immigrants from the great migratory wave that occurred between 1880 and 1924 were incorporated chiefly via this mode, while in the case of racial minorities, exclusion rather than incorporation characterized their relationship to the core.

Multiculturalism arose as a repudiation of hyphenation. As Alexander (2006, p. 450) puts it, "Only very recently in democratic societies has such a possibility for [civic] repair emerged. It opens a new chapter in the history of social integration." What differentiates it from the other two modes is that rather than individuals extirpating themselves from their particularistic ethnic identities, either totally or partially, those identities are revalorized and permitted to enter the civil sphere. In the process, the separation between the private and public realms becomes increasingly blurred. Although he does not put it this way, Alexander's argument suggests that it is not only individuals who enter the civil sphere, but minority groups, too. This occurs in a process whereby rather than purifying polluted individuals, it entails the purification of qualities (Alexander, 2006, p. 451). The result is an enlarged, increasingly complex, fragmented, and heterogeneous civil society that makes possible the expansion of democratic participation.

This produces a new relationship between the universal and the particular, which in the other two modes were seen as antithetical. In a multicultural society, "incorporation is not celebrated as inclusion, but as the achievement of diversity" (Alexander, 2006, p. 452). This then makes possible a politics of difference in place of the previous goal of a unified and homogeneous core. In this regard, there is a clear family resemblance to Alexander's views and those of liberal multiculturalists. Like them, he is convinced that difference can be respected and solidarity across difference can be achieved. Like them, he knows that this is not inevitable, as heated group attachments can prevent people across groups from developing a sense of a shared humanity and similarly shared core values that valorize and promote trust, mutual respect, justice, and equality. Given the relative newness of multiculturalism, its potential is not fully apparent. However, the promise it offers is as an alternative to the failure of hyphenation to solve the problem of race—where the prospect of invisibility is not an option (other than for the few who can "pass"). One might add that religion, too, can raise the prospect of not being invisible, as some would especially argue in the case of Islam (Modood & Ahmad, 2007; Modood, Triandafyllidou, & Zapata-Barrero, 2006).

In their effort to map multiculturalism sociologically, Douglas Hartmann and Joseph Gerteis (2005) build on Alexander's framework, but, as can be seen in Figure 6.1, elaborate it to identify four rather than three varieties of incorporation. They do so by considering both the social and cultural bases of societal cohesion. To use Durkheimian language, they do so by distinguishing between social integration and moral regulation. With these two dimensions

**Bases of Cohesion**

| | Substantive Moral Bonds | Procedural Norms |
|---|---|---|
| Individual in Society | Assimilation | Cosmopolitanism |
| Mediating Groups | Interactive Pluralism | Fragmented Pluralism |

*Bases for Association* (left axis label)

**Figure 6.1**    Types of Integration

*Source:* Adapted from Hartmann and Gerteis (2005, p. 224).

in place, they constructed a two-by-two grid containing four distinct types of incorporation: assimilation, cosmopolitanism, fragmented pluralism, and interactive pluralism. From their perspective, the last three can all appropriately be considered as types of multiculturalism. Although Hartmann and Gerteis intend their model to be useful in distinguishing competing theoretical perspectives on multiculturalism rather than existing incorporation regimes, we would suggest that it sheds light on the latter, too.

Social integration—or association—occurs either via the singular interactions of autonomous individuals or through the activities of mediating groups. Moral regulation occurs either due to the existence of substantive moral bonds or procedural norms. The former constitutes a "thick" form of regulation, while the latter is a "thin" form. Factored into this framework is the need to consider the respective strengths of both internal group boundaries and of external boundaries that out-groups confront.

With this in mind, their view of assimilation parallels that of Alexander. This mode of incorporation stresses the individual rather than the mediating group. At the same time, it involves a thick form of regulation based on "mutual responsibilities" that connect the individuals to the center while detaching them from the ethnic group. This type is possible insofar as internal group boundaries are sufficiently weak to permit individuals to exit, while the boundaries of the society as a whole (read: the nation) are strong enough to keep individual members bounded and bonded to shared values. As with

Alexander, Hartmann and Gerteis contend that this assimilative incorporation regime demands the absence of particularism in the civil sphere, but is generally prepared to permit it in the realm of private life. They are speaking about theories and not real-world examples of their types. However, based on their description, it would be reasonable to conclude that France is perhaps the exemplar of this particular type of society—its republican ideal being antithetical to multiculturalism (Kivisto, 2002, pp. 170–184).

Cosmopolitan multiculturalism is akin in many respects to Alexander's interstitial category, ethnic hyphenation—although with one significant difference. A cosmopolitan multiculturalism is one that values diversity. As with assimilation, the individual rather than the mediating group serves as the basis of association, and therefore in this version of multiculturalism, neither group rights nor the constraining impact of groups over individuals is endorsed. Instead, the operative terms characterizing such a society are fluidity and hybridity as individuals exercise their ethnic options, picking and choosing which aspects of their ethnic cultures to embrace and which to discard. This occurs in a dialectical process whereby both newcomers and existing core members of the civil sphere exhibit a willingness to change as a result of interacting with others. This is a society where ethnic attachments are thin and the manifestations of ethnicity are typically symbolic rather than instrumental. The main difference between Alexander's hyphenation and cosmopolitanism is that in the former, the public and private clearly divide the place where the particular can be acted out. In a cosmopolitan setting, by contrast, individuals can in various ways manifest their distinctiveness in the public sphere. Toleration of difference, if not valorization, is the order of the day in such a setting. Invisibility is not a requirement. Again, if one were to point to an existing society that most closely resembles this type, the United States or Britain could be identified.

By contrast, fragmented pluralism is depicted as being furthest removed from the assimilation model. Here the center does not hold, as mediating groups take on a salience not evident in the other models. Incorporation means inclusion into group membership, or as Hartmann and Gerteis (2005, p. 231) put it, fragmented pluralism is "assimilation *into* group difference." This type is far removed from Bhikhu Parekh's (2000a, p. 219) earlier-noted assertion that multiculturalism cannot exist without being grounded in a broadly shared culture. It is also a prospect that Alexander would object to on both moral and empirical grounds.

At the theoretical level, they (concurring with Alexander) depict Young's work as perhaps most reflective of this perspective. They also point to Afrocentrism. However, their empirical example derived from the idea of "segmented assimilation" is problematic. They depict segmented assimilation as amounting to entry into distinctive sectors of society that both in terms of related patterns of cultural values and social interaction function in isolation from other sectors. In the first place, we think this is a misreading of what Portes and others associated with the idea of segmented assimilation meant. Furthermore, as the work of Elijah Anderson (2000) makes clear, the adversarial culture of the streets exists in dialectical relationship and tension with the culture of "decent people." Likewise, for scholars of the new immigrants, while the civil society they enter is fragmented, there are nonetheless linkages that prevent the society's sectors from being totally isolated from each other. There is no existing society among the world's liberal democratic regimes that fits this model. Indeed, to the extent that multiculturalism in a product of elite decision making—political and/or cultural elites—it is inconceivable that any elites would actively endorse or promote such societal balkanization.

The third type of multiculturalism is dubbed "interactive pluralism." Hartmann and Gerteis (2005, pp. 231–235) consider this type to be what both Alexander and Taylor mean when they speak about multiculturalism. One might add that it also appears to be the form most closely resembling the perspectives advanced by Kymlicka and Parekh. Here mediating groups play a central role in defining associative patterns, but in such a society, not only do group members interact with nonmembers; the groups themselves enter into dialogue and interaction with other groups. Not only is such a society characterized by the politics of recognition, but groups, like individuals, open themselves to being influenced and changed by the very process of intergroup interaction. Interactive pluralism shares with assimilation a premium placed on substantive moral bonds as a basis of societal cohesion. It differs insofar as those bonds—indeed, the character of the core culture itself—are subject to redefinition through what Hartmann and Gerteis (2005, p. 232) refer to as a "democratic hermeneutics in which understanding the 'other' involves a new understanding of the self." The two nations that come closest to this version of multiculturalism are Canada and, to a somewhat lesser extent, Australia.

Multiculturalism, in either of its two viable forms—cosmopolitan or interactive—constitutes a political project. The former can be viewed as a thinner version of multiculturalism, with its emphasis on individuals and its resistance to the idea of group rights. The latter, by contrast, offers a thicker version that is prepared to entertain the idea of group rights in addition to individual rights. Whether and to what extent the project of institutionalizing either of these forms of multiculturalism is realized in any particular society depends on the outcome of the dialectical tension between the competing demands of outsiders seeking incorporation and states seeking to manage diversity on their own terms. There is nothing inevitable about multiculturalism, and it ought not to be construed as an achievement that once settled is permanent. Rather, if it exists, it does so only as long as it is an ongoing accomplishment, revised and reconstituted in response to historical contingencies. In this regard, Kymlicka (2007) has recently pointed out that the institutionalization of multiculturalism has been increasingly influenced by the role of international intergovernmental organizations.

Both Alexander and Hartmann and Gerteis point out that liberal democratic states have an older mode of incorporation available to them: assimilation. It may well be the case that some states, like France, will continue to resist multiculturalism in favor of assimilation (despite the shock of the events in that nation during the fall of 2005), while others who took steps toward becoming multicultural will retreat and return to assimilation (Brubaker, 2001; Kivisto, 2005), witnessed in the Netherlands, for example, after the murder of Theo van Gogh (see Vasta, 2007, for an account of the shift away from multiculturalism in the Netherlands as a consequence of the legacy of pillarization, which downplayed the integrative aspects of multiculturalism). What they don't mention, but which is yet another option, is the development of policies that result in the exclusion and/or marginalization of the racial or ethnic other. Such a course of action would ratchet up the level of societal conflict (Esman, 2004). In other words, states can resist pursuing any mode of incorporation altogether. For their part, the ethnic or racial outsider may decide to reject or resist incorporation because the society is viewed as unjust, illegitimate, or morally suspect. If this was an avowed group or partial group claim, it could be seen as the quest for fragmented pluralism.

While the main task of this chapter has been to lay out a conceptual framework for making sense of multiculturalism as an incorporation regime, it should be noted at the end that there is a moral dimension to the argument. Alexander (2001, p. 247) concludes his discussion of multiculturalism by asserting, "Multiculturalism is a project that can be attempted only in a situation of increasing, not diminishing, feelings of common humanity." The recognition of individuals not only as individuals but as members of distinct groups, along with the desire to create more just and egalitarian societies, constitutes the moral basis of multiculturalism (Kivisto & Faist, 2007). Whether or not citizens acting in concert—in cooperative and conflictual situations—manage to advance the ethos of a common humanity characterized nevertheless by differences that can be respected and valorized will prove to be crucial to the prospects of the project.

# SECTION III

## Control

# 7

# The State and Immigration Control

Who should get in? While many people in immigrant-receiving nations ask (and sometimes have strong opinions about) this question, it is states alone that maintain a monopoly on providing definitive and enforceable answers to it. States are responsible for enacting policies that ultimately determine who does and who does not get in. They determine the criteria by which potential entrees will either be accepted or rejected. Furthermore, states are responsible for enforcing immigration laws, which includes dealing with people who enter countries without legal permission to do so. When summarized in such a succinct fashion, it is clear that states play a major role in shaping immigration flows. Nevertheless, as James Hollifield (2000) has contended, political scientists (and, we might add, political sociologists) have been slower to address the topic of immigration than their social scientific counterparts in sociology and economics. The net result, he contends, is that the role of states has been underanalyzed, and thus he has issued a call to "bring the state back in" (a similar call was made by Aristide Zolberg, 1981, years earlier). This chapter and the following one do precisely that.

Prior to the 18th century, borders were not subject to widespread and systematic management. States had not yet established the highly bureaucratized formal systems of border control that became a characteristic feature of the contemporary world, though precursors to such elements of control as the modern passport system can be traced back as far as Ancient Egypt and the Roman Empire. Travel across borders often took place with relative ease and informality. Often, letters of introduction sufficed to permit movement from one jurisdiction to another. Some date the birth of the modern passport system to the latter part of the 17th century, when Louis XIV required identification papers for all individuals seeking to either leave or enter France. The passport reinforced the distinction between citizen and noncitizen while also serving to enhance the surveillance capabilities of states—providing not only personal identification information about the passport holder but also monitoring the individual's movement outside the state (Torpey, 2000). Citizens are required to possess a passport if they seek to travel outside of their nation, and they cannot reenter without it. Likewise, their passports can be confiscated in some circumstances, such as when they are accused of a crime and judged to be potential flight risks while out on bail.

Noncitizens must be in possession of a valid passport from the nation where they derive their citizenship. Beyond that, states require visas for entry and have considerable discretion in either granting or denying visas. In the post-9/11 United States, for instance, this has led to a growing tendency to deny access or to delay the review process in ways that make travel into the country increasingly difficult. This situation has received media attention, but only insofar as it has affected entertainers. This applies to high-profile performers such as the British singer Amy Winehouse, who has a history of illicit drug use and as a consequence was originally denied a visa that she sought in order to attend the Grammy awards, where she was an award nominee. However, it also affects others who are not so well known and who do not appear to have histories of legal problems. This includes artists in theater, film, music, and dance (Lee, 2008). But the issue goes far beyond entertainers. Aware of the fact that some of the individuals involved in the terrorist attack on the World Trade Center and the Pentagon were in the United States with expired student visas, in the intervening years it has become far more difficult to obtain such documents. This has led critics of government policy to contend that since 9/11, it has done much to promote a "fortress America" mentality—an inward-focused society, wary of the larger world.

Immigration legislation and policy needs to be understood in this larger context. It should be construed as a subset of a larger state agenda to set the parameters for legitimate movement across national borders. In this regard, Aristide Zolberg (1999a) has argued that in recent decades, on the continuum between advocating open borders and closed borders, wealthy states have opted for positions closer to the latter. The case for open borders advocated by free market spokespersons of a libertarian streak, such as those affiliated with the Cato Institute, has not managed to gain political traction in policy circles. Even less influential in public debates is the case made on behalf of a populist version of globalization, such as the case advanced by Jonathan Moses (2006), to abolish all immigration restrictions. Despite what appears with a cursory examination of public opinion to be a preference for more- rather than less-restrictive immigration policies, the flow of migrants—legal and undocumented—continues apace, resulting in what some see as a disjunction between aspiration and reality (Freeman, 1995).

Some link this situation to what Martin Heisler (1986) has referred to as the "diminished autonomy of the modern democratic state." This diminishment has been attributed by some to the presumed growing significance of trans-state entities such as the United Nations, the European Union, and congeries of INGOs that are responsible for promoting a global human rights regime. The result, according to Heisler (1986, p. 162), is that states have not been replaced by such organizations, but rather have less room to initiate new actions and thus are left "muddling along." Not everyone agrees with this assessment or with the conclusion that the diminishment is inevitable (see, for example, Beckfield, 2008). Gary Freeman (1994), for one, contends that the capacity of states to control migration, though somewhat variable from state to state and from one time period to another, has in general grown rather than declined in recent decades. Thus, the implementation of points systems has created a new mode of control of legal migrants, enhancing the ability to choose selectively. Moreover, when states focus on reducing the number of immigrants entering under family reunification schemes, states have greater control. Writing during the last decade of the 20th century, he contends that the reason for high levels of illegal immigration is that states have simply not made use of the power they have to contain their borders and to reduce the number of permanent immigrants by implementing temporary workers schemes. He considers regularization efforts less a sign of state weakness and more a realistic response to employer needs. The bottom line for Freeman (1994, p. 29) is that "democracies have more and better means to control their borders, monitor foreigners within their territories, and manage international flows than they did twenty, fifty, or one hundred years ago." Suffice it to say, this view has been challenged by many other scholars and diverges from commonly held views of the public at large.

## Controlling Immigration

Postville, Iowa, a rural town of about 2,200 located in the rolling hills of northeast Iowa, would appear to be an unlikely epicenter for a debate over immigration control. However, when Immigration and Customs Enforcement (ICE—formerly known as the Immigration and Naturalization

Service) agents stormed into the Agriprocessors kosher meatpacking plant—the largest in the nation—and detained 389 workers, it was thrust into the spotlight. This proved to be the largest immigration raid in the nation's history ("Iowa Lawsuit," 2008, p. 15). A majority of those detained were from Guatemala, with a sizeable contingent from Mexico, as well. Among the charges leveled against the workers were felony violations for aggravated identity theft and the false use of social security numbers. Rather than being arrested and quickly deported, the workers faced serious prison time if convicted of these charges.

Like many other small farming communities in the Midwest, Postville's population had been declining for decades after World War II, and business closures were common. This changed in the mid-1980s when a Brooklyn butcher and member of the Chabad-Lubavitch movement purchased a vacant meat processing plant and reopened it as a kosher plant. A Hasidic community developed as several hundred former urbanites (many from Crown Heights in Brooklyn) settled in Postville, setting off what journalist Stephen Bloom (2000) has described as a "clash of cultures." At the same time, they hired workers at the plant chiefly from the ranks of Mexican and Central American immigrants, which further increased the community's population base and added to its cultural diversity. While the Jewish community created a separate sphere of social life for itself, including religious schools, the Latino population sent their children to public schools and attended mass at the local Catholic church. Although cultural tensions were very real, many established residents of Postville were keenly aware of the fact that these newcomers had introduced new vitality into what had been a declining community.

It is within this background that the ICE raid needs to be located. A report by a court-appointed interpreter, reinforced by additional evidence, raised serious questions about rights violations against the undocumented workers, leading to an editorial in the *New York Times* ("Shame of Postville," 2008, p. 11) that accused the government of "abusing and terrorizing undocumented immigrant workers," noting that "there is a profound difference between stealing people's identities to rob them of money and property, and using false papers to merely get a job." This raises a question about ICE's motives. What does it say about their approach to undocumented immigrants? The removal of all of the undocumented is a persistent demand of the extremist fringe of the anti-immigration movement, seen in such organizations as the Minute Men, the American Immigration Control Foundation, and the Federation for American Immigration Reform. There is little evidence that such a goal is the objective of the federal government. Not only is it administratively and politically unfeasible to remove millions of people, but it would prove to be economically costly. Two alternative explanations appear to be more likely, and these are not either/or propositions. First, the agency might want to instill fear in the undocumented community nationwide that it hopes might translate into a voluntary decision to return home. Second, it may be treating the raid in symbolic terms rather than as a genuine effort to reduce the total number of undocumented nationwide in an attempt to shore up support from the most vocal anti-immigration elements in the Republican Party. This raises another question: has the state lost control of its borders or is it content to allow somewhat porous borders to persist because key officials know that reducing the number of immigrants—including the undocumented—would be economically detrimental? One thing is clear: the impact of the raid in Postville proved damaging to both the workers and the local community. Most of the arrested served 5-month prison sentences and were then deported. Meanwhile, the slaughterhouse declared bankruptcy (Preston, 2008). The closure of the plant has had such a negative impact on the local economy that officials from the town actually sought (unsuccessfully) disaster relief from state and federal authorities.

Were the consequences of the raid for the local community factored into the federal government's decisions? Or were the results the unintended consequences of policies implemented with different objectives in mind? These are the larger questions to which we now turn. While our first case study will focus on the United States, the same issues pertain to the other advanced industrial nations.

In an influential book on *Controlling Immigration*, the editors structured the collection of essays around two "hypotheses": the gap hypothesis and the convergence hypothesis (Cornelius et al., 2004). The first refers to the disjuncture—or gap—between policy objectives and their outcomes. While much of the attention on gaps focuses on the matter of stemming the flow of unwanted or undesirable immigrants, it can also refer to the incapacity to attract sufficient numbers of immigrants with needed skills and experience. Cornelius and Tsuda (2004, p. 5) identify two types of policy gaps, one resulting from "the unintended consequences of policy" and the other "caused by inadequate implementation or enforcement of policy."

The convergence hypothesis contends that there is a growing similarity in both the articulation and implementation of immigration laws and policies among the world's liberal democracies. While there are more scholars prepared to question this hypothesis compared to the former one, for those who see convergence occurring, the question arises: why? Among the possible explanations, Cornelius and Tsuda (2004, pp. 17–19) identify five that can operate either independently or in tandem. The first is *parallel path development*, which means that the nations in question are sufficiently alike in terms of structural conditions and cultural perspectives to lead to common views regarding what should be construed as beneficial approaches to immigration. The second explanation is *policy emulation,* whereby one state learns from another's experience. A good example of this can be seen in Australia's implementation of a multicultural policy. Policymakers there explicitly patterned their plans along the lines of the Canadian model. A third explanation involves *regional integration.* While the example par excellence is the European Union, the relationship between Australia and New Zealand could also be considered. Whether something comparable is in evidence in North America between Canada and the United States is an open question. While in many respects, the answer would appear to be that such evidence does not exist, the significance over time of NAFTA might possibly change that by moving in the direction of the European Union. A fourth explanation involves the impact of *global events and geopolitics.* Cornelius and Tsuda point to two such events during the past several decades: the economic dislocations resulting from the OPEC oil embargo in 1973 and the securitization of immigration as a consequence of 9/11 and its aftermath (reinforced by the subsequent bombings in Bali, Madrid, and London). Finally, *public opinion* can play a role. While it is quite clear that immigration policies are not directly and explicitly shaped by the public's opinions du jour, politicians and policy administrators cannot simply ignore the sentiment of voters. This can be seen in many cases, including recently the rethinking of multiculturalism in the Netherlands.

## The Gap Hypothesis: Case Study

In order to appreciate the complexity of state efforts aimed at controlling immigration, we turn in this chapter to two case studies. The focus of the first is the United States. This section will address the question of why the efforts to reform immigration laws during the first decade of the current century—during the second Bush administration—have thus far proven to be unsuccessful. In other words, it takes up the question of whether or not the gap hypothesis accurately accounts for the situation. We will first review immigration policy from 1965 through the rest of the 20th century. This will set the stage for an examination of the fate of "The Fair and Secure Immigration Reform" proposal floated by the administration's congressional sponsors, which will be followed by a review of the ensuing legislative stalemate and its impact.

As noted in Chapter 3, the current wave of immigration to the United States—the third major wave in the nation's history—commenced shortly after the passage of the landmark Immigration Reform Act of 1965, which, referring to its Congressional sponsors, is also known as the Hart-Cellar Act. The legislation was passed during the heady days of the Johnson administration's Great Society program, at a time of considerable social upheaval, chiefly due to the combined impact of the Viet Nam War and the civil rights movement. As a consequence, relatively little attention was paid to this legislation at the time by the public at large or by policymakers. It would appear that the sponsors and supporters of the legislation did not envision that the act would become a stimulus for a major migratory wave. Nor did they think that the major source of immigration would shift from Europe to the developing nations of the world. As Daniel Tichenor (2002, p. 18) notes, "Senator Edward Kennedy, one of the bills' principal stewards, assured skeptics that the reform 'would not inundate America with immigrants from any one country or area or the most populated and deprived nations of Africa and Asia'."

## Locating the 1965 Act in Historical Perspective

Gary Freeman (1995; see also Zolberg, 1999b) contends that immigration policy is shaped by the contest of competing interests. In the case of the Hart-Cellar Act, there is a need to locate its policy implications over time in terms of the nation's two-party system—parties with internal divisions and competing interests. In short, both parties have simultaneously contained both pro-immigration and anti-immigration elements (Tichenor, 2002, p. 8). The Republicans have long been home to both free marketers with a desire for expansive immigration laws and cultural conservatives calling for immigration restriction in the interest of cultural unity. On the other hand, the Democrats have had within their ranks both pro-immigration cosmopolitans and economic protectionists (especially, until recently, labor unions). All of these forces were present at the passage of the 1965 legislation, but as became clear, the free market proponents in the Republican Party and the cultural cosmopolitans in the Democratic Party got the upper hand. They were successful because they managed in this instance to forge a cross-party alliance. Perhaps the most significant feature of the act was that it eliminated the essentially racist character of existing law, which had established a rank order of preferred groups based on ethnicity, or to be more specific, on national origin.

Before turning to the new law's specific provisions, it is useful to place it in historical perspective. As a classic settler nation that needed population growth for economic development to occur, the United States has had, comparatively speaking, relatively liberal immigration laws for much of its history. However, the operative word is comparatively. In fact, from the period after the Civil War until the passage of the National Origins Quota of 1924, Congress passed a series of legislative measures that were increasingly restrictive and intended to offer preferential treatment to certain nationality groups at the expense of others (Zolberg, 2006). The first such enactment occurred in 1882, when in response to an anti-Chinese movement that was both growing and becoming increasingly virulent, Congress passed the Chinese Exclusion Act. This particular piece of legislation had a 10-year limit. After that time, new laws were passed that were even more draconian in their effort to put a halt to immigration from China (Lyman, 1974, pp. 63–85).

The nation entered a major wave of new European immigration around this time, but the newcomers came increasingly from origins in Europe that heretofore had not provided immigrants: from southern and eastern Europe. Catholics, Jews, and Orthodox Christians predominated among these groups instead of Protestants. Moreover, given the racial views of the era, many of these newcomers were not considered to be white and thus posed a challenge to the hegemony of white Anglo-Saxon Protestants. As a consequence, an organized movement designed to stem the tide of immigration took form. This movement is chronicled in John Higham's (1970) classic study of nativist responses to "strangers in the land." This included organizations ranging from those operating within the legal system through lobbying efforts, such as the American Protective Association, to violence-prone groups such as the Ku Klux Klan. With the rise of a powerful anti-immigrant movement, Congress enacted a series of laws designed to reduce the flow of immigrants, including a series of literacy test bills that were intended to reduce the number of southern and eastern Europeans from entering the country. This trend to restrict immigrant flows from what were deemed to be undesirable points of origin culminated in the passage of the earlier-noted National Origins Quota. This legislation was actually a revision of a law passed 3 years earlier that imposed numerical limits on immigrants based on their nation of origin, calculated on the basis of the composition of the white population of the United States in 1910. The 1924 law recalculated the quotas based on the 1890 census, in effect further restricting the numbers of permitted immigrants from eastern and southern Europe.

The result of this law, in conjunction with the negative impact on migration of the Great Depression and World War II, was that the migratory wave ended. For the following four decades, the number of foreign-born entering the nation declined significantly. During this period, a variety of laws shaped migration policies. For example, in 1943, a system of contract labor was created that allowed employers to hire Mexican workers for specified periods of time, after which they were expected to return to Mexico. Known as the Bracero Program, this was the U.S. version of what would later be called in western Europe a "guest worker program." This program, which was increasingly opposed by the Mexican American community, was finally terminated in

1964. In the wake of World War II, the flight of people from nations that had fallen under the control of the Soviet Union prompted the passage of the Displaced Persons Act of 1948. The most significant piece of legislation leading up to the 1965 act was the Immigration and Nationality Act of 1952 (also known as the McCarran-Walter Act). While that act reaffirmed the national quota system, it reclassified existing quotas. For example, it ended Japanese exclusion and instituted a small quota for the Asia-Pacific region. It also created a preferential system based on worker skills and on family reunification (Bean & Stevens, 2003, pp. 17–19).

## Hart-Cellar's Content and Impact

With this background, it is evident that the 1965 act represented a significant departure from the past because it eliminated the quota system. In its place was a set of universal selection criteria that commentators such as Christian Joppke (2005, p. 19) have seen as congruent with the ethos of modern liberal democracies. His view is shared by those who focus on the role of rights in immigration policy, such as Hollifield (2000; see Wong, 2006).

The law established a set of criteria that would rank order selective preferences. Originally, it called for 170,000 visas per year for immigrants from the Eastern Hemisphere and 120,000 from the Western Hemisphere. In the former case, a 20,000 maximum limit per country was imposed (Schuck, 2003, p. 85). In the first place, the premium attached to family reunification meant that spouses, minor children, and the parents of U.S. citizens were exempt from these caps, so in effect there was no limit to the number of people falling into these categories who could obtain a visa. Then, seven criteria were established, each being accorded a percentage limit of the total number of visas to be allotted. These seven criteria and the respective percentages of the total are as follows: (1) unmarried adult children of U.S. citizens (20%); (2) spouses and unmarried children of permanent resident aliens (20%); (3) professionals, with preferences given to gifted scientists and artists (10%); (4) married children of U.S. citizens (10%); (5) brothers and sisters of U.S. citizens over the age of 21 (24%); (6) skilled and unskilled workers who are needed to meet specific labor shortages (10%); and (7) refugees (6%).

Contrary to the predictions of the bill's sponsors, the act, when it took effect in 1968, unleashed a major wave of immigration. In fact, during the last decade of the 20th century, more newcomers entered the nation than during any other decade in the nation's history, surpassing the totals from the first decade of that century, heretofore the peak decade. The arrivals came overwhelmingly from Latin America and Asia (but not, partially supporting Kennedy's prediction, Africa). About 75% of the totals originated in these regions during the 1970s and much of the 1980s, with the percentage rising to over 80% thereafter. According to the 2000 Census, over 31 million legal immigrants resided in the United States, representing about 11% of the total population, a figure not reached since 1930 (U.S. Census Bureau, 2002). It should be noted that immigrants represent a smaller percentage of the overall population than they did a century ago. In addition, because until after the turn of the new century, they were heavily concentrated in six states—California, Florida, Illinois, New Jersey, New York, and Texas—their impact in those localities has been profound, while in other locales it was minimal. Perhaps one of the most significant transformations that has occurred due to the new wave of immigration is that African Americans no longer constitute the largest non-European origin group, having been surpassed by Latinos. This has sometimes been referred to in public discourse as the "browning of America."

The impact of immigration during the last three decades of the past century is even more significant than this cursory summary would suggest, for in addition to the influx of legal immigrants, two other categories of newcomers have also contributed to the heightened diversity of American society. The first category is that of nonimmigrant entrants who, rather than becoming permanent residents, are granted visas to be in the country for a specified period of time. While tourists and diplomats fall into this category, by far the two largest groups are temporary workers and students. Many workers in this category are holders of H-1B visas, which permit employers to hire foreign-born skilled workers and allow those workers to remain in the country for 6 years. The enabling legislation contained in the Immigration Act of 1990 allows 200,000 such workers into the country each year. By far, a substantial majority of workers possessing these visas come from Asia and work in the high-tech sector. Since its implementation, the law has been liberalized in various ways, including a provision that allows workers to move from one employer to another. By the end of the 20th century, there were 31.4 million nonimmigrant entrants, a figure roughly equivalent to the number of permanent immigrants. Peter Schuck (2003, p. 89) points out that with the assistance of their employers, "many will become permanent residents despite the program's explicit temporary character and without having to leave the country or even interrupt their employment."

The second category consists of illegal or undocumented immigrants. This includes both persons who entered the country illegally ("EWI's"—entered without inspection—in ICE parlance) and those who entered legally but overstayed their visas (what ICE calls "visa-overstays"). While it is extremely difficult to accurately measure the size of the undocumented population, Schuck (2003, p. 89) writes that estimates based on the 2000 census put the figure at somewhere between 8 and 9 million, with approximately half originating from Mexico and the bulk of the remainder coming heavily from Asia and other Latin American nations. The question this raises is whether or not there is a gap between policy and outcomes. To address this issue, it is necessary to review subsequent immigration policies.

## Policy Refining and Revising Since 1965

Legislation enacted since 1965 has been designed to address two distinct concerns. The first focuses on refugee policy, while the second is intended to both control the flow of labor migrants in general and to deal with the problem of undocumented migrants in particular. Refugee policy was influenced by the exigencies of Cold War politics. Thus, the Cuban Refugee Act of 1966 was in fact a continuation of refugee policies that U.S. administrations had implemented since the communist victory in Cuba and the beginning of the long era of rule by Fidel Castro. The presence of a Marxist government 90 miles off the shore of Florida proved to be a powerful symbol of competing ideologies in the struggle between the United States and the Soviet Union. Not surprisingly, the U.S. government received these political exiles warmly. The 1975 Indochina Refugee Act was passed in response to the U.S. defeat in Vietnam and the subsequent exodus of Vietnamese and other Southeast Asians who had sided with the Americans. This act, in effect, began a resettlement program for these exiles. Two years later, the act was refined to specify that 174,988 Indochinese refugees would be admitted.

The Refugee Act of 1980 was not targeted to specific groups, but rather sought to provide a more coherent set of criteria that could be used universally. The act adopted the definition of "refugee" that the United Nations had developed. In addition, it expanded the annual number of asylum seekers admitted to the country and established procedures by which the Attorney General could facilitate a shift in status from temporary refugee to permanent resident (Tichenor, 2002, pp. 246–249). Despite the effort to standardize and rationalize the system, critics contended that during the Reagan presidency, refugee policies were employed in a discriminatory manner, as asylum seekers from communist-controlled countries—such as Nicaragua—had a relatively easy time of being accepted while those fleeing right wing dictatorships—such as exiles from El Salvador and Guatemala— were frequently denied admission.

Turning to the other type of post-1965 immigration legislation, the first significant initiative was a series of amendments to the Hart-Cellar Act, passed in 1976, that established 20,000 per year as a per country cap on immigrants, applicable to both the Western and Eastern Hemispheres. This was intended to limit the flow of immigrants from some of the major migrant-exporting nations—especially Mexico. Undocumented immigrants became the focus of attention in the Immigration Reform and Control Act of 1986. The key provision of this act was to offer a general amnesty to 3 million undocumented residents under certain conditions. The amnesty made it possible for these individuals to obtain legal permanent residence status. The product of intense negotiating between pro-immigration and anti-immigration camps, the legislation sought to offer something for both sides. On the one hand, it included a provision that imposed sanctions against employers who hired illegal workers (these sanctions proved to be very weak). It also included the creation of a special program for agricultural workers, and it required the establishment of an office within the Justice Department that was created to deal with charges of discrimination against immigrants. The act also contained a provision intended to expand the diversity of the immigrant pool by creating the NP-5 program for residents of nations that had favorable quotas prior to 1965. The three major beneficiaries of this program were Canada, Ireland, and the United Kingdom. Criticism of the Eurocentric character of this program led to a comparable program for other nations in 1988, called the OP-1 program. In both cases, visa recipients were chosen by lottery.

The Immigration Act of 1990 increased the immigration cap to 675,000. Family reunification immigrations continued to receive preferential treatment under the terms of the act. In addition, it contained refined employment-based criteria, including expanding the number of skilled immigrants entering the country. Finally, it also had a "diversity" lottery system, known as the AA-1 system, which replaced both the NP-5 and OP-1 programs (Tichenor, 2002, pp. 244–245).

Anti-immigrant sentiment grew during the 1990s, with a particular focus on the undocumented. The passage of Proposition 187 in California signaled this change, for the referendum called for denying undocumented immigrants various social services, including educational benefits for their children. The Personal Responsibility Act of 1996 followed suit by limiting the access of immigrants—legal and illegal—to public welfare benefits, including Temporary Assistance for Needy Families, food stamps, Medicaid, and Supplemental Social Security (Bean & Stevens, 2003, pp. 66–67). In the same year, Congress passed the Illegal Immigration Reform and Responsibility Act. It was intended to increase border security and to streamline the process for deportation. Employer sanctions were increased (though again, in practice, these proved to be relatively weak and were perceived by many employers as simply a cost of doing business).

## *Immigration Reform in the 21st Century*

This context serves to locate the ensuing battles over immigration legislation in the present century. On January 7, 2004, President George W. Bush announced that he would ask Congress to pass an immigration reform measure that was described as "The Fair and Secure Immigration Reform" bill. The announcement came as plans were being developed for a March 6 meeting with his Mexican counterpart, President Vincente Fox, over border security, immigration control, revisions to the North American Free Trade Agreement (NAFTA), and discussions about the creation of a Central American free trade zone. The announcement also came at a time when the presidential election campaign season was beginning to heat up, and when public opinion polls suggested that it was too early to tell whether economic issues, particularly those associated with the jobless recovery that had resulted in the loss of over 3 million jobs during the Bush presidency's first term, or war and security would be paramount in the minds of voters. The Bush administration played a delicate balancing act, attempting to craft a bill that would garner needed votes from vital constituencies, or at least not alienate them, which included both pro-immigration and anti-immigration forces. According to Carolyn Wong (2006, p. 18), "The Bush proposal was vague, but reflected the demands of the Essential Worker Immigration Coalition (EWIC), which in 2004 represented thirty-six of the nation's largest business and trade associations, including the Chamber of Commerce."

In the words of the White House Web site (www.whitehouse.gov), the Fair and Secure Immigration Reform bill called for the implementation of a

> new temporary worker program to match willing foreign workers with willing U.S. employers where no Americans could be found to fill the jobs. The program would be open to new foreign workers and to the undocumented men and women currently employed in the U.S. This new program would allow workers who currently hold jobs to come out of hiding and participate in America's economy while not encouraging further illegal behavior.

The announced goals of the reform were threefold: (1) to create a more prosperous American economy, (2) to enhance homeland security, and (3) to construct a more compassionate system than the current one.

The Web site went on to describe five principles that were seen as underpinning the plan. The first reflected the administration's effort to frame virtually all of its policy initiatives in light of 9/11 and the claim that the administration has made the nation more secure since the tragedy. Thus, the first principle involves "protecting the homeland by controlling our borders."

Second, the measure was intended to bolster the American economy by matching foreign workers to specific employers in an efficient and timely manner. Third, reiterating the campaign theme of "compassionate conservatism" when Bush first ran for president, the measure was intended to promote compassion by preventing exploitation (it should be noted that the proposal was evasive about how exactly this would be accomplished) and allowing temporary workers to travel back and forth between the United States and their country of origin. Fourth, the plan was designed to provide incentives for temporary workers to return to their homelands after their work period had ended. In this regard, the plan called for a 3-year period of temporary worker status, with the possibility of renewal for an additional 3-year term, after which time the worker would be expected to leave the United States. Finally, the legislation was intended to protect the rights of legal immigrants. What this meant was that the transformation of undocumented workers to documented ones would not place them in the front of the queue for citizenship. This was not, the administration insisted, an amnesty program, for if it was, it would do what critics claimed it did: reward past illegal behavior and encourage such conduct in the future.

Specific provisions of the proposed legislation called for requiring that employers "make every reasonable effort to find an American to fill a job before extending job offers to foreigners." Employers who violated existing workplace laws pertaining to the hiring of illegal workers would confront increased governmental enforcement of those laws. It should be noted that the law did not call for increased penalties, simply for increased enforcement of existing penalties. An incentive to return home—only one—could be identified on the Web site. It was based on what was described as an effort on the part of the U.S. government to forge agreements with migrant exporting countries that would allow temporary workers to receive credit in their nation's retirement system and to promote the establishment of tax-preferred savings accounts that workers could collect once they returned home.

The proposal did not rule out the possibility that some temporary workers might be able to seek U.S. citizenship, but it stated that a temporary worker card did not put the individual on the path to a green card, which is needed if a person is going to be permitted 5 years later to apply for citizenship. There was a studied ambiguity about this aspect of the plan. Without specifying who would be eligible and under what conditions, the Web site stressed two features of what was touted as a "fair and meaningful citizenship process." The first stressed a point made earlier, namely that formerly undocumented workers would be placed at the end of the waiting list. Second, without providing any detail, it appeared that new candidates for citizenship would have an additional hurdle added to the process insofar as they would have an "obligation to learn the facts and ideals that have shaped America's history." One feature of the plan not mentioned in this list, but which was addressed in a section dealing with frequently asked questions, concerned the family members of temporary workers. Family members would be able to receive temporary visas, but only if the worker was able to indicate that he or she could financially support them.

Seen in terms of the recent past, it is evident that the Bush administration's 2004 proposal fell into a familiar pattern of policy and legislative initiatives undertaken during the past three decades. It was framed in a way that sought to avoid alienating either of the Republican Party's key constituencies: anti-immigration forces and business interests intent on having a steady supply of immigrant labor—either as cheap labor or because of their educations and skills. The potential divisiveness of the plan led the administration to back away from it leading up to 2004 elections. Indeed, some thought that the proposal was dead on arrival once it reached Congress. Opposition to the plan developed very quickly. A review of some of the criticisms is instructive, for it highlights the political fault lines within American society and speaks to the limits to enacting significant changes in current immigration law.

Organizations that are advocates for immigrant labor, such as the National Employment Law Project (www.nelp.org), contended that the plan focused on the needs of employers and not workers, defining it as a contemporary version of the Bracero Program. NELP was equally critical of the Clear Law Enforcement for Criminal Alien Removal (CLEAR) Act proposed by conservative Republican Congressman Charles Norwood that was pitched as part of homeland security measures, but which was seen by this organization as an attempt to get state and local police authorities involved in enforcing immigration laws, something they do not do at the present time. NELP was more sympathetic to a bipartisan reform bill offered by then–Democratic Senate leader Tom Daschle and Republican Senator Charles Hagel.

The National Network for Immigrant and Refugee Rights (www.nnirr.org) echoed the reaction of NELP, accusing the President of peddling "false hopes," intended to ensure that there was a large pool of cheap labor to perform 3D jobs. It was described on the organization's Web site as no more than a guest worker program designed to benefit certain categories of employers. The fact that the plan would have been overseen by the Department of Homeland Security was faulted because this recently created cabinet-level department established in the aftermath of the 9/11 attacks was not seen as an agency particularly concerned with protecting individual rights. The bureaucratic location of this proposal, in other words, raised concerns about whether the President was being sincere about his oft-stated desire to be a "compassionate conservative."

Faith-based groups, particularly mainline Protestant and Roman Catholic churches, voiced similar concerns. Some groups working with immigrants expressed skepticism about whether the plan would actually address the human rights problem associated with human trafficking, particularly along the Mexican-U.S. border. The American Friends Service Committee (www.afsc.org) argued that the proposals offered by the administration plan "fall well short of the evolving demands of international law and ethics of global justice." Moreover, it linked the plan to both NAFTA and the proposed Free Trade Area of the Americas (FTAA), which are depicted as "causes of upheaval and cruelty." The Mennonite Central Committee declared that the current immigration system was broken and the president's plan would do nothing to fix it. The Catholic Legal Immigration Network faulted the plan for not having a provision for permanent residency. These are typical reactions on the part of liberal religious organizations. To our knowledge, fundamentalist church bodies have not taken a stand on this particular issue, perhaps reflecting the fact that it has not been a front-burner issue for them (their major issues being at the moment abortion and gay marriage).

What about organized labor? John Sweeney (www.aflcio.org), speaking as head of the AFL-CIO, the largest labor organization in the country, took a position similar to that of liberal religious denominations. In stark contrast to the position of organized labor as recently as a quarter of a century ago, he stressed the need for worker solidarity by stating that the Bush administration's plan was

> a hollow promise for hardworking, undocumented workers, people seeking to immigrate to the U.S. and American workers alike. It creates a permanent underclass of workers who are unable to fully participate in democracy. The plan deepens the potential for abuse and exploitation of these workers, while undermining wages and labor protections for all workers.

Sweeney's criticism was echoed by United Farm Workers of America president Arturo Rodriquez (the organization is an affiliate of the AFL-CIO), who criticized the proposal for its failure to offer a "path for hardworking immigrants to earn a green card" (www.ufs.org). Similarly, the Farmworker Justice Fund found the proposal to be "ill-conceived."

What about the organizational voice of various ethnic groups? Among Asian immigrants, one found both the Asian Pacific American Labor Alliance and the National Asian Pacific American Legal Consortium expressed disappointment over the plan. The National Federation of Filipino American Associations described its reservations and its clear preference for two bipartisan bills that were at the time working their way through Congress, the

AgJobs bill which would have permitted 500,000 undocumented agricultural workers already in the United States to become legal residents, and the Dream Act, which allowed the children of undocumented workers to be eligible for in-state college tuition costs and would allow them to pursue a path to citizenship. The National Korean American Service and Education Consortium concluded that the administration's plan failed "to address the legitimate concerns of immigrant communities," and as a result it would result in the legalization of "a system of cheap and exploitable labor."

Within the Latino community, which would have been most impacted by the proposed legislation, there was evidence of a division of opinion. The oldest Mexican-centered Latino organization in the United States is the League of United Latin American Citizens (LULAC). The organization's president was in the audience at the White House when President Bush made his January 7 announcement. The Mexican American Legal Defense and Educational Fund viewed the plan as a "step in the right direction," but voiced concern that Mexicans were not receiving their due share of permanent residency green cards. Both of these groups represent the established Mexican American community—with many members tracing their ancestry in the United States back several generations—which has often been ambivalent about more recent immigrants, particularly the undocumented, because they are sometimes seen either as a competitive threat in the labor market or as a cause for depressed wage levels.

On the other hand, the National Council of La Raza was highly critical of the Bush plan for reasons little different from the other critics cited previously. In addition, the organization accused the administration of playing election-year politics, offering a plan that appeared in some ways on the surface to be generous in order to appeal to Latino voters—who were seen as an important part of the electoral mix in several key states, including California, Florida, and Texas.

As would be expected, certain business interests were the most enthusiastic supporters of the guest worker aspect of the plan. This was certainly the case with agricultural growers and with corporations that employ substantial numbers of immigrant workers, particularly those in the food and apparel industries. Perhaps the largest example is Tyson's Foods, where a substantial majority of workers at the corporation's meat processing plants are immigrants. It had long been an employer of undocumented workers, though the company denied that it knowingly hired workers who had violated immigration laws. Tyson's is an example of those business firms that had given generously to the Bush campaign. They sought substantial numbers of workers at the low-skilled end of the spectrum, and given a general strategy of preventing unionization of such workers to occur, the idea of a temporary guest worker program was unusually attractive, for such workers are generally perceived by management to be compliant. Since their work permits are dependent on employers stating that there is a need for their services, it is unlikely that they would engage in confrontational tactics concerning wages, benefits, or work conditions.

At the same time, the most assertive anti-immigrant organizations in the country are also part of the Republican Party's political base. A number of Republican legislators in some key immigrant-receiving states have sponsored a variety of anti-immigrant measures. This included Save Our State in California and Protect Arizona Now, which was supported by over 80% of registered Republican voters in that state. A measure wound its way through the Colorado legislature that would have added to the list of services already denied to undocumented immigrants by barring such immigrants from immunizations and library cards. Conservatives supporting these measures were critical of any effort that would allow taxpayer dollars to support undocumented immigrants in any way. In contrast to left-of-center citizens who saw the Bush plan as unfair to immigrants, this constituency saw it as being unduly generous. This being said, many on both sides of the debate agreed on one thing: to them the plan appeared to be part of a larger approach to immigration control, which Douglas Massey, Jorge Durand, and Nolan Malone (2002) have referred to as policy of "smoke and mirrors."

Given this constellation of constituencies and the ideological predilections of the Bush administration, it could perhaps have been predicted that its immigration reform plan would take the form that it did. What was perhaps most significant about it was that it promoted a type of contract labor that was designed principally with unskilled immigrants from Mexico and Central America in mind. As some critics had pointed out, it bore an uncanny resemblance to the Bracero Program that functioned between 1942 and 1964 to supply employers with unskilled labor for specified periods of time. The program was intended to offer a tap on/tap off approach to meeting the immigrant labor needs of certain U.S. employers. Temporary workers who were ineligible for citizenship meant that there was no need to worry about whether they would assimilate or not. Problems arose when these "guests" were "asked" to return to their homeland and refused. Thus, during the recession of the early 1950s, the Immigration and Naturalization Service engaged in draconian roundups of those who had overstayed their contracts—in a now infamous campaign known as Operation Wetback. The Bracero Program came under increasing attack during the early 1960s, as spokespersons for the temporary workers increasingly posed their plight in terms of a campaign for fundamental civil rights—rights that were associated with citizenship.

## A Legislative Impasse

In this light, the Bush administration's plan would in many ways appear to be simply repeating history. But the historical context was different (Jaret, 1999; Swain, 2007). For one thing, immigrants today have considerably more organized support—particularly from faith-based organizations, civil rights groups, and organized labor—than their earlier historical counterparts (see, for example, Hondagneu-Sotelo, 2007, on the role of organized religion). Of particular significance is the turnabout of organized labor. Once a powerful voice in support of immigration restriction, the union movement has become increasingly sympathetic to immigrants, whom labor sees as potential new recruits rather than as enemies. Second, the United States operates in a world of transnational organizations that have increasingly shaped the discourse about fundamental human rights. Thus, the nation cannot operate in a vacuum, however unilateralist the Bush administration often attempted to be. A third and related difference is that the nations of origin of many immigrant groups have become involved in the lives of their emigrants, as we noted in the analysis of transnationalism in Chapter 5. In particular, given the unique significance of the Mexican population in the United States, that government's decision to legalize dual citizenship combined with its creation of centers designed in various ways to assist their émigré community must be factored into the equation.

While it might have appeared that some sort of immigration reform package would have been passed, this did not occur. In the run-up to the 2006 Congressional elections, many Republican legislators chose immigration legislation as one instance where they could distance themselves from an increasingly unpopular president. A bipartisan deal unraveled along party lines and it became clear that no legislation would be passed by a Congress in which both houses had Republican majorities (Hulse & Swarns, 2006). When Democrats took control in 2006, it was thought that immigration legislation would be back on the table, and indeed it was (Archibold, 2006). However, intense negotiations in 2007 ended in futility, with the result being that a lack of movement in Washington prompted state and local government officials to pass 244 pieces of legislation, the result being "a legal patchwork for immigrants" (Preston, 2007).

## The Role of Public Opinion

Was the legislative impasse a reflection of public opinion, or did legislators largely discount the views of the public? This is a difficult question to answer, in no small part because pollsters reveal a public that can best be described as ambivalent about immigration. The Gallup Organization found that Americans believe that in the abstract, immigration has had a beneficial impact on the nation. Thus, 60% of respondents thought that on the whole, immigration is a "good thing," with 33% seeing it as a "bad thing." These figures are little changed from the beginning of the present century up to 2007. At the same time, immigration is not a top priority issue for most Americans, being located near the bottom on a list of 12 social issues (www.institution.gallup.com; see Simon & Lynch, 1999, for a comparative portrait of the preceding decade).

When asked whether immigration levels should be reduced, kept the same, or increased, the public is divided. While 45% would like to see levels decreased, 35% support current levels and 16% would like to see the level increased. This could be read to mean that by the slightest of majorities, the American public supports liberal immigration policies, though it is also clear that a sizeable plurality takes a restrictionist stance. Turning to illegal immigrants, respondents were asked how important an issue this was for them. Only 11% think it is not very or not at all important. The largest percentage— 35%—see it as extremely important, while 27% think it is very important and 26% see it as "somewhat" important. When anti-immigration cheer-leaders, such as CNN's commentator Lou Dobbs, argue that the "system is broken," they are referring to the fact that undocumented immigrants have come to constitute such a significant part of the migrant population.

When asked how best to respond to illegal immigrants, half of respondents called for the passage of new laws, while 46% thought this could be accomplished by enforcing existing laws (4% had no opinion). Addressing specific topics of concern, a majority of people thought that immigrants have made the crime situation in the country worse. On the other hand, a majority concluded that their presence has not had much effect on job opportunities. A slightly larger percentage thought that immigrants did not have much effect on social and moral values (41%), while 37% thought their presence had made things worse and 19% thought they had made things better. Finally, although a majority of respondents said they had followed the proposed immigration reform package closely or somewhat closely, 58% said they did not know enough about the legislation to determine whether they were in favor of it or opposed to it.

This leads, then, to a question: do these findings suggest that there is a gap between U.S. immigration policy and public opinion? If answered in terms of the disjuncture between the stated limits to immigration in existing law and the actual number of undocumented immigrants, there is an obvious gulf. But is there a gulf between public opinion and existing law? A majority of Americans are concerned about the level of undocumented immigrants, and this might be taken to indicate a gap. However, when it comes to how this translates into proposed legal responses to the situation, half think new laws are in order while nearly as large a figure thinks simply that current laws need to be better enforced. In other words, one group thinks that the gap is due to flaws with existing law while the other group sees the gap in terms of a failure to implement existing law. Given that a solid majority of the public could not decide whether it supported or was opposed to the Bush plan, it is unclear to what extent one can talk about a gulf between proposed legislation and the will of the public.

We thus return to Freeman's (1995) argument regarding interest group politics. The proposed legislation would have accomplished the goal of the business and trade associations who wanted legislation that would guarantee a continuing supply of workers under the terms of a guest worker program. This aspect of the program was criticized by immigrant rights groups and by organized labor. However, this feature of the plan was not the aspect that troubled the public at large. Rather, their concern—voiced vociferously by immigration restriction spokespersons—has to do with whether or not the plan actually provided amnesty for the currently undocumented. To the extent that it was perceived to do so, many were opposed to it because it was described as condoning illegal behavior. The fact that in the end the campaign marshaled by business interests resulted in a legislative deadlock can be read as an indication of the significance of public opinion. That a divided and ambivalent public shaped an election campaign that in the end led to a legislative impasse is not surprising. In other words, public opinion cannot be simply or readily discounted by political and economic elites, as some adherents of the gap hypothesis would suggest.

Our conclusion parallels that of Gallya Lahav (2004), who explored the role of public opinion regarding immigration in the European Union. Using the findings of the Eurobarometer, Lahav questioned the disjuncture between European public opinion and policies enacted at both the national and EU levels. She contends that there are good grounds to conclude that public opinion does matter for policy formulation. Insofar as this is true, the presumed "disconnect between elite and public preferences" stressed by Freeman is an overstatement of "a more complex and diffuse" picture (Lahav, 2004, p. 1159).

## The Convergence Hypothesis: Case Study

In this section, we explore the convergence hypothesis, using the European Union as our case study, beginning by noting that in comparison to other policy areas, migration and settlement issues have only recently begun to acquire a pan-European dimension. During the past two decades, significant changes in the direction of stronger EU regulation have occurred, accompanied by a transfer of administrative competencies from the national to the European level as well as shifts in the modes of European policy making. We contend that what began originally as intergovernmental cooperation among member states about immigration-related issues has over time become a form of "intensive transgovernmentalism" (Lavenex & Wallace, 2005).

During this time, all European countries with significant levels of immigration have overhauled their national immigration policies. Thus, Germany revamped its asylum policy in 1992 and introduced its first-ever comprehensive immigration act in January 2005. In the United Kingdom, four major immigration acts have been produced since 1999. Likewise, the Spanish "Alien Law" has undergone three major reforms in recent years. The government of Poland, one of the European Union's newest members, introduced legislative reforms to existing immigration policies in 2001 and again in 2003. Turkey, which is not a member of the European Union but is seeking entry, has begun to work on a new "Law of Settlement" that would replace the existing act, which dates back to 1934.

Immigration experts have devised a number of models to explain the varieties of national immigration policies (for a review, see Hollifield, 2000). However, comparatively little is known about the impact of international and, in particular, European influences, on these and other legislative reforms. What role does and what role can the European Union play in the increasingly multilevel approach to regulating migration? If there is a distinctive European influence, what is its nature? Specifically, can we detect a growing convergence of national policies due to the impact of EU membership? Are national immigration policies moving toward a similar, shared model, or does the Europeanization of national policies lead to greater divergence? Studies indicate that the process of the Europeanization of policy in other areas has led to a great variety of outcomes from country to country. The issue at hand is whether these findings hold true for immigration policies as well, and if so, how these differences in the impact of Europeanization can be explained.

Finally, past discussions of the European integration of immigration policies have concluded that national political constraints and tensions have often provided a major rationale for policymakers to "escape to Europe." In other words, if caught in the sort of policy impasse described in the preceding U.S. case study, political leaders in the European Union are tempted to do something their U.S. counterparts don't have the option of doing: moving from the state to the EU level to seek a resolution. If this is the course of action chosen by policymakers, it raises the matter of discerning the impact of a harmonized policy at the EU level on the domestic politics of immigration. The research to date offers contradictory accounts and is quite thin. Indeed, there is "little systematic empirical research on how European developments 'hit home' at the national level" (Vink, 2005a, p. 4).

## A Brief History of the Europeanization of Immigration Policies

The European integration of national immigration policies has developed over the course of four distinct historical periods following the creation of the European Community. The first, which occurred over a three-decade period from 1957 to 1986, was characterized by minimal involvement on the part of the European Union in national immigration policies. Immigration policies remained firmly and entirely under national control, and initiatives by the European Commission that were designed to promote closer EU cooperation within the traditional method of decision making were routinely declined. During this period, however, significant cooperation on these questions took place outside of the European Union's established structures. For example, the Trevi group was established by member states during the 1970s, with the goal being to find a modus operandi for cooperating on internal security measures. A second and more crucial example was the 1985 Schengen Agreement, which was concerned with achieving consensus about the objective of achieving the mutual abolition of internal border controls and the development of compensating internal security measures.

These intergovernmental forms of cooperation helped shape cooperative actions during the second period, which ran from 1986 until 1993. That period was characterized by what might be defined as informal intergovernmentalism, in which representatives from the respective member states engaged in a process that led to closer cooperation than was the case earlier. Examples of how this played out include the creation of the Ad Hoc Working Group on Immigration in 1986 and the work of the group of coordinators who were responsible for preparing the Palma Programme, which dealt with the security implications of the free-movement measures in the Union's Single Europe Act. The third period ran from 1993 to 1999. It was shaped by the Maastricht Treaty and its structure of formal intergovernmental cooperation. At this stage, the three-pillar structure of the European Union made genuinely integrated immigration policies under the auspices of the European Union a reality, and recognized that immigration issues should be treated as common interests shared by all member states. The decision-making structures in the third pillar, however, ensured that cooperation remained strictly intergovernmental.

The current period, beginning in the late 1990s, has been characterized by increasing communitarization, marked by the Treaty of Amsterdam. Determined to increase the degree of integration, the European Council summit in Tampere, Finland, in 1999 set out a 5-year action plan that was to move in the direction of a common European immigration policy. After 5 years of such efforts, the Commission published its final report in which it assessed the original plan, concluding that "substantial progress has been made in most areas." However, because of the intergovernmental decision-making procedure, which required unanimous decisions, "it was not always possible to reach agreement at the European level for the adoption of certain sensitive measures relating to policies which remain at the core of national sovereignty" (Commission of the European Communities, 2004, pp. 3–4). In order to overcome the limitation imposed by unanimous voting, this policy was changed to a system of qualified majority voting. In part, the motive for making this possible derived from concerns about migrants entering the European Union illegally through the Spanish enclaves of Ceuta and Melilla. This lent urgency to the goal of further integration, by revealing the weakness of a policy that focused primarily on migration control while neglecting the root causes of migration (Boswell, 2003).

## The Extent and Modes of Europeanization

In a study conducted by Thomas Faist and Andreas Ette (2007), two main findings emerged. The first concerns differences between countries in the extent to which what they refer to as Europeanization has had an impact on national immigration policies. This involves examining a spectrum ranging from no change or minor changes in domestic policies to substantive and comprehensive changes at the other end. Six EU nations were included in the study: Germany, Greece, Poland, Spain, Sweden, and the United Kingdom. In addition, two nations currently seeking membership into the European Union were also examined: Albania and Turkey. These eight nations can be placed at various points along this continuum, the most extreme positions being those of the United Kingdom, with only minor alterations to their laws, and Poland at the other end, with major changes to its policy. In between are Germany and Sweden, which are closer to the British pole, and Greece and Spain, which are closer to the Polish experience. Furthermore, the study showed that a reciprocal relationship exists between the mode and extent of Europeanization: discursive modes of interaction lead to greater national policy change in the case of older EU member states, while prescriptive modes result in a greater degree of Europeanization in the case of new member states.

The United Kingdom showed the least EU influence on the original British approach to immigration control, although the situation has evolved over time. Overall, the influence of European policy approaches on Britain's immigration and asylum policies was greater during the 1990s, prior to the Amsterdam Treaty. Examples from this period include changes to British asylum law that came as a result of European initiatives that became established in what became known as the Dublin Conventions. In contrast, after the turn of the century, there have been minimal national policy changes resulting from EU initiatives. The sole exception involves policies on human trafficking and smuggling, for which the United Kingdom adopted the European policy framework, in the absence of an existing British policy on the matter.

In the case of all other European policies, the British government responded to European requirements by introducing minor changes or by opting out. The British case provides a prime example of the usefulness of the modes of Europeanization in explaining the European impact on national immigration policies. The relationship between the extent and the mode of Europeanization is even more obvious in the case of Germany. It is often seen as the "poster child" of European integration, actively participating in the process of European integration in general and showing particular interest in a common European immigration policy. In line with this image, EU activities during the 1990s profoundly altered Germany's immigration policy. In particular, the fundamental revamping of the nation's asylum policy with the change in its Basic Law can be directly attributed to EU influence. The Amsterdam Treaty, however, marked a turning point for its involvement in a common immigration policy, with Germany changing "from a laggard to a vanguard" (Hellmann, Baumann, Bösche, Herborth, & Wagner, 2005, p. 143). In contrast to the earlier period, European developments after 1999 have not, overall, significantly affected Germany's immigration policies. Neither are any major changes expected to come of recently drafted bills before the German Bundestag.

At the other end of the spectrum is Poland, a relatively new member state that joined the European Union in the first round of eastern enlargement in 2004. Generally, those countries that have joined the "club" recently have experienced the most comprehensive Europeanization of their domestic immigration policies. Again, the mode of Europeanization seems an important predicator for the extent of policy change stimulated by the European Union. Unlike the situation for the older member states, however, the impact of the European Union is greater where Europeanization is prescriptive in nature. In fact, the EU influence on Poland's immigration laws was actually felt even earlier, due to the need for policy after the collapse of the Warsaw Pact. While the influence was considerable during the early

1990s, it grew even more significant after 1997, when negotiations on EU ascension were launched. In the early 1990s, the EU influence was evident when Poland joined the Geneva Convention on refugees and the European Convention for the Protection of Human Rights and Fundamental Freedoms. Those developments were finally given expression in the 1997 Alien Act, which introduced a range of measures that had been discussed at the European level at the time, including, for example, temporary residency permits, carrier sanctions, and what was known as the safe third-party concept. The European influence grew thereafter, with many European proposals being directly transposed into Polish policy. As a highly motivated candidate for EU membership, Poland willingly accepted the requirements concerning its immigration policies.

The assessment of the extent to which immigration policies have been Europeanized can be examined in countries currently seeking ascension to the EU, such as Turkey and Albania. The situation in both countries can be likened to that in Poland between 1997 and 2004—highly coercive and prescriptive modes of Europeanization governed by conditionality. Both of these nations have a keen interest in joining the European Union, and it is likely that they will follow Poland's example in acceding to EU demands for revisions in current policies. Overall, the impact of the European Union on nonmembers is weaker than it is on Poland because the institution is able to exert more pressure on member states. Given that both Turkey and Albania are not as certain of future membership as Poland was, they have somewhat less incentive to be as compliant to EU dictates as preascension Poland was.

The second finding from Faist and Ette's research concerns the variations in the European impact on the politics—as opposed to the policies—of immigration. As we have seen, the Europeanization of national immigration policies has had far-reaching consequences for some countries. By contrast, the European impact on the national politics of immigration is far weaker and follows a largely different logic. Whereas the extent of the Europeanization of the policies of immigration is best explained by the mode of Europeanization, with regard to the politics of immigration, it is the degree of compatibility between national and European structures of policy making that plays a stronger role. Faist and Ette suggest that two factors account for the difference.

The first factor focuses on the general characteristics of immigration policies with regard to the importance of different actors in the policy-making and decision-making processes, as well as the general findings of the impact of the European Union on national politics. Despite recent debates about the importance of interest groups and the judiciary in immigration policy making (see, for example, Freeman, 2006, and Guiraudon, 2000), immigration politics and other policy areas in justice and home affairs are generally regarded as elite dominated and are seen as a policy sector in which the executive has a strong prerogative, at the expense of the legislatures, political parties, and interest groups (Hammar, 1985; Statham & Geddes, 2006). In recent years, the dominance of the executive has increased even further. The growing significance of the migration-security nexus, the continuing securitization of immigration, and the mingling of external and internal security with immigration issues have strengthened the grasp of the executive in this policy area (Faist, 2005). These developments in the politics of immigration confirm the findings of studies of the European Union's overall impact on national politics, which indicate that the European impact on national politics tends to strengthen the executive at the expense of the legislature (Andersen & Burns, 1996).

The second explanation for the comparatively weak impact of the European Union on national politics is based on country-specific institutional arrangements that are clearly visible in politics but not so obvious in the policy dimension. National institutional frameworks for politics are much harder to Europeanize than the more contingent regulatory approaches in the policy dimension (Maurer, Mitag, & Wessels, 2003). In line with these expectations, the findings of all of Faist and Ette's individual country studies indicated that the extent of Europeanization with regard to politics is, indeed, small compared to the impact on policy. It can be said that in general there has been little EU impact on the national politics of immigration in any of the subject countries. A prime example is Sweden, which has traditionally had a strong parliament with considerable influence in shaping policy. In this case, the Europeanization of policy-making processes has clearly strengthened the executive, and on European issues, the parliamentary committees have had difficulty making their influence felt in the government. Similar problems have been reported in the process of transposing EU policies into the national arena. The implementation of EU directives into Swedish law is generally prepared by expert commissions and working groups in the ministries rather than in the parliament itself, which contributes to a further weakening of this institution. Another good example supporting the same trend is the Spanish case. In this country, with its traditionally strong executive, the European influence actually serves to reinforce the classic features of the Spanish political system. With the European Union "pushing" and the government "pulling" for a more restrictive policy, the parliamentary opposition and interest groups have great difficulty promoting their position.

Despite these findings, which illustrate the reinforcement of traditional national patterns of policy making, there are a number of cases in which the European Union has provided for new configurations in the national politics of immigration. The United Kingdom, for example, is seen as a country where a strong executive and weak judicial control have made a very stringent immigration control regime possible. Overall, the politics of immigration in the United Kingdom has not been transformed by the country's participation in the development of a broader European immigration policy. Nevertheless, the British adoption of the European Convention on Human Rights (ECHR) could in the long term significantly alter these established ways of doing things. Indeed, Faist and Ette conclude that there is evidence to support such a development in the future.

The most striking results, however, are again to be seen in the new member states such as Poland, and in potential future states such as Turkey and Albania. In the Polish case, the institutional framework of immigration policy making has not changed in substance for more than 15 years. There is a clear executive dominance over such policy, with the parliament and interest groups being largely excluded from the process. Europeanization has hardly changed this institutional framework. Instead, what has happened is that the political discourse of Polish elites has been Europeanized to a large extent. The perception of uncontrolled immigration as a threat and a "fortress Europe" approach has been effectively transplanted to the Polish context, even though the number of immigrants in Poland remains quite small. Overall, Faist and Ette's analysis of the Europeanization of national policies and politics of immigration has revealed that the European Union has over time become an increasingly important player. In particular, it has become a successful venue for longtime EU member states to exercise influence on the newer states' policies and politics.

Thus, it is reasonable to speak about a convergence of approaches to immigration in Europe due to the singular role of the European Union. Insofar as this is the case, it is an example of convergence brought about by regional integration (Cornelius & Tsuda, 2004, p. 18). But what does this suggest about the rest of the advanced industrial nations? To date, there is no regional counterpart to the European Union. Certainly, NAFTA does not serve the same function. In this instance, the United States and Canada are immigrant-receiving nations, while Mexico is a major exporter. While the United States has increasingly promoted get-tough policies, Canada's official stance calls for the need to increase the size of the population via immigration. Australia and New Zealand have various regional ties, but this has not resulted in the same convergence effect as that within the European Union. Japan, meanwhile, largely goes it alone, to large extent failing to grapple with the need for comprehensive immigration policies. In this regard, Cornelius and Tsuda (2004, pp. 38–40) contend that there is at present a convergence between Japan and South Korea due to the latter's attempts at policy emulation. This is a reminder that regional integration is but one of five factors that can contribute to convergence. A more comprehensive exploration of the other four would be necessary before one could arrive at a fully rounded portrait of the impact of convergence on contemporary immigration policies.

## The Open Question

Authoritarian states do not have perfect track records, but they can point to considerable success in controlling movement into and outside of their borders (see, for example, Dowty, 1987, on the closed borders of eastern European regimes before 1989). That such nations are politically unattractive for would-be immigrants combined with economic shortcomings makes immigration unattractive. But even when people want to enter these countries, they often confront considerable brutality, are consigned to an underground existence, and live with the constant threat of being deported to a homeland where their lives might be at risk. North Korea, in many respects a failed nation, does not have an "immigration problem." China does, insofar as some North Koreans manage to find their way into that nation. Its record to date suggests that the Chinese state has a high capacity for controlling unwanted immigration. Indeed, at the moment, controlling internal migration poses a far bigger challenge for the Chinese government.

The question that remains unanswered is whether the world's liberal democracies have comparable capabilities. Recall that Freeman (1994) thought that the ability to control immigration had increased rather than decreased over the past century or so. Others are not so sure, seeing in democratic states a challenge to the capacity to control that does not exist in authoritarian states. A conclusion that one could reasonably draw from Hollifield's (2000) "liberal state thesis" is that a central feature of such states can pose a built-in constraint to the capacity to control: the recognition of rights. If it is true, as we indicated in our discussion of immigration flows in Chapter 2, that economic forces and networks are the main causes of immigration, rights can serve as both an additional stimulus to migrate and a constraint on the state's ability to control the flow and address the problem of "unwanted" immigrants. The aftermath of the Postville raid discussed earlier in the chapter is a case in point. Lawyers and immigrant rights groups have subsequently challenged the government's actions on the basis of various violations of rights—pitched both at the national level (as in workers' rights enshrined in U.S. labor law) and in terms of universal human rights (Fujiwara, 2005). This is a complex and evolving issue that has not received the level of scholarly attention that it merits, but that will certainly be on the front burner of research agendas in the future.

# 8

# Citizenship and the State in a Globalizing World

Who should be permitted to stay—and on what terms? This is the inevitable question that arises after the question that introduced the preceding chapter (Who should get in?) has been answered. Once immigrants are allowed into a country, their status in that country needs to be sorted out. Is their entrance contingent on the assumption that at some specified point in time they will return to their country of origin? Or will they be permitted to reside permanently in the settlement state? If the latter is the case, will they be afforded the opportunity to become full-fledged citizens of that state? These are the questions that will be addressed in this chapter.

The focus will be on issues related to citizenship, but at the outset this needs to be placed into context, for there are three distinct legal statuses relevant to immigrants: alienship, denizenship, and citizenship. In contrast to an earlier phase of immigration studies, in which aliens and citizens were posed in dichotomous terms, the tripartite scheme that adds denizens to the mix has shaped recent research since this term was first advanced by Swedish sociologist Thomas Hammar (1990). That being said, the three categories reflect an older understanding, one that dates to the Greek city-states. In that historical setting, it was customary to distinguish between the citizen (*politai*), resident alien (*katoikoi*), and foreigner (*xenoi*). In contemporary parlance in the world of the nation-state, the resident alien becomes the denizen, while the foreigner becomes the alien. As Figure 8.1 indicates, aliens include temporary workers, asylum seekers and those who are claiming refugee status, and the undocumented. Denizens, in turn, include migrants with permanent resident status

| Legal Status | Immigrant Categories |
|---|---|
| Alienship | • Migrants with temporary residence and work permits (e.g., seasonal workers)<br>• Asylum seekers, defacto refugees<br>• Undocumented aliens, illegal immigrants |
| Denizenship | • Labor migrants with permanent residence status and their dependents<br>• Recognized refugees |
| Citizenship | • Citizens of immigration nation-states<br>• Citizens of EU member states<br>• Citizens of autonomous regions |

**Figure 8.1**    Immigrant Types

and officially recognized refugee status. Finally, while citizenship's most obvious unit remains the nation-state, immigrants also need to contend in some jurisdictions with what citizenship entails at the subnational and supranational levels (Faist, 2000b). Thus, immigrants in Quebec or Catalonia must reckon with the fact that the regional autonomy of these political entities has implications for citizens that might be quite distinct from those for immigrants living elsewhere in Canada or Spain. Similarly, in the European context, supranational citizenship is relevant insofar as being a member of the European Union has a number of implications, including the freedom of mobility of EU citizens and their access to jobs within the organization's 27 member states.

## Why Is Citizenship Important?

Before turning to the topic of citizenship and immigration, it is necessary to locate this particular subject in terms of the field of citizenship studies as a whole. Once a neglected theme in the social sciences, citizenship studies is at present a burgeoning field of inquiry. A review of the now-vast literature on the topic reveals that underlying this efflorescence of interest are two assumptions: (1) citizenship is important and (2) it is taking new forms. In an effort to capture what is deemed to be novel about the present situation, a proliferation of adjectives is evident in the literature aimed as describing the peculiar features and contours of contemporary citizenship. Thus, we find treatments of world citizenship (Heater, 2002), global citizenship (Falk, 1994), universal citizenship (Young, 1989), cosmopolitan citizenship (Linklater, 1998), multiple citizenship (Held, 1995), postnational citizenship (Soysal, 1994), transnational citizenship (Bauböck, 1994; Johnston, 2001), dual citizenship (Miller, 1991), nested citizenship (Faist, 2000a), multilayered citizenship (Yuval-Davis, 2000), cultural citizenship (Stevenson, 1997), multicultural citizenship (Delgado-Moreira, 2000; Kymlicka, 1995), cybercitizenship (Tambini, 1997), environmental citizenship (Jelin, 2000), feminist citizenship (Lister, 1997), gendered citizenship (Seidman, 1999), flexible citizenship (Ong, 1999), differentiated citizenship (Bloemraad, 2006), intimate citizenship (Plummer, 2003), consuming citizenship (Park, 2005), and protective citizenship (Gilbertson & Singer, 2003). This is far from an inclusive sampling of recent takes on citizenship.

However different from one another they may be, all of these types of citizenship call into question two assumptions that have been part and parcel of classical citizenship theory. The first assumption involves a presumed congruence between state territory, a people (nation), and state authority (Benhabib, 2008; Faist, 2004). The second assumes the relative homogeneity among the people, especially in terms of such features as ethnicity and religion. When British social theorist T. H. Marshall (1964) argued that the rise of social citizenship was necessitated by the fact that capitalist economies generated unacceptably high levels of inequality that were viewed as a threat to social solidarity, he had in mind states that were divided by class, but not in significant ways by ethnicity and religion. From his perspective, social citizenship constituted a historical compromise between labor and capital, which also amounted to a compromise between market results based on the principle of contract and the principle of status in the solidarity collective of the nation-state. Most important, regarding the assumption of relative homogeneity, the new forms of citizenship listed previously signal a heightened attention to the reality of heterogeneity, which cuts in a number of ways, such as due to ethnicity or national origin, gender, religion, age, and so forth.

One of the unintended consequences of the expansive character of new thinking about citizenship is that a certain level of conceptual inflation has crept in. For that reason, it is useful at the outset to go back to basics, outlining its most elemental characteristics. Citizenship can be defined in terms of two component features. First, it constitutes membership in a polity, and, as such, it inevitably involves a tension between inclusion and exclusion, between those deemed eligible for citizenship and those who are denied the right to become members. In its earliest form in ancient Greece, as noted earlier, the polity in question was the city-state. In the modern world, it was transformed during the era of democratic revolutions into the nation-state (Fahrmeir, 2007; see also Hobsbawm, 1962; Markoff, 1996). Second, membership brings with it a reciprocal set of duties and rights, both of which vary by place and time, though some are universal. Thus, paying taxes and obeying the law are among the duties expected of all citizens in all countries, while the right to participate in the political process in varying ways—by voting, running for elective office, debating, petitioning, and so forth—is an inherent feature of democratic citizenship.

This leads to the final point: citizenship exists only in democratic regimes, for in nondemocratic ones, people are subjects rather than citizens—even though the language of citizenship is often used by nondemocratic regimes. Thus, we concur with Juan Linz and Alfred Stepan's (1996, p. 28) assertion that "without a state, there can be no citizenship; without citizenship, there can be no democracy." In essence, citizenship so conceived builds on notions of collective self-determination, which is the essence of democracy. In this regard, there are three crucial features that characterize the democratic political system: (1) the right to participate in the public sphere; (2) limitations on the power of government over the individual; and (3) a system based on the rule of law, not the arbitrary rule of rulers.

The principal fault lines used to define the boundaries of inclusion versus exclusion have historically been based on three major social divisions: class, gender, and race. And, indeed, though much has changed, these divisions remain significant—and in fact tend to be intersecting. During the formative period of all the modern democratic regimes, beginning in the 18th century, the privileged white property-owning male citizens were intent on disqualifying a majority of their nation's residents from citizenship rights. Confronted with a disjunction between the egalitarian ideals of democratic theory and the desire to exclude from full societal membership certain categories of persons who did not share their class, gender, or racial identities, they responded by creating justifications for social exclusion, seeking to use the boundaries of citizenship to effect social closure (Murphy, 1988). For their part, the white working class, women, and nonwhites responded, always in difficult circumstances and with varying degrees of success, by creating social movements aimed at acquiring the political voice that had been denied them—engaging in what Alexander (2006, pp. 193–209) refers to as efforts aimed at "civil repair" that expand the bases of solidarity. The white working class had, by the late 19th century, succeeded in being included, though not as genuine equals. A similar inclusion would come slower for women and racial and ethnic minorities; in many cases, this did not occur until the latter part of the 20th century. Thus, American blacks did not overcome the barriers created by Jim Crow until the 1960s; Australia's Aboriginal population did not receive the right to vote until the same time; and in some Swiss cantons, women did not acquire the right to vote until 1990.

As with inclusion, the development of the rights of citizens entails a dynamic historical process. Analyses of this process are generally framed in terms of the thesis advanced by T. H. Marshall (1964), who distinguished between three types of rights: civil, political, and social. In his view, these types are distinct not only analytically, but also historically. Civil rights refer to such aspects of individual freedom as free speech, freedom of religious expression, and the right to engage in economic and civic life. Political rights involved those rights that ensure the ability to actively participate in the realm of politics. Finally, social rights involve the rights to various welfare provisions designed to guarantee to all a minimum standard of living necessary for the other two rights to be meaningful. Included are guarantees of educational opportunities, health care, decent and affordable housing, pensions, and so forth.

Marshall thought that civil rights in Britain emerged in the 18th century, political rights in the 19th century, and social rights in the 20th century, with the birth of the modern welfare state. He also assumed that a similar pattern could be detected in other democratic regimes. Although the historical record calls into question the unilateral depiction of the evolution of rights, it is the case that all the world's liberal democracies sooner or later, more expansively or less so, developed welfare states guaranteeing various types of social rights. In Marshall's view, whereas the other two rights do not challenge capitalism's production of unacceptable levels of inequality, social rights are intended to do precisely that. Inequality does not cease to exist, but by being reduced it becomes less consequential in shaping the life chances of individuals and impeding the goal of the equality of people qua citizens. The historical record indicates that welfare states have not actually managed to achieve this goal. Moreover, during the past quarter of a century, the neoliberal assault on the welfare state has resulted in an increase in levels of inequality (Gilbert, 2004; Schierup, Hansen, & Castles, 2006; Somers, 2008).

Debates over the duties of citizens have pitted advocates of republicanism (and communitarianism) against liberalism's spokespersons. The former position calls for an involved citizenry, while the latter is less inclined to ask or require citizens to be too actively engaged in politics. For example, republicans would be inclined to support universal conscription into military service or some alternative form of public service, while liberals would not. Nevertheless, both positions contend that for democracies to succeed, they need an informed and active citizenry. The distinction between the two traditions has much to do with differing perspectives on the levels of activity required. By the latter part of the 20th century, a lively discourse emerged about the presumed tendency on the part of citizens in the United States, and to a somewhat lesser degree elsewhere, to withdraw from civic and political involvement, as evidenced, for instance, in the widespread interest in the Harvard political scientist Robert Putnam's (2000) "bowling alone" thesis.

Citizenship entails the construction of a distinction between the "we," members of the political community, and "they," those who remain outsiders. Thus, it is apt to speak about national citizenship as entailing social closure around the political community (Murphy, 1988). This is true even though denizens make the divide somewhat fuzzier insofar as they are often accorded social rights similar to citizens and in some instances are even granted political voice via voting at the local level. However, they are in the end defined as outsiders without access to the full political voice accorded to citizens. It is in this context that the matter of naturalization needs to be located, for it is via this process that immigrants move from outsiders to insiders. From the perspective of immigrants, what is to be gained by being an insider? What incentive to pursue naturalization is there if denizens are granted essentially the same social rights as citizens, as is the case in some polities? Or, what happens to the incentive to become a citizen in the neoliberal era characterized by the erosion of social rights? Likewise, what happens to the incentive when, in the post-9/11 era of the security state, civil rights (including the right to privacy) become threatened? Turning from rights to duties, what are the implications of seeking to acquire political voice in a state where the general population has increasingly withdrawn from the public sphere? Finally, what is the underlying motive for seeking to become a citizen? Is it purely or primarily instrumental, or is there an emotional attachment at play helping to foster loyalty to the new homeland?

## Immigrants, Citizenship, and Democracy

These issues, in a different way, also shape how states address the matter of naturalized citizens. From experience, the Western liberal democracies provide ample evidence that levels of naturalization vary, from relatively low rates in countries such as Germany and Switzerland to high rates in Australia and the Netherlands (Castles & Davidson, 2001). Some may be more inclined to be restrictive in their naturalization policies, while others may be quite liberal—with the historic settler states located in the latter category. It is generally agreed that the nations of western Europe have on the whole become more inclusive over time, though, as we will discuss later, some suggest that since 2000 there is evidence of more restrictive tendencies. The 1999 German citizenship law is seen as a particularly significant case, for it reversed the nation's long-standing restrictive naturalization requirements and made Germany's law among the most liberal on the continent. But this liberalizing trend is not uniformly the case, as is evident in Britain's 1981 Nationality Act, which made it more difficult for residents of former British colonies to naturalize, and the Irish referendum that eliminated the *jus soli* right to citizenship for children born to non-Irish nationals (Weil, 2001).

States make use of varied admixtures of a range of criteria in adjudicating applications for citizenship acquisition. Among the main criteria are the following: (1) a residency requirement; (2) good character; (3) absence of criminal convictions; (4) a loyalty oath; (5) renunciation of prior citizenship; (6) sufficient income; (7) knowledge of the nation's main language(s); and (8) knowledge of the nation's history, political system, and culture. Some states have implemented more stringent requirements than other states, reflecting in part the differing nature of current debates over the inclusion of newcomers. In the states requiring more of newcomers than other states, it is frequently the case that those who are most suspicious of their loyalty to the new homeland have gotten the upper hand in the battle over public opinion and policy formulation. Thus, they have been successful in advancing the claim that the "patriotic assimilation of immigrants" must precede the granting of citizenship rights (see, for example, Fonte, 2005).

For their part, those immigrants in a position to do so have to decide whether or not to naturalize. In determining how to proceed, they need to consider whether citizenship will serve to attenuate economic inequality and reduce power differentials that lead to marginalization. Immigrants need to assess both their own circumstances and the situation of the most vulnerable among the citizenry. As Bill Jordan and Frank Düvell (2003, p. 146) put it, "The key questions are therefore which non-nationals are most vulnerable to which kinds of domination or exploitation, and which citizens are exposed to new risks under the new global order."

But this is a two-way street insofar as immigrants respond to their perception of whether or not the host nation is welcoming. If it is perceived to be welcoming, it is more likely that immigrants will exhibit higher levels of identification with the host society, which in turn impacts levels of political and civic involvement. Pontus Odmalm's (2005) comparative study of five European nations—Britain, France, Germany, the Netherlands, and Sweden—provides empirical support for this relationship. Unfortunately, there has been relatively little research that has focused primarily on the ways specific states either encourage or discourage immigrants to identify with the polity and the larger society.

The most intriguing study to date on this topic is Irene Bloemraad's (2006) comparative study of Portuguese immigrants and Vietnamese refugees in Canada and the United States. She found that both groups revealed higher naturalization rates in Canada compared to their neighbor to the south.

Contending that citizenship is more than a legal status entailing rights and duties, she stresses the fact that it can be "an invitation to participate in a system of mutual governance," and that, as such, it can constitute "an identity that provides a sense of belonging" (Bloemraad, 2006, p. 1). From this framework, she advances an argument that the differences in naturalization rates are due to differing institutional and policy environments. Specifically, the pro-active multicultural policy combined with coherent assistance programs characteristic of the Canadian government's approach creates a hospitable and encouraging setting that is lacking in the United States' more laissez-faire orientation.

Underlying Bloemraad's (2006, p. 251) thesis is the belief that "democratic governance demands participatory citizenship." A contrasting argument has been advanced by Ron Hayduk (2006), who contends that voting rights need not only be for citizens. His argument is that in the interest of advancing "democracy for all," noncitizens—including immigrants—should be permitted to vote. He contends that this is not a pie-in-the-sky goal, but rather has both historical and contemporary precedent. Focusing historically on the United States, he provides evidence that from the founding of the republic to shortly after World War I, noncitizens were not only permitted to vote at the local and state levels, but were also granted this right in some instances at the federal level. Moreover, many immigrants ran for and held elective offices. At present, he contends that more than 40 countries allow permanent resident noncitizens to vote. This includes all of the member states of the European Union, who, under the terms of the 1993 Maastricht Treaty, grants the right to all EU citizens to vote in EU countries other than their own (Hayduk, 2006, p. 5).

Whether the issue is to encourage naturalization or to grant voting rights, the assumption of both Bloemraad and Hayduk is that the potential for achieving political voice is an essential facet of immigrant inclusion. Thus, if there is a larger societal goal of facilitating inclusion and expanding the boundaries of solidarity, the specific role of the state is clearly to adopt policies that encourage citizenship acquisition and promote the democratic participation of newcomers. One proposal that links voting rights to naturalization does so by granting the former in order to allow immigrants to demonstrate their fitness for citizenship. Rodolfo de la Garza and Louis DeSipio have proposed giving immigrants the right to vote for a nonrenewable period of 5 years. Those immigrants who regularly voted would be deemed appropriate candidates for naturalization. Although they realize that their proposal is unlikely to be enacted, they nonetheless see it as a reasonable approach in a situation characterized by relatively low voter turnout rates for the native-born and naturalized alike (DeSipio, 2001, p. 100). Such a plan would, in effect, amount to a form of civic education for newcomers.

## Challenges to the Nation-State

These discussions about immigrant inclusion have been increasingly framed in terms of recent developments brought about by globalization (Spiro, 2007). Nation-states in the modern era have claimed a monopoly on defining the specific parameters of citizenship regimes and establishing the ground rules for inclusion and exclusion (Tilly, 2007). However, recent challenges to the container concept of citizenship have arisen, whereby the nation-state is viewed as the ultimate arbiter of both questions concerning membership and the content of citizen rights and duties (Faist, 2001a, 2004, 2006; Münch, 2001). This discourse arises in the context of the growing interdependency of nations—economically for certain, but also politically and culturally. Located in terms of what scholars variously refer to as transnationalism (Faist, 2000b, 2000c, 2004; Kivisto, 2001) or globalization (Lechner & Boli, 2005), new modes and loci of belonging that transcend existing political borders have begun to arise. It should be noted that the novelty of this discourse is such that it is a relatively new topic in the social sciences (Turner, 2006) and likewise at the level of public policy. In those nations that have entered into parliamentary discussions about the viability of expansion, the topic has percolated into public discourse, while in other places where such initiatives have not taken place, it has not become a topic of public interest.

Seyla Benhabib (2004, p. 1) describes contemporary developments in the following way:

> The modern nation-state system has regulated membership in terms of one principal category: national citizenship. We have entered an era when state sovereignty has been frayed and the institution of national citizenship has been disaggregated or unbundled into diverse elements. New modalities of membership have emerged, with the result that the boundaries of the political community, as defined by the nation-state system, are no longer adequate to regulate membership.

Although the rapidly growing literature on the new modalities of citizenship is rich and complex, we think that the discussions can be divided into two central themes about the way citizenship is coming to be redefined. The first shift concerns the impact of the rapid proliferation of dual citizenship (Faist, 2006;

Faist & Kivisto, 2007), while the second entails the emergence of various modes of what might be referred to as supranational citizenship. In terms of the latter, there are two distinct foci. One looks at *nested citizenship,* which implies a set of two or more memberships located in concentric circles, where national identities do not disappear but become embedded in the larger, overarching trans-state entity (Faist, 2000a; Faist & Ette, 2007). The second focus is on what has variously been described as global, world, or cosmopolitan citizenship (Lechner & Boli, 2005).

It should be noted at the outset that dual citizenship does not challenge the nation-state per se, but rather calls into question any one state's right to claim a monopoly on the membership of its citizenry. On the other hand, although nested citizenship is also an empirical phenomenon that requires scrutiny, it is solely confined to Europe, for there is no truly parallel regional counterpart to the European Union in any other part of the world. Thus, this is a more circumscribed topic, though given the importance of Europe as an immigration destination, its significance cannot be underestimated. When, at the conclusion, we briefly touch upon the debates about global citizens, we increasingly enter the realm of speculation, addressing issues that can only be understood as phenomena that exist, where they do, in embryonic form.

## Immigrant Inclusion and Dual Citizenship

Dual citizenship increased dramatically in the latter decades of the 20th century, and this trend has continued unabated in the present century. An ever-increasing number of nation-states, for a range of reasons, have come to accept, or at least tolerate, dual citizenship. On the face of it, this is a surprising trend because in the not-too-distant past it was widely assumed that citizenship and political loyalty to sovereign states were thought to be indivisible. This new development casts doubt on the assumption that overlapping membership violates the principle of popular sovereignty and that multiple ties and loyalties on the part of citizens in border-crossing social spaces contradict or pose a serious challenge to state sovereignty (Faist, 2004).

To appreciate this fact, we will explore dual citizenship by first examining its history, with an eye to identifying factors that have contributed to its rapid expansion. Second, we offer a brief review of the role played by international law and covenants. Finally, we will summarize what is known at present about the number of dual citizens in the world today. This discussion is intended to offer us some clues about future trends.

# Causal Forces Promoting Dual Citizenship

What are the major reasons that dual citizenship in the past has been viewed negatively, as something that should be both prohibited and avoided? One primary reason has been a concern that issues of diplomatic protection of dual nationals could result in conflict between nations. Peter Spiro (2002, p. 22) contends that, contrary to what might be assumed, this negative attitude toward dual citizenship resulted not from cases of "disloyalty and deceit, divided allegiances and torn psyches." Rather, countries were much less concerned about the dual nationals themselves, and much more about how they could treat their dual nationals. In a time before international human rights agreements, nations did whatever they wished to their own citizens, but were limited in terms of what they could do to citizens of other countries. Conflicts between nations over citizens of both states could result in war. For example, the War of 1812 between Britain and the United States was in part instigated over a disagreement concerning the treatment of individuals claimed as nationals by both countries.

Such issues were problematic for the United States in particular during the founding period of the republic due to the fact that many European nations did not acknowledge the naturalization of their citizens in the new nation. As Spiro (2002, p. 23) observes, "At times the issue even inflamed the public imagination, as when Britain put several naturalized Irish-Americans on trial for treason as British citizens." The United States also confronted a number of cases wherein naturalized citizens returned permanently to their countries of origin, but demanded that the United States afford them diplomatic protection. This historical backdrop notwithstanding, despite the early emphasis on international relations, much of the subsequent rhetoric against dual nationality has focused on the individual's presumed divided loyalties—which were commonly seen as being tantamount to political bigamy.

A second and related concern about dual citizenship involved the matter of military service. Referring again to the War of 1812, one of the precipitating factors that led to war was the decision of British military officers to press naturalized Americans of British descent into their military. Other nations attempted to similarly induct naturalized Americans from their particular nations when those nationals ventured back to their respective homelands. This included France, Spain, Prussia, and various other German states (Koslowski, 2003, p. 158). In the German case, issues surrounding military service became increasingly knotty by the middle of the 19th century. In 1849, the U.S. Ambassador to the Northern German Federation,

George Bancroft, made a vigorous case against the idea of dual citizenship, arguing that countries should "as soon tolerate a man with two wives as a man with two countries; as soon bear with polygamy as that state of double allegiance which common sense so repudiates that it has not even coined a word to express it" (quoted in Koslowski, 2003, p. 158).

What Bancroft was reacting to was the fact that according to German law at the time, German citizenship could not be lost. Thus, even as German emigrants became naturalized citizens of their new homeland, they also remained German citizens. Germany was not unique in this regard. U.S. opposition to dual citizenship led to a series of diplomatic initiatives with Germany and other states, spearheaded by Bancroft. In 1868, a treaty was entered into between the United States and Germany that provided for the right of a German national to expatriate after 5 years residence in the United States (Koslowski, 2003, pp. 158–159). Clearly, by the second half of the 19th century, the idea that dual citizenship was a situation to be avoided gained adherents among political leaders in both immigrant-exporting and -receiving nations. Thus, similar agreements, known as the Bancroft Treaties, were entered into between the United States and 26 other nations, including Austria-Hungary, Belgium, Britain, Denmark, Norway, and Sweden. These treaties served chiefly to establish a situation in which one nationality would be gained at the expense of the other; dual citizenship was construed as an undesirable and, in general, an impermissible outcome.

The Bancroft Treaties were emblematic of an increasingly shared position among political elites about the need to prevent dual citizenship whenever possible. Nevertheless, while not always welcomed, dual citizenship has long existed due to differing criteria employed by various nations in granting citizenship. To make sense of these differences, it is important to realize that specific states responded in various ways to the following four criteria. The first criteria is *jus soli*, or birthplace, which means that citizenship is extended to all individuals born within a nation's borders—generally including territories or protectorates under the jurisdiction of the state in question. The second criteria is *jus sanguinis*, which refers to citizenship determined by lineage, which typically has meant that it is determined by parentage, but sometimes has meant that it can be acquired on the basis of a more distant familial relationship. Third, marital status can serve as a criterion. Marriage to a citizen of a different nation can affect one's own national affiliation in two ways. In some instances, marriage can result in the loss of citizenship, while in other instances it can mean the acquisition of a new citizenship (in any particular case, either one or the other or both can occur). Fourth, residential location can be a criterion. Living in a country of which one is not a citizen for a specified length of time in some cases alters one's citizenship ties to both the nation of origin and the nation of residence (Hansen & Weil, 2002, p. 2).

The interaction of these four criteria can and has resulted in legitimacy being accorded to dual citizenship. For example, *jus soli* and *jus sanguinis* criteria in tandem can readily result in dual nationality as the result of population movements from one state to another. If a child of parents who are nationals of a country granting citizenship on the basis of ancestry is born in a nation operating with *jus soli,* then that child automatically has two citizenships from birth. While this scenario is not a new one, the number of children attaining two nationalities from birth in this way rises with population mobility (Hansen & Weil, 2002, p. 2). In practice, many countries use a combination of these two criteria, and in fact none use *jus soli* exclusively. Immigrant-receiving nations tend to favor *jus soli,* as this best reflects the needs of both the nation for new settlers and for the settlers themselves. On the other hand, emigrant-sending nations—including most European nations historically—tend to favor *jus sanguinis.* What this illustrates is the fact that although the desire to unify citizenship attainment policy across nations in order to cut down on the incidence of dual nationality has been strong, each nation has its own interests in mind in creating its own distinctive policies related to citizenship (Martin, 2003, p. 9).

In an effort to avoid granting dual citizenship to the offspring of couples with differing citizenships, it was customary for citizenship laws in the 19th century and first part of the 20th to dictate that a woman marrying a citizen of another country lose her original citizenship and attain that of her husband. Therefore, any children born to them would be citizens of a single nation. However, such explicitly gender-biased laws have increasingly been challenged. Feminist demands have led to the revision of such laws to allow women to retain their former citizenship ties; hence, children born out of such unions have dual nationality (Spiro, 2002, p. 20). In fact, if a child was born of two nationals of different *jus sanguinis* nations in a third *jus soli* nation of which neither parent was a citizen, the offspring could potentially have three citizenships. Many nations have attempted to prevent such a situation from arising from the passing down of nationalities from parent to child by requiring dual- (or multiple-) national children to choose a single nationality upon reaching adulthood. Germany, for example, in its passage in 1999 of what is arguably the most liberal citizenship law in Europe, mandated such a requirement. Nonetheless, as David Martin (2003, p. 10) has noted, even where such legal provisions exist, they are typically not vigorously enforced.

Stephen Legomsky (2003, p. 81) succinctly summarizes the factors at play in creating the preconditions for dual citizenship despite opposition to it in principle. He describes three maxims that interact in a variety of ways to yield dual or plural citizenship: (1) "each state decides who its own nationals are"; (2) "a state typically provides alternative multiple routes to nationality"; and (3) "the rules vary from state to state."

Within this framework, one can point to a variety of reasons that dual nationality is increasingly accepted—if not necessarily legally sanctioned. In the first place, one can point to globalizing forces. As noted previously, most of the world was quite averse to the idea of dual citizenship until about three decades ago, when a profound shift of opinion became evident. Martin (2003, p. 4) contends that this move toward growing (if sometimes grudging) acceptance of this shift has resulted from "the expanding interconnection of the world community." While dual nationality has always existed due to a lack of uniformity of nationality laws from nation to nation, the dramatic increase in international mobility, marriage, and commerce has elevated the number of dual citizens, and with it, the growing call for accepting dual citizenship. A substantial number of people today live in countries of which they are not citizens, desiring to naturalize, but also desiring to continue to be citizens of their countries of origin, with which they continue to maintain ties (Martin, 2003, p. 5).

Legomsky (2003, p. 82) points to the centrality of increased levels of migration as contributing to the proliferation of dual citizenship, which has been spurred by "technological advances in information, communication, and transportation, combined with sizeable economic disparities among nations, widespread armed conflicts, systematic violations of fundamental human rights, and other worldwide forces." Looking specifically at western Europe, which had in the 19th century exported more people than it imported and during that time had preferred to define nationality along ancestry lines, Weil (2001) notes that after World War II, these nations were forced to rethink such policies. The result was the dramatic increase in the number of dual nationals within their borders.

A second factor contributing to the growth of dual nationality is the fact that concerns over diplomatic protection no longer have the same relevance that they did in the 19th century. While it may be too much to contend, as some have, that the historic concern over conflicts of diplomatic protection have become virtually obsolete, it is the case that in an era of international sensitivity to human rights, whether or not individuals are a nation's own citizens makes less difference than it did in the past in terms of the country's treatment of them due to the growing significance of an international human rights regime. As Spiro (2002, p. 25) points out, if Germany is treating a German citizen badly, members of the international community will protest even though they have no nationality ties to the individual.

The women's movement represents the third factor. This is particularly the case in nations where nationality is transmitted by ancestry. Although it has traditionally been the rule that children born in wedlock take their father's nationality and those born outside of marriage take that of their mother, thus in both instances discouraging dual nationality, the push for women's equality during the past century has resulted in the increase in the number of nations that legitimize the passing on of both nationalities to offspring (Koslowski, 2003, p. 161). One result, perhaps unintended, has been that efforts to promote gender equality have made it more difficult for women to take their spouse's nationality.

As noted earlier, many older nationality laws granted foreign women automatic citizenship upon marrying a citizen of that country (and many also automatically stripped a woman's citizenship upon her marriage to a foreigner). The general trend during the 20th century was to repeal such laws, beginning in the 1930s in some nations and continuing until the last decade of the past century in other nations. Spouses of both genders now often have to be a resident of a country for a specified number of years and undergo the same naturalization processes. Weil (2001, p. 28) has noted that a stimulus for this change is the desire to avoid "false marriages" that are designed to expedite the acquisition of citizenship.

The fourth factor contributing to the expansion of dual citizenship involves the shifting interests of immigrant-sending countries. During the 19th and early 20th centuries, political and cultural (including religious) elites tended to be opposed to emigration; this situation has changed dramatically during the past several decades. In part, the reversal from opposition to general support of the idea of dual citizenship has arisen as a result of demands made on the part of overseas nationals to their native homelands. However, state elites would not likely have been prompted to support the desires of their expatriates, particularly when they were motivated by the fact that immigrants who naturalize enjoy more rights and benefits than do foreign residents. Realizing that the retention of homeland nationality is largely an identity issue, they came to see that if they could maintain ties with a constituency abroad, it might be to the state's benefit. For one thing, dual nationals with a favorable orientation toward their homeland might in various ways use their political influence (voting, lobbying, and the like) in their new nation to promote policies favoring the homeland. In other words, nations of emigration have a vested interest in promoting political transnationalism (Guarnizo, Portes, & Haller, 2003).

Another, and perhaps more significant, reason that countries of emigration want to encourage enduring ties with their foreign nationals is economic in nature. If allowed to remain citizens even after naturalizing elsewhere, emigrants will be more likely to continue traveling back to the country of origin and maintain close ties with individuals and institutions there, which as Martin (2003, p. 7) points out, "might foster continued [economic investment] or charitable donations in the country of origin, thus boosting the national economy." On the one hand, developing nations seek to encourage immigrant entrepreneurs to create and sustain economic networks with the homeland. As Portes, Haller, and Guarnizo (2002, p. 294) contend, although the percentage of immigrants who are entrepreneurs is quite small, nonetheless the "transnational firms" they create "can be viewed as bridges helping to keep ties alive with the home countries and even strengthening them over time." In addition, remittances have become a major factor contributing to the GDP in many developing nations.

Fifth, the dissolution of empires and nations has led to the expansion of dual citizenship. When colonial empires crumbled after World War II and former colonies became independent nations, many former empires allowed their own citizens who had settled in the colonies to exercise full citizenship in these newly formed nations while simultaneously preserving their citizenships in the motherland—either by formal treaty or more informally. For example, with the demise of Spain as a colonial power, it entered into treaties with Chile, Peru, Paraguay, Nicaragua, Guatemala, Bolivia, Ecuador, Costa Rica, Honduras, the Dominican Republic, and Argentina. In a different era and context, when the Soviet Union disintegrated, 25 million people of Russian ancestry found themselves residing in non-Russian states. To allow these people to be part of the new Russia, dual citizenship was legitimated (Koslowski, 2003, p. 161).

Miriam Feldblum (2000, p. 478) summaries the factors that have led to a progressive loosening of restrictions on dual citizenship, particularly since the 1980s, as follows: "increased migrations, gender equity reforms in nationality transmission and retention, reforms in nationality criteria, informal policy practices to ignore the ban on dual nationality, and actual legislation to lift the traditional ban on dual nationality." Koslowski (2003, p. 160) adds to these internal causes the following external forces when he contends that the "trend toward increasing toleration of dual nationality is enabled by international security factors such as post-war European integration, North Atlantic security structures, the end of the Cold War, and the decline of conscription." At the same time, it is useful to observe that despite these internal and external forces contributing to a profound shift in the way states and publics view dual citizenship, many of the old laws, nonetheless, remain unchanged (de la Pradelle, 2002, p. 194).

## Overview of International Laws and Conventions

The Bancroft Treaties noted earlier became something of a model insofar as they ratified the generally agreed on opposition to dual citizenship on the part of governments. The Convention on the Status of Naturalized Citizens, entered into by many Western nations in 1906, declared that naturalized individuals who left the country in which they naturalized and returned permanently to their original homeland lost their naturalized citizenship (Aleinikoff & Klusmeyer, 2001, pp. 73–74).

Of particular significance was the 1930 Hague Convention Concerning Certain Questions Relating to the Conflict of Nationality. In part a consequence of conflicts arising over military service in World War I, the convention's preamble states, "it is in the interest of the international community to secure that all members should have a nationality and should have one nationality only" (quoted in Koslowski, 2003, p. 159). Although the United States supported this ideal, in the end it did not sign the convention because it failed to provide that a woman's nationality should be considered independently of her husband's and that her citizenship should not be automatically revoked upon marrying a foreign national. The convention was intended to deal with the issue of the diplomatic protection of dual nationals. In principle, a state cannot afford protection to a dual national against the other country whose citizenship the individual holds. Since this guideline was established, there have been many exceptions on the grounds of universal human rights, and in many cases arbitration between the nations involved has been employed to resolve disputes. Frequently, the nation with which the individual has stronger ties is permitted to intervene on that individual's behalf (Hailbronner, 2003, pp. 22–23).

The Hague Convention was intended to promote single nationality. However, in declaring that each state had the right to determine who were and who were not its citizens and in offering no uniform guidelines for such determinations, it actually did very little to curb the incidence of dual citizenship (Aleinikoff & Klusmeyer, 2001, p. 72). Thus, it is not surprising that over the next several decades the issues posed by the Hague Convention were revisited again and again. The effort to reduce the number of dual citizens and to sort out military obligations in the case of dual citizenship were addressed both by the United Nations and by the Council of Europe as the emergence of the European Union raised questions about the impact of greater labor mobility within western European nations and the opening of borders to new immigrants from outside of the European Union. However, at the same time, the move to reduce gender discrimination in citizenship laws, such as the 1979 UN Convention on the Elimination of All Forms of Discrimination against Women, inevitably meant that there was a greater openness to dual nationality. At the same time, there was a concern about people who were stateless. The Hague Convention argued that every person should have one nationality, but some displaced persons lost their citizenship of origin and were not readily granted citizenship by the nations that offered them asylum. This, for example, was a problem confronting western Europe after World War II as political refugees fled Warsaw Pact nations.

By the end of the 20th century, the primacy accorded to preventing dual nationality had eroded considerably. Thus, Aleinikoff and Klusmeyer (2001, p. 73) note that the European Convention on Nationality of 1997 no longer sought to reduce or eliminate dual nationality, which had been the chief goal of its 1963 convention. Rather than being primarily concerned about split national allegiances and security, this convention was much more focused on achieving "greater unity between its members," the "legitimate interests" of individuals, averting statelessness and discrimination, and determining "the rights and duties of multiple nationals" (Council of Europe, 1997, p. 5). In addition to the EU signatories of this convention, several non-EU members were also signatories, including Albania, Bulgaria, the Czech Republic, Hungary, Moldova, Poland, Russia, Slovakia, and the former Yugoslav Republic of Macedonia (Koslowski, 2003, p. 170).

## How Many Dual Citizens?

Given the growing openness to dual nationality, it is clear that the number of dual citizens in the developed nations has grown significantly in recent decades. However, just how many dual citizens reside in these nations is far from clear. Spiro (2002, p. 21) summarizes the situation in the United States as follows: "No national or international statistical surveys of the incidence of dual nationality have been conducted to date, but the trend . . . has clearly been upward." The same can be said of the other industrial nations. States typically only register their own citizens, not even attempting to count the number of other citizenships those citizens might possess. In part, this is due to the fact that people with two or more citizenships may keep quiet about this fact in order to avoid administrative difficulties and bureaucratic hurdles.

Germany is one state that has attempted to determine the number of dual citizens in the case of naturalization. Between 2000 and 2006, it determined that about 45% of all naturalizations involved new citizens who were allowed to keep their original citizenship. This would suggest that the German state has a fairly precise handle on the level of dual citizenships, but this overstates the case. If one is interested in the total number of dual citizens residing on German territory, then dual citizenships arising from other circumstances, such as the children of binational couples, also have to be factored into the figures. In looking at the overall picture, the situation becomes considerably less certain.

The number of individuals marrying outside of their own nationality as well as moving about from one nation to another is increasing, hence increasing the number of dual citizens (Schuck, 2002, p. 66). Worldwide, there are tens of millions of people who find themselves in situations where, laws permitting, they could be eligible for dual citizenship (Aleinikoff & Klusmeyer, 2001, p. 79). Add to this the fact that worldwide, the number of nations permitting dual nationality is growing. Renshon (2001, pp. 234–236) refers to previous studies that concluded, for example, that in 1996 there were 40 nations granting dual nationality. Two years later another estimate placed the figure at 55. Renshon (2001, p. 236) himself found that at the turn of the century there were 93 nations that allowed dual citizenship, albeit in most instances with some restrictions.

Turning to specific countries, it is estimated that there are between 4 and 5 million American citizens residing permanently in other countries, many of whom already have or likely will obtain dual citizenship in the nation of residence (Spiro, 2002, p. 21). Meanwhile, the number of dual nationals residing in the United States is due in part simply to increased naturalization in the United States. To illustrate this fact, Spiro (2002, p. 21) notes, "More individuals naturalized in 1997 than in the entire decade of the 1970s." Aleinikoff and Klusmeyer (2001, p. 63) report that "more than a half million children born each year in the United States have at least one additional nationality." Renshon (2001, p. 234) observes that the United States, like most countries, fails to keep track of how many of its citizens are dual nationals. He reports that between 1961 and 1997, 17,437,607 immigrants entered the United States from nations that permitted dual nationality. Theoretically, all of these immigrants are potential dual nationals. At this point, we simply do not know how many of them have pursued this option; however, the figure suggests that the pool of those who might at some point in the future become a dual national is large and growing over time (Renshon, 2001, pp. 268–269).

Both Feldblum (2000, p. 478) and Zappala and Castles (2000, p. 56) concur that by the early 20th century, Australia had about 5 million dual nationals. This is a remarkable figure given that it represents nearly a quarter of the total Australian population. Koslowski (2003, p. 162) estimates that there are over a million French citizens who maintain dual nationality. Looking at western Europe as a whole, Feldblum (2000, p. 478) estimates that the figure is "at least several million and rising." However imprecise these estimates are, they clearly point to the fact that dual nationality is a significant phenomenon in the world's liberal democracies, and is likely to increase in significance over time.

## Dual Citizenship and Immigrant Incorporation

Are the consequences of dual citizenship on the whole positive or negative for the receiving nation? What about the sending nation? Is dual citizenship beneficial or detrimental to the dual citizen? Despite the pronounced trend toward increased levels of dual citizenship and the recasting of state policies regarding dual citizens, there is still considerable uncertainty about its implications. Those who have a positive view of the phenomenon contend that allowing immigrants to retain their original citizenship can actually lead to increased rates of naturalization, insofar as the immigrant is not required to make a choice between one of two citizenships. This, for example, is the conclusion of Michael Jones-Correa's (2001) study of immigrants from the Western Hemisphere who have settled in the United States. He found that immigrants from those countries permitting dual nationality exhibited higher levels of naturalization in the United States than their counterparts from countries that do not recognize dual nationality. Similarly, he contends that dual citizenship is an inducement to greater levels of civic and political participation. Finally, the acceptance of dual citizenship is considered to be an aspect of multiculturalism, and insofar as it is, it can contribute to immigrant self-respect and is congruent with the "politics of recognition" (Taylor et al., 1992), while at the same time it serves as an endorsement of transnational ties.

According to critics, this is precisely the problem with dual citizenship. One issue that these critics pose is whether dual voting ought to be condoned. For example, in the debates over dual citizenship in Sweden, the potential violation of the "one person, one vote" principle was what opponents of liberalizing citizenship laws regarded as the most important problem. Dual voting is connected to the two broader and clearly intertwined problems that critics point to. The first raises the specter of a failure to integrate immigrants. By remaining connected to the homeland, it is argued, immigrants refuse to set stakes in the host society and to fit into its social fabric. Closely connected to this concern is the claim that dual citizenship can easily lead to dual allegiances, which reflect a lack of loyalty to the new polity. While in the past this fear was voiced in terms of nation-states that might at some point be belligerents, since 9/11, it typically focuses on immigrants from Muslim countries who are viewed as a suspect fifth column.

Related to these concerns is the claim that dual citizenship contributes to the general devaluation of national citizenship. Peter Spiro (2007) has made this case in terms of U.S. citizenship, but similar concerns have been voiced elsewhere. He contends that citizenship increasingly is incapable of defining and fostering a shared national identity that is defined by a level of loyalty that would entail the prospect of genuine sacrifice. Instead, it is seen as an increasingly instrumental identity, such as by people collecting passports in order to grease the wheels of transnational contacts or by people seeking to take advantage of generous welfare systems.

In responding to such criticisms, David Martin and T. Alexander Aleinikoff contend that the alarm is unwarranted. Governments, they argue, are quite capable of managing the risks while encouraging the benefits. Referring to the old charge that dual citizenship amounted to bigamy, they contend that this claim "adapts the wrong family analogy. Marriage makes a person a member of two families: one's own and one's spouse's. To give love or loyalty to the second does not require subtracting it from the first" (Martin & Aleinikoff, 2002, p. 81).

In fact, the state of empirical research on dual citizenship is in its infancy, having entered the research agenda in the social and political sciences only very recently (see, for example, Dahlin & Hironaka, 2008). So far, most studies have been concerned with the perspective of nation-states, focusing on policies intended to facilitate immigrant integration and on citizenship law in general. Very few studies have explored the perspectives of immigrants, and thus we know little about their vocabularies of motives and their actual social practices. Bloemraad's (2006) previously cited study is one of the main contributions to date. A comparable edited volume examines immigrants in several select European countries (Kalekin-Fishman & Pitkänen, 2006).

## Nested Citizenship

If dual citizenship is a pervasive feature of a majority of the world's nations, developed and developing states alike, nested citizenship is a far more limited and circumscribed phenomenon. It refers specifically to the newly emerging citizenship regime created by the constituent members of the European Union. What is nested citizenship? It is a form of supranational citizenship. British Commonwealth citizenship is an example of a supranational form of citizenship that arose during the colonial era (Gilbertson, 2006, p. 4). In the specific contemporary case of the European Union, nested citizenship calls to mind an image of Russian dolls, with smaller dolls contained in larger and larger dolls. Juan Díez Medrano and Paula Guitiérrez (2001, p. 757) succinctly describe the relationship in the following way: "Nested identities are lower- and higher-order identities such that the latter encompass the former." Nested citizenship is a form of multiple citizenship, but one in which multiple citizenship connotes full membership on multiple governance levels (Faist, 2001b; Faist & Ette, 2007). Elizabeth Meehan (1993, p. 1) defines the new and evolving citizenship in the European Union as "neither national nor cosmopolitan, but . . . multiple in the sense that the identities, rights, and obligations associated . . . with citizenship are expressed through an increasingly complex configuration of common community institutions, states, national and transnational voluntary associations, regions, and alliances of regions." The notion of nested citizenship presumes that the different levels of citizenship are interconnected, rather than operating autonomously.

Thus, immigrants in locales that have become autonomous regions (smaller, subnational dolls contained within the larger national dolls), such as Scotland and Wales in Britain and the Basque region and Catalonia in Spain, can operate with the assumption that citizenship laws and policies within both Britain and Spain apply uniformly throughout the nation. In other words, they can assume that autonomous regions have not been granted the authority to establish their own citizenship regimes, though they may have to contend with the fact that the regime manifests itself somewhat differently in such regions (as, for example, in regard to language). Similarly, immigrants can assume that certain human rights provisions that have become institutionalized at the EU level will be applicable anywhere within its 27 member states. For example, they will know that nowhere within the European Union will they be subject to courts imposing the death penalty. In posing the relationship between and among the levels of nested citizenship, we seek to make clear that national sovereignty has been and remains the fulcrum, making possible the legitimacy of both subnational and supranational political institutions.

## Competing Perspectives

Nested citizenship offers a perspective about what citizenship in the European Union means that differs from two competing perspectives, which we refer to as intergovernmentalism and postnationalism. The first position contends that EU citizenship is largely residual insofar as the primary function of the European Union is to promote the market and to assist in the coordination of the economic activities of the member states. If this is true, it means that the European Union is not to any significant extent engaged in policies aimed at redistribution or welfare provision, leaving such activities overwhelmingly to the member states. It is argued that the most notable involvement in the promotion of social rights has been regulatory in nature, such as the requirement for equal pay for equal work, health and safety standards, and migration policy. These activities can be seen as being chiefly designed to establish uniform standards across member states in order to achieve economic integration. However, in so doing, they have impacts that lead to greater similarities across states than would otherwise be the case. The Treaty of Amsterdam will most likely over time add to the substance of EU membership by formally declaring that the basis of the European Union lies in the recognition of fundamental human and social rights (Faist & Ette, 2007; Roche, 1997).

The second perspective is the antithesis of the former and it has had a larger influence in recent scholarly discourses on citizenship, generally under the rubric of postnationalism (Jacobson, 1996; Soysal, 1994). The central thesis of postnationalist thought is that the nation-state is weakening, being replaced by supranational constructs. Insofar as this is the case, the historic association of modern citizenship with the nation-state is seen as eroding, while simultaneously, supranational entities have stepped in to reconfigure and expand the territorial boundaries of citizenship. In this regard, the postnational musings that appeared on the scene during the past decade often suggested that we were witnessing the dawn of a nationless era. A more modified form does not see the state as disappearing entirely, but its salience as eroding appreciably. This is the position advanced by Damian Tambini (2001, p. 212), who contends that "no one can seriously propose that the nation as an institutional form is about to disappear. Neither, however, can it continue in the classical nineteenth-century form. Rather, the meaning and content of national belonging will be transformed as the structural basis of national citizenship continues to be undermined."

There are three main claims associated with this perspective. First, liberal democracies have increasingly come to respect the human rights of all persons irrespective of citizenship (Jacobson, 1996). Second, international human rights discourses and international and supranational institutions have prompted nation-states to grant rights to previously excluded groups, such as immigrants from outside the European Union who have taken up residence in one of its member states (Soysal, 1994). Third, institutions such as the European Court of Justice (ECJ) have developed common rights for all residents, such that, at present, there are relatively few differences in social rights and the salience of social citizenship between permanent residents and citizens of EU member states. For this reason, the distinction between citizenship and what some have called denizenship has been blurred (Hammar, 1990). To the extent that permanent legal residents who are not citizens—those dubbed denizens—acquire rights that are increasingly congruent with the rights traditionally associated with citizenship status, the salience of national citizenship is called into question.

The central idea is that the two prime components of citizenship—rights and obligations on the one hand and collective identity on the other—have increasingly decoupled over the past few decades. Thus, for example, human rights, formerly tightly connected to nationality, nowadays also apply to noncitizen residents. In other words, settled noncitizens also have access to significant human, civil, and social rights. To the extent that this is true, citizenship as a "right to have rights" (Arendt, 1968; see also Benhabib, 2004, pp. 49–69; Somers, 2008) is not any longer the fundamental basis for membership in political communities. Instead, discourses tied to interstate norms such as the various charters of the United Nations are viewed as contributing to postnational membership (Soysal, 1994).

This is a problematic claim. There are, in fact, no supranational institutions conferring the status of formal membership irrespective of a prior nationality—including the European Union. The postnational perspective fails to appreciate the democratically legitimated aspect of citizenship status. As a consequence, it is no coincidence that analysts operating from this framework tend to speak of postnational *membership* instead of *citizenship*. For example, political rights are still almost exclusively tied to formal citizenship. The popular legitimation of membership in political communities, of utmost importance for any democratic regime, gets lost. Instead, the focus is on courts that uphold interstate norms, or what Jacobson (1996) refers to as "rights across borders."

If the intergovernmental approach downplays the significance of suprastate institutions, the postnational position treats such institutions as increasingly becoming more consequential than nation-states. From our perspective, neither offers a convincing portrait of the European Union in its present form. Rather, it is our view that the idea of nested citizenship offers the most compelling account of the relationship between the European Union and its constituent member states. At the same time, we should note that the European Union has evolved over time, and continues to do so. With this proviso, the characteristics of nested citizenship become clearer when we look at an example of how the different levels interact in changing the "rules of the game."

This particular illustration concerns the increased portability of social rights across national borders for German retirees and beneficiaries of long-term care insurance. During the past two decades, on average about 30,000 pensioners from Germany have lived year-round in Spain. A problem arose when these pensioners became invalids and required increasing levels of health care. To be eligible for social assistance or long-term health care, they were expected to return to Germany. This changed when the ECJ determined that the social benefits of EU member states are portable across national borders of member states. In this case, the ECJ had made a determination that required the German government to establish bureau-cratic procedures designed to ensure the portability of these particular social rights.

As this example suggests, nested citizenship entails an interactive system of political choices and policy decisions occurring at both the state and suprastate levels. The web of governance operates on multiple levels, and in the process, the European Union becomes the site of building new concep-tions of rights. The European Union does not function as a compensatory mechanism for deficiencies in the social rights regimes of the respective mem-ber states. It does, however, function to coordinate and harmonize those regimes. This can be seen in a variety of ways. For example, the European Union is concerned with the regulation of safety and health policies, as well as those regulating the condition of economic production. As early as the agreement arrived at in Messina in 1955, there was an expressed attempt to harmonize social standards regarding the work week, overtime pay, vacation time, the free movement of labor, and the overall coordination of social pol-icy (Moravcsik, 1999). At the same time, the member states retain sole purview over their social security systems and the social service institutions tasked to oversee such provision. Indeed, most conventional social policies remain solidly ensconced within the borders of the respective member states, albeit with somewhat reduced levels of autonomy and sovereignty than before the creation of the European Union.

## What Is EU Citizenship?

What does this mean for EU citizenship? Are there rights that accrue to EU citizens that go beyond those possessed as a consequence of membership in a specific member state? It is worth quoting Benhabib's (2004, pp. 148–149) summary of what individuals derive from EU membership:

Not just a passive status, it is also intended to designate an active civic identity. Citizens of the EU states can settle anywhere in the union, take up jobs in their chosen countries, and vote as well as stand for office in local elections and in elections for the parliament of Europe. They have the right to enjoy consular and diplomatic representation in the territory of a third country in which the member state whose nationals they are may not be represented. They have the right to petition the European Parliament and to apply to the European Ombudsman. As monetary and economic integration progresses, EU members are debating whether union citizenship should be extended to an equivalent package of social rights and benefits, such as unemployment compensation, health care, and old age pensions, which members of EU states would be able to enjoy whichever EU country they take up residency in.

All of this raises the question: how ought we to characterize the European Union and to what extent is it meaningful to speak about EU citizenship? By introducing the term *citizenship*, the institution has been transformed into a polity, albeit one where the link between political rights and the articulation of those rights in terms of state boundaries since the Treaty of Westphalia had been, if not undone, at least partially uncoupled. As a multilevel governance system, the European Union clearly reaches beyond a low-profile interstate regime, although it has not at this point developed into a coherent suprastate institution—a United States of Europe—as some of its elite proponents would prefer. Related to this fact, the extent to which ordinary citizens of Europe perceive themselves to be citizens of the European Union appears to be rather attenuated. The reverse of this is also true: despite the existence of the European Union for a half century, there is little evidence to conclude that national citizenship is becoming a hollow shell, replaced by the more expansive citizenship at the EU level. Maarten Vink's (2005b) study of the Netherlands and Fiorella Dell-Olio's (2005) comparative analysis of Britain and Italy both arrive at the same conclusion, which is that national identity remains robust in spite of the growing significance of the European Union at an institutional level.

Given its historical uniqueness, it is difficult to use traditional categories to describe the European Union. Reflective of this fact, while it is quite accurate to describe the European Union as a suprastate and federative governance network with mixed intergovernmental and common authorities, such a description emphasizes the fact that the European Union is sufficiently novel that our typical categories do not quite do it justice. The principal architects of the European Union appear to have been aware of this situation when they created the European Economic Community (EEC) in the 1957 Treaty of Rome. Rather than attempting to create an explicitly suprastate institution, they opted for a more pragmatic approach, establishing instead an entity designed to foster the economic integration of Europe. Nevertheless, since that time, the framework evolved from a purely economic institution to an intergovernmental one, becoming by the 1990s a collective actor on the global scene. Indeed, as Kalypso Nicolaidis (2005, p. 11) observes, "By the turn of the millennium, the EU had many prerogatives associated with sovereign states: various police powers, border controls, currency regulation, and cooperative (at least partly) foreign policy."

However, by introducing the idea of citizenship at a level that transcends the nation-state, the uniqueness of the European Union comes into focus. As Benhabib (2004) emphasizes, the focus of much of the discussion about EU citizenship revolves around the question of rights—rights for both those who are already defined as citizens of member states and the rights of those who are not. Insofar as this is the case, such a discourse highlights the fact that in its current form, the European Union suffers from a democratic deficit and from an imprecise understanding of collective affiliation. As long as the European Union functioned well and questions of national sovereignty were not raised, these deficits were largely ignored. Many complained about the faceless bureaucrats in Brussels who were seen as the power behind the European Parliament. However, this did not deter the expansion of the role played by both the parliament and the ECJ.

The gulf between the ordinary citizens of the member states' perceptions of the rationale for the European Union and that of the Eurocrats who ran the institution has for some time been a topic of concern in some quarters. Thus, in British politics, a powerful strain of "Euroscepticism" has been evident in both the Tory and Labour Parties, and recently led to the creation of a single-issue party led by a popular television presenter who wants the United Kingdom to exit the European Union altogether. Recently, the gulf has taken, from the point of view of supporters of the European Union, a disturbing turn. From its inception, the European Union operated without a formal constitution. However, with the passage of the Treaty of Nice in 2000, not only did the member states agree to an expansion of the European Union, but they also committed to the creation of a constitution—a constitution, as Nicolaidis (2005, p. 12) put it, "not for a nation but *among* nations."

This raised an interesting question, for it was not clear which voices were necessary to ratify the constitution—which proved to be a 300-page-long text as befits a document written by bureaucrats. Many of the member states decided that their national legislatures would determine whether or not to approve the constitution, while in other cases it was decided that the decision would be put to the nation's voters in referenda. In the latter camp were two of the original members of the EEC, France and the Netherlands. After nearly half of the legislatures of the member states had approved the constitution, it appeared to be headed for approval. However, in the summer of 2005, the voters of France and the Netherlands resoundingly rejected the proposed constitution despite the coordinated efforts of political elites from the center left and center right in both countries to gain an electoral victory.

Despite victories among the voters in Spain and Luxemburg, there was a general sense that the proposed constitution had failed and, for the more pessimistic advocates of the European Union, that the institution itself had entered into crisis that might spell the end of the European Union as we have known it. This is a highly improbable scenario given the fact that during its half-century of existence, it has become institutionally embedded and cannot readily be undone. Indeed, despite the anti-EU stance of a minority in all the member states, there is actually very little political will to pursue such a course. While some of the more pragmatically minded supporters of the European Union are prepared to return to the status quo ante, arguing that a constitution is not necessary, others have instead suggested that if this version of the constitution is ultimately to be approved, it may be necessary to modify the rules required for approval.

At the same time, this impasse has prompted reflection about the distinctiveness of the European Union. In a commentary in *The Guardian*, sociologists Ulrich Beck and Anthony Giddens (2005, p. 28), both forceful defenders of the constitution and supporters of expansion, including the ultimate inclusion of Turkey, made the following bold claim:

> The European Union is the most original and successful experiment in political institution-building since World War II. It has reunited Europe after the fall of the Berlin Wall. It has influenced political change as far away as Ukraine and Turkey—not, as in the past, by military, but by peaceful means. Through its economic innovations, it has played a part in bringing prosperity to millions, even if its recent level of growth has been disappointing. It has helped one of the very poorest countries in Europe, Ireland, to become one of the richest. It has been instrumental in bringing democracy to Spain, Portugal, and Greece, countries that had previously been dictatorships.

They go on to make clear that they think the European Union has much unfinished business to attend to, and that an inward-looking nationalism on the part of critics of the European Union works against the best interests of the member states, individually and collectively. In making their case, Beck and Giddens (2005, p. 28) offer their own understanding of what precisely the European Union is, suggesting that it ought not to be viewed as an "unfinished nation" or an "incomplete federal state." Stressing that the European Union is not a threat to the sovereignty of the member nation states and does not signal either a postnationalist institution that transcends the nation-state or leads to cultural homogenization, they consider it to be "a new type of cosmopolitan project." We would only add that at this particular time, the pressing need is to create a new democratic legitimation of the project—one that manages to bridge the gulf between elite proponents and skeptical, apathetic, or antagonistic ordinary citizens.

## Fortress Europe and Immigration

While Beck and Giddens voice their concern about the potential deleterious consequences of parochial nationalism, they do not speak to a similar threat of an overly insular Europe. Yet within the recently expanded European Union, the distinction between what are referred to as second-country nationals versus third-country nationals becomes increasingly significant. The former refers to citizens of the various EU member states. Given their ability to move freely within the European Union, as well as work and reside where they choose to do so, whether they can be viewed as migrants in the conventional sense is an open question. Certainly, the movement of Bulgarians and Romanians westward to countries such as Germany, France, and Britain represents a different sort of movement of people compared to the years prior to these two eastern European nations' ascension to the European Union. Put another way, while they are in fact moving beyond a border, the nature of the border is qualitatively different for them at present compared to the recent past.

While the ability of eastern Europeans to move freely into western Europe may not be quite the same as an American from Connecticut moving to California, it is also starkly different from the situation confronting third-country nationals, a term referring to nationals from countries that are not part of the European Union—or, in other words, the rest of the world. This includes not only legal labor immigrants, but the undocumented and, in growing numbers, asylum seekers.

In recent years, particularly since the beginning of the present century, a debate has been underway in Europe pitting those who advocate more restrictive immigration and citizenship policies against opponents of what has become known as "fortress Europe." A key to this debate hinges on the matter of whether or not third-country nationals can (or should) be integrated into the European Union, a topic that cannot be divorced from the question of whether or not a more expansive form of civil solidarity is being forged within Europe, linking in a salient way the citizens of all the European Union's member states. In this regard, Jürgen Habermas, a critic of fortress Europe, has argued that immigration can actually serve to promote European solidarity. As he put it,

> Integration is not a one-way street. When it is successful, it can inspire strong national cultures to become more porous, more sensitive and more receptive both domestically and abroad. In Germany, for example, when the more harmonious coexistence with citizens of Turkish origin becomes a matter of course, the better we will be able to understand other European citizens—from the Portuguese winegrower to the Polish plumber. In opening up domestically, self-contained cultures can also open up to each other. (Habermas, 2006, p. 2)

While this may be true, it is also possible that the forces of immigration restriction have proven to be sufficiently powerful that rather than proceeding along the lines proposed by Habermas, in fact, Europe has taken a restrictive turn. This possibility was recently explored by the European Parliament's Directorate General for Internal Policies. In a report prepared for the committee, three phases in nationality laws since World War II were identified (de Hart, 2008). During the first, which extended until the 1980s, nationality laws changed very little. However, during the last two decades of the past century, when it became clear that immigrants have become a permanent feature of Europe, a convergence of opinion among policy elites across the European Union occurred, whereby the goal of naturalization was to facilitate the integration of newcomers. The general thrust of changes to existing laws was one of liberalization, the goal being to lower the barriers to naturalization.

The third phase began around the turn of the century, when more restrictive naturalization policies were implemented in a number of EU states. Among the ways that this occurred include reducing the use of *jus soli* rules, decreasing the number of immigrants entering countries on the basis of family reunification, and establishing criteria related to language, civics knowledge, and the proof of liberal values as preconditions for naturalization. Joppke (2008) contends that such policies amount to coercive integration. In his view, one of the reasons that EU countries have opted for more restrictive naturalization policies is that they have not implemented immigration policies that stress selectivity for such things as occupational skills and language facility. He distinguishes Europe from Canada and Australia in this regard, arguing that the two historical settler nations have not had to resort to coercive naturalization policies because of their ability to be selective at the point of entry (Joppke, 2007a).

Just as with border policy, which EU member states have increasingly come to see requires coordinated action, so too with integration models. In the case of who gets in, it is obvious that if the borders of some states, such as those on the European Union's eastern frontier or along the Mediterranean, are porous, the impact will be felt throughout the European Union. Likewise with integration: Joppke (2007a, 2007b) contends that despite national variations (for example, Dutch multiculturalism versus French republicanism), there is clear evidence of a convergence of approaches to integration, which he sees as based on the aforementioned coercive integration model coupled with antidiscrimination legislation. He stresses that this is a direction one can find in all the world's liberal democracies, brought about in part by the fact that nations have exhibited an interest in employing a "best practices" approach to the issue. While Joppke does not want to place too much emphasis on the role played by the European Union itself in shaping this new approach, we would contend that it has in fact proven to be a significant agent. This can be seen perhaps most clearly in examining the expansion of antidiscrimination laws into states, particularly new member states, that have not in the past placed much stock in such legislation.

At this juncture, the question arises about the relationship between citizenship rights and universal human rights. Can immigrants rely increasingly on the rights that accrue from the former to combat deficits in the latter? In addressing this question, we locate it in terms of contemporary discussions concerning the prospects of global, world, or cosmopolitan citizenship.

## Can Immigrants Become Global Citizens?

Given the current challenges confronting the European Union, it would appear that any effort to expand the idea of citizenship to the global level has very little probability of success in the foreseeable future. Terms such as *global* or *world citizenship* are often used so indiscriminately that their meaning is far from clear. Certainly, in terms of law, including international law, there is no such status as a world or global citizen. Derek Heater (2002), one of the most ardent spokespersons on behalf of "world citizenship," is cognizant of this reality.

Nonetheless, he and other like-minded thinkers argue that there are incipient indications that such a prospect might in the long run take hold. For instance, in contemporary international law there exist the rudiments of something resembling a world law, including important precedents that emerged out of the military tribunals that tried German and Japanese war criminals after the conclusion of World War II. The International War Crimes Tribunal, and more recently the International Criminal Court, constitute further developments along these lines, efforts, in effect, to articulate the content, the scope, and the nature of a universal human rights regime. Clearly, a landmark in this regard was the ratification of the Universal Declaration of Human Rights in 1948. It and its subsequent covenants on economic, social, and cultural rights likewise point to the seeds of a conceptualization of the global citizen.

Connected to the emergence of a global human rights framework is the growth of a global civil society, for such institutions are viewed as primary carriers of a universal human rights regime. Considerable attention has been paid recently to the dramatic expansion of INGOs, including human rights international nongovernmental organizations (HRINGOS), though the focus of such research has often been more concerned with their growth and not their impact on existing political regimes and cultural milieus (Tsutsui & Wotipka, 2004). The assumption is that what has been evolving since the second half of the 20th century is what Rainer Bauböck (2002) has referred to as a "political community beyond the nation state."

Given the incipient and protean character of the present situation, and the resistance of nation-states to challenges to their authority, it is not difficult to appreciate the skepticism some voice about contemporary prospects for a political community beyond the nation state (Benhabib, 2004; Spiro, 2007; Turner, 2006). After all, it is quite clear that at this time the institutional structures undergirding a universal human rights regime remain woefully underdeveloped. Nevertheless, it is useful to be reminded of the fact that citizenship began at the level of the city-state, and only centuries later was the boundary redefined as the nation-state. We do not find it inconceivable that in various ways the future might spell a similar redefinition that moves beyond the confines of the nation-state. We would stress that this is a long-term possibility, not something that is going to develop in the lifetimes of today's immigrants or that of their children. That being said, it is difficult to predict where the future might lead. When considering the formidable challenges that any project aimed at promoting global citizenship inevitably faces, it is easy to sympathize with Jost Halfmann's (1998) contention that at present, "Kant's vision of a world civil society is a remote, if not highly improbable prospect in the future."

What this means for contemporary immigrants is obvious: citizenship at the level of the nation-state remains the major vehicle for the acquisition and preservation of civil, political, and social rights. This means that the millions of flesh and blood counterparts to Biju, Arjun, and Nazneen, the fictional immigrants introduced at the beginning of this book, will need to be transformed from aliens into fellow citizens if they are to have a chance at living in a world shaped by the twin goals of justice and equality. Much will depend on the dictates of global capitalism, on the ongoing role of states protective of their sovereignty, and on the ability of a global human rights regime to become a more significant force in the world. It depends, too, on the mobilized efforts of immigrants. But it also depends on the willingness of ordinary people in receiving societies to treat the strangers in their midst as potential neighbors, friends, and companions.

# References

Abu-Lughod, J. (1991). *Before European hegemony: The world system A.D. 1250–1350.* New York: Oxford University Press.

Adepoju, A. (2006). Internal and international migration within Africa. In P. Kok, D. Gelderbloom, J. O. Oucha, & J. van Zyl (Eds.), *Migration in South and Southern Africa: Dynamics and determinants* (pp. 26–45). Cape Town, SA: HSRC Press.

Alba, R. (1990). *Ethnic identity: The transformation of white America.* New Haven, CT: Yale University Press.

Alba, R. (1995a). Assimilation's quiet tide. *Public Interest, 119*(Spring), 3–16.

Alba, R. (1995b). Comment. *Journal of American Ethnic History, 14*(2), 82–90.

Alba, R. (1998). Assimilation, exclusion or neither? Models of the incorporation of immigrants in the United States. In P. H. Schuck & R. Munz (Eds.), *Paths to inclusion: The integration of migrants in the United States and Germany* (pp. 1–31). New York: Berghahn Books.

Alba, R. (1999). Immigration and the American realities of assimilation and multiculturalism. *Sociological Forum, 14*(1), 3–25.

Alba, R. (2005). Bright vs. blurred boundaries: Second-generation assimilation and exclusion in France, Germany, and the United States. *Ethnic and Racial Studies, 28*(1), 20–49.

Alba, R. (2006). On the sociological significance of the American Jewish experience: Boundary blurring, assimilation, and pluralism. *Sociology of Religion, 67*(4), 347–358.

Alba, R. (2008). Why we still need a theory of mainstream assimilation. *Kölner Zeitschrift für Soziologie und Sozialpsychologie, 48*, 37–56.

Alba, R., & Nee, V. (1997). Rethinking assimilation theory for a new era of immigration. *International Migration Review, 31*(4), 826–874.

Alba, R., & Nee, V. (2003). *Remaking the American mainstream: Assimilation and contemporary immigration.* Cambridge, MA: Harvard University Press.

Alba, R., & Silberman, R. (2002). Decolonization immigrations and the social origins of the second generation: The case of North Africans in France. *International Migration Review, 36*(4), 1169–1193.

Aleinikoff, T., & Klusmeyer, D. (2001). Plural nationality: Facing the future in a migratory world. In T. A. Aleinikoff & D. Klusmeyer (Eds.), *Citizenship today: Global perspectives and practices* (pp. 63–88). Washington, DC: Carnegie Endowment for International Peace.

Alexander, J. C. (2001). Theorizing the "modes of incorporation": Assimilation, hyphenation, and multiculturalism as varieties of civil participation. *Sociological Theory, 19*(3), 237–249.

Alexander, J. C. (2006). *The civil sphere.* New York: Oxford University Press.

Alexander, J. C., & Smelser, N. J. (1999). Introduction: The ideological discourse of cultural discontent. In N. J. Smelser & J. C. Alexander (Eds.), *Diversity and its discontents: Cultural conflict and common ground in contemporary American society* (pp. 3–18). Princeton, NJ: Princeton University Press.

Ali, A. H. (2007). *Infidel.* New York: Free Press.

Ali, M. (2003). *Brick Lane: A novel.* New York: Scribner.

Andersen, S., & Burns, T. (1996). The European Union and the erosion of parliamentary democracy: A study of post-parliamentary governance. In S. Andersen & K. Eliassen (Eds.), *The European Union: How democratic is it?* (pp. 48–73). London: Sage.

Anderson, E. (2000). *Code of the street: Decency, violence, and the moral life of the inner city.* New York: W.W. Norton.

Ang, I. (2005). Multiculturalism. In T. Bennett, L. Grossberg, & M. Morris (Eds.), *New key words: A revised vocabulary of culture and society* (pp. 34–37). Malden, MA: Blackwell.

Appadurai, A. (1993). Patriotism and its futures. *Public Culture, 2*(1), 1–24.

Appadurai, A. (1996). *Modernity at large: Cultural dimensions of globalization.* Minneapolis: University of Minnesota Press.

Appiah, K. A. (2005). *The ethics of identity.* Princeton, NJ: Princeton University Press.

Appleyard, R. (1991). *International migration: Challenges for the nineties.* Geneva: International Organization for Migration.

Aranda, E. (2007a). *Emotional bridges to Puerto Rico: Migration, return migration, and the struggles of incorporation.* Lanham, MD: Rowman & Littlefield.

Aranda, E. (2007b). Struggles of incorporation among the Puerto Rican middle class. *The Sociological Quarterly, 48*(2), 199–228.

Archibold, R. C. (2006, November 10). The 2006 elections: Democratic victory raises spirits of those favoring citizenship for illegal aliens. *New York Times,* p. 27.

Arendt, H. (1968). *The origins of totalitarianism.* New York: Harcourt, Brace, & Jovanovich. (Original work published 1951)

Baily, S. L. (1999). *Immigrants in the lands of promise: Italians in Buenos Aires and New York City, 1870–1914.* Ithaca, NY: Cornell University Press.

Baines, D. E. (1995). *Emigration from Europe, 1815–1930.* Cambridge, UK: Cambridge University Press.

Bangladeshis in Assam flee anti-migrant drive. (2005, May 20). *International Herald Tribune.*

Barkan, E. (1995). Race, religion, and nationality in American society: A model of ethnicity—from contact to assimilation. *Journal of American Ethnic History, 14*(2), 38–75.

Barkan, E. (2004). America in the hand, homeland in the heart: Transnationalism and translocal immigrant experiences in the American West. *Western Historical Quarterly, 35*(Autumn), 331–354.

Barkan, E. (2006). Introduction: Immigration, incorporation, assimilation, and the limits of transnationalism. *Journal of American Ethnic History, 25*(2–3), 7–32.

Barry, B. (2001). *Culture and equality: An egalitarian critique of multiculturalism.* Cambridge, UK: Polity.

Barth, F. (1969). Introduction. In F. Barth (Ed.), *Ethnic groups and boundaries: The social organization of cultural difference* (pp. 9–38). Boston: Little, Brown.

Basch, L., Glick Schiller, N., & Szanton Blanc, C. (1994). *Nations unbound: Transnational projects, postcolonial predicaments, and deterritorialized nation-states.* Basel, Switzerland: Gordon & Breach.

Bauböck, R. (1994). *The integration of immigrants.* Strasbourg: Council of Europe.

Bauböck, R. (2002). Political community beyond the sovereign state, supranational federalism, and transnational minorities. In S. Vertovec & R. Cohen (Eds.), *Conceiving cosmopolitanism: Theory, context, and practice* (pp. 110–136). Oxford, UK: Oxford University Press.

Bauman, Z. (1998). *Globalization: The human consequences.* Oxford: Polity.

Bean, F. D., & Stevens, G. (2003). *America's newcomers and the dynamics of diversity.* New York: Russell Sage Foundation.

Beck, U. (2000). *What is globalization?* Cambridge: Polity.

Beck, U., & Giddens, A. (2005, October 4). Nationalism has now become the enemy of Europe's nations. *The Guardian,* p. 28.

Beckfield, J. (2008). The dual world polity: Fragmentation and integration in the network of intergovernmental organizations. *Social Problems, 55*(3), 419–442.

Bell, D. (1973). *The coming of post-industrial society: A venture in forecasting.* New York: Basic Books.

Benhabib, S. (2002). *The claims of culture: Equality and diversity in a global era.* Princeton, NJ: Princeton University Press.

Benhabib, S. (2004). *The rights of others: Aliens, residents, and citizens.* Cambridge, UK: Cambridge University Press.

Benhabib, S. (2008). *Another cosmopolitanism* (Robert Post, Ed.). New York: Oxford University Press.

Berkson, I. (1920). *Theorizing of Americanization: A critical study with special reference to the Jewish group.* New York: Teachers College.

Berlin, I. (2000). *Many thousands gone: The first two centuries of slavery in North America.* Cambridge, MA: Belknap Press of Harvard University Press.

Best, J. (2001). *Damned lies and statistics: Untangling numbers from the media, politicians, and activists.* Berkeley: University of California Press.

Bibby, R. (1990). *Mosaic madness: Pluralism without a cause.* Toronto: Stoddart.

Bissoondath, N. (2002). *Selling illusions: The cult of multiculturalism in Canada.* Toronto: Penguin.

Blackburn, R. (1998). *The making of new world slavery: From the baroque to the modern, 1492–1800.* London: Verso.

Bloemraad, I. (2006). *Becoming a citizen: Incorporating immigrants and refugees in the United States and Canada.* Berkeley: University of California Press.

Bloom, S. G. (2000). *Postville: A clash of cultures in heartland America.* New York: Harcourt.

Bluestone, B., & Harrison, B. (1982). *The deindustrialization of America: Plant closings, community abandonment and the dismantling of basic industry.* New York: Basic Books.

Bodnar, J. (1985). *The transplanted: A history of immigrants in urban America.* Bloomington: Indiana University Press.

Bogardus, E. (1933). A social distance scale. *Sociology and Social Research, 17*(January–February), 265–271.

Boli, J., & Thomas, G. W. (1997). World culture in the world polity: A century of non-governmental organization. *American Sociological Review, 62*(2), 171–190.

Bommes, M. (2005). *Transnationalism or assimilation?* Retrieved May 31, 2006, from http://www.sowi-onlinejournal.de/2005-1/transnationalism_assimilation_bommes.htm

Borjas, G. (1989). Economic theory and international migration. *International Migration Review, 23*(3), 457–485.

Borjas, G. (1990). *Friends or strangers: The impact of immigrants on the U.S. economy.* New York: Basic Books.

Bosniak, L. (2006). *The citizen and the alien: Dilemmas of contemporary membership.* Princeton, NJ: Princeton University Press.

Boswell, C. (2003). *European migration policies in flux: Changing patterns of inclusion and exclusion.* Oxford, UK: Blackwell.

Bourne, R. (1916). Trans-national America. *Atlantic Monthly, 118*, 86–97.

Bourque, G., & Duchastel, J. (1999). Erosion of the nation-state and the transformation of national identities in Canada. In J. L. Abu Lughod (Ed.), *Sociology for the twenty-first century: Continuities and cutting edges* (pp. 183–198). Chicago: University of Chicago Press.

Boyd, M. (2002). Educational attainments of immigrant offspring: Success or segmented assimilation? *International Migration Review, 36*(4), 1037–1060.

Braudel, F. (1972). *The Mediterranean and the Mediterranean world in the age of Philip II, Volumes I and II.* New York: Harper & Row.

Breton, R. (1986). Multiculturalism and Canadian nation-building. In A. Cairns & C. Williams (Eds.), *The politics of gender, ethnicity, and language in Canada* (pp. 27–66). Toronto: University of Toronto Press.

Brettell, C. B. (2006). Introduction: Global spaces/local places: Transnationalism, diaspora, and the meaning of home. *Identities, 13*(3), 27–34.

Brettell, C. B., & & Hollifield, J. F. (2000). Migration theory: Talking across disciplines. In C. B. Brettell & J. F. Hollifield (Eds.), *Migration theory: Talking across disciplines* (pp. 1–26). New York: Routledge.

Brubaker, R. (1992). *Citizenship and nationhood in France and Germany.* Cambridge, MA: Harvard University Press.

Brubaker, R. (2001). The return of assimilation? Changing perspectives on immigration and its sequels in France, Germany, and the United States. *Ethnic and Racial Studies, 24*(4), 531–548.

Brubaker, R. (2005). The "Diaspora" diaspora. *Ethnic and Racial Studies, 28*(1), 1–19.

Brubaker, R., Feischmidt, M., Fox, J., & Grancea, L. (2006). *Nationalist politics and everyday ethnicity in a Transylvanian town.* Princeton, NJ: Princeton University Press.

Bulmer, M., & Warwick, D. P. (Eds.). (1993). *Social research in developing countries: Surveys and censuses in the third world*. London: Routledge.

Căglar, A. (2006). Hometown associations, the rescaling of state spatiality and migrant grassroots transnationalism. *Global Networks, 6*(1), 1–22.

Camarota, S. A. (2005). *Immigrants at mid-decade: A snapshot of America's foreign-born population in 2005*. Washington, DC: Center for Immigration Studies.

*Canada's ethnocultural portrait: The changing mosaic.* (n.d.). Retrieved March 14, 2007, from http://www12.statcan.ca/english/census01/products/analytic/companion/etoimm/contents.cfm

*Canadian immigration statistics.* (2007). Retrieved March 14, 2007, from http://www.canadaimmigrants.com/statistics.asp

Caponia, T. (2008). (Im)Migration research in Italy: A European comparative perspective. *The Sociological Quarterly, 49*(3), 445–464.

Castells, M. (1996). *The rise of network society: Vol. I. The information age: Economy, culture, and society*. Oxford: Blackwell.

Castells, M. (1997). *The power of identity: Vol. II. The information age: Economy, culture, and society*. Oxford: Blackwell.

Castles, S. (1997). Multicultural citizenship: A response to the dilemma of globalization and national security. *Journal of Intercultural Studies, 18*(1), 5–22.

Castles, S. (2002). Migration and community formation under conditions of globalization. *International Migration Review, 36*(4), 1143–1168.

Castles, S., & Davidson, A. (2001). *Citizenship and migration: Globalization and the politics of belonging*. New York: Routledge.

Castles, S., & Miller, M. J. (2004). *The age of migration: International population movements in the modern world* (4th ed.). New York: Guilford Press.

Chatelard, G. (2004). *Jordan: A refugee haven. Migration information source*. Washington, DC: Migration Policy Institute.

Chen, H.-S. (1992). *Chinatown no more: Taiwan immigrants in contemporary New York*. Ithaca, NY: Cornell University Press.

Chiswick, B. R., Lee, Y. W., & Miller P. W. (2005). A longitudinal analysis of immigrant occupational mobility: A test of the immigrant assimilation hypothesis. *International Migration Review, 39*(2), 332–353.

Clark, X., Hatton, T. J., & Williamson, J. G. (2002). *Where do U.S. immigrants come from and why?* (Working paper 8998). Cambridge, MA: National Bureau of Economic Research.

Cohen, Y., & Haberfeld, Y. (2007). Self-selection and earnings assimilation: Immigrants from the former Soviet Union in Israel and the United States. *Demography, 44*(3), 649–668.

Collins, R. (2001). Ethnic change in macro-historical perspective. In E. Anderson & D. S. Massey (Eds.), *Problem of the century: Racial stratification in the United States* (pp. 13–46). New York: Russell Sage Foundation.

Colombo, A., & Sciortino, G. (2004). Italian immigration: The origins, nature, and evolution of Italy's migratory systems. *Journal of Modern Italian Studies, 9*(1), 49–70.

Commission of the European Communities. (2004). *Towards a common European Union immigration policy*. Brussels: European Commission Directorate-General.

Constable, N. (1997). *Maid to order in Hong Kong: Stories of Filipina workers.* Ithaca, NY: Cornell University Press.

Conzen, K. (1976). *Immigrant Milwaukee, 1836–1860.* Cambridge, MA: Harvard University Press.

Cornelius, W. A., Espenshade, T. J., & Salehyan, I. (Eds.). (2001). *The international migration of the highly skilled: Demand, supply, and development consequences in sending and receiving countries.* La Jolla, CA: Center for Comparative Immigration Studies, University of California, San Diego.

Cornelius, W. A., & Tsuda, T. (2004). Controlling immigration: The limits of government intervention. In W. A. Cornelius, T. Tsuda, P. Martin, & J. Hollifield (Eds.), *Controlling immigrants: A global perspective* (pp. 3–48). Stanford, CA: Stanford University Press.

Cornelius, W. A., Tsuda, T., Martin, P., & Hollifield, J. (Eds.). (2004). *Controlling immigration: A global perspective.* Stanford, CA: Stanford University Press.

Cornell, S., & Hartmann, D. (2004). Conceptual confusions and divides: Race, ethnicity, and the study of immigration. In N. Foner & G. M. Fredrickson (Eds.), *Not just black and white: Historical and contemporary perspectives on race and ethnicity in the United States* (pp. 34–41). New York: Russell Sage Foundation.

Coser, L. (1974). *Greedy institutions: Patterns of undivided commitment.* New York: Free Press.

Council of Europe. (1997). *European Convention on Nationality: An explanatory report.* Strausbourg, France: Author.

Curtin, P. (1969). *The Atlantic slave trade.* Madison: University of Wisconsin Press.

Dahlin, E. C., & Hironaka, A. (2008). Citizenship beyond borders: A cross-national study of dual citizenship. *Sociological Inquiry, 28*(1), 54–73.

Daniels, R. (1990). *Coming to America: A history of immigration and ethnicity in American life.* New York: HarperCollins.

Daniels, R. (2004). *Guarding the golden door.* New York: Hill & Wang.

Dannecker, P. (2004). Transnational migration and the transformation of gender relations: The case of Bangladeshi labour migrants. *Current Sociology, 53*(4), 655–674.

Deaux, K. (2006). *To be an immigrant.* New York: Russell Sage Foundation.

de Bruijn, M., van Dijk, R. A., & Foeken, D. (Eds.). (2001). *Mobile Africa: Changing patterns of movement in Africa and beyond.* Leiden: Brill.

DeConde, A. (1992). *Ethnicity, race, and American foreign policy: A history.* Boston: Northeastern University Press.

de Haas, H. (2006). *Engaging diasporas: How governments and development agencies can support diaspora involvement in the development of origin countries* [A study for Oxfam Novib, Oxford: International Migration Institute, James Martin 21st Century School]. New York: University of Oxford.

de Haas, H. (2007, June). *Migration and development: A theoretical perspective.* Paper presented at the conference on Transnationalism and Development(s): Toward a North-South Perspective, University of Bielefeld, Bielefeld, Germany.

de Hart, B. (2008). *Recent trends in European nationality laws: A restrictive turn?* Brussels: European Parliament, Policy Department C.

de la Pradelle, G. (2002). Dual nationality and the French citizenship tradition. In R. Hansen & P. Weil (Eds.), *Dual nationality, social rights, and federal citizenship in the U.S. and Europe: The reinvention of citizenship* (pp. 191–212). New York: Berghahn Books.

Delgado-Moreira, J. M. (2000). *Multicultural citizenship of the European Union.* Aldershot, UK: Ashgate.

Delgado-Wise, R., & Márquez Covarrubias, H. (2005). *The reshaping of Mexican labor exports under NAFTA: Paradoxes and challenges.* Zacatecas, Mexico: Program in Development Studies, Autonomous University of Zacatecas.

Dell'Olio, F. (2005). *The Europeanization of citizenship: Between the ideology of nationality, immigration, and European identity.* Burlington, VT: Ashgate.

Department of Immigration and Citizenship. (2007). *Immigration update.* Australia: Research at Statistics Section, Department of Immigration and Citizenship.

Department of Immigration and Multicultural Affairs. (2001). *Immigration: Federation to century's end, 1901–2000.* Australia: Statistics Section, Department of Immigration and Multicultural Affairs.

Desai, K. (2006). *The inheritance of loss.* New York: Grove Press.

DeSipio, L. (2001). Building America, one person at a time: Naturalization and political behavior in contemporary American politics. In G. Gerstle & J. Mollenkopf (Eds.), *E pluribus unum? Contemporary and historical perspectives on immigrant political incorporation* (pp. 67–106). New York: Russell Sage Foundation.

Dewing, M., & Leman, M. (2006). *Canadian multiculturalism. Parliamentary Information and Research Service, Library of Parliament.* Retrieved March 10, 2007, from www.parl.gc.ca/information/library/PRBpubs/936-e.htm

Dignan, D. (1981). Europe's melting pot: A century of large-scale immigration into France. *Ethnic and Racial Studies, 4*(2), 137–152.

Dowty, A. (1987). *Closed borders: The contemporary assault on freedom of movement.* New Haven, CT: Yale University Press.

Dufoix, S. (2008). *Diasporas.* Berkeley: University of California Press.

Elliott, J. L. (Ed.). (1983). *Two nations, many cultures.* Scarborough, ON: Prentice-Hall of Canada.

Erickson, C. (1972). *Invisible immigrants: The adaptation of English and Scottish immigrants in nineteenth-century America.* Coral Gables, FL: University of Miami Press.

Esman, M. J. (2004). *An introduction to ethnic conflict.* Malden, MA: Blackwell.

Espiritu, Y. L., & Tran, T. (2002). "Viêt Nam, nuoc tôi" (Vietnam, my country): Vietnamese Americans and transnationalism. In P. Levitt & M. C. Waters (Eds.), *The changing face of home: The transnational lives of the second generation* (pp. 367–398). New York: Russell Sage Foundation.

Esser, H. (2004). Does the "new" immigration require a "new" theory of intergenerational integration? *International Migration Review, 38*(3), 1126–1159.

Evans, P. (2000). Fighting marginalization with transnational networks: Counter-hegemonic globalization. *Contemporary Sociology, 29*(1), 230–241.

Fahrmeir, A. (2007). *Citizenship: The rise and fall of a modern concept.* New Haven, CT: Yale University Press.

Fairchild, H. (1925). *Migration: A world movement and its American significance.* New York: Putnam.

Faist, T. (1998). Transnational social spaces out of international migration: Evolution, significance, and future prospects. *Archives of European Sociology, 39*(2), 213–247.

Faist, T. (2000a). *The volume and dynamics of international migration and transnational social spaces.* Oxford: Oxford University Press.

Faist, T. (2000b). Transnationalization in international migration: Implications for the study of citizenship and culture. *Ethnic and Racial Studies, 23*(2), 189–222.

Faist, T. (2000c). *Social citizenship in the European Union: Residual post-national and nested membership.* Unpublished manuscript, Institut für Interkulturelle und Internationale Studien, Arbeitspapier, Wr. 17/2000.

Faist, T. (2004). Dual citizenship as overlapping membership. In D. Joly (Ed.), *International migration in the new global millennium: Global movement and settlement* (pp. 210–231). Burlington, VT: Ashgate.

Faist, T. (2005). The migration-security nexus: International migration and security before and after 9/11. In Y. M. Bodemann & Gökçe (Eds.), *Migration, citizenship, ethnos: Incorporation regimes in Germany, Western Europe, and North America* (pp. 83–102). London: Palgrave Macmillan.

Faist, T. (Ed.). (2006). *Dual citizenship in Europe.* Aldershot, UK: Ashgate.

Faist, T. (2007). *Dual citizenship in Europe: From nationhood to societal integration.* Aldershot: Ashgate.

Faist, T., & Ette, A. (Eds.). (2007). *The Europeanization of national immigration policies: Between autonomy and the European Union.* Basingstoke: Palgrave Macmillan.

Faist, T., & Kivisto, P. (Eds.). (2007). *Dual citizenship in a global perspective: From unitary to multiple citizenship.* Basingstoke, UK: Palgrave Macmillan.

Falk, R. (1994). The making of global citizenship. In B. Van Steenbergen (Ed.), *The condition of citizenship* (pp. 42–61). London: Sage.

Fargues, P. (2006, May). *International migration in the Arab region: Trends and policies.* Paper presented at the United Nations Expert Group Meeting on International Migration and Development in the Arab Region, Beirut.

Farrant, M., Grieve, C., & Sriskandarajah, D. (2006). *Irregular migration in the UK.* London: Institute for Public Policy Research.

Favell, A. (1998). *Philosophies of integration.* Basingstoke, UK: Macmillan.

Feldblum, M. (2000). Managing membership: New trends in citizenship and nationality policy. In T. A. Aleinikoff & D. Klusmeyer (Eds.), *From migrants to citizens: Membership in a changing world* (pp. 475–499). Washington, DC: Carnegie Endowment for International Peace.

Ferenczi, I. (1933). Migrations, modern. In E. R. A. Seligman (Ed.), *Encyclopedia of the social sciences* (pp. 433–438). New York: Macmillan.

Ferenczi, I., & Wilcox, W. (1929). *International migrations.* New York: National Bureau of Economic Research.

Fischer, C. S. (1992). *America calling: A social history of the telephone to 1940.* Berkeley: University of California Press.

Fitzgerald, D. (2004). Beyond "transnationalism": Mexican hometown politics in an American labour union. *Ethnic and Racial Studies, 27*(2), 228–247.

Flinn, M. W. (1985). *The European demographic system, 1500–1820*. Baltimore, MD: Johns Hopkins University Press.

Foner, N. (2001). Immigrant commitment to America, then and now: Myths and realities. *Citizenship Studies, 5*(1), 27–40.

Foner, N. (2005). *In a new land: A comparative view of immigration*. New York: New York University Press.

Fong, T. P. (2000). The first suburban Chinatown: The remaking of Monterey Park, California. In P. Kivisto & G. Rundblad (Eds.), *Multiculturalism in the United States: Current issues, contemporary voices* (pp. 369–380). Thousand Oaks, CA: Pine Forge Press.

Fonte, J. (2005, November). *Dual allegiance: A challenge to immigration reform and patriotic assimilation*. Washington, DC: Center for Immigration Studies.

Fouron, G. E., & Glick Schiller, N. (2002). The generation of identity: Redefining the second generation within a transnational field. In P. Levitt & M. C. Waters (Eds.), *The changing face of home: The transnational lives of the second generation* (pp. 168–208). New York: Russell Sage Foundation.

Francis, E. K. (1947). The nature of the ethnic group. *American Journal of Sociology, 52*(5), 393–400.

Fraser, N. (1995). From redistribution to recognition? Dilemmas of justice in a postsocialist age. *New Left Review, 212*(July/August), 68–93.

Freeman, G. (1994). Can liberal states control unwanted migration? *Annals of the American Academy of Political and Social Science, 534*(July), 17–30.

Freeman, G. (1995). Modes of immigration politics in liberal democratic states. *International Migration Review, 29*(4), 881–902.

Freeman, G. (2006). National models, policy types, and the politics of immigration in liberal democracies. *West European Politics, 29*(2), 227–247.

Friedman, T. L. (2006). *The world is flat: A brief history of the twenty-first century*. New York: Farrar, Straus, & Giroux.

Fuchs, L. H. (1990). *The American kaleidoscope: Race, ethnicity, and the civic culture*. Hanover, NH: Wesleyan University Press.

Fujiwara, L. H. (2005). Immigrant rights are human rights: The reframing of immigrant entitlement and welfare. *Social Problems, 52*(1), 79–101.

Gabaccia, D., & Iacovetta, F. (Eds.). (2002). *Women, gender, and transnational lives: Italian workers of the world*. New Providence, NJ: BPR Publishers.

Galligan, B., & Roberts, W. (2003). *Australian multiculturalism: Its rise and demise*. Paper presented at the Australasian Political Association Conference, University of Tasmania, Hobart, Tasmania.

Gans, H. (1979). Symbolic ethnicity: The future of ethnic groups and cultures in America. *Ethnic and Racial Studies, 2*(1), 1–20.

Gans, H. (1992a). Ethnic invention and acculturation: A bumpy-line approach. *Journal of American Ethnic History, 12*(1), 45–52.

Gans, H. (1992b). Second-generation decline: Scenarios for the economic and ethnic futures of the post-1965 American immigrants. *Ethnic and Racial Studies, 15*(2), 173–192.

Gans, H. (1997). Toward a reconciliation of assimilation and pluralism: The interplay of acculturation and ethnic retention. *International Migration Review, 31*(4), 875–892.

Gans, H. (1999a). *Making sense of America: Sociological analyses and essays.* Lanham, MD: Rowman & Littlefield.

Gans, H. (1999b). The possibility of a new racial hierarchy in the twenty-first century United States. In M. Lamont (Ed.), *The cultural territories of race* (pp. 371–390). Chicago and New York: University of Chicago Press and Russell Sage Foundation.

Gans, H. J. (2007). Acculturation, assimilation, and mobility. *Ethnic and Racial Studies, 30*(1), 152–164.

Gerstle, G. (2001). *American crucible: Race and nation in the twentieth century.* Princeton, NJ: Princeton University Press.

Giddens, A. (1984). *The constitution of society: Outline of the theory of structuration.* Berkeley: University of California Press.

Giddens, A. (1990). *The consequences of modernity.* Stanford, CA: Stanford University Press.

Giddens, A. (1999). *Runaway world: How globalization is reshaping our lives.* London: Profile Books.

Gilbert, N. (2004). *The transformation of the welfare state: The silent surrender of public responsibility.* New York: Oxford University Press.

Gilbertson, G. (2006). Citizenship in a globalized world. Retrieved June 6, 2008, from www.migrationinformation.org/Feature/print.cfm?ID=369

Gilbertson, G., & Singer, A. (2003). The emergence of protective citizenship in the USA: Naturalization among Dominican immigrants in the post-1966 welfare reform era. *Ethnic and Racial Studies, 26*(1), 25–51.

Gilroy, P. (1987). *There ain't no black in the Union Jack: The cultural politics of race and nation.* Chicago: University of Chicago Press.

Gilroy, P. (1992). *The empire strikes back: Race and racism in 70's Britain.* London: Routledge.

Gilroy, P. (2005). *Postcolonial melancholia.* New York: Columbia University Press.

Gitlin, T. (1995). *The twilight of common dreams: Why America is wracked by culture wars.* New York: Metropolitan Books.

Gjerde, J. (1985). *From peasants to farmers: The migration from Balestrand, Norway to the Upper Middle West.* Cambridge: Cambridge University Press.

Glazer, N. (1993). Is assimilation dead? *Annals of the American Academy of Political and Social Science, 530*(November), 122–136.

Glazer, N. (1997). *We are all multiculturalists now.* Cambridge, MA: Harvard University Press.

Glazer, N. (2000). On beyond the melting pot, 35 years after. *International Migration Review, 34*(1), 270–276.

Glazer, N., & Moynihan, D. P. (1963). *Beyond the melting pot.* Cambridge, MA: MIT Press and Harvard University Press.

Glazer, N., & Moynihan, D. P. (1975). Introduction. In N. Glazer & D. P. Moynihan (Eds.), *Ethnicity: Theory and experience* (pp. 1–26). Cambridge, MA: Harvard University Press.

Gleason, P. (1964). The melting pot: Symbol of fusion or confusion? *American Quarterly, 16*(1), 20–46.

Gleason, P. (1983). Identifying "identity": A semantic history. *Journal of American History, 69*(4), 910–931.

Glenn, D. (2004, February 13). Scholars cook up a new melting pot. *Chronicle of Higher Education,* pp. A10–A12.

Glick Schiller, N. (1997). The situation of transnational studies. *Identities, 4*(2), 155–166.

Glick Schiller, N. (1999). Transmigrants and nation-states: Something old and something new in the U.S. immigrant experience. In C. Hirschman, P. Kasinitz, & J. DeWind (Eds.), *The handbook of international migration: The American experience* (pp. 94–119). New York: Russell Sage Foundation.

Glick Schiller, N. (2005). Transnational social fields and imperialism: Bringing a theory of power to transnational studies. *Anthropological Theory, 5*(4), 439–461.

Glick Schiller, N. (2007, May). *Beyond the nation-state and its units of analysis: Toward a new research agenda for migration studies.* Paper presented at the Conference on Transnationalism and Development, Centre for Interdisciplinary Research, Bielefeld University, Bielefeld, Germany.

Glick Schiller, N., Basch, L., & Szanton Blanc, C. (1992). Transnationalism: A new analytic framework for understanding migration. In N. Glick Schiller, L. Basch, & C. Szanton Blanc (Eds.), *Towards a transnational perspective on migration: Race, class, ethnicity, and nationalism reconsidered* (pp. 1–24). New York: New York Academy of Sciences.

Glick Schiller, N., Basch, L., & Szanton Blanc, C. (1995). From immigrant to transmigrant: Theorizing transnational migration. *Anthropological Quarterly, 68*(1), 48–63.

Glick Schiller, N., & Levitt, P. (2006). *Haven't we heard this somewhere before? A substantive review of transnational migration studies by way of a reply to Waldinger and Fitzgerald* (Working Paper #06-01). Princeton, NJ: Center for Migration and Development, Princeton University.

Gold, S. J. (2007). Israeli emigration policy. In N. L. Green & F. Weil (Eds.), *Citizenship and those who leave: The politics of emigration and expatriation* (pp. 283–304). Urbana: University of Illinois Press.

Goldring, L. (2002). The Mexican state and transmigrant organizations: Negotiating the boundaries of membership and participation. *Latin American Research Review, 17,* 55–99.

Gordon, M. M. (1964). *Assimilation and American life: The role of race, religion, and national origins.* New York: Oxford University Press.

Gordon, M. M. (1978). *Human nature, class, and ethnicity.* New York: Oxford University Press.

Goulbourne, H. (1998). *Race relations in Britain since 1945.* London: Macmillan.

Gray, J. (2004). Monolithic secularism is not suited to today's Europe. *New Perspectives Quarterly, 21*(2), 14–15.

Greeley, A. (1971). *Why can't they be like us? America's white ethnic groups.* New York: E. P. Dutton.

Greeley, A. (1974). *Ethnicity in the United States: A preliminary reconnaissance.* New York: John Wiley & Sons.

Greeley, A., & McCready, W. C. (1975). The transmission of cultural heritages: The case of the Italians and the Irish. In N. Glazer & D. P. Moynihan (Eds.). *Ethnicity: Theory and experience* (pp. 209–235). Cambridge, MA: Harvard University Press.

Grosfoguel, R. (1997). Colonial Caribbean migrations to France, the Netherlands, Great Britain, and the United States. *Ethnic and Racial Studies, 20,* 595–609.

Guarnizo, L. E. (1997). The emergence of a transnational social formation and the mirage of return migration among Dominican transmigrants. *Identities, 4*(2), 281–322.

Guarnizo, L. E., Portes, A., & Haller, W. J. (2003). Assimilation and transnationalism: Determinants of transnational political action among contemporary migrants. *American Journal of Sociology, 108*(6), 1211–1248.

Guglielmo, T. A. (2003). *White on arrival: Italians, race, color, and power in Chicago, 1890–1965.* New York: Oxford University Press.

Guibernau, M. (1999). *Nations without states: Political communities in a global age.* Cambridge: Polity.

Guiraudon, V. (2000). The Marshallian triptych reordered: The role of courts and bureaucracies in furthering migrants' social rights. In M. Bommes & A. Geddes (Eds.), *Immigration and welfare: Challenging the borders of the welfare state* (pp. 46–71). London: Routledge.

Habermas, J. (2006). *Opening up fortress Europe.* Retrieved June 14, 2008, from http://print.signandsight.com/features/1048.html

Hagerstrand, T. (1976). *Innovation as a spatial process.* Chicago: University of Chicago Press.

Hahn, H. P., & Klute, G. (Eds.). (2008). *Cultures of migration: African perspectives.* Berlin: LIT Verlag.

Hailbronner, K. (2003). Rights and duties of dual nationals: Changing concepts and attitudes. In D. A. Martin & K. Hailbronner (Eds.), *Rights and duties of dual nationals: Evolution and prospects* (pp. 19–26). The Hague: Kluwer Law International.

Halfmann, J. (1998). Citizenship, universalism, migration and the risks of exclusion. *British Journal of Sociology, 49*(4), 513–533.

Hall, G. M. (2007). *Slavery and African ethnicities: Restoring the links.* Chapel Hill: University of North Carolina Press.

Hamilton, B., & Whaley, J. (1984). Efficiency and distributional implications of global restrictions on labor mobility. *Journal of Development Economics, 14,* 61–75.

Hamilton, K., Simon, P., & Veniard, C. (2004). *The challenge of French diversity.* Migration Information Source. Retrieved February 8, 2006, from www.migrationinformation.org/Profiles/display.cfm?id=266

Hammar, T. (1985). *European immigration policy: A comparative study.* Cambridge, UK: Cambridge University Press.

Hammar, T. (1990). *Democracy and the nation-state: Aliens, denizens, and citizens in a world of international migration.* Aldershot, UK: Gower.

Handlin, O. (1941). *Boston's immigrants, 1790–1880: A study in acculturation.* Cambridge, MA: Harvard University Press.

Handlin, O. (1973). *The uprooted* (2nd ed.). Boston: Little, Brown.

Hansen, M. L. (1938). *The problem of the third generation immigrant.* Rock Island, IL: Augustana Historical Society.

Hansen, M. L. (1940). *The immigrant in American history.* Cambridge, MA: Harvard University Press.

Hansen, R., & Weil, P. (2002). Dual citizenship in a changed world: Immigration, gender and social rights. In R. Hansen & P. Weil (Eds.), *Dual nationality, social rights and federal citizenship in the U.S. and Europe: The reinvention of citizenship* (pp. 1–15). New York: Berghahn Books.

Hannerz, U. (1996). *Transnational connections: Culture, people, places.* London: Routledge.

Hargreaves, A. (1995). *Immigration, "race," and ethnicity in contemporary France.* London: Routledge.

Harles, J. C. (1997). Integration before assimilation: Immigration, multiculturalism, and the Canadian polity. *Canadian Journal of Political Science, 30*(4), 711–736.

Harris, J. R., & Todaro, M. P. (1970). Migration, unemployment, and development: A two-sector analysis. *American Economic Review, 60*(2),126–142.

Hartmann, D., & Gerteis, J. (2005). Dealing with diversity: Mapping multiculturalism in sociological terms. *Sociological Theory, 23*(2), 218–240.

Harvey, D. (1989). *The condition of postmodernity.* Oxford: Blackwell.

Harvey, D. (1996). *Justice, nature, and the geography of difference.* Malden, MA: Blackwell.

Hatton, T. J., & Williamson, J. G. (1998). *The age of mass migration: Causes and economic impact.* New York: Oxford University Press.

Hawkins, F. (1989). *Critical years in immigration: Canada and Australia compared.* Kingston and Montreal, CA: McGill-Queen's University Press.

Hayduk, R. (2006). *Democracy for all: Restoring immigrant voting rights in the United States.* New York: Routledge.

Heater, D. (2002). *World citizenship: Cosmopolitan thinking and its opponents.* London: Continuum.

Heilig, G., Buttner, T., & Lutz, G. (1990). Germany's population: Turbulent past, uncertain future. *Population Bulletin, 45*(4), 28–29.

Hein, J. (2006). *Ethnic origins: The adaptation of Cambodian and Hmong refugees in four American cities.* New York: Russell Sage Foundation.

Heisler, M. (1986). Transnational migration as a small window on the diminished autonomy of the modern democratic state. *Annals of the American Academy of Political and Social Science, 485*(May), 153–166.

Held, D. (1995). *Democracy and the global order: From the modern state to cosmopolitan governance.* Cambridge: Polity Press.

Held, D., McCrew, A., Goldblatt, D., & Perraton, J. (1999). *Global transformations: Politics, economics, and culture.* Cambridge: Polity.

Hellmann, G., Baumann, R., Bösche, M., Herborth, B., & Wagner, W. (2005). De-Europeanization by default? Germany's EU policy in defense and asylum. *Foreign Policy Analysis, 1*(1), 143–164.

Higham, J. (1982). Current trends in the study of ethnicity in the United States. *Journal of American Ethnic History, 2*(1), 1–11.

Higham, J. (1970). *Strangers in the land.* New York: Atheneum.

Higham, J. (1990). From process to structure: Formulations of American immigration history. In P. Kivisto & D. Blanck (Eds.), *American immigrants and their generations* (pp. 11–41). Urbana: University of Illinois Press.

Hillebrand, E. (2008, March). Europe's failing left. *Prospect,* 42–45.

Hirschman, A. (1958). *The strategy of economic development.* New Haven, CT: Yale University Press.

Hirschman, A. (1970). *Exit, voice, and loyalty: Responses to decline in firms, organizations, and states.* Cambridge, MA: Harvard University Press.

Hirschman, C. (1983). America's melting pot reconsidered. *Annual Review of Sociology, 9,* 397–423.

Hirschman, C. (2001). The educational enrollment of immigrant youth: A test of the segmented-assimilation hypothesis. *Demography, 38*(3), 317–336.

Hirschman, C., Kasinitz, P., & DeWind, J. (Eds.). (1999). *The handbook of international migration: The American experience.* New York: Russell Sage Foundation.

Hobsbawm, E. J. (1962). *The age of revolution: 1789–1848.* New York: Mentor Books.

Hobsbawm, E. J. (1969). *Industry and empire.* New York: Penguin.

Hoerder, D. (2002). *Cultures in contact: World migrations in the second millennium.* Durham, NC: Duke University Press.

Hollifield, J. F. (2000). The politics of international migration: How can we bring the state back in. In C. B. Brettell & J. F. Hollifield (Eds.), *Migration theory: Talking across disciplines* (pp. 137–185). New York: Routledge.

Hollifield, J. F. (2004). The emerging migration state. *International Migration Review, 38*(3), 885–912.

Hollinger, D. (1995). *Postethnic America: Beyond multiculturalism.* New York: Basic Books.

Hollinger, D. (2003). Amalgamation and hypodescent: The question of ethnoracial mixture in the history of the United States. *American Historical Review, 108*(5), 1363–1390.

Hondagneu-Sotelo, P. (Ed.). (2007). *Religion and social justice for immigrants.* New Brunswick, NJ: Rutgers University Press.

Horne, G. (2007). *The deepest South: The United States, Brazil, and the African slave trade.* New York: New York University Press.

Huff, T. E., & Schluchter, W. (Eds.). (1999). *Max Weber and Islam.* New Brunswick, NJ: Transaction.

Hulse, C., & Swarns, R. L. (2006, April 8). Blame and uncertainty as immigration deal fails. *New York Times,* p. 1.

Human Rights Watch. (2006). *The response of other countries to Iraqis fleeing war and persecution.* Retrieved May 22, 2006, from www.hrw.or/reports/2006/jordan/1106/8.htm

Huntington, S. P. (2004). *Who are we? The challenges to America's national identity.* New York: Simon & Schuster.

Hutchinson, E. P. (1956). *Immigrants and their children, 1850–1950.* New York: John Wiley & Sons.

Iowa lawsuit filed over raid. (2008, May 17). *New York Times,* p. 15.

Isaacs, H. (1975). *Idols of the tribe: Group identity and political change.* New York: Harper & Row.

Jackson, K. T. (1985). *Crabgrass frontier: The suburbanization of America.* New York: Oxford University Press.

Jacobson, D. (1996). *Rights across borders: Immigration and the decline of citizenship.* Baltimore: Johns Hopkins University Press.

Jacobson, M. F. (2006). *Roots too: White ethnic revival in post-civil rights America.* Cambridge, MA: Harvard University Press.

Jacoby, T. (Ed.). (2004). *Reinventing the melting pot: The new immigrants and what it means to be American.* New York: Basic Books.

Jaret, C. (1999). Anti-immigrant attitudes and action during two eras of mass immigration. *Journal of American Ethnic History, 18*(3), 9–39.

Jelin, E. (2000). Towards a global environmental citizenship. *Citizenship Studies, 4*(1), 47–63.

Johnston, P. (2001). The emergence of transnational citizenship among Mexican immigrants in California. In T. A. Aleinikoff & D. Klusmeyer (Eds.), *Citizenship today: Global perspectives and practices* (pp. 253–277). Washington, DC: Carnegie Endowment For International Peace.

Jones, M. (1960). *American immigration.* Chicago: University of Chicago Press.

Jones, M. (1976). *The old world ties of American ethnic groups.* London: Macmillan.

Jones, D. (1992). Comments on rethinking migration: A transnational perspective. In N. Glick Schiller, L. Basch, & C. Szanton Blanc (Eds.), *Towards a transnational perspective on migration: Race, class, ethnicity, and nationalism reconsidered* (pp. 221–225). New York: New York Academy of Sciences.

Jones-Correa, M. (2001). Under two flags: Dual nationality in Latin America and its consequences for naturalization in the United States. *International Migration Review, 35*(4), 997–1029.

Jones-Correa, M. (2002). The study of transnationalism among the children of immigrants: Where we are and where we should be headed. In P. Levitt & M. C. Waters (Eds.), *The changing face of home: The transnational lives of the second generation* (pp. 221–241). New York: Russell Sage Foundation.

Joppke, C. (1999). How immigration is changing citizenship: A comparative view. *Ethnic and Racial Studies, (22)*4, 629–652.

Joppke, C. (2001a). Immigration. In N. J. Smelser & P. B. Baltes (Eds.), *International encyclopedia of the social and behavioral sciences, Vol. II* (pp. 7208–7211). Amsterdam: Elsevier.

Joppke, C. (2001b). Multicultural citizenship: A critique. *Archives européenes de sociologie/European Journal of Sociology, XLII*(2), 431–447.

Joppke, C. (2004). The retreat of multiculturalism in the liberal state: Theory and policy. *British Journal of Sociology, 55*(2), 237–257.

Joppke, C. (2005). *Selecting by origin: Ethnic migration in the liberal states.* Cambridge, MA: Harvard University Press.

Joppke, C. (2007a). Beyond national models: Civic integration policies for immigrants in Western Europe. *West European Politics, 30*(1), 1–22.

Joppke, C. (2007b). Transformation of civic integration: Civic integration and antidiscrimination in the Netherlands, France, and Germany. *World Politics, 59*(January), 243–273.

Joppke, C. (2008). Comparative citizenship: A restrictive turn in Europe? *Journal of Law and Ethics of Human Rights, 2*(1), 1–41.

Joppke, C., & Morawska, E. (2003). Integrating immigrants in liberal nation-states: Policies and practices. In C. Joppke & E. Morawska (Eds.), *Toward assimilation and citizenship: Immigrants in liberal nation-states* (pp. 1–36). Basingstoke, UK: Palgrave Macmillan.

Jordan, B., & Düvell, F. (2003). *Migration: The boundaries of equality and justice.* Cambridge, UK: Polity Press.

Jureidini, R. (2003). *Migrant workers and xenophobia in the Middle East.* Geneva: United Nation Research Institute for Social Development.

Kaldor, M. (1999). *New and old wars: Organized violence in a global era.* Stanford, CA: Stanford University Press.

Kalekin-Fishman, D., & Pitkänen, P. (Eds.). (2006). *Multiple citizenship as a challenge to European nation-states.* Rotterdam: Sense Publications.

Kallen, H. (1924). *Culture and democracy in the United States: Studies in the group psychology of the American people.* Salem, NH: Ayer.

Kapur, D. (2005). Remittances: The new development mantra? In S. M. Maimbo & D. Ratha (Eds.), *Remittances: Development impact and future prospects* (pp. 331–360). Washington, DC: World Bank.

Kasinitz, P., Mollenkopf, J. H., & Waters, M. C. (2002). Becoming American/Becoming New Yorkers: Immigrant incorporation in a majority minority city. *International Migration Review, 36*(4), 1020–1036.

Kasinitz, P., Mollenkopf, J. H., & Waters, M. C. (Eds.). (2004). *Becoming New Yorkers: Ethnographies in the new second generation.* New York: Russell Sage Foundation.

Kasinitz, P., Mollenkopf, J. H., Waters, M. C., & Holdaway, J. (2008). *Inheriting the city: The children of immigrants come of age.* Cambridge, MA and New York: Harvard University Press and Russell Sage Foundation.

Kaufman, J., & Patterson, O. (2005). Cross-national cultural diffusion: The global spread of cricket. *American Sociological Review, 70*(1), 82–110.

Kazal, R. A. (1995). Revisiting assimilation: The rise, fall, and reappraisal of a concept in American ethnic history. *American Historical Review, 100*(2), 437–471.

Kelly, P. (Ed.). (2002). *Multiculturalism reconsidered.* Cambridge, UK: Polity Press.

Kenny, M. (2004). *The politics of identity.* Cambridge, UK: Polity.

Keohane, R. O., & Nye, J. S. (1977). *Power and interdependence: World politics in transition.* Boston: Little, Brown.

Kindleberger, C. P. (1967). *Europe's postwar growth: The role of labor supply.* Cambridge, MA: Harvard University Press.

Kivisto, P. (1984). *Immigrant socialists in the United States: The case of Finns and the left.* Rutherford, NJ: Fairleigh Dickinson University Press.

Kivisto, P. (1990). The transplanted then and now: The reorientation of immigration studies from the Chicago School to the new social history. *Ethnic and Racial Studies, 13*(4), 455–481.

Kivisto, P. (2001). Theorizing transnational immigration: A critical review of current efforts. *Ethnic and Racial Studies, 24*(4), 549–577.

Kivisto, P. (2002). *Multiculturalism in a global society.* Malden, MA: Blackwell.

Kivisto, P. (2003). Social spaces, transnational immigrant communities, and the politics of incorporation. *Ethnicities, 3*(1), 5–28.

Kivisto, P. (2004). What is the canonical theory of assimilation: Robert E. Park and his predecessors. *Journal of the History of the Behavioral Sciences, 40*(2), 1–15.

Kivisto, P. (2005). *Incorporating diversity: Rethinking assimilation in a multicultural age.* Boulder, CO: Paradigm.

Kivisto, P. (2007a). What would a racial democracy look like? In H. Vera & J. Feagin (Eds.), *Handbook of the sociology of racial and ethnic relations* (pp. 219–239). New York: Springer.

Kivisto, P. (2007b). Poverty intolerance and migration networks: Review symposium on Ivan Light's deflecting immigration. *Ethnic and Racial Studies, 30*(6), 1156–1159.

Kivisto, P., & Blanck, D. (Eds.). (1990). *American immigrants and their generations.* Urbana: University of Illinois Press.

Kivisto, P., & Faist, T. (2007). *Citizenship: Discourse, theory, and transnational prospects.* Malden, MA: Blackwell.

Kok, P., Gelderblom, D., Oucho, J. O., & van Zyl, J. (Eds.). (2006). *Migration in South and Southern Africa.* Cape Town, SA: HSRC Press.

Koslowski, R. (2003). Challenges of international cooperation in a world of increasing dual nationality. In D. A. Martin & K. Hailbronner (Eds.), *Rights and duties of dual nationals: Evolution and prospects* (pp. 157–182). The Hague: Kluwer Law International.

Kriesberg, L. (1997). Social movements and global transformation. In J. Smith, C. Chatfield, & R. Pagnucco (Eds.), *Transnational social movements and global politics* (pp. 3–18). Syracuse, NY: Syracuse University Press.

Kunzru, H. (2004). *Transmission.* New York: Dutton.

Kurien, P. A. (2007). *A place at the multicultural table: The development of an American Hinduism.* New Brunswick, NJ: Rutgers University Press.

Kymlicka, W. (1995). *Multicultural citizenship: A liberal theory of minority rights.* Oxford: Oxford University Press.

Kymlicka, W. (2001). *Politics in the vernacular: Nationalism, multiculturalism, and citizenship.* Oxford: Oxford University Press.

Kymlicka, W. (2005, September 29). *Remaking multiculturalism after 7/7.* Open Democracy. Retrieved June 4, 2007, from www.openDemocracy.net/conflict-terrorism/multiculturalism_2879.jsp

Kymlicka, W. (2007). *Multicultural odyssey: Navigating the new international politics of diversity.* New York: Oxford University Press.

Lahav, G. (2004). Public opinion toward immigration in the European Union: Does it matter? *Comparative Political Studies, 37*(10), 1151–1183.

Lal, B. B. (1990). *The romance of culture in an urban civilization: Robert E. Park on race and ethnic relations in cities.* London: Routledge.

Lamont, M., & Molnár, V. (2002). The study of boundaries in the social sciences. *Annual Review of Sociology, 28,* 167–195.

Lavenex, S., & Wallace, W. (2005). Justice and home affairs: Towards a "European public order?" In H. Wallace, W. Wallace, & M. Pollack (Eds.), *Policy-making in the European Union* (pp. 104–132). Oxford, UK: Oxford University Press.

Lechner, F., & Boli, J. (2005). *World culture: Origins and consequences.* Malden, MA: Blackwell.

Leclerc, E., & Meyer, J.-B. (2007). Knowledge diasporas and development: A shrinking space for skepticism. *Asian Population Studies, 3*(3), 245–261.

Lee, E. (1966). A theory of migration. *Demography, 3*(1), 47–57.

Lee, F. R. (2008, April 3). New bill may speed U.S. visas for artists. *New York Times,* pp. A1, A10.

Legomsky, S. (2003). Dual nationality and military service: Strategy number two. In D. A. Martin & K. Hailbronner (Eds.), *Rights and duties of dual nationals: Evolution and prospects* (pp. 79–126). The Hague: Kluwer Law International.

Lemert, C. (2004). Can the world be changed?: On ethics and the multicultural dream. *Thesis Eleven, 78,* 46–60.

Levitt, P. (2001a). Transnational migration: Taking stock and future directions. *Global Networks, 1*(3), 195–216.

Levitt, P. (2001b). *The transnational villagers.* Berkeley: University of California Press.

Levitt, P. (2003). Keeping feet in both worlds: Transnational practices and immigrant incorporation in the United States. In C. Joppke & E. Morawska (Eds.), *Toward assimilation and citizenship: Immigrants in liberal nation-states* (pp. 177–194). Basingstoke, UK: Palgrave Macmillan.

Levitt, P., & Glick Schiller, N. (2004). Conceptualizing simultaneity: A transnational social field perspective on society. *International Migration Review, 38*(4), 1002–1039.

Levitt, P., & Jaworsky, B. N. (2007). Transnational migration studies: Past developments and future trends. *Annual Review of Sociology, 33,* 129–156.

Levitt, P., & Waters, M. C. (Eds.). (2002). *The changing face of home: The transnational lives of the second generation.* New York: Russell Sage Foundation.

Lewis, A. (1954). *Theory of economic growth.* London: Unwin.

Lie, J. (2001). *Multiethnic Japan.* Cambridge, MA: Harvard University Press.

Light, I. (2006). *Deflecting immigration: Networks, markets, and population in Los Angeles.* New York: Russell Sage Foundation.

Linklater, A. (1998). Cosmopolitan citizenship. *Citizenship Studies, 2*(1), 23–41.

Linz, J., & Stepan, A. (1996). *Problems of democratic transition and consolidation: Southern Europe, South America, and post-communist Europe.* Baltimore, MD: Johns Hopkins University Press.

Lipset, S. M., & Marks, G. (2000). *It didn't happen here: Why socialism failed in the United States.* New York: W.W. Norton.

Lister, R. (1997). *Citizenship: Feminist perspectives.* New York: New York University Press.

Lustick, I. S. (2004, June). Recent trends in emigration from Israel: The impact of Palestinian violence. Paper presented at the Association for Israel Studies, Jerusalem, Israel.

Lyman, R. (2006, August 15). New data show immigrants' growth and reach. *New York Times,* pp. Al, A16.

Lyman, S. M. (1972). *The black in American sociological thought: A failure of perspective.* New York: Capricorn Books.

Lyman, S. M. (1974). *Chinese Americans.* New York: Random House.

Mahler, S. J., & Pessar, P. R. (2001). Gendered geographies of power: Analyzing gender across transnational spaces. *Identities, 7*(4), 441–459.

Maimbo, S. M., & Ratha, D. (2005). Remittances: An overview. In S. M. Maimbo & D. Ratha (Eds.), *Remittances: Development impact and future prospects* (pp. 1–16). Washington, DC: World Bank.

Malik, K. (2002, Summer). Against multiculturalism. *New Humanist.* Retrieved October 2, 2002, from http://www.Rationalist.org.uk/newhumanist/issue02 summer/malik.shtml

Markoff, J. (1996). *Waves of democracy.* Thousand Oaks, CA: Pine Forge Press.

Marshall, T. H. (1964). *Class, citizenship, and social development.* Garden City, NY: Doubleday.

Martin, D. A. (2003). Introduction: The trend toward dual nationality. In D. A. Martin & K. Hailbronner (Eds), *Rights and duties of dual nationals: Evolution and prospects* (pp. 3–18). The Hague: Kluwer Law International.

Martin, D. A., & Aleinikoff, T. A. (2002). Double ties. *Foreign Policy, 133*(November/December), 80–81.

Martin, P. L. (1991). *The unfinished story: Turkish labour migration in Western Europe, with special reference to the Federal Republic of Germany.* Geneva: International Labour Office (ILO).

Marx, K. (1973). *Grundrisse: Foundations of the critique of political economy.* New York: Vintage Books.

Massey, D. (Ed.). (2008). *New faces in new places: The changing geography of American immigration.* New York: Russell Sage Foundation.

Massey, D. S., Arango, J., Hugo, G., Kouaouci, A., Pellegrino, A., & Edward, T. J. (1993). Theories of international migration: A review and appraisal. *Population and Development Review, 19*(3), 431–466.

Massey, D. S., Arango, J., Hugo, G., Kouaouci, A., Pellegrino, A., & Edward, T. J. (1994). An evaluation of international migration theory: The North American case. *Population and Development Review, 20*(4), 699–751.

Massey, D., Durand, J., & Malone, N. J. (2002). *Beyond smoke and mirrors: Mexican immigration in an era of free trade.* New York: Russell Sage Foundation.

Massey, D., & Taylor, J. E. (Eds.). (2004). *International migration: Prospects and policies in a global market.* New York: Oxford University Press.

Matthews, F. (1977). *Robert E. Park and the Chicago School*. Montreal: McGill-Queen's University Press.

Maurer, A., Mitag, J., & Wessels, W. (2003). National systems' adaptation to the EU system: Trends, offers, and constraints. In B. Kohler-Koch (Ed.), *Linking EU and national governance* (pp. 23–41). Oxford, UK: Oxford University Press.

Mayo-Smith, R. (1894). Assimilation of nationalities in the United States. *Political Science Quarterly, 9*(3), 426–444 and 9(4), 649–670.

McKee, J. (1993). *Sociology and the race problem: The failure of a perspective*. Urbana: University of Illinois Press.

Medrano, J. D., & Gutiérrez, P. (2001). Nested identities: National and European identity in Spain. *Ethnic and Racial Studies, 24*(5), 753–778.

Meehan, E. (1993). *Citizenship and the European community*. London: Sage.

Merton, R. K. (1987). Three fragments from a sociologist's notebook: Establishing the phenomena, specified ignorance, and strategic research materials. *Annual Review of Sociology, 13*, 1–28.

Miller, J. C. (1996). *Way of death: Merchant capitalization and the Angolan slave trade, 1730–1830*. Madison: University of Wisconsin Press.

Miller, K. A. (1985). *Emigrants and exiles: Ireland and the Irish exodus to North America*. New York: Oxford University Press.

Miller, M. (1991). Dual citizenship: A European norm? *International Migration Review, 33*(4), 245–257.

Miller, S. (1974). *The radical immigrant*. New York: Twayne.

Modood, T. (2005). *Multicultural politics: Racism, ethnicity, and Muslims in Britain*. Minneapolis: University of Minnesota Press.

Modood, T. (2007). *Multiculturalism*. Cambridge, UK: Polity.

Modood, T. (2008, February 14). Multicultural citizenship and the anti-Sharia storm. Retrieved April 2, 2008, from www.openDemocracy.net/node/35790/print

Modood, T., & Ahmad, F. (2007). British Muslim perspectives on multiculturalism. *Theory, Culture, & Society, 24*(2), 187–213.

Modood, T., Triandafyllidou, A., & Zapata-Barrero, R. (Eds.). (2006). *Multiculturalism, Muslims, and citizenship: A European approach*. London: Routledge.

Moller, H. (1964). Introduction. In H. Moller (Ed.), *Population movements in modern European history* (pp. 1–12). New York: Macmillan.

Moravcsik, A. (1999). *The choice for Europe: Social purpose and state power from Messina to Maastricht*. Ithaca, NY: Cornell University Press

Morawska, E. (1985). *For bread with butter: The life-worlds of East Central Europeans in Johnstown, Pennsylvania, 1890–1940*. Cambridge: Cambridge University Press.

Morawska, E. (1989). Labor migrations of Poles in the Atlantic economy, 1880–1914. *Comparative Studies in Society and History, 31*(2), 237–272.

Morawska, E. (1990). The sociology and historiography of immigration. In V. Yans-McLaughlin, V. (Ed.), *Immigration reconsidered: History, sociology, and politics* (pp. 187–238). New York: Oxford University Press.

Morawska, E. (1994). In defense of the assimilation model. *Journal of American Ethnic History, 13*(2), 76–87.

Morawska, E. (1999, May). *The sociology and history of immigration: Reflections of a practitioner*. Paper presented at the European University Institute Workshop: Reflections on Migration Research, Florence.

Morawska, E. (2001). Immigrants, transnationalism, and ethnicization: A comparison of this great wave and the last. In G. Gerstle & J. Mollenkopf (Eds.), *E pluribus unum?: Contemporary and historical perspectives on immigrant incorporation* (pp. 175–212). New York: Russell Sage Foundation.

Morawska, E. (2003). Immigrant transnationalism and assimilation: A variety of combinations and the analytic strategy it suggests. In C. Joppke & E. Morawska (Eds.), *Toward assimilation and citizenship: Immigrants in liberal nation-states* (pp. 133–176). New York: Palgrave Macmillan.

Morawska, E. (2008). Research on immigration/ethnicity in Europe and the United States. *The Sociological Quarterly, 49*(3), 465–482.

Moses, J. W. (2006). *International migration: Globalization's last frontier*. London: Zed Books.

Moya, J. C. (1998). *Cousins and strangers: Spanish immigrants in Buenos Aires, 1850–1930*. Berkeley: University of California Press.

Moya, J. C. (2005). Immigrants and associations: A global and historical perspective. *Journal of Ethnic and Migration Studies, 31*(5), 831–864.

Muenz, R. (2007). *Europe: Population and migration in 2005*. Migration Policy Institute. Retrieved April 7, 2007, from www.migrationinformation.org

Münch, R. (2001). *National citizenship in the global age: From national to transnational ties and identities*. New York: Palgrave.

Murphy, R. (1988). *Social closure: The theory of monopolization and exclusion*. New York: Oxford University Press.

Myrdal, G. (1957). *Rich lands and poor*. New York: Harper & Row.

Nahirny, V. C., & Fishman, J. A. (1965). American immigrant groups: Ethnic identification and the problem of generations. *Sociological Review, 13*(November): 311–326.

Naïr, S. (1997). *Rapport de bilan et d'orientations sur la politique de co-développment liée aux flux migratoires*. Paris: Unpublished manuscript.

Nicolaidis, K. (2005, Fall). The struggle for Europe. *Dissent*, 11–17.

Nee, V., & Sanders, J. (2001). Understanding the diversity of immigrant incorporation: A forms-of-capital model. *Ethnic and Racial Studies, 24*(3), 386–411.

Noriel, G. (1990). *Workers in French society in the 19th and 20th centuries*. New York: Berg.

Noriel, G. (1996). *The French melting pot: Immigration, citizenship, and national identity*. Minneapolis: University of Minnesota Press.

Novak, M. (1972). *The rise of the unmeltable ethnics: Politics and culture in the seventies*. New York: Macmillan.

Nugent, W. (1992). *Crossings: The great transatlantic migrations, 1870–1914*. Bloomington: Indiana University Press.

Nyberg-Sørensen, N. (2000, June). Notes on transnationalism to the panel of devil's advocates: Transnational migration—useful approach or trendy rubbish? Paper presented at the Conference on Transnational Migration, Oxford University.

Nye, J. S., & Keohane, R. O. (1971). Transnational relations and world politics: An introduction. *International Organization, 25*(3), 329–346.

Odmalm, P. (2005). *Migration policies and political participation.* Basingstoke, UK: Palgrave Macmillan.

Oezcan, V. (2004). *Germany: Immigration in transition.* Migration Information Source. Retrieved November 17, 2005, from http://migrationinformation.net/feature/print.cfm

Oliveira, M. (2008, June 5). Canada could lose multiculturalism, critics warn. *Toronto Star.* Retrieved August 12, 2008, from www.thestar.com/printArticle/413212

Omi, M. A., & Winant, H. (1994). *Racial formation in the United States: From the 1960's to the 1980's.* New York: Routledge.

Ong, A. (1999). *Flexible citizenship: The cultural logic of transnationality.* Durham, NC: Duke University Press.

Ostergren, R. C. (1988). *A community transplanted: The trans-Atlantic experience of a Swedish immigrant settlement in the Upper Middle West, 1835–1915.* Madison: University of Wisconsin Press.

Oxford University Press. (2003). *Oxford dictionary of English* (2nd ed.). Oxford: Author.

Özden, Ç., & Schiff, M. (2007). Overview. In Ç. Özden & M. Schiff (Eds.), *International migration, economic development, and policy* (pp. 1–16). Washington, DC, and Basingstoke, UK: World Bank and Palgrave Macmillan.

Papastergiadis, N. (2000). *The turbulence of migration.* Cambridge: Polity.

Parekh, B. (2000a). *Rethinking multiculturalism: Cultural diversity and political theory.* London: Macmillan.

Parekh, B. (2000b). *The future of multi-ethnic Britain: The Parekh report.* London: Profile Books.

Parekh, B. (2008). *A new politics of identity: Political principles for an interdependent world.* Basingstoke, UK: Palgrave Macmillan.

Park, L. S.-H. (2005). *Consuming citizenship: Children of Asian immigrant entrepreneurs.* Stanford, CA: Stanford University Press.

Park, R. E. (1914). Racial assimilation in secondary groups, with particular reference to the Negro. *American Journal of Sociology, 19*(5), 606–623.

Park, R. E. (1926). Behind our masks. *Survey Graphic, LVI* (May):135–139.

Park, R. E. (1930). Assimilation, social. In E.R.A. Seligman & A. Johnson (Eds.), *Encyclopedia of the social sciences* (pp. 281–283). New York: Macmillan.

Park, R. E. (1950). *Race and culture: Essays in the sociology of contemporary man.* New York: Free Press. (Original work published 1935)

Park, R. E., & Burgess, E. W. (1969). *Introduction to the science of sociology.* Chicago: University of Chicago Press. (Original work published 1921)

Parsons, T. (1971). *The system of modern societies.* Englewood Cliffs, NJ: Prentice-Hall.

Passel, J. S. (2005). *Unauthorized migrants: Numbered characteristics.* Washington, DC: Pew Hispanic Center.

Pearson, D. (2001). *The politics of ethnicity in settler societies: States of unease.* New York: Palgrave.

Peignard, E. (n.d.) *Immigration in France*. Embassy of France in the United States. Retrieved October 2006 from www.ambafrance-us.org

Pérez, N. O. (2003). *Spain: Forging an immigration policy*. Migration Information Source. Retrieved April 10, 2005, from www.migrationinformation.org/Profiles/pring.cfm

Perlmann, J. (2002). Second-generation transnationalism. In P. Levitt & M. C. Waters (Eds.), *The changing face of home: The transnational lives of the second generation* (pp. 216–220). New York: Russell Sage Foundation.

Perlmann, J. (2005). *Italians then, Mexicans now: Immigrant origins and second-generation progress, 1890–2000*. New York: Russell Sage Foundation.

Perlmann, J., & Waldinger, R. (1997). Second generation decline: Children of immigrants past and present—a reconsideration. *International Migration Review, 31*(4), 893–922.

Perlmann, J., & Waldinger, R. (1998). Are the children of today's immigrants making it? *The Public Interest, 132*(Summer), 73–96.

Persons, S. (1987). *Ethnic studies at Chicago, 1905–45*. Urbana: University of Illinois Press.

Petersen, W. (1958). A general typology of migration. *American Sociological Review, 23*(3), 256–266.

Phillips, A. (1993). *Democracy and difference*. Cambridge, UK: Polity.

Phillips, A. (2007). *Multiculturalism without culture*. Princeton, NJ: Princeton University Press.

Piore, M. J. (1979). *Birds of passage: Migrant labor in industrial societies*. Cambridge: Cambridge University Press.

Plummer, K. (2003). *Intimate citizenship: Private decisions and public dialogues*. Seattle: University of Washington Press.

Porter, J. (1965). *The vertical mosaic: An analysis of social class and power in Canada*. Toronto: University of Toronto Press.

Portes, A. (1995). Children of immigrants: Segmented assimilation. In A. Portes (Ed.), *The economic sociology of immigration* (pp. 248–280). New York: Russell Sage Foundation.

Portes, A. (1996a). Global villagers: The rise of transnational communities. *American Prospect, 25*, 74–77.

Portes, A. (1996b). Transnational communities: Their emergence and significance in the contemporary world-system. In R. P. Korzeniewicz & W. C. Smith (Eds.), *Latin America in the world-economy* (pp. 151–168). Westport, CT: Greenwood Press.

Portes, A. (1998). Divergent destinies: Immigration, the second generation, and the rise of transnational communities. In P. H. Schuck & R. Munz (Eds.), *Paths to inclusion: The integration of migrants in the United States and Germany* (pp. 33–57). New York: Berghahn Books.

Portes, A. (1999a). Conclusion: Toward a new world—The origins and effects of transnational activities. *Ethnic and Racial Studies, 22*(2), 463–477.

Portes, A. (1999b). Immigration theory for a new century: Some problems and opportunities. In C. Hirschman, P. Kasinitz, & J. DeWind (Eds.), *The handbook of international migration: The American experience* (pp. 21–33). New York: Russell Sage Foundation.

Portes, A. (2001). Introduction: The debates and significance of immigrant transnationalism. *Global Networks, 1*(3), 181–194.

Portes, A. (2003). Conclusion: Theoretical convergences and empirical evidence in the study of immigrant transnationalism. *International Migration Review, 37*(3), 874–892.

Portes, A. (2007). Migration, development, and segmented assimilation: A conceptual review of evidence. *Annals of the American Academy of Political and Social Science, 610*(March), 73–97.

Portes, A. (2009). Migration and development: Reconciling opposite views. *Ethnic and Racial Studies, 32*(1), 5–22.

Portes, A., & Bach, R. L. (1985). *Latin journey: Cuban and Mexican immigrants in the United States.* Berkeley: University of California Press.

Portes, A., Escobar, C., & Arana, R. (2008). Bridging the gap: Transnational and ethnic organizations in the political incorporation of immigrants in the United States. *Ethnic and Racial Studies, 31*(6), 1056–1090.

Portes, A., Escobar, C., & Radford, A. W. (2005). *Immigrant transnational organizations and development: A comparative study* (CMD Working Paper #05-07). Princeton, NJ: Center for Migration and Development Working Paper Series, Princeton University.

Portes, A., Fernandez-Kelly, P., & Haller, W. (2005). Segmented assimilation on the ground: The new second generation in early adulthood. *Ethnic and Racial Studies, 28*(6), 1000–1040.

Portes, A., Guarnizo, L. E., & Landolt, P. (1999). The study of transnationalism: Pitfalls and promise of an emergent research field. *Ethnic and Racial Studies, 22*(2), 217–237.

Portes, A., Haller, W., & Guarnizo, L. E. (2002). Transnational entrepreneurs: An alternative form of immigrant economic adaptation. *American Sociological Review, 67*(2), 278–298.

Portes, A., & Jensen, L. (1989). The enclave and entrants: Patterns of ethnic enterprise in Miami before and after Mariel. *American Sociological Review, 54*(16), 929–949.

Portes, A., & Rumbaut, R. (2001). *Legacies: The story of the immigrant second generation.* Berkeley: University of California Press.

Portes, A., & Rumbaut, R. (2005). Introduction: The second generation and the children of immigrants longitudinal study. *Ethnic and Racial Studies, 28*(6), 983–999.

Portes, A., & Rumbaut, R. (2006). *Immigrant America: A portrait* (3rd ed.). Berkeley: University of California Press.

Portes, A., & Zhou, M. (1993). The new second generation: Segmented assimilation and its variants. *Annals of the American Academy of Political and Social Science, 530*(November), 74–96.

Portes, A., & Walton, J. (1981). *Labor, class, and the international system.* New York: Academic Press.

Portes, A., & Zhou, M. (1999). Entrepreneurship and economic progress in the 1990s: A comparative analysis of immigrants and African Americans. In F. D. Bean & S. Bell-Rose (Eds.), *Immigration and opportunity: Race, ethnicity, and employment in the United States* (pp. 143–171). New York: Russell Sage Foundation.

Postma, J. M. (1990). *The Dutch in the Atlantic slave trade, 1600–1815*. New York: Cambridge University Press.

Preston, J. (2007, November 30). States take up immigration issue. *New York Times*, p. A17.

Preston, J. (2008, November 6). Large meatpacker in illegal immigrant raid files for bankruptcy. *New York Times*, p. A21.

Pridemore, W. A., & Kim, S.-W. (2007). Socioeconomic change and homicide in a transitional society. *The Sociological Quarterly, 48*(2), 229–251.

Pries, L. (2004). Determining the causes and durability of transnational labour migration between Mexico and the United States: Some empirical findings. *International Migration, 42*(2), 3–39.

Pries, L. (2005). Configurations of geographic and social spaces: A sociological proposal between "methodological nationalism" and the "spaces of flows." *Global Networks, 5*(2) 167–190.

Profile: Ayann Hirsi Ali. (2007, June 29). *BBC*.

Putnam, R. (2000). *Bowling alone: The collapse and revival of American community*. New York: Simon & Schuster.

Ramachandran, S. (2005). *Indifference, impotence, and intolerance. Transnational Bangladeshis in India* (Global Migration Perspectives, No. 42). Geneva, Switzerland: Global Commission on International Migration.

Ratha, D. (2005). Workers' remittances: An important and stable source of external development finance. In S. M. Maimbo & D. Ratha (Eds.), *Remittances: Development impact and future prospects* (pp. 19–51). Washington, DC: World Bank.

Rauch, J. (2001). Business and social networks in international trade. *Journal of Economic Literature, 34*, 1177–1204.

Ravenstein, E. G. (1885). The laws of migration. *Journal of Royal Statistical Society, 48*(1), 167–227.

Ravenstein, E. G. (1889). The laws of migration. *Journal of the Royal Statistical Society, 52(2)*, 241–305.

Renshon, S. A. (2001). Dual citizenship + multiple loyalties = one America? In S. Renshon (Ed.), *One America? Political leadership, national identity, and the dilemmas of diversity* (pp. 232–282). Washington, DC: Georgetown University.

Richmond, A. H. (1981). Immigrant adaptation in a postindustrial society. In M. M. Kritz, C. B. Keely, & S. M. Tomasi, (Eds.), *Global trends in migration: Theory and research on international population movements* (pp. 298–319). New York: Center for Migration Studies.

Rieder, J. (1985). *Canarsie: The Jews and Italians of Brooklyn against liberalism*. Cambridge, MA: Harvard University Press.

Risse-Kappen, T. (1995). Bringing transnational relations back in: Introduction. In T. Risse-Kappen (Ed.), *Bringing transnational relations back in: Non-state actors, domestic structures, and international institutions* (pp. 3–33). Cambridge: Cambridge University Press.

Roberts, B. (1995). Socially expected durations and the economic adjustment of immigrants. In A. Portes (Ed.), *The economic sociology of immigration* (pp. 42–86). New York: Russell Sage Foundation.

Robertson, R. (1992). *Globalization: Social theory and global culture.* London: Sage.

Roche, M. (1997). Citizenship and exclusion: Reconstructing the European union. In M. Roche & R. van Berkel (Eds.), *European citizenship and social exclusion* (pp. 3–22). Aldershot, UK: Ashbury.

Roediger, D. (2005). *Working toward whiteness: How America's immigrants became white: The strange journey from Ellis Island to the suburbs.* New York: Basic Books.

Rosenbaum, G. (1973). *Immigrant workers: Their impact on American radicalism.* New York: Basic Books.

Rudolph, S. H. (1997). Religion, states, and transnational civil society. In S. H. Rudolph & J. Piscatori (Eds.), *Transnational religion and fading states* (pp. 1–27). Boulder, CO: Westview Press.

Rumbaut, R. (1997). Assimilation and its discontents: Between rhetoric and reality. *International Migration Review, 31*(4), 923–960.

Rumbaut, R. (1999). Assimilation and its discontents: Ironies and paradoxes. In C. Hirschman, P. Kasinitz, & J. DeWind (Eds.), *The handbook of international migration* (pp. 172–195). New York: Russell Sage Foundation.

Rumbaut, R. (2001). Assimilation of immigrants. In N. J. Smelser & P. B. Bales (Eds.), *International encyclopedia of the social and behavioral sciences* (pp. 845–849). New York: Elsevier.

Rumbaut, R. (2002). Severed or sustained attachments? Language, identity, and immigrant communities in the post-immigrant generation. In P. Levitt & M. C. Waters (Eds.), *The changing face of home: The transnational lives of the second generation* (pp. 43–95). New York: Russell Sage Foundation.

Rumbaut, R. (2005). The melting and the pot: Assimilation and variety in American life. In P. Kivisto (Ed.), *Incorporating diversity: Rethinking assimilation in a multicultural era* (pp. 154–173). Boulder, CO: Paradigm.

Sanders, J., & Nee, V. (1987). Limits of ethnic solidarity in the enclave. *American Sociological Review, 52*(5), 745–767.

Sassen, S. (1988). *The mobility of labor and capital: A study in international investment and labor flow.* Cambridge: Cambridge University Press.

Sassen, S. (1996). *Losing control? Sovereignty in an age of globalization.* New York: Columbia University Press.

Sassen, S. (1999). *Guests and aliens.* New York: New Press.

Saxenian, A. L. (2002). The Silicon Valley connection: Transnational networks and regional development in Taiwan, China, and India. *Science, Technology, and Society, 7*(1), 117–132.

Sayad, A. (2004). *The suffering of the immigrant.* Cambridge: Polity.

Schierup, C.-U., Hansen, P., & Castles, S. (2006). *Migration, citizenship, and the European welfare state.* Oxford: Oxford University Press.

Schlesinger, A., Sr. (1924). The significance of immigration in American history. *American Journal of Sociology, 27*(1), 71–78.

Schlesinger, A., Jr. (1992). *The disuniting of America: Reflections on a multicultural society.* New York: W. W. Norton.

Schmitter, B. H. (2000). The sociology of immigration: From assimilation to segmented assimilation, from the American experience to the global arena. In

C. B. Brettell & J. F. Hollifield (Ed.), *Migration theory: Talking across disciplines* (pp. 77–96). New York: Routledge.

Schneider, D. (2007). The United States government and the investigation of European immigration in the open door era. In N. Green & F. Weil (Eds.), *Citizenship and those who leave: The politics of emigration and expatriation* (pp. 195–210). Urbana: University of Illinois Press.

Schuck, P. (2002). Plural citizenships. In R. Hansen & P. Weil (Eds.), *Dual nationality, social rights and federal citizenship in the U.S. and Europe* (pp. 61–99). New York: Berghahn Books.

Schuck, P. (2003). *Diversity in America: Keeping government at a safe distance.* Cambridge, MA: Belknap Press of Harvard University Press.

Schuster, L. (2004). *The exclusion of asylum seekers in Europe* (Center on Migration, Policy, and Society Working Paper No. 1, Wp-04-01). Oxford: University of Oxford.

Sciortino, G. (2003). From homogeneity to difference? Comparing multiculturalism as a description and a field for claim-making. *Comparative Social Research, 22,* 263–285.

Seidman, G. (1999). Gendered citizenship: South Africa's democratic transformation and the constitution of a gendered state. *Gender & Society, 13*(3), 287–307.

The shame of Postville, Iowa. (2008, July 13). *New York Times,* p. 11.

Shelley, L. (1995). Transnational organized crime: An imminent threat to the nation-state? Transcending national boundaries. *Journal of International Affairs, 48*(2), 463–489.

Shibutani, T., & Kwan, K. (1965). *Ethnic stratification.* New York: Macmillan.

Shokeid, M. (1988). *Children of circumstances: Israeli emigrants in New York.* Ithaca, NY: Cornell University Press.

Siebert, H. (2003). *Germany: An immigration country* (Keil Working Paper No. 1189, 1—24). Kiel, Germany: Kiel Institute for World Economics.

Silberman, R., Alba, R., & Fournier, I. (2007). Segmented assimilation in France? Discrimination in the labour market against the second generation. *Ethnic and Racial Studies, 30*(1), 1–27.

Simmel, G. (1955). *Conflict and the web of group-affiliations.* New York: Free Press.

Simmel, G. (1971). *On individuality and social forms* (D. N. Levine, Ed.). Chicago: University of Chicago Press. (Original work published 1911)

Simon, R., & Lynch, J. (1999). A comparative assessment of public opinion toward immigrants and immigration policies. *International Migration Review, 33*(2), 455–467.

Simons, S. (1901–1902). Social assimilation. *American Journal of Sociology, 6*(6), 790–822; 7(1), 53–79; 7(2), 234–248; 7(3), 386–404, and 7(4), 539–556.

Sklair, L. (2001). *The transnational capitalist class.* Oxford: Blackwell.

Skrentny, J. D. (2002). *The minority rights revolution.* Cambridge, MA: Belknap Press of Harvard University Press.

Smelser, N. J. (1998). The rational and the ambivalent in the social sciences. *American Sociological Review, 63*(1), 1–16.

Smith, J. (2001). Global civil society? Transnational social movement organizations and social capital. In B. Edwards, M. W. Foley, & M. Diani (Eds.), *Beyond*

*Tocqueville: Civil society and the social capital debate in comparative perspective* (pp. 194–206). Hanover, NH: New England Press for Tufts University.

Smith, M. P., & Guarnizo, L. E. (Eds.). (1998). *Transnationalism from below.* New Brunswick, NJ: Transaction.

Smith, R. C. (2006). *Mexican New York: Transnational lives of new immigrants.* Berkeley: University of California Press.

Solberg, C. E. (1987). *The prairies and the pampas: Agrarian policy in Canada and Argentina, 1880–1930.* Stanford, CA: Stanford University Press.

Solomos, J. (2003). *Race and racism in Britain* (3rd ed.). London: Palgrave.

Solomos, J., & Back, L. (1995). Marxism, racism, and ethnicity. *American Behavioral Scientist, 38*(3), 407–420.

Somers, M. (2008). *Genealogies of citizenship: Markets, statelessness and the right to have rights.* Cambridge: Cambridge University Press.

Soysal, Y. N. (1994). *Limits of citizenship: Migrants and postnational membership in Europe.* Chicago: University of Chicago Press.

Soysal, Y. N. (2000). Citizenship and identity: Living in diasporas in post-war Europe? *Ethnic and Racial Studies, 23*(1), 1–15.

Spickard, P. (2005). Race and nation, identity and power: Thinking comparatively about ethnic systems. In P. Spickard, (Ed.), *Race and nation: Ethnic systems in the modern world* (pp. 1–29). New York: Routledge.

Spiro, P. (2002). Embracing dual nationality. In R. Hansen & P. Weil (Eds.), *Dual nationality, social rights, and federal citizenship in the U.S. and Europe: The reinvention of citizenship* (pp. 19–33). New York: Berghahn Books.

Spiro, P. (2007). *Beyond citizenship: American identity after globalization.* New York: Oxford University Press.

Sriskandarajah, D., & Road, F. H. (2005). *United Kingdom: Rising numbers, rising anxieties.* Migration Information Source. Retrieved February 9, 2006, from www.migrationinformation.org/Profiles/display.cfm

Staples, C. (2008). Cross-border acquisitions and board globalization in the world's largest TNCs, 1995–2005. *The Sociological Quarterly, 49*(1), 31–51.

Stark, O. (1991). *The migration of labor.* Cambridge, MA: Basil Blackwell.

Statham, P., & Geddes, A. (2006). Elites and the "organized public": Who drives British immigration politics and in what direction? *West European Politics, 29*(2), 248–269.

Steinbeck, J. (1967). *The grapes of wrath.* New York: Viking Press. (Original work published 1940).

Steinberg, S. (1981). *The ethnic myth: Race, ethnicity, and class in America.* New York: Atheneum.

Steinberg, S. (2007). *Race relations: A critique.* Stanford, CA: Stanford Social Sciences of Stanford University Press.

Stevenson, N. (1997). Globalization, national cultures, and cultural citizenship. *The Sociological Quarterly, 38*(1), 41–66.

Struyck, R. J. (2002). Management of transnational think networks. *International Journal of Politics, Culture, and Society, 15*(4), 625–638.

Suárez-Orozco, M. M. (2002). Everything you ever wanted to know about assimilation but were afraid to ask. In R. A. Schweder, M. Minow, & H. R. Marcus (Eds.), *Engaging cultural differences: The multicultural challenge to liberal democracies* (pp. 19–42). New York: Russell Sage Foundation.

Suhrke, A., & Zolberg, A. R. (1999). Issues in contemporary refugee policies. In A. Bernstein & M. Weiner (Eds.), *Migration and refugee policies: An overview* (pp. 143–180). London: Pinter.

Susser, S. M. (2004, July 1–2). Strangers in our midst: The abuse of foreign workers in Israel. *Jewish Currents.* Retrieved January 15, 2006, from www.jewishcurrents .org/2004-july-susser.htm

Swain, C. M. (Ed.). (2007). *Debating immigration.* Cambridge, UK: Cambridge University Press.

Takaki, R. (1993). *A different mirror: A history of multicultural America.* Boston: Little, Brown.

Takaki, R. (1989). *Strangers from a different shore: A history of Asian Americans.* Boston: Little, Brown.

Tambini, D. (1997). Universal cybercitizenship, In *Cyberdemocracy: Technology, cities, and civic networks* (pp. 84–109). London: Routledge

Tambini, D. (2001). Post-national citizenship. *Ethnic and Racial Studies, 24*(2), 195–212.

Taylor, C. (1998). The dynamics of democratic exclusion. *Journal of Democracy, 9*(4), 143–156.

Taylor, C., Gutmann, A., Rockefeller, S. C., Walzer, M., & Wolf, S. (1992). *Multiculturalism and "the politics of recognition."* Princeton, NJ: Princeton University Press.

Taylor, P. (1971). *The distant magnet: European emigration to the U.S.A.* New York: Harper & Row.

Thistlethwaite, F. (1960). Migration from Europe overseas in the nineteenth and twentieth centuries. *XI Congres Des Sciences Historiques, Rapports-60, 5,* 2–60.

Thomas, B. (1954). *Migration and economic growth: A study of Great Britain and the Atlantic economy.* Cambridge: Cambridge University Press.

Thomas, W. I., & Znaniecki, F. (1918–1920). *The Polish peasant in Europe and America, 5 volumes.* Chicago: University of Chicago Press.

Thornton, J. (1998). *Africa and Africans in the making of the Atlantic world, 1440– 1800.* Cambridge: Cambridge University Press.

Tichenor, D. J. (2002). *Dividing lines: The politics of immigration control in America.* Princeton, NJ: Princeton University Press.

Tilly, C. (1990). Transplanted networks. In V. Yans-McLaughlin (Ed. ), *Immigration reconsidered: History, sociology, and politics* (pp. 79–95). New York: Oxford University Press.

Tilly, C. (2007). *Coercion, capital, and European states, AD 990–1992.* Malden, MA: Blackwell.

Tilove, J. (2002). *Rethinking dual citizenship in the post-September 11 world.* Retrieved March 11, 2002, from www.newhouse.com/archieve/story/a062002.html

Todaro, M. P. (1969). A model of labor migration and urban unemployment in low-developed countries. *American Economic Review, 59*(1), 138–148.

Todaro, M. P. (1976). *Internal migration in developing countries*. Geneva: International Labor Office.

Todaro, M. P., & Maruszku, L. (1987). Illegal immigration and U.S. immigration reform: A conceptual framework. *Population and Development Review, 13*(1), 104–114.

Torpey, J. (2000). *The invention of the passport: Surveillance, citizenship, and the state*. New York: Cambridge University Press.

Torpey, J. (2007). Leaving: A comparative perspective. In N. L. Green & F. Weil (Eds.), *Citizenship and those who leave: The politics of emigration and expatriation* (pp. 13–32). Urbana: University of Illinois Press.

Touraine, A. (1971). *Post-industrial society*. New York: Random House.

Tseng, Y.-F. (2000). The mobility of entrepreneurs and capital: Taiwanese capital-linked migration. *International Migration, 38*(2), 143–166.

Tsutsui, K., & Wotipka, C. M. (2004). Global civil society and the international human rights movement: Citizen participation in human rights international non-governmental organizations. *Social Forces, 83*(2), 587–620.

Turner, B. S. (2006). Classical sociology and cosmopolitanism: A critical defence of the social. *British Journal of Sociology, 57*(1), 133–151.

Turner, F. J. (1893). *The significance of the frontier in American history*. Lecture presented at the American Historical Association's meeting at the World's Columbia Exposition, Chicago, IL.

Ullah, A. K. M. A., & Panday, P. K. (2007). Remitting money to Bangladesh: What do migrants prefer? *Asian and Pacific Migration, 16*(1), 121–138.

United Nations. (2006). *The state of world population*. United Nations Population Fund.

United Nations. (2008). *Eliminating female genital mutilation: An interagency statement*. Retrieved August 22, 2008, from www.popline.org/docs/1789/325496.html

Urry, J. (2000). *Sociology beyond societies: Mobilities for the twenty-first century*. London: Routledge.

U.S. Census Bureau. (2002). *Census 2000: Demographic profiles*. Washington, DC: Government Printing Office.

van den Berghe, P. (1981). *The ethnic phenomenon*. New York: Elsevier.

Van Hook, J., Bean, F., & Passel, J. (2005). *Unauthorized migrants living in the United States: A mid-decade portrait*. Washington, DC: Migration Policy Institute.

Vasta, E. (2007). From ethnic minorities to ethnic majority policy: Multiculturalism and the shift to assimilationism in the Netherlands. *Ethnic and Racial Studies, 30*(5), 713–740.

Vecoli, R. (1995). Comment. *Journal of American Ethnic History, 14*(2), 76–81.

Vecoli, R., & Sinke, S. M. (1991). *A century of European migrations, 1830–1930*. Urbana: University of Illinois Press.

Vertovec, S. (1999). Conceiving and researching transnationalism. *Ethnic and Racial Studies, 22*(2), 447–462.

Vertovec, S. (2004). Cheap calls: The social glue of migrant transnationalism. *Global Networks, 4*(2), 219–224.

Vertovec, S., & Cohen, R. (Eds.). (2002). *Conceiving cosmopolitanism: Theory, context, and practice.* Oxford, UK: Oxford University Press.

Vink, M. (2005a, March). *European integration and domestic immigration policies.* Paper presented at the An Immigration Policy for Europe? conference, Florence, Italy.

Vink, M. (2005b). *Limits of European citizenship: European integration and domestic immigration policies.* Basingstoke, UK: Palgrave Macmillan.

Waldinger, R. (2003). Foreigners transformed: International migration and the remaking of a divided people. *Diaspora, 12*(2), 247–272.

Waldinger, R. (2007a). Debating deflection: Review symposium on Ivan Light's deflecting immigration. *Ethnic and Racial Studies, 30*(6), 1159–1162.

Waldinger, R. (2007b). Did manufacturing matter? The experience of yesterday's second generation: A reassessment. *International Migration Review, 41*(1), 3–39.

Waldinger, R. (2007c). The bounded community: Turning foreigners into Americans in twenty-first century L.A. *Ethnic and Racial Studies, 30*(3), 341–374.

Waldinger, R. (2007d, October 25). *Between here and there: How attached are Latino immigrants to their native country?* Washington, DC: Pew Center.

Waldinger, R., & Feliciano, C. (2004). Will the new second generation experience "downward assimilation"? Segmented assimilation reassessed. *Ethnic and Racial Studies, 27*(3), 376–402.

Waldinger, R., & Fitzgerald, D. (2004). Transnationalism in question. *American Journal of Sociology, 109*(5), 1177–1195.

Waldinger, R., Popkin, E., & Magana, H. A. (2008). Conflict and contestation in the cross-border community: Hometown associations reassessed. *Ethnic and Racial Studies, 31*(5), 843–870.

Wallerstein, I. (1974). *The modern world-system: Capitalist agriculture and the origins of the European world-economy in the 16th century.* New York: Academic Press.

Wallerstein, I. (1980). *The modern world-system II: Mercantilism and the consolidation of the European world-economy, 1600–1750.* New York: Academic Press.

Wallerstein, I. (1989). *The modern world-system III: The second era great expansions of the capitalist world-economy, 1730–1840.* New York: Academic Press.

Wallerstein, I. (1998). *Utopistics: Or historical choices for the twenty-first century.* New York: New Press.

Walton-Roberts, M. (2004). Transnational migration theory in population geography: Gendered practices in networks linking Canada and India. *Population, Space, and Place, 10*, 361–373.

Ward, R. (1978). *The Australian legend.* Melbourne: Oxford University Press.

Warner, R. S. (2007). The role of religion in the process of segmented assimilation. *Annals of the American Academy of Political and Social Sciences, 612*, 102–115.

Warner, W. L., & Srole, L. (1945). *The social systems of American ethnic groups.* New Haven, CT: Yale University Press.

Waters, M. (1995). *Globalization.* London: Routledge.

Waters, M. C. (1990). *Ethnic options: Choosing identities in America.* Berkeley: University of California Press.

Waters, M. C., & Jiménez, T. (2005). Assessing immigrant assimilation: Empirical and theoretical challenges. *Annual Review of Sociology, 31,* 105–125.

Weil, P. (2001). Access to citizenship: A comparison of twenty-five nationality laws. In T. A. Aleinikoff & D. Klusmeyer (Eds.), *Citizenship today: Global perspectives and practices* (pp. 17–35). Washington, DC: Carnegie Endowment for International Peace.

White, H. C. (1970). Stayers and movers. *American Journal of Sociology, 76*(2), 397–324.

Wieviorka, M. (1998). Is multiculturalism the solution? *Ethnic and Racial Studies, 21*(5), 881–910.

Wiley, N. (1986). Early America sociology and the Polish peasant. *Sociological Theory, 4*(Spring), 537–556.

Williams, E. (1994). *Capitalism and slavery.* Chapel Hill: University of North Carolina Press. (Original work published 1944)

Williams, R. (1976). *Keywords.* New York: Oxford University Press.

Williamson, J. G. (1974). Migration to the new world: Long term influences and impact. *Explorations in Economic History, II,* 357–390.

Wimmer, A. (2008). The making and unmaking of ethnic boundaries: A multilevel process theory. *American Journal of Sociology, 113*(4), 970–1022.

Wimmer, A., & Glick Schiller, N. (2002). Methodological nationalism and beyond: Migration and the social sciences. *Global Networks, 2*(4), 301–334.

Winant, H. (2001). *The world is a ghetto: Race and democracy since World War II.* New York: Basic Books.

Wirth, L. (1928). *The ghetto.* Chicago: University of Chicago Press.

Wolfe, A. (2003). The costs of citizenship: Assimilation v. multiculturalism in liberal democracies. *Responsive Community, 13*(3), 23–33.

Wong, C. (2006). *Lobbying for inclusion: Rights politics and the making of immigration policy.* Stanford, CA: Stanford University Press.

Wyman, M. (1993). *Round-trip to America: The immigrants return to Europe, 1880–1930.* Ithaca, NY: Cornell University Press.

Yans-McLaughlin, V. (1977). *Family and community: Italian immigrants in Buffalo, 1880–1930.* Ithaca, NY: Cornell University Press.

Yinger, J. M. (1994). *Ethnicity: Source of strength? Source of conflict?* Albany: State University of New York Press.

Young, I. M. (1989). Polity and group difference: A critique of the ideal of universal citizenship. *Ethics, 99*(2), 250–274.

Young, I. M. (1990). *Justice and the politics of difference.* Princeton, NJ: Princeton University Press.

Young, I. M. (2000). *Inclusion and democracy.* Cambridge, UK: Cambridge University Press.

Yuval-Davis, N. (2000). Multi-layered citizenship and the boundaries of the "nation state." *International Social Science Review, 1*(1), 112–127.

Zappala, G., & Castles, S. (2000). Citizenship and immigration in Australia. In T. A. Aleinikoff & D. Klusmeyer (Eds.), *From migrants to citizens: Membership in a changing world* (pp. 32–81). Washington, DC: Carnegie Endowment for International Peace.

Zhou, M. (1997). Segmented assimilation: Issues, controversies, and recent research on the new second generation. *International Migration Review, 31*(4), 975–1108.

Zhou, M., & Logan, J. (1989). Return on human capital in ethnic enclaves: New York City's Chinatown. *American Sociological Review, 54*(5), 809–820.

Zimmer, K. (2007). *How labor migration is changing Ukraine.* Retrieved April 7, 2007, from www.businessweek.com/print/globalbiz/content/jan2007/htm

Zolberg, A. R. (1981). International migration in political perspective. In M. M. Kritz, C. Kelly, & S. Tomasi (Eds.), *Global trends in migration: Theory and research on international population movements* (pp. 3–27). New York: Center for Migration Studies.

Zolberg, A. R. (1989). The next waves: Migration theory for a changing world. *International Migration Review, 23*(3), 403–430.

Zolberg, A. R. (1999a). The politics of immigration policy. *American Behavioral Scientist, 42*(9), 1276–1279.

Zolberg, A. R. (1999b). Matters of state: Theorizing immigration policy. In C. Hirschman, P. Kasanitz, & J. DeWind (Eds.), *The handbook of international migration: The American experience* (pp. 71–93). New York: Russell Sage Foundation.

Zolberg, A. R. (2006). *A nation by design: Immigration policy in the fashioning of America.* New York and Cambridge, MA: Russell Sage Foundation and Harvard University Press.

Zolberg, A. R. (2007). The exit revolution. In N. Green & F. Weil (Eds.), *Citizenship and those who leave: The politics of emigration and expatriation* (pp. 33–60). Urbana: University of Illinois Press.

Zolberg, A. R., & Woon, L. L. (1999). Why Islam is like Spanish: Cultural incorporation in Europe and the United States. *Politics and Society, 27*(1), 5–38.

Zúñiga, V., & Hernández-León, R. (Eds.). (2005). *New destinations: Mexican immigration in the United States.* New York: Russell Sage Foundation.

Zunz, O. (1985). American history and the changing meaning of assimilation. *Journal of American Ethnic History, 4*(2), 53–81.

# Index

# About the Authors

**Peter Kivisto** is the Richard A. Swanson Professor of Social Thought and Chair of Sociology at Augustana College and Finland Distinguished Professor at the University of Turku. His current research involves a collaborative project on multiculturalism with colleagues in Finland. His interests include immigration, social integration, citizenship, and religion. Among his recent books are *Key Ideas in Sociology* (Pine Forge, 3rd edition, in press); *Illuminating Social Life* (Pine Forge, 5th edition, in press); *Citizenship: Discourse, Theory and Transnational Prospects* (Blackwell, 2007, with Thomas Faist); *Intersecting Inequalities* (Pearson Prentice Hall, 2007, with Elizabeth Hartung); and *Incorporating Diversity* (Paradigm, 2005). He is the immediate past editor of *The Sociological Quarterly.* He serves on the editorial boards of *Contexts, Ethnic and Racial Studies* and *Journal of Intercultural Studies* and on the publication committee for *Sociology of Religion.*

**Thomas Faist** is Professor of Transnational and Development Studies at the Department of Sociology, Bielefeld University. His research interests focus on international migration, immigrant integration, citizenship, social policy, and development studies. He formerly directed International Studies in Political Management at the University of Bremen, and has held visiting professorships at Malmö University and the University of Toronto. Currently, his work centers on environmental degradation and migration and on the transnational social question. He serves on the editorial boards of *Ethnic and Racial Studies, Migration Letters,* and the *Indian Journal of Diaspora.* He recently published *Dual Citizenship in Europe: From Nationhood to Social Integration* (Ashgate, 2007); *Dual Citizenship in Global Perspective: From Unitary to Multiple Citizenship* (Palgrave Macmillan, 2007, with Peter Kivisto); and *The Europeanization of National Immigration Politics and Policies* (Palgrave Macmillan, 2007).